ETHNIC GROUPS OF AMERICA: THEIR MORBIDITY, MORTALITY AND BEHAVIOR DISORDERS

Volume I - The Jews

ETHNIC GROUPS OF AMERICA: THEIR MORBIDITY, MORTALITY AND BEHAVIOR DISORDERS

Volume I - The Jews

Edited by

AILON SHILOH

*Professor of Anthropology
in Public Health
Graduate School of Public Health
University of Pittsburgh
Pittsburgh, Pennsylvania*

and

IDA COHEN SELAVAN

CHARLES C THOMAS • PUBLISHER

Springfield • Illinois • U.S.A.

Published and Distributed Throughout the World by
CHARLES C THOMAS • PUBLISHER
BANNERSTONE HOUSE
301–327 East Lawrence Avenue, Springfield, Illinois, U.S.A.

© *1973, by* CHARLES C THOMAS • PUBLISHER

ISBN 0–398–02610–6 (cloth)
ISBN 0–398–02619–X (paper)

Library of Congress Catalog Card Number: 72–81717

Printed in the United States of America

BB-14

This work is dedicated to our parents.

CONTRIBUTORS

E.D. ACHESON, D.M., F.R.C.P.
*Dean of Medicine and Professor
of Clinical Epidemiology
The University of Southampton
England*

J. AGMON, M.D.
*Beilinson Hospital
Petah Tikva, Israel*

DAVID ALLALOUF, Ph.D.
*Endocrinology Department
The Rogoff-Wellcome Medical
Research Institute
Beilinson Hospital
Petah Tikva, Israel*

STANLEY M. ARONSON, M.D.
*Brown University
Providence, Rhode Island*

P.S. BAYANI-SIOSON
*Associate Professor
Head, Basic Sciences and
Research Section
College of Dentistry
University of the Philippines
Manila, The Philippines*

ARTUR BER, M.D.
*Head, Endocrinology Department
The Rogoff-Wellcome Medical
Research Institute
Beilinson Hospital
Petah Tikva, Israel*

BERTHE BERTINI, M.D., M.SC.
*Endocrinology Department
Beilinson Hospital
Petah Tikva, Israel*

NAVAH BLOCH-SHTACHER,
M.SC.
*Instructor, Department of Human
Genetics
Tel Aviv University Medical School
Tel-Hashomer Government Hospital
Israel*

PETER W. BRUNT, M.B., CH.B.
*Division of Medical Genetics
Department of Medicine
Johns Hopkins University
Baltimore, Maryland*

JULIAN CASPER*
*Department of Pathology (now J.
Casper Department of Pathology)
Beilinson Hospital
Petah Tikva, Israel*

AHARON M. COHEN, M.D.
*Department of Medicine B
Hadassah-University Hospital
Jerusalem, Israel*

HAROLD W. DEMONE, JR.,
Ph.D.
*Executive Director
United Community Services of
Metropolitan Boston
Boston, Massachusetts*

VICTOR DEUTSCH, M.D.
*Department of Surgery and
Radiology
Tel Hashomer Government Hospital
Israel*

* Deceased in 1969

HAROLD F. DORN, Ph.D.**
Biometrics Branch
National Heart Institute
National Institutes of Health
Bethesda, Maryland

LUCIA J. DUNHAM, M.D.
Laboratory of Pathology
National Cancer Institute
National Institutes of Health
Bethesda, Maryland

JOHN H. EDGCOMB, M.D.
Laboratory of Pathology
National Cancer Institute
National Institutes of Health
Bethesda, Maryland

BEATRICE ELIAN, M.D.
Department of Surgery and
Radiology
Tel-Hashomer Government Hospital
Israel

PHILIP E. ENTERLINE, Ph.D.
Professor of Biostatistics
Graduate School of Public Health
University of Pittsburgh
Pittsburgh, Pennsylvania

HENRY J. FARKAS
Division of Medical Genetics
Department of Medicine
Johns Hopkins University
Baltimore, Maryland

S. JOSEPH FAUMAN, Ph.D.
Professor of Sociology
Eastern Michigan University
Ypsilanti, Michigan

K. FRIED, M.D., Ph.D.
Dept. of Human Genetics
Western General Hospital
Edinburgh, Scotland, U.K.

ROBERT GIBSON, Ph.D.
Research Associate
Department of Sociology
and Department of Social and
Preventive Medicine
State University of New York
at Buffalo
Buffalo, New York

MAX M. GLATT, M.D.
St. Bernard's Hospital
Southall, Middlesex, England
Editor, British Journal of Addiction

CALVIN GOLDSCHEIDER, Ph.D.
Associate Professor of Demography
Kaplan School of Economics and
Social Science
The Hebrew University
Jerusalem, Israel

ELISABETH GOLDSCHMIDT,*
Ph.D.
Department of Zoology
The Hebrew University
Jerusalem, Israel

RICHARD M. GOODMAN, M.D.
Acting Chairman and Associate
Professor of Human Genetics
Tel Aviv University Medical School
Tel-Hashomer Government Hospital
Israel

** Deceased

* Deceased, May 1970

SAXON GRAHAM, Ph.D.
*Professor, Department of Sociology
and Department of Social and
Preventive Medicine
State University of New York
at Buffalo
Buffalo, New York*

J.J. GROEN, M.D.
*Professor
Psychiatrische Kliniek
Rijksuniversiteit Leiden
"Jelgersma—Kliniek"
The Netherlands*

J. GUREVITCH*
*Department of Microbiology
Hadassah-University Hospital
Jerusalem, Israel*

BERTRAM HERMAN, SC.D.
*Chief Epidemiologist
Netherlands Institute for Preventive
Medicine
T.N.O., Leiden, Netherlands*

D. HERMONI, Ph.D.
*Department of Clinical Microbiology
Hadassah-University Hospital
Jerusalem, Israel*

ELIZABETH KASEY, M.P.H.
*Principal Associate
Harvard Medical School
Harvard University
Cambridge, Massachusetts*

AHARON KATCHALSKY-
KATZIR, Ph.D.**
*Director, Polymer Department
Weizman Institute
Rehovoth, Israel
President, National Academy of
Science in Israel*

* Deceased, October 1960
** Deceased, 1972

MARK KELLER, Ph.D.
*Editor, Quarterly Journal of Studies
on Alcohol
Rutgers Center of Alcohol Studies
Rutgers, The State University
New Brunswick, New Jersey*

MORTON LEVIN, M.D., DR.
P.H., F.A.P.H.A.
*Visiting Professor
Johns Hopkins University
Baltimore, Maryland*

ABRAHAM LILIENFELD, M.D.,
M.P.H., F.A.P.H.A.
*Professor of Epidemiology
Johns Hopkins University
Baltimore, Maryland*

MOHSEN MAHLOUDJI, M.B.,
CH.B.
*Division of Medical Genetics
Department of Medicine
Johns Hopkins University
Baltimore, Maryland*

BENJAMIN MALZBERG, Ph.D.
*Principal Research Scientist
State of New York Department of
Mental Hygiene
Albany, New York*

EMMANUEL MARGOLIS, M.D.
*Department of Social Medicine
Hadassah-University Hospital
Jerusalem, Israel*

ALBERT J. MAYER, Ph.D.
*Professor
Arizona State University
Tempe, Arizona*

VICTOR A. McKUSICK, M.D.
Professor of Medicine,
Epidemiology and Biology
Johns Hopkins University
Baltimore, Maryland

MARK MOZES, M.D.
Department of Surgery and
Radiology
Tel-Hashomer Government Hospital
Israel

NTINOS C.
MYRIANTHOPOULOS, Ph.D.
Head, Section on Epidemiology and
Genetics
Perinatal Research Branch
National Institute of Neurological
Diseases and Stroke
National Institutes of Health
Bethesda, Maryland

ROBERT A. NORUM, M.D.
Fellow in Division of Medical
Genetics
Department of Medicine
Johns Hopkins University
Baltimore, Maryland

RICHARD H. POST, Ph.D.
Department of Human Genetics
University of Michigan
Ann Arbor, Michigan

JOSEPH RACKOWER, M.D.
Associate Professor of Chest
Diseases
Hadassah-University Medical School
Chief of Pulmonary Unit
Hadassah-University Hospital
Jerusalem, Israel

IRWIN D. RINDER, Ph.D.
Professor, Department of Sociology
and Anthropology
Macalester College
St. Paul, Minnesota

ERICH ROSENTHAL, Ph.D.
Professor of Sociology
Queens College of the City
University of New York
Flushing, New York

DONALD CLARE ROSS, Ph.D.
Staff Psychologist
Hillside Hospital
Glen Oaks, New York

YAACOV ROTEM, M.D.
Tel-Hashomer Government Hospital
Israel

A. SANDOR
Department of Human Genetics
University of Michigan
Ann Arbor, Michigan

VICTOR D. SANUA, Ph.D.
Associate Professor, The School
of Education
The City College of the City
University of New York
New York, New York

LEONARD SCHUMAN, M.D.,
M.P.H., F.A.P.H.A.
Professor of Epidemiology
University of Minnesota
Minneapolis, Minnesota

HERBERT SEIDMAN
Chief, Statistical Analyses
Department of Epidemiological
and Statistical Research
American Cancer Society, Inc.
New York, New York

CHAIM SHEBA, M.D.*
Tel-Hashomer Government Hospital
(Now the Chaim Sheba Hospital)
Israel

H. ELDON SUTTON, Ph.D.
Chairman, Department of Zoology
The University of Texas at Austin
Austin, Texas

HAROLD L. STEWART, M.D.
Laboratory of Pathology
National Cancer Institute
National Institutes of Health
Bethesda, Maryland

ALEXANDER SYMEONIDES,
M.D.
Department of Pathology
Aristotelian University School of
Medicine
Thessaloniki, Greece

CAROLINE BEDELL THOMAS,
M.D.
Professor Emeritus
Department of Medicine
The Johns Hopkins University
School of Medicine
Baltimore, Maryland

LOUIS B. THOMAS, M.D.
Laboratory of Pathology
National Cancer Institute
National Institutes of Health
Bethesda, Maryland

DENISE THUM, Ph.D.
Research Associate
The Medical Foundation, Inc.
Boston, Massachusetts

MORDECHAI TOOR, M.D.*
Director, Heart Institute
Beilinson Hospital
Petah Tikva, Israel

HENRY WECHSLER, Ph.D.
Director of Research
The Medical Foundation, Inc.
Boston, Massachusetts

ABRAHAM A. WEINBERG, M.D.
Israel Foundation for the Study
of Adjustment Problems
Jerusalem, Israel

* Deceased, 1971

* Deceased

ACKNOWLEDGMENTS

The development of this volume was considerably aided by the Graduate School of Public Health of the University of Pittsburgh in providing a General Research Support Grant from the National Institutes of Health (NIH). Miss Barbara Beck was responsible for providing prompt and courteous secretarial work. Mr. Pete Finley and Mrs. Betty S. Woodward, of Charles C Thomas, are particularly thanked for so kindly and efficiently directing the manuscript through to publication.

A.L.
I.C.S.

INTRODUCTION

There has been only recently an increasing awareness of the relevance of ethnicity as a factor in American morbidity, mortality and behavior disorders. The original recognition of ethnicity as a criterion of significance for ill-health analyses soon gave way under the influence of the "melting pot" hypothesis to an almost complete negation of ethnicity as a potentially operative causality factor for medicine. So serious has been this negation that as late as 1965 Dr. Leona Baumgartner could publish an article in the *American Journal of Public Health* noting, in dismay, the lack of documented studies in the degree and range of health problems of the ethnic minorities of America. While studies have been made on incidences of certain diseases in some groups, she went on, the data are still scattered throughout hundreds of scientific journals and there have been very few attempts to arrange these bits and pieces of information into meaningful and functional health profiles.

Recent medical investigators are manifesting a growing interest in what may be termed the "ethnic variable" in American morbidity, mortality and behavior disorders. This interest may have been generated by the probing investigations of genes which are revealing, among other things, that specific gene-linked diseases have an affinity for certain ethnic groups. The sophisticated blood typing techniques of our generation are also revealing ethnic variable differentials. Demographers, too, are no longer explaining differing ethnic group fertility and mortality rates as due simply to the social class variable. Furthermore, behavior disorders such as alcoholism, drug addiction and mental illness are now also being considered from the position of the individual's sub-culture—his ethnic group.

The entire study of ethnicity as a documented and determined factor in the variety of American morbidity, mortality and behavior disorders is, however, still in its earliest scientific stages.

There are still too few sound research publications confronting inter-ethnic as well as cross-ethnic ill-health manifestations, and the theoretical hypotheses to test for the interactions of culture and genetics in ethnicity have scarcely been delineated. This entire promising field of research and therapy, with its analysis of the inter-relationships of the medical sciences, the behavioral sciences, and the science of genetics, is still in its intellectual infancy.

The purpose of these volumes is to bring together under one cover current sound, documented, and relevant research articles concerning the morbidity, mortality and behavior disorders of specific ethnic groups of America. This volume deals with the Jews and further volumes are now being prepared which study other ethnic groups.

These proposed health profiles of ethnic groups of America can serve an important pioneering function in centralizing, correlating and stimulating research, training and therapy in what we consider to be a most relevant factor in American medicine today—the ethnic variable.

For historical, geographical, linguistic, religious and cultural reasons, the Jews are often characterized as comprising a variety of subpopulations, such as Ashkenazim and Sephardim. As the criteria for these sub-populations are not finally determined and fixed, the reader will note that there are differences in orthography, geography and historic criteria for the various subgroups cited. It is hoped that, derived from the genetic, morbidity and mortality studies cited herein, more precise criteria may be ascertained.

CONTENTS

PART ONE

DEMOGRAPHY

PART TWO

BLOOD GROUPING

PART THREE

GENETIC DISORDERS

PART SIX

BEHAVIOR DISORDERS

ETHNIC GROUPS OF AMERICA: THEIR MORBIDITY, MORTALITY AND BEHAVIOR DISORDERS

Volume I - The Jews

PART ONE
DEMOGRAPHY

The two basic facts of life are birth and death. The science which translates these facts into figures as statistics of populations, including birth and death and fertility rates, is known as demography. Demographers have frequently encountered difficulties in attempting to analyze Jewish population figures, due to the scarcity and inconsistency of the available material.

In his survey of countries with Jewish populations, Rosenthal in Chapter 1 describes the various categories under which Jews are listed, as, for example, religion, ethnic group, mother tongue, nationality. Since these categories are not used consistently, it is difficult to estimate the numbers of Jews living in most countries, let alone the world. Rosenthal has made a comprehensive attempt to do so, however, by using a variety of sources and he has made a major contribution to Jewish population research by collecting, inventorying and citing available sources of data.

The population explosion is considered to be one of the major threats facing our world. Within the Jewish population of the United States, however, there appears to be a decrease, rather than an increase, in numbers of children per family. Goldscheider (Chap. 2) reviews the existing literature on American Jewish fertility and documents the fact that there has been a trend toward smaller families among American Jews since the 1880's. Additionally, in his discussion Goldscheider places the analysis of Jewish fertility in the context of assimilation and acculturation to American society.

How old Jews are when they die, that is, age specific mortality rates, cannot ordinarily be analyzed from government data. Accordingly, most efforts to compile statistics relating to Jewish mortality rates have had to rely upon such cultural phenomena as sentiment. Jewish families, even those not observant of religious ritual, tend to bury their dead in Jewish cemeteries via Jewish funeral homes. Fauman and Mayer, accordingly, use this aspect of American Jewish behavior to derive their data in Chapter 3. They combine the studies of the Jewish population of three cities to produce the most recent and comprehensive estimates of American Jewish mortality rates.

4

Chapter 1

JEWISH POPULATIONS IN GENERAL DECENNIAL POPULATION CENSUSES, 1955–61: A BIBLIOGRAPHY

E. ROSENTHAL

Demographers engaged in the study of Jewish populations have frequently expressed concern about the paucity of adequate data.[1] This bibliography[2] is presented here to make recent demographic data on Jewish communities in general population censuses more easily accessible and to serve as a more or less complete inventory of all such data. This task could not have been accomplished without the work of the Statistical Office of the United Nations. It has brought together in *Demographic Yearbook, 1962, 1963,* and *1964* the results of scores of recent population censuses from all parts of the globe.[3]

Data relevant for Jewish populations have been compiled in three tables, dealing with religion, ethnicity, and language. The information on religion will be found in *Demographic Yearbook, 1963,* Table II entitled "Population by religion and sex: each census, 1956–63," and in *Demographic Yearbook, 1964,* Table 32 (supplement to Table II). The census returns for ethnicity and language will be found in Tables 9 and 10 of the *Yearbook, 1963* and in supplementary Tables 30 and 31 of *Yearbook, 1964.* Countries whose censuses returned Jews either in terms of religion, nationality, or language are listed in the reference tables accompanying this article. The returns for Argentina, Morocco, and for a 1957 sample survey for the United States were added to the *Yearbook* list.

This article first appeared in *Jewish J Soc,* 11:31–39, 1969, and is reprinted by permission of the Editor.

The tables published in the *Demographic Yearbook* contain the date on which the population enumeration took place and the total number of persons of a given religion, nationality, or language, classified by sex. The reference tables presented here have omitted the classification by sex but have added the precise reference to each census and a summary of the content of the published data.

A perusal of the list of countries in the reference tables reveals that significant Jewish communities are not represented. In Europe, census returns are not available for, among others, France, Great Britain, and Hungary. In the western hemisphere such information is missing for, among others, Brazil and Uruguay. It appears that in some countries a question on religion, ethnicity, and mother tongue was not included in the census schedule, while in others the answers to one or more of them were not published. In the United States the 1960 decennial census enumerated mother tongue but not religion. Religion was enumerated in the above-mentioned 1957 sample survey.[4]

Of the 34 countries listed in the reference tables, 14—or 41 percent—held their enumerations in the first year of the decade (1960), while 10—or nearly 30 percent—arranged theirs in the second year (1961). The virtual coincidence in time of enumerations in over two-thirds of the countries listed should be especially helpful to the student of international migrations in general and, in view of recent sudden relocations of Jewish communities, to the student of Jewish migrations in particular.

In countries where a cooperative relationship exists between communal Jewish agencies and the government bureau charged with the administration of the next decennial population census in 1970 or 1971, arrangements for the inclusion of proper questions and for special tabulations should have been completed by the summer of 1968. In countries where surveys of the Jewish population are undertaken by private Jewish communal agencies every effort should be made to synchronize these surveys with the official enumeration of the total population so that maximum comparability between governmental and privately sponsored data can be secured.

True comparability will be achieved if the operational definitions of a Jew are identical. Most commonly, Jews are categorized in terms of religion or a combination of ethnic nationality and mother tongue. A glance at the reference tables reveals that in most parts of the world, population censuses have defined the Jewish population in terms of religion. Canada is the only country which produces returns for all three categories.

Religion, ethnicity, and mother tongue are "soft" categories, and it is difficult to set up operational definitions that will yield a uniform response in any one country. Since definitions often vary from country to country, it is difficult to make international comparisons.

According to the *Demographic Yearbook, 1963*[5] the data on religion

> represent—in unknown proportions—religious belief or religious affiliation; the latter may be of recent origin or dating from childhood. No criterion is used by the enumerator to determine church 'membership' and none is possible to verify 'belief.' Moreover, there is a definite tendency for this question to remain unanswered on a large number of census schedules; in some countries such as New Zealand, respondents have the statutory right to refuse to answer the question on religion. Therefore these statistics . . . must be used only as rough indicators of the distribution of population by broad religious designations.

Similarly, the category "ethnic composition" relates[6]

> to a series of categories which are not uniform in concept or terminology. Rather they represent a variety of characteristics or attributes, variously designated by countries as race, colour, tribe, ethnic origin, ethnic group, ethnic nationality (as distinct from legal nationality), etc. . . . By and large the[se] statistics . . . have one advantage over country-of-birth or citizenship data as indicators of ethnic composition. The attributes on which they are based do not change even though their interpretation may be subject to variation. Thus, they may serve as the best indicators of the ethnic composition of populations and, hence, of cultural and social heterogeneity or homogeneity.

Mother tongue is usually defined as "the language spoken in the individual's home in his early childhood"; it is considered a very sensitive index "because linguistic differences tend to persist until complete cultural assimilation has taken place."[7] Since "the census question on which the statistics are based is essentially the same in each country" this category yields a high degree of comparability between countries.[8] The return of "Jewish" for this category means Yiddish for all countries except Turkey where the return is Ladino.

The designation given to Jews varies from country to country. Most frequently they are identified by the term "Jew." Sometimes the term "Hebrew" or "Israelite" is used. While individuals who identify themselves in these terms are most probably members of the religio-ethnic group known as Jews, one cannot take it for granted that this is the case in every single instance, as the recent Mexican experience has shown. The 1960 census of Mexico enumerated 100,750 "Israelitas." However, according to the Mexican correspondent of the *American Jewish Year Book*, members of several Protestant sects had identified themselves as "Israelitas" in the enumeration, thus inflating the actual number of Jews residing there. Jewish communal agencies have estimated the number of Jews in Mexico from a minimum of 30,000 to a maximum of 45,000.[9]

This experience illustrates the first difficulty of attempting to analyze census returns from a distance. The second difficulty arises from the fact that the outsider is in no position to judge the quality of each population enumeration in general or the reliability of response to questions on religion, nationality, and language—subjects that often are charged with political, social, and psychological dynamite.[10]

Since government publications are notorious for baffling the researcher, full bibliographical details have been added to the reference tables, wherever possible, in order to ease access to the published data.[11] The tabulations were inspected and their content summarized with the aid of categories developed by the *UN Yearbook*.[12] It will be seen that the most frequently published data, after population size, concern the distribution of the population by major civil divisions (provinces, states, etc.) and its sex composition.

Census data are often obsolete by the time they are published, and demographers need access to them as soon as they are available. The *Population Index*[13] renders a valuable service by giving this information in its section "Official Statistical Publications." (The *Index* refers to religion, ethnicity, and mother tongue explicitly only if these categories appear in the title of a government publication.)

The difficulty of "locating information about the tabulations contained in many censuses" has motivated a research group at Duke University to explore the feasibility of a census information retrieval system.[14] The basic purpose of the research group was "neither data storage nor bibliography, but an index which will tell a researcher what censuses provide information on particular population characteristics and how these characteristics are defined, mapped, cross-indexed, compared and discussed."[15] I suggest that a project be set up which would establish such a retrieval system for Jewish population data from official and private sources.

Research workers interested in historical demography will find *Jewish Demography and Statistics*[16] and the recently completed *International Population Censuses Bibliography*[17] indispensable. The latter lists the population censuses of each country from the first published census up to 1960; however, as in the case of the *Population Index*, specific references to religion and nationality occur only if they appear in the title of a census publication.

NOTES AND REFERENCES

1. R. Bachi: Recent progress in demographic research on the Jews. *The Jewish Journal of Sociology*, 8:142–9, 1966.

2. I acknowledge gratefully the assistance of my daughter, Barbara, in the preparation of the tabular material.

3. New York, United Nations, 1963, 1964, 1965.

4. Erich Rosenthal: Five million American Jews. *Commentary*, 26:499–507, 1958.

5. *Demographic Yearbook, 1963*, p. 41.

6. Ibid., p. 38.

7. Ibid., p. 39.

8. Ibid., p. 40.

9. Seymour B. Liebman: Mexico. *The American Jewish Year Book*, 66:352–3, 1965.

10. For a discussion of the accuracy of returns and a presentation of accuracy ratings see *Demographic Yearbook, 1963*, pp. 18–21.

11. I used the special library of the Statistical Office of the United Nations in the Department of Economic and Social Affairs in New York.

12. *Demographic Yearbook, 1963,* Table B, p. 4.

13. Office of Population Research, Woodrow Wilson School of Public and International Affairs, Princeton University.

14. Sarah Hobbs, Reynolds Farley, and Halliman H. Winsborough: A design for a census information retrieval system. *Demography, 4:*331–40, 1967.

15. Ibid., p. 331.

16. Schmelz, O. (Ed.): *Jewish Demography and Statistics: Bibliography for 1920–1960.* Jerusalem, Institute of Contemporary Jewry, The Hebrew University, July 1961.

17. University of Texas. Population Research Center, Austin, Texas, 1965–7.

Reference Tables

JEWS IN GENERAL POPULATION CENSUSES OF THE WORLD BY DATE OF CENSUS, TYPE OF IDENTIFICATION, SOURCE AND NATURE OF TABULATIONS, 1955–61

LEGEND

a: size of population
b: population trend
c: major civil divisions
d: minor civil divisions
e: capital and large cities
f: locality size groups
g: urban–rural residence
i: sex composition

j: age composition
l: marital status
m: occupation and industry
n: intermarriage
o: literacy and employment status
p: birthplace and occupation
q: citizenship
x: census not available for inspection

TABLE 1-I

AFRICA

County	Date of Census	Religion			Ethnicity			Mother Tongue		
		Jews Number	Source	Content	Jews Number	Source	Content	Jewish Number	Source	Content
Morocco	June 1960	159,806	1	a, c, e						
Rhodesia (Southern Rhodesia)	26 September 1961	7,057	2	a						
South Africa	6 September 1960	116,189	3	a, b, c, i, m						
Tunisia	1 February 1956	8,561	5	x						
United Arab Republic	20 September 1960				57,792	4	a, c, d			
Zambia (Northern Rhodesia)	26 September 1961	852	6	a, i						

1. Royaume du Maroc. Ministere de l'économie nationale. Division de la coordination économique et du plan. Recensement demographique. (Juin 1960.) Population légale du Maroc. Table E, pp. 91–2.
2. Rhodesia. 1961 Census of the European, Asian, and Coloured Population. Central Statistical Office, Salisbury, Rhodesia. Table 15, p. 44.
3. Republic of South Africa. Bureau of Statistics. Population Census, 6 September 1960. Volume 3: Religion. Tables 1–4.
4. Service des Statistiques. Recensement général de la population de la Tunisie du 1 février 1956: Répartition géographique de la population.
5. Census not available for inspection.
6. Government of the Republic of Zambia. Final Report of the September 1961 Censuses of Non-Africans. Appendix II: September 1961 Census of Non-African Population. Table 6. Religion by race and sex, p. 55. Lusaka, Central Statistical Office, August 1965.

TABLE 1-II
AMERICA, NORTH AND SOUTH

Continent and Country	Date of Census	Religion — Jews Number	Source	Content	Ethnicity — Jews Number	Source	Content	Mother Tongue — Jewish Number	Source	Content
America, North										
Bermuda	23 October 1960	21	1	a, d, i						
British Honduras	7 April 1960	1,101	2	a, c, d, i						
Canada	1 June 1961	254,368	3		117,344	4	a, b, c, d, f, g, i	82,448	5	a, b, c, d, e, g, i
Jamaica	7 April 1960	600	6	a, d, i						
Mexico	8 June 1960	100,750	7	a, b, c, i						
Netherlands Antilles:										
Aruba	27 June 1960	188	8	x						
United States	1957	5,000,000	9	a, c, g, i, j, n						
United States	1 April 1960							503,605	10	a, b, c, e, g, i, j
America, South										
Argentina	30 September 1960	275,913	11	a, c, d						
Chile	29 November 1960	11,700	12	x						

1. Census of Bermuda. Table 27.
2. West Indies Population Census. Census of British Honduras. Volume II, Table 2.
3. Dominion Bureau of Statistics. 1961 Census of Canada. Population. Religious Denominations: Bulletin SP-3. Ottawa, 1963.
4. Dominion Bureau of Statistics. 1961 Census of Canada. Population. Ethnic Groups: Bulletin 1.2-5. Ottawa, 1962. Religion by Ethnic Groups: Bulletin 1.3-8. Ottawa, 1964.
5. Dominion Bureau of Statistics. 1961 Census of Canada. Population. Official Language and Mother Tongue: Bulletin 1.2-9. Ottawa, 1963. Language by Ethnic Groups: Bulletin 1.3-10. Ottawa, 1963.
6. West Indies Population Census. Census of Jamaica. Volume II, Part A, Book 1. Table 4.
7. Estados Unidos Mexicanos. Dirección General de Estadística. VIII Censo General de Población, 1960. Resumen General. Table 18.
8. Census not available for inspection.
9. United States Bureau of the Census, Current Population Reports. Series P-20, No. 79. Washington, D.C., 2 February 1958.
10. U.S. Bureau of the Census. U.S. Census of Population: 1960 Volume 1, Characteristics of the Population, Part 1, U.S. Government Printing Office, Washington, D.C., 1964, Tables 70 and 111. Mother Tongue of the Foreign Born, Final Report PC (2)—IE, Washington, D.C., 1966.
11. República Argentina. Dirección Nacional De Estadística Y Censos. Censo Nacional De Población 1960. Volume 1, Table 35. The returns for major and minor civil divisions will be found in standard Table 35 of Volumes 2-9.
12. Census not available for inspection.

TABLE 1-III
ASIA, OCEANIA, AND USSR

Continent and Country	Date of Census	Religion			Ethnicity			Mother Tongue		
		Jews Number	Source	Content	Jews Number	Source	Content	Jewish Number	Source	Content
Asia										
Aden	7 July 1955	65,232	2	a, c, g, i						
Iran	1–15 November 1956	4,906	3	x	831	1	a, b, c			
Iraq	12 November 1957							100,120	5	a, i, j
Israel	22 May 1961				1,932,357	4	a, b, c, d, g, i, j, l			
Turkey	23 October 1960	43,926	6	a, c, f, i, o				19,399	7	a, c, f, i
Oceania										
Australia	30 June 1961	9,329	8	a, b, c, e, f, i, j, l, p						
New Zealand	18 April 1961	4,006	9	a, b, c, g, i, j						
Union of Soviet Socialist Republics										
USSR	15 January 1959				2,267,814	10	a, c, e, g, i	407,900	11	a
Byelorussian SSR	15 January 1959				150,084	12	a, c, e, g, i	142,143	12	a
Ukrainian SSR	15 January 1959				840,311	12	a, c, e, g, i	32,910	12	a

1. Aden Colony. Census Report, 1955. Summary Table 8, p. 11.
2. Ministry of Interior. Public Statistics. Teheran, Iran. National and Province Statistics of the First Census of Iran. Volume II. Social and Economic Characteristics of the Inhabitants of Iran and the Census Provinces. Tables 11 and 12.
3. Census not available for inspection.
4. State of Israel. Central Bureau of Statistics. Demographic Characteristics of the Population. Part I. Population and Housing Census. Table 1.
5. State of Israel. Population and Housing Census 1961, Part 15. Language, Literacy and Educational Attainment. Part I, Table 1. (Language usually spoken Yiddish. The census also enumerated 24,095 persons whose mother tongue was Spanish, including Ladino.)
6. Republic of Turkey. State Institute of Statistics. Census of Population 1960. Population of Turkey. Tables 17 and 18. (Publication No. 452.)
7. ibid., Table 12. (Language usually spoken in the home: Ladino.)
8. Commonwealth Bureau of Census and Statistics, Canberra, Australia, Census of the Commonwealth of Australia. Volume VIII. Chapter 15, pp. 206–25.
9. New Zealand. Population Census 1961. Volume 3, Religious Professions, Tables 1–8.
10. Tsentralnoye Statisticheskoye Upravleniye pri Sovyete Ministrov SSSR, Itogi Vsesoyuznoy Perepisi Naseleniya 1959 Goda, SSSR: Svodniy Tom. (Results of the All-Union Census of Population of 1959, USSR: Summary Volume) Moscow, Gosstatizdat, 1962. Table 53.
11. ibid.
12. ibid., Table 55.

TABLE 1-IV
EUROPE

Country	Date of Census	Religion Jews Number	Religion Source	Religion Content	Ethnicity Jews Number	Ethnicity Source	Ethnicity Content	Mother Tongue Jewish Number	Mother Tongue Source	Mother Tongue Content
Bulgaria	1 December 1956				6,027	1	x			
Germany (Federal Republic)	6 June 1961	22,700	2	a, b, c, i, j						
Gibraltar	3 October 1961	654	3	a, b, i						
Ireland	9 April 1961	3,255	4	a, b, c, d, e, f, g, i, j, l						
Liechtenstein	1 December 1960	37	5	a, b, g						
Luxemburg	31 December 1960	643	6	x						
Netherlands	31 May 1960	14,503	7	a, c, d, e						
Norway	1 November 1960	841	8	a, d, g						
Romania	21 November 1956				146,264	9	a, c, g	34,337	10	a c,
Switzerland	1 December 1960	19,984	11	a, b, c, f, i, n, q						

1. Not available for inspection.
2. Statistisches Bundesamt Wiesbaden. Volks- und Berufszählung vom 6. Juni 1961. Heft 5: Bevölkerung nach der Religionszugehörigkeit, pp. 19, 32, 33.
3. Government of Gibraltar. Report on the Census of Gibraltar. Table 9.
4. Central Statistics Office. Census of Population of Ireland. Volume VII. Part I: Religions.
5. Not available for inspection.
6. Luxemburg. L'office de la statistique générale. Annuaire statistique: 1964. Table 13: Population suivant le culte.
7. The Netherlands Central Bureau of Statistics. 13th Census of Population. Volume 7: Religion.
8. Central Bureau of Statistics of Norway. Population Census 1960. Volume VIII. Table 1.
9. Republica Populara Romina. Recensamintul Populatiei din 21 Februarie 1956. Structura Demografica a Populatiei. Summary Table, p. XXXIV.
10. ibid, Summary Table, p. XXXVI.
11. Switzerland. Eidgenössisches Statistisches. Amt. Volkszählung 1960. Volume 27, Part I, Table 33.

Chapter 2

FERTILITY OF THE JEWS

C. GOLDSCHEIDER

INTRODUCTION

Since the turn of the century, research in the United States has pointed to the unmistakable conclusion that Jews have lower fertility than members of other religious groupings. The major fertility studies undertaken during the last decade have consistently confirmed this finding for a wide variety of fertility measures, including fertility behavior, aspiration, and planning success.

However, a careful review of the literature on fertility trends and differentials within the Jewish population reveals contradictory findings and inconsistent explanations. This is partly a function of the fact that conclusions have been based on a small number of Jewish couples included in the samples of fertility surveys. Moreover, demographers have not placed the analysis of fertility in a cogent and coherent sociological frame of reference which would integrate findings concerning Jewish fertility with other social behavior characterizing the Jewish population. Thus, the data that are available and the explanations that have been offered are too limited to allow for an analysis and understanding of Jewish fertility trends and differentials.

To fill partially the gap in our knowledge concerning Jewish fertility trends and differentials, information on family size, age at marriage, and birth spacing[1] was obtained in a 1963 sample

Reprinted in edited version with permission from *Demography,* 4:(no. 1) 1967, published by the Population Association of America.

Funds from Hadassah and the National Foundation for Jewish Culture are gratefully acknowledged.

survey of the Jewish population of the Providence metropolitan area. The survey covered 1,603 Jewish households, a 25 percent sample of the total Jewish population.

The highlights of these data will be summarized in the ensuing discussion.

JEWISH AND NON-JEWISH FERTILITY

Recent research in American fertility patterns has emphasized religious differentials and, particularly, the lower fertility of Jewish couples. However, smaller family size, delayed age at marriage, and extensive and efficient use of contraception have characterized the Jewish population in the United States since the latter part of the nineteenth century.

In 1889, Billings' study of over ten thousand Jewish families revealed that the Jewish birth rate was lower than the non-Jewish birth rate.[2] The only example of a state census which obtained information on religion and related this to family size—the Rhode Island census of 1905—showed that the average family size of native-born Jewish women was 2.3 compared to an average family size of 3.2 for native-born Catholics and 2.5 for native-born Protestants.[3] Although smaller family size characterized only the native-born Jewish women in Rhode Island, Jaffe in the late 1930's found that the net reproduction rates of foreign-born and native-born Jews were lower than the rate of economically comparable Protestants.[4]

Related evidence on contraceptive practices during the 1930's indicates that a higher proportion of Jews used contraceptives, planned their pregnancies, used more efficient methods of birth control, and began the use of contraception earlier in marriage than Protestants or Catholics.[5]

The United States census in a 1957 sample population survey obtained for the first time information on religion as related to number of children ever born per 1,000 women of different age groups. Although only limited cross-tabulations were published, the results confirm the lower fertility of Jews. First, Jewish children under age 14 constituted only 22 percent of the Jewish population, compared to 28 percent and 27 percent for the

Catholic and white Protestant population, respectively. Second, the cumulative fertility rate of Jewish women 45 years of age and older was 2,218 per 1,000, compared to 3,056 per 1,000 Catholic women and 2,753 per 1,000 Protestant women. Lower fertility also characterized Jewish women 15 to 44. Even controlling for area of residence, the fertility rate for Jewish women was 14 percent below the fertility rate for urban women of all religions.[6]

Comparisons between the fertility ratios of Jews and the total population in over a dozen Jewish communities in the United States point to similar lower Jewish fertility.[7] For the Jewish population in the Providence metropolitan area, there were 450 children under five years of age for every 1,000 women aged 20 to 44. This fertility ratio is significantly lower than the fertility ratio of the total population in the Providence metropolitan area (620) or the total white urban American population (635).

The results of the "Growth of American Families Study" indicate that in 1955 the average family size of Catholic and Protestant couples was 2.1, compared to an average family size of 1.7 for Jewish couples, and that Jews expected significantly fewer children (2.4) than either Protestants (2.9) or Catholics (3.4). In summary, the authors point out that Jews have the smallest families, marry later, expect and desire to have the smallest families, approve the use of contraception most strongly, are most likely to have used contraception, are most likely to plan the number and spacing of all their children, and are most likely to use effective appliance methods of contraception.[8] The 1960 GAF study reported similar findings. Jews expected and desired smaller families than either Protestants or Catholics. Moreover, a larger proportion of Jewish women completely planned their families, used the most efficient contraceptives, and in general had greater success in regulating family size.[9]

Consistent with these findings are those which resulted from the Princeton fertility studies of 1957 and 1960. They found that Jews, when compared to Protestants and Catholics, desired fewer children, planned their pregnancies more successfully, had a third child less often, and had an unplanned pregnancy in fewer instances. Fully 92 percent of the Jewish couples used

the most efficient contraceptive methods, compared to 66 percent
of the Protestants and 35 percent of the Catholics. As a result,
Jews had the lowest contraceptive failure rate of any religious
group.[10] Moreover, most of these findings applied even with
control for social class differences between the three religious
groupings. The authors state:

> The degree to which Jewish couples practice more effective con-
> traception than either Protestants or Catholics both in the periods
> preceding and following first pregnancy strains credulity. Not only
> do the Jewish couples of this sample rely more exclusively on the
> most effective methods, but they apparently manage these methods
> with unusual efficiency.[11]

Much of the current research on religious differentials in
fertility has focused on American couples. As a consequence,
the illusion is created that the pattern of low fertility characterizing the Jewish population is confined to Jews living in the United
States. However, the pattern of lower Jewish fertility is not unique
to the American experience. Even a casual perusal of the literature indicates that Jews in other countries have lower fertility
than non-Jews.

Utilizing Canadian census data, which include information on
religion, Spiegelman shows that as early as 1926 the Jewish
birth rate was only 70 percent of that of the total population.[12]
In 1941, the average size of Jewish families in Canada was 3.6,
decreasing to 3.2 by 1951. The family size of non-Jews for the
same years was 3.9 and 3.7, respectively. Of the eight largest
ethnic groups in Canada, Jews reported the smallest family size.[13]
Although the Jewish population in Canada, as in the United
States, is concentrated in urban areas which are characterized
by lower fertility, Goldberg shows that the Jewish fertility rate
is lower than the non-Jewish urban fertility rate.[14]

In Great Britain, Fanning's analysis of 3,281 hospital interviews
(of which 108 were Jews) suggested that a higher proportion
of Jewish couples used birth-control methods and used more
efficient contraception than women of other religious groups.[15]
It was estimated that the Jewish birth rate for 1945–47 in Great
Britain was 11.6 per 1,000, compared to 16.8 per 1,000 for the

total population in the same period.[16] Although reliable data are not available, Maurice Freedman suggests that Jewish fertility in Great Britain follows the prevalent middle-class pattern but exaggerates the tendency toward the deliberate restriction of childbearing.[17]

Similar findings of lower Jewish fertility have been reported for Switzerland, Italy (since 1851), and Holland.[18] Engleman shows that in Rumania, Bulgaria, Poland, Galicia, Lithuania, Hungary, Prussia, Vienna, Amsterdam, and Leningrad, the Jewish birth rate for the first 30 years of the twentieth century was lower than the general birth rate.[19] Controlling for urban residence, Hersch uncovers similar trends for Berlin (1851–1923), St. Petersburg (1910–20), Budapest (1896–1934), Warsaw (1900–1936), and other Polish towns (1931–32).[20]

The evidence on the lower fertility of Jews in a variety of countries for at least the last 75 years suggests that there may be a relationship between the position of the Jew in Western societies and his fertility behavior. Certainly, lower Jewish fertility is not a recent phenomenon, nor is there anything unique about the American situation that can account for the lower fertility of the Jewish population.

TRENDS AND DIFFERENTIALS IN JEWISH FERTILITY

Trends and Generation Status

Few systematic data are available for the examination of trends in Jewish fertility. An indirect approach to uncover change is to compare the fertility of the native-born and foreign-born at one point in time. The assumption is that the fertility of the native-born represents the changes that will occur as an immigrant group acculturates. Available evidence suggests that native-born Jews have lower fertility than foreign-born Jews, and this indirectly implies a decline in fertility behavior.

These changes are similar to the general downward trend in family size during this period. Yet some have argued that the decline was greater for Jews than for the total population. For example, Goldberg, using United States census data on Polish and Russian women who reported Yiddish as their mother tongue, shows that in the 20 years to 1940 the Jewish birth rate fell 37 percent, compared to a decline of only 15 percent for the native white population. The reduction in fertility occurred not only in average family size but also in the proportion of women with five or more children.[21]

Although the evidence on the decline in Jewish fertility can be indirectly obtained from the literature, no data are available to determine whether and to what extent Jews participated in the "baby boom" following World War II. Basing their conclusion on a limited number of Jewish couples from the Detroit area studies, Goldberg and Sharp suggest that "Jewish families seem to be relatively unaffected by the post-World War II 'baby boom.' "[22]

The data collected on the Jewish population of Providence shed some light both on the downward trend in Jewish fertility and post-World War II recovery.[23] Marriage cohort data showed a steady decline in family size from those marrying before 1910 to those marrying during the years 1920–24, which stabilized at two children for the four cohorts marrying 1925–44. Although complete data were available for only two observation periods (1945–49 and 1950–54), the postwar marriage cohorts showed a definite gradual increase in family size, which clearly indicates the participation of Jews in the baby boom.

It appears, however, that the pre-World War II decline in Jewish fertility was sharper than that in the general population. Those marrying during the 20-year-period between 1925 and 1945 maintained very small family patterns. Furthermore, the recovery in Jewish fertility after World War II began later than it did for the general population and increased less. This was observed not only in the smaller average size of Jewish families but also in the small proportion of Jewish women with four or more children.

Although the marriage-cohort analysis reveals fertility trends which can be indirectly compared to similar changes in the general population, an additional analysis is needed to measure fertility changes in the context of other social and economic changes that have taken place within the Jewish community. An analysis of Jewish fertility by generation status provides such a measure. This is especially important for a minority group whose acculturation patterns are intertwined with generation status.

Whether generation was measured by nativity (foreign-born, native-born of foreign-born parents, native-born of native-born parents), with control for age, or approximately by age groupings, similar results appeared. First-generation Jews had larger families, married at younger ages, and had shorter first and second birth intervals than second-generation Jewish couples. Furthermore, the family size of third-generation Jews was 22 percent larger than the family-size patterns of the second generation, and third-generation Jews married earlier and had their first and second child sooner after marriage than Jews of the second generation.

These findings are meaningful considering the social and demographic situation of the three generations. First-generation Jews had little formal education, were unskilled, and were imbued with the traditional values associated with Eastern European ghetto living. These factors in general are associated with higher fertility. In contrast, most second-generation Jews were economically mobile, had the benefits of a secular education, and desired assimilation. Coupled with the economic depression of the 1930's, these factors led to reductions in the family size of second-generation Jewish families and to many delayed marriages. The economic depression alone, however, does not account for the fertility decline. Our data showed that there were generational differentials within the same marriage cohort. Second-generation Jews marrying before and during the depression had smaller families than first-generation Jews marrying at the same time.

Third-generation Jews, secure in their middle-class backgrounds, with college educations and in high white-collar occupations, participated, as did other middle-class couples, in the baby boom. The increases in fertility from the second to the third generation are partially the result of the stabilization of social and economic status among third-generation Jews.

Socioeconomic Status

The existing data are not consistent on the relationship between measures of socioeconomic status and Jewish fertility. Some limited studies have found no relationship between occupation and Jewish fertility.[24] Nevertheless, Engleman's study in 1938 of the Jewish community of Buffalo, New York, clearly showed an inverse relationship between occupation and Jewish fertility— the average completed family size of professional Jews was 2.9, in contrast to the family size of 3.2 for businessmen, 3.5 for artisans, and 3.7 for peddlers.[25] Based on a small number of Jewish couples, the "Princeton Fertility Study" found little association between occupation and Jewish fertility, although professionals were found to desire slightly larger families than managers or salesmen.

When socioeconomic status is measured by education, similar inconsistent findings have been reported. In a limited survey of fertility of the parents of Jewish college students, Greenberg found an inverse relationship between education and Jewish fertility—college-educated Jews had smaller families than those with only a grammar-school education.[26] The Princeton study reported no association between education and family-size preferences for Protestants, but for Catholics and Jews there was a definite positive correlation. Moreover, despite the exercise of effective control in family planning, better-educated Jews desired larger families.[27] In the reinterview stage of the Princeton study, the authors reported a higher positive correlation between number of children desired and education of wife among Jews than among the other religious groupings.[28]

One possible explanation of the discrepancy between Engleman's and Greenberg's findings of an inverse relationship between measures of socioeconomic status and Jewish fertiliity and the direct relationship found by the Princeton study may be that they focused on different generations. Higher-status groupings of the older generation were upwardly mobile, rejected the ghetto way of life, and broke with the traditional culture of their contemporaries. This acculturation pattern would lead to lower fertility. The lower-status groupings of the earlier generations were less socially and economically mobile and were associated with Eastern European ghetto culture. These factors would probably result in their higher fertility. Thus, Greenberg and Engleman have reported an inverse relationship of measures of socioeconomic status and Jewish fertility. However, this inverse relationship of socioeconomic status to Jewish fertility may not characterize the younger generations. Following the suggestion of the Princeton study, younger Jewish couples in higher-status positions may have higher fertility than those in lower-status positions. This conforms to patterns of the socioeconomic differential in the fertility of couples who rationally plan their families and efficiently use contraceptive methods.

Nevertheless, reliable data for the confirmation of generational changes in socioeconomic differentials in Jewish fertility have been lacking. Most of the speculation seems to be that there is little or no socioeconomic differential in Jewish fertility. Goldberg suggests that "there is apparently no correlation between socioeconomic status and the birth rate in the case of the Jewish group."[29] Indirect evidence seems to suggest that contraction of socioeconomic differentials in Jewish fertility may have taken place.

In the Princeton study as well as in the GAF study, religion was found to be a more significant differentiator in fertility than class. In the former study, class yielded significant differences *in all religious groups in their survey except the Jewish group.*[30]

The Princeton study pointed out that rural background affects the relationship of socioeconomic status in Protestant fertility but does not at all affect the Catholic population.[31]

The Providence fertility data showed a clear inverse relationship between socioeconomic status and fertility among first-generation Jews.[32] This pattern was found using three measures of socioeconomic status—education of wife, education of husband, and occupation of husband. However, patterns of socioeconomic differentials in Jewish fertility were unclear and differences were smaller for second-and third-generation Jewish couples. Nevertheless, a measure of social class that combined the three individual socioeconomic measures into a unitary index indicated that a reversal of the inverse relationship of social class and

Jewish fertility characterizing first-generation Jews had occurred for second-and third-generation Jews. Higher-status Jews of the second and third generations had larger families than lower-status Jews of the respective generations.

Thus, these data tentatively confirm the explanation offered earlier on generational changes in the relationship of social class to Jewish fertility. Moreover, the data clearly indicated the trend toward convergence and homogeneity in the fertility patterns of socioeconomic groupings within the Jewish population. The contraction of socioeconomic differentials may be viewed as the result of the wide-spread rationality with which the majority of contemporary Jews plan their families, the absence of the rapid upper mobility characteristic of earlier generations, and the greater homogeneity of contemporary Jewish social structure. Third-generation Jews are concentrated in the college-trained group and in white-collar occupations. The lack of wide class distinctions among third-generation Jews within the Jewish community may account for the absence of striking fertility differences within the Jewish population.[33]

Ideological Differentials

There are no reliable data available on the relationship between the religious commitment of Jews and fertility. However, two available studies arrived at conflicting conclusions concerning the nature and role of religious ideological factors in Jewish fertility.

The first study, carried out during the spring of 1946, indicated that Orthodox (presumably more religious) Jews had slightly larger families than Conservative or Reform Jews.[34] In explanation of this finding, the author suggests that ideological factors are important in understanding Jewish fertility—those who identify more strongly with Judaism have a deeper feeling of responsibility for the Jewish people and this influences them to have larger families.[35]

The Princeton study showed that more religious-minded Jewish couples (measured by formal as well as informal religious orientation) had more success in planning their families than less religious-minded Jewish couples. They concluded that non-Catholic religious ideology stresses "social responsibility in parenthood."[36]

Whatever the merits or weaknesses of the two studies, their conclusions are conflicting, since traditional Jewish ideology cannot at the same time encourage large families and rationally planned small families. It is unwarranted to explain the larger families of Orthodox Jews (Greenberg) and the greater family planning success of "religious" Jews (Princeton study) in terms of ideological factors that are unknown and inoperative on the personal level or at best interrelated with generation, degrees of assimilation, and social class.

An alternative and more consistent explanation of the respective findings of the two studies mentioned, assuming the validity of their results, may lie in the consideration that there have been generational shifts in the religious division differential in Jewish fertility. The pattern found by Greenberg referred to first- and second-generation Jews, while the Princeton study was mostly concerned with third-generation Jews. The explanation of their findings may not reside in the realm of ideology but possibly in the social class concentrations of the three religious divisions of Judaism and, more broadly, in the changing relationship of the social class differential to Jewish fertility.

This hypothesis was tested and confirmed with the data on the Providence Jewish community.[37] The data indicated that there have been generational shifts in the religious divisional differential in Jewish fertility. On the one hand, Orthodox Jews of the first generaton had larger families, married at earlier ages, and had shorter birth intervals than first-generation Conservative or Reform Jews. On the other hand, second- and third-generation Orthodox-identified Jews had lower fertility than Conservative or Reform Jews. This pattern is similar to the changes in the social class differential in Jewish fertility discussed earlier.

In illustration of the argument that religious divisional identification reflects social class differences, we found that Orthodox Jews in each generation were concentrated in the lower social classes, Reform Jews in the higher social classes, and Conservative Jews were in an intermediate position. When social

class was controlled, family-size difference between those identifying with various religious divisions disappeared. Thus, we
may conclude that ideology and religious divisional differences
have little relationship to Jewish fertility and that few differences
appear that cannot be explained by social class factors.

Moreover, data on frequency of synagogue attendance, kind
and extent of Jewish education, and membership in Jewish and
non-Jewish organizations showed little relationship to Jewish
fertility. In most cases, the weak relationship between these
measures of religiosity and Jewish fertility was eliminated when
social class was controlled. In general, the secular nature of religion for the modern Jew implies that Judaism as a religion
plays a minor role in determining his fertility.

THE EXPLANATION OF JEWISH FERTILITY

The prevalent explanation of the patterns of Jewish fertility
is that Jewish fertility is unique only insofar as the Jewish population is characterized by a peculiar combination of residential,
social, and economic attributes. The authors of the "Growth of
American Families Studies" suggest that the long urban experience of the Jews and their high educational and economic status
would lead us to expect that Jews would have lower fertility than
Protestants or Catholics.[38] Similarly, Petersen argues that "the
small family size of Jews derives from their concentration in
cities, especially in those urban occupations that are always
associated with low fertility."[39]

The data on the characteristics of the Jewish population in the
United States suggest that these normally lead to lower fertility.
According to the 1957 Current Population Survey, 96 percent of
the Jewish population is concentrated in urban areas, compared
to 78.8 percent of the Catholic population and 56.6 percent of
the Protestant population.[40] Moreover, the high educational and
occupational achievements of Jews relative to other religious
groupings are well documented. Thus, Freedman, Whelpton,
and Smit state:

> The fertility norms and behavior of the Jews appear to be con
> sistent with their distinctive social and economic characteristics.

They have fertility characteristics we would expect to be associated with their high educational, occupational, and income status, their high concentration, in metropolitan areas and the small amount of farm background in their recent history. These social and ecomic characteristics have been associated generally in both theoretical discussions and in empirical work with low fertility, low fertility values and high rationality in family planning.[41]

To support this, the authors of the GAF study precision-matched on selected variables the 66 Jewish couples in their 1955 sample with Protestants and Catholics with similar characteristics. Comparisons between the matched groups indicated that the fertility complex for Protestants is very much like that for Jews when they have similar social and economic characteristics.[42] In addition, in the twelve largest cities of their national sample, Protestants and Jews expected the same number of children (2.3).[43] As a result, the authors of the GAF study speculate that the pattern of Jewish fertility may foreshadow what may, in the future, come to characterize the Protestant population as social and economic differences between these groups diminish.

Empirically, as well as theoretically, this approach to the understanding of Jewish fertility is incomplete. First, the findings of the "Princeton Fertility Studies" disprove the basic formulation. They found that with control for metropolitan size, social class, and other variables, Jews varied significantly from Catholics and Protestants on a wide range of fertility variables. Similarly, when the data on the Jewish population of Providence were compared to national data on Catholics and non-Catholics (controlling for age and education), Jews had the smallest family size. Second, the "characteristics" explanation of Jewish fertility would have to assume that Jews in other Western countries have had, for at least the last century, the same matrix of characteristics as Jews in the United States—or factors unique to their circumstances—contributing to their lower fertility. Moreover, it would similarly have to be assumed that Jews in the United States since 1880 have had these same social and economic characteristics. Empirical evidence, however, shows the very opposite; that is, contemporary Jews do not have the same matrix of characteristics that their fathers and grandfathers had. The "chacteristics" approach represents an *ad hoc* explanation which fails to account for existing evidence on Jewish fertility and thus generates little in the way of meaningful hypotheses.

An alternative explanation which not only accounts for the existing data but integrates the study of Jewish fertility with other social behavior characterizing the Jewish population is the analysis of the relationship between the changing nature of Jewish social structure in the process of acculturation and Jewish fertility.[44] This approach treats the Jew as a member of a minority group that is conscious of discriminations, feels insecure, and lacks full acceptance in the non-Jewish world. The long history of low Jewish fertility in many countries may be explained by the minority position of Jews and cross-culturally-shared Jewish values. Although the "characteristics" of Jews at the turn of the century were not the ones usually associated with low fertility, the aspirations of Jews for social mobility, their desire for acceptance in American society, and the insecurity of their minority status tended to encourage small family size. Moreover, generational changes in fertility can be understood in relationship to other significant social changes accompanying acculturation and assimilation.

This approach does not overlook the social and economic characteristics of Jews. However, it adds the structural and cultural dimensions to these characteristics. Furthermore, it posits a uniqueness based, not only on a particular matrix of social and economic attributes, but on the minority position of the Jew in the social structure. It appears that an examination of the combination of minority status, cultural values, and social characteristics of Jews provides a more fruitful direction for understanding Jewish fertility.

SUMMARY

This paper has reviewed the available literature on Jewish fertility and summarized recent fertility data obtained on the Jewish population of the Providence metropolitan area. Three major themes were covered: (1) differences in the fertility of

Jews and non-Jews, (2) fertility trends and differentials within the Jewish population, and (3) the explanation of Jewish fertility.

The literature on fertility differences between Jews and non-Jews clearly and consistently reveals that Jews have smaller families and in general plan their families more "rationally" than Protestants or Catholics. Moreover, lower Jewish fertility is neither a recent phenomenon nor confined to Jews in the United States. Available data since the 1880's in the United States and for the last 75 years in a variety of European countries indicate lower fertility patterns for the Jewish population.

Previous studies, based on a small number of Jewish couples, have reached contradictory conclusions concerning fertility trends and differentials within the Jewish population. A summary of fertility data on the Providence Jewish population shed light on the patterns of Jewish fertility and indicated the prewar decline in Jewish fertility and the participation of Jewish couples in the baby boom. Moreover, generational changes in Jewish fertility indicated that first-generation Jews had high fertility followed by sharp decreases in the second generation and by increases in the third generation. These generational changes fit well with the expected fertility patterns of a minority group in the process of acculturation and assimilation, given the lack of ideological factors encouraging high fertility.

Socioeconomic differentials in Jewish fertility showed an inverse relationship among first-generation Jews, and a direct relationship was found between social class and fertility for second- and third-generation Jewish couples. There were no significant patterns of religiosity differences in Jewish fertility that were not eliminated when social class was controlled.

Finally, previous explanations of Jewish fertility in terms of the social characteristics of the Jewish population or ideological factors neither accounted for existing data nor generated meaningful hypotheses. An alternative explanation that combines the social characteristics of Jews with their minority status was suggested. This integrated the study of Jewish fertility with the broader sociological analyses of the changing social behavior of Jews in the process of acculturation and assimilation.

NOTES AND REFERENCES

1. Family size was measured by the total number of children ever born excluding stillbirths. Birth spacing was measured in three ways: (1) months between marriage and birth, (2) months between marriage and second birth, and (3) months between first and second birth. Age at marriage refers to median age at first marriage for women.

2. Billings, John S.: Vital statistics of the Jews in the United States. Census Bulletin, no. 19, December 30, 1889, pp. 4–9.

3. Calculated from the Rhode Island Census of 1905, "Conjugal Conditions, Maternity Tables," bulletin 4, part 1, of the annual report for 1907, Table 7, pp. 551. The data are limited since they include number of children born to women 15 to 44 and not completed families. J.J. Spengler: *The Fecundicity of Native and Foreign Women in New England.* Washington, D.C., The Brooking Institute, 1930.

4. Jaffee, A.J.: Religious differentials in the net reproduction rate. *J Am Stat Assoc, 24:*335–342, 1939.

5. Stix, R.K. and Frank Notestein: *Controlled Fertility.* Baltimore, Williams and Wilkins, 1940. Raymond Pearl: *The Natural History of Population.* New York, Oxford University Press, 1939.

6. The main report is contained in United States Bureau of the Census, Current Population Report, Series P–20, no. 79, 1958. The fertility data were only published in the Statistical Abstract of the United States, 1958, p. 41, Table 40. See also Paul Glick: Intermarriage and fertility patterns among persons in major religious groups. *Eugenics Q, 7:*31–38, 1960.

7. See the review in Ben Seligman and Aaron Antonovsky: Some aspects of Jewish demography. In Marshall Sklare (Ed.): *The Jews.* Glencoe, Ill., Free Press, 1958. Also, *Council of Jewish Federations and Welfare Funds, Council Reports.* New York, 1963, p. 3; and Sidney Goldstein: *The Greater Jewish Providence Community: A Population Survey.* General Jewish Committee of Providence, 1964, p. 66.

8. Freedman, Ronald, Pascal K. Whelpton and John W. Smit: Socioeconomic factors in religious differential in fertility. *Am Soc Rev, 26:*608–610, 1961.

9. *Ibid.,* pp. 71–72, 90–91, 247–252 and Tables 33 and 46.

10. Westoff, Charles F., Robert G. Potter, Jr., and Philip C. Sagi: Some selected findings of the Princeton fertility study: 1961. *Demography, 1:*134, 1964.

11. *Ibid.,* p. 102.

12. Spiegelman, Mortimer: The reproductivity of Jews in Canada, 1940–42. *Population Studies, 4:*299–313, 1950.

13. Rosenberg, Louis: The demography of the Jewish community in Canada. *Jewish J Soc, 1:*217–233, 1959.

14. Goldberg, Nathan: The Jewish population in Canada. In *Jewish*

People, Past and Present, vol. II. New York, Central Yiddish Culture Organization, 1949.

15. Lewis-Fanning, E.: Report on an inquiry into family limitation and its influence on human fertility during the past fifty years. London, Papers of the Royal Commission on Population, H.M.S.O., p. 82.

16. Neustatter, Hannah: Demographic and other statistical aspects of Anglo-Jewry. In Maurice Freedman (Ed.): *A Minority in Britain.* London, Vallentine, Mitchell and Co., 1955.

17. Freedman, Maurice: The Jewish population of Great Britain. *Jewish J Soc,* 4:95, 1962.

18. See Kurt B. Mayer: Recent demographic developments in Switzerland. *Soc Res,* 24:350–351, 1957; Roberto Bachi: The demographic development of Italian Jewry from the seventeenth century. *Jewish J Soc,* 4:184, 1962; Dutch Jewry: A demographic analysis. *Jewish J Soc,* 3:195–243, 1961.

19. Engelman, Uriah Z.: Sources of Jewish statistics. In Louis Finkelstein (Ed.): *The Jews: Their History, Culture and Religion,* 2nd ed. Philadelphia, Jewish Publication Society, 1960.

20. Hersch, Liebman: Jewish population trends in Europe. In *Jewish People, Past and Present,* vol. 2, Table 10.

21. Goldberg, Nathan: Jewish population in America. *Jewish Rev,* 5:36–48, 1948.

22. Goldberg, David and Harry Sharp: Some characteristics of Detroit area Jews and non-Jewish adults. In Sklare (Ed.), *op. cit.,* p. 110.

23. For a more detailed discussion and presentation of the data, see Calvin Goldscheider: Nativity, generation, and Jewish fertility. *Soc Anal,* 26:137–147, 1965; and Trends in Jewish fertility. *Sociology and Social Res,* 50:173–186, 1966.

24. See Erwin S. Solomon: Social characteristics and fertility. *Eugenics Q,* 3:101, 1956; Myer Greenberg: The reproductive rate of the families of Jewish students at the University of Maryland. *Jewish Soc Studies,* 10:230, 1948.

25. Engelman, Uriah Z.: A study of the size of families in the Jewish population of Buffalo. University of Buffalo Series, 16:29, 1938.

26. Greenberg, *op. cit.,* pp. 231–232.

27. Westoff, Potter, Sagi and Mishler, *op. cit.,* pp. 215–261.

28. Westoff, Potter and Sagi, *op. cit.,* p. 115.

29. Goldberg, Nathan: Demographic characteristics of American Jews. In Jacob Fried (Ed.): *Jews in the Modern World,* vol. 2. New York, Twayne Publishers, 1962.

30. Westoff, Potter, Sagi and Mishler, *op. cit.,* p. 80.

31. Westoff, Potter and Sagi, *op. cit.,* p. 134.

32. For a fuller discussion and presentation of data, see Calvin Goldscheider: Socio-ecnomic status and Jewish fertility. *Jewish J Soc,* 7:221–237, 1965.

33. Freedman, Ronald: American studies of family planning and fertility: A review of major trends. In Clyde V. Kiser (Ed.): *Research in Family Planning*. Princeton, University Press, 1962; Kurt B. Mayer: Fertility changes and population forecasts in the United States. *Soc Res*, 26:347–366, 1959.

34. Greenberg, *op. cit.*, p. 233. Neither generational status nor social class was considered or controlled.

35. *Ibid., p. 234.*

36. Westoff, Potter, Sagi and Mishler, *op. cit.*, pp. 196–198. In the reinterview phase, similar findings are reported. This time, however, caution was introduced in interpreting the findings of higher fertility among more "religious Jews" and the authors suggest that this relationship might be related to socioeconomic security (Westoff, Potter and Sagi, *The Third Child*, p. 87).

37. For a more detailed discussion of ideological factors in Jewish fertility and the presentation of the data, see Calvin Goldscheider: Ideological factors in Jewish fertility differentials. *Jewish J Soc*, 7:92–105, 1965.

38. Freedman, Whelpton and Campbell, *op. cit.*, p. 104; Whelpton, Campbell and Patterson, *op. cit.*, pp. 72–73.

39. Petersen, William: *Population*. New York, Macmillian Co., 1961, p. 223. See also Ralph Thomlinson: *Population Dynamics*. New York, Random House, 1965, p. 179. For a similar approach see Erich Rosenthal: Jewish fertility in the United States. *Eugenics Q*, 8:198–217, 1961.

40. United States Bureau of the Census, *op. cit.*, p. 7, Table 3.

41. Freedman, Whelpton and Smit, *op cit.* p. 608.

42. *Ibid.*, p. 612. Their findings may be explained by the different relationships between socioeconomic status and fertility for Protestants, Catholics and Jews. See Westoff, Potter and Sagi, *The Third Child*, p. 227, Table 112 and footnote 5; and Goldscheider, Socioeconomic status and Jewish fertility, *op. cit.*, pp. 221–237.

43. Freedman, Whelpton and Campbell, *op. cit.*, p. 287; Whelpton, Campbell and Patterson, *op. cit.*, p. 73.

44. Goldberg, Nathan: The Jewish population in the United States. In *Jewish People, Past and Present, op. cit.*, pp. 28–29 Nathan Goldberg: Jewish population in America. *Jewish Rev*, pp. 30–55; Charles F. Westoff: The social-psychological structure of fertility. International Population Conference, Vienna, 1959, pp. 361–362.

Chapter 3

JEWISH MORTALITY IN THE UNITED STATES

S. J. Fauman and A. J. Mayer

Over half a century ago it was argued[2] from the evidence available that Jewish death rates were lower than the death rates for the population among whom Jews lived. Fishberg suggested that the relationship varied with age and social factors, with the Jewish population having far lower death rates than non-Jews among infants and in early adult life. At the advanced ages he suggested that death rates were higher for Jews because so many had in fact survived the hazards of early life. Since that study three widely separated areas have been studied, Canada in 1941,[8] New York City in 1925, and Berlin in the years 1924-26. In each instance the same pattern has been observed: the Jewish population experience lower death rates than the non-Jewish population for ages under 50 years of age and higher death rates for ages over 50.

This study develops current mortality data for Jews in the U. S. and examines mortality experience of the Jewish and non-Jewish populations in selected communities.

To compute age specific mortality rates for a population, it is necessary to have a count of living persons and of deaths, both by age and sex. In the case of Jews, official statistics in the U. S. yield neither. These are the only data known to us with both deaths and populations obtained by individual effort. Only one prior study has met these requirements: a study of the Jewish population of Greater Providence, Rhode Island.[3] Studies of Jewish mortality patterns have been made by Seidman[7] in New York, in St. Louis by Gorwitz,[4] in Detroit by Fauman and Mayer,[1] and in Canada by Spiegelman.[8] In the case of the U. S.

Reprinted with permission from *Hum Biol*, 41:416–426, 1969.

cities cited, the population count was lacking and in the Canadian study deaths by age were estimated.

The present study analyzes patterns of Jewish mortality in three cities: Providence, Rhode Island; Milwaukee, Wisconsin; and Detroit, Michigan. In each case mortality rates were calculated from data gathered in a similar manner. Jewish deaths were derived (in all three cities) from the records of "Jewish" funeral directors. Experience has shown that with rare exception all Jewish persons in each of the three communities are buried by specific funeral directors, one in Providence, two in Milwaukee and three in Detroit. The death records gathered in this way are assumed to be complete. Jewish population data were obtained by sample surveys in Detroit and Providence and by a complete census in Milwaukee. The first two enumerations are subject to sampling error, but the Providence sample was one household in four; thus the error in this case would be small.

The deaths have some inherent sampling error. The Detroit Jewish deaths numbered 4,590, Jewish deaths in Milwaukee numbered 1,457, both covering a five year period (1961-1965). The number of Jewish deaths in Providence was only 397 covering a two year period. Obviously the N in both Milwaukee and Providence was not very large, and the stability of the age-sex specific death rates, particularly in the younger age groupings, is questionable. This is largely the reason that data from the three communities were added to produce a combined life table, which can be considered to be the most reliable estimate of mortality rates in the Jewish population of the United States.

DATA FOR INDIVIDUAL AREAS

The individual areas can be compared if the possibility of substantial sampling variations are kept in mind. It can be seen in Table 3-I that among males the expectation of life for each sex at the ages shown is higher in Providence than in either Detroit or Milwaukee; the difference amounts to over three years at birth. Most of the difference is attributable to lower mortality rates for persons over 25 years of age, and particularly over 45 years of age. Among Jewish males, Detroit and Milwaukee have mortality rates and life expectancies so similar that the small differentials are not worthy of discussion.

The same pattern of lower Jewish death rates in Providence compared with Detroit and Milwaukee is also observed among females, but the difference in expectation of life is only 1.8 years at birth and never rises above two years at any age. Between 45 and 75 years of age only small differences in life expectancy among females are observed among the three areas. After age 75, death rates among females in Providence are again lower than in Detroit and Milwaukee. Too much should not be made of these differences due to the relatively small size of the population involved.

With the data in hand it is fruitful to consider a life table for all three cities combined. Such a life table is based on a total population of 126,000 and 6,444 deaths. Since the Jewish population of Detroit is almost twice as large as both Milwaukee and Providence combined, it contributes the major weight to the combined life table. Combining the three areas does, however, give some weight to other geographic areas, and their health conditions. The result may be tentatively regarded as a U. S. Jewish mortality experience. The combined life tables for males and females given in Table 3-II need no separate discussion for they are obviously much like the previously discussed Detroit life tables. However, they are presented in fuller detail so that they may serve as a basis for further demographic analysis.

COMPARISON OF U.S. JEWISH MORTALITY WITH RELEVANT POPULATIONS

Table 3-III compares the life expectancy and Table 3-IV contains the comparative rates of survivorship for the U. S. Jewish population, the U. S. white population and the white population of three states, the Canadian Jewish population, the total Canadian population, Israel, and Sweden. Thus there are two instances of Jewish populations and the larger populations among whom they live (U.S. and Canada); Israel, an almost entirely Jewish nation; and Sweden which has almost no Jews, but which has long had very low death rates. With these data, the U.S.

Jewish mortality picture can be viewed in a pattern of relevant mortality rates.

In 1960, the U.S. male Jewish population had an expectation of life at birth less than that of any of the other populations, Jewish or non-Jewish. Between birth and 65 years of age male Jewish expectation of life in the U.S. is slightly less than among the Canadian Jews and over a year less than for Swedish males. It is slightly higher than for Israel, nearly two years higher than for all white males in the U.S., more than a year greater than for the male whites in the three comparable states, and nearly two years greater than for all Canadian males. But by 65 years of age U.S. Jewish male life expectancy is substantially less than that of *any of the other populations*. Among Jewish females the same pattern, even more intensified, is observed.

In the 1950 period the life expectancy at birth of the Detroit Jewish male population (the only observation of U.S. Jewish mortality known to the authors for that time) was about the same as that of the Canadian and U.S. white male populations and somewhat less than that of the male population of Israel or Sweden. The life expectancy between birth and 65 years of age for Detroit Jewish males was greater than that of any other population listed. But, over 65 years of age Detroit Jewish male life expectancy was far less than that of the other male populations listed. Again the same situation was observed for females.

In 1940 the life expectancy at birth for Detroit Jewish males and Canadian Jewish males was considerably more than for U.S. white males or Canadian males and about the same as males in Sweden. By age 65 this advantage had disappeared.

To summarize, in past years the Jewish population of the U.S. and Canada has had a greater total expectation of life at birth than the corresponding non-Jewish population due to lower mortality rates at ages below 65 years. By age 65 this advantage disappeared for their mortality rates were higher than those for the total population at age 65. With the decrease in mortality rates among the total population of the U.S. and Canada and the emergence of higher mortality rates among older males and females in the U.S. and Canadian Jewish populations, the total expectation of life of Jews, male and female alike, in the U.S.

and Canada has fallen behind that for the U.S. white, the total Canadian, the Swedish, and the Israeli.

The survivorship rates for the life tables under consideration are compared in Table 3-IV. In 1960 U.S. and Canadian Jews of both sexes up to age 55 have the same or better chances of survival as any of the other relevant population groups, except Sweden. However, by age 65 there are fewer survivors among the U.S. Jews than there are in any group except U.S. white males, and by age 75 they have far fewer survivors than any other of the populations. This pattern is repeated for Jewish males and females in 1960, but to a lesser degree. It was not true for males in 1940. At that time both U.S. and Canadian Jews in both the male and female categories survived in numbers equal to or greater than those of any of the populations compared except Sweden.

DISCUSSION

The principal conclusion is only suggestive in view of the approximate nature of the life tables for American Jews. The mortality experience of American Jews is somewhat better than the general population up to about 55 years of age for both males and females. It then becomes increasingly poor with advancing age. A completely parallel case in Canada yields exactly the same results. Israel does not show this pattern, nor does Sweden, a country with low mortality as well as only a small minority of Jews. When the 1960's are compared with the 1950's and the 1940's it is evident that the pattern of higher Jewish mortality at advancing ages has become more intensified.

There are a number of possible explanations for this. First of course is the possibility of technical error due to limited data, sample error in the population estimates, etc. for the U.S. data. Could the variations between Jews and the U.S. life table data used be due to the fact that the Jewish data are all metropolitan data and the white data are state data with both rural and metropolitan populations included? This is possible but highly improbable. The Rhode Island total population is almost entirely urban and metropolitan. Data for Michigan[5] show that for males at age 65, expectation of life varies less than three-tenths of a year between rural, non-metropolitan, and metropolitan areas while the differences between Jewish and all white males in expectation of life at age is two and one half years. Canadian data show a similar pattern. Although the basic Canadian data come from official sources, technical error is possible although unlikely. We suggest that the phenomenon is real and not a product of chance or technical error.

Working with the assumption that the mortality of American Jews from middle age onward is conspicuously higher than it need be, a number of hypotheses can be advanced. Genetic factors may be responsible. This seems unlikely. The population of Israel, which came out of the same gene pool as the Canadian and the American Jews, does not share the high mortality at older ages. The hypothesis that dysgenic selection has occurred because of low infant and child mortality rates in the American Jewish population for many years which has "saved" persons of weaker constitution only to have them die in middle age does not stand up either. The Swedes, also have had low infant mortality for as long, if not longer, than American and Canadian Jews and they are not in the least affected by this.

The hypothesis that both genetic weakness and selection operate in combination is a possibility and should perhaps be the object of further scrutiny.

The most feasible hypothesis is that environmental factors arising from the way of life of the American Jew are the principal cause of the unfavorable mortality for older Jewish persons. Over abundant diet and sedentary habits have been mentioned by Muhsam[6] and indeed these are important possibilities. The obvious or seemingly obvious clues are not always correct. Perhaps the real causes are more complex and subtle. One reason for doubt lies in the fact that Jewish males and females are similarly affected. This fact largely demolishes the hypothesis that any factors directly associated with occupation are casual. Evidently the causes are bound up with a total life style. The possibility that faulty medical care and medical technology can be casual does not hold up either, for U.S. white and Canadian populations receive the same, if not less medical care, and they are not affected. The implications of these findings are far reaching. While the phenomenon seems confined to the U.S. and Canadian Jew, since the causes are unknown, it might be something that can reach beyond the confines of this group. For example in the Canadian mortality study made available by Zayachkowski[9] from which the data on Canadian Jews were drawn, the British nationality group also shared with the Jewish group high mortality at advanced ages and low mortality in childhood. An investigation of U.S. Episcopalians might be fruitful.

Even if the case of the Jews is unique, it would be desirable to pursue it further. When clinical data on the precise medical causes of death are available an examination of death rates for specific causes by age, sex, and religion seems very much called for. This, of course, will require a larger population base than the three relatively small Jewish populations used here. Several cities have large Jewish populations. A total U.S. population base of perhaps a million persons could be obtained. A Canadian base although much smaller also could be assembled as a control. Of course, the U.S. and Canadian total populations and Israel, and Swedish data are available for comparison by cause and age.

Thus it is technically possible to carry this study further and to isolate the precise medical causes of this differential mortality among older Jewish persons. Once such specific mortality causes by age, sex, and religion have been secured it will be feasible to investigate the relationships between life style and specific mortality rates.

SUMMARY AND ABSTRACT

Records of Jewish deaths by age and sex from 1961-1965 were collected for Detroit, Michigan and Milwaukee, Wisconsin, and from 1962-1964 for Providence, Rhode Island. Almost every Jewish death in these communities is handled by six funeral directors from whom these records were secured. Jewish population data by age and sex was secured by sample surveys in Detroit and Providence and by complete census in Milwaukee. Canadian Jewish data were secured from the Dominion Bureau of Statistics. Life Tables were prepared by age and sex for the

Jewish populations. Life expectancy and Life Table Survivorship at various ages was compared for each sex, the Jewish populations, total white populations of Michigan, Rhode Island and Wisconsin, the U.S., Canada, Sweden and Israel through time. A decrease in life expectancy at age 65 was found for Jews between 1940 and 1963 while the reverse was true for the other populations. Expectation of life from birth through age 64 was higher for Jews than the total white populations to whom they were compared. At age 65 expectation of life for Jews was lower than among total white populations with whom they were compared. These findings hold for both males and females.

NOTES AND REFERENCES

1. Fauman, S.J. and A.J. Mayer: Estimation of Jewish population by the death rate method. *Jewish Social Studies* 17:315–322, 1955.

2. Fishberg, Maurice: *The Jews*. New York, Charles Scribner's Sons, 1911, pp. 225–267.

3. Goldstein, Sidney: Jewish mortality and survival patterns: Providence, Rhode Island, 1962–64. *Eugenics Q, 13*:48–61, 1966.

4. Gorwitz, Kurt: Jewish mortality in St. Louis and St. Louis County 1955–1957. *Jewish Social Studies, 24*:248–254, 1962.

5. Indra, R. Raja: *Michigan Population Handbook*. Michigan Department of Public Health, 1965, pp. 118–120.

6. Muhsam, H.V.: Mode of life and longevity in Israel. Reprinted in Papers in Jewish Demography Part III. The Hebrew University, Jerusalem, 1967, pp. 39–48.

7. Seidman, H., L. Garfinkel and L. Craig: Death rates in New York City by socio-economic class and religious group and by country of birth, 1949–51. *Jewish J Soc* 8:254–272, 1962.

8. Spiegelman, Mortimer: The longevity of the Jews in Canada 1940–42. *Population Studies*, 2:292–304, 1948.

9. Zayachkowski, W.: Data for Canadian Jews are based on information recorded on official death registration forms for the Canadian provinces with the following exceptions: Newfoundland which has never asked for ethnic origin on the forms; British Columbia and Ontario which discontinued collecting such information in 1960. Deaths for 1960–62 by ethnc origin and 1961 census data by ethnic origin were used to calculate the life tables for Canadian Jews. Life Table data for eight ethnic groups and for all Canadians were calculated for 1960–1961 from official data by Mr. W. Zayachkowski and generously furnished to us in private communication by Mr. H.G. Page, Dominion Bureau of Statistics.

TABLE 3–I

SELECTED LIFE TABLE FUNCTIONS FOR DETROIT, MILWAUKEE AND PROVIDENCE 1963

Age	Mx				lx				e°x			
	Det.	Mil.	Prov.	Total	Det.	Mil.	Prov.	Total	Det.	Mil.	Prov.	Total
Male												
0	16.4	9.8	10.9	13.7	1000	1000	1000	1000	66.6	67.5	70.8	67.0
1	1.7	1.5	—	1.4	983	990	989	986	66.7	67.2	70.6	66.9
5	.4	.3	.5	.4	977	984	989	981	63.2	63.6	66.6	63.3
15	1.3	.9	—	1.0	973	981	984	977	53.4	53.8	56.9	53.6
25	1.5	2.4	.6	2.4	963	972	984	966	43.9	44.2	46.9	44.1
35	2.5	3.1	2.4	2.6	948	961	978	947	34.5	34.7	37.2	34.9
45	8.3	10.2	4.6	8.0	925	932	955	923	25.3	25.6	27.9	25.7
55	24.5	22.3	17.2	22.9	851	843	912	852	16.9	17.7	19.0	17.3
65	67.4	61.9	55.8	64.3	664	668	768	674	10.2	11.0	11.6	10.6
75	191.8	143.9	124.4	166.8	327	352	433	344	5.7	6.6	6.8	6.0
Total Population	40510	11120	9673	61303								
Total Deaths	2654ª	802ª	205ᵇ	3661								
Female												
0	12.6	8.9	14.3	12.4	1000	1000	1000	1000	71.6	72.0	73.4	71.9
1	1.2	1.0	.9	.9	987	991	986	988	71.5	71.6	73.4	71.8
5	.2	.1	.2	.1	983	987	986	984	67.9	67.9	69.4	68.0
15	.5	.1	.8	.5	981	986	984	982	58.0	58.0	60.0	58.2
25	1.4	1.2	—	1.2	976	985	976	977	48.3	48.0	50.0	48.4
35	1.9	2.5	.7	1.8	962	974	976	966	38.9	38.5	40.0	38.9
45	5.4	4.8	3.2	4.9	944	950	969	946	29.5	29.4	30.3	29.6
55	12.3	9.8	13.2	11.9	895	905	938	901	20.8	20.6	21.1	20.9
65	42.1	43.3	43.6	42.6	793	813	822	797	12.9	12.2	13.4	12.9
75	164.4	155.2	84.7	145.9	508	516	528	514	6.9	6.3	8.0	7.0
Total Population	43360	11899	9922	65181								
Total Deaths	1936ª	655ª	192ᵇ	2783								

ª Five years.
ᵇ Two years.
Mx is observed mortality rate.
lx is the number surviving to exact age x out of 100,000 born alive.
e°x is the complete expectation of life, or mean after lifetime at age x.
Source: Data for Detroit and Milwaukee collected by the authors, for Providence see Goldstein, *op. cit.*

TABLE 3-II

ABRIDGED LIFE TABLE FOR U.S. JEWISH POPULATION (1961–1965)

| | Male | | | | | | | Female | | | | | |
Age	Mx	Qx	lx	dx	Lx	Tx	e°x	Mx	Qx	lx	dx	Lx	Tx	e°x
0	13.68	13.68	100000	1368	99009	6702194	67.02	12.36	12.36	100000	1236	99105	7188277	71.88
1	1.41	5.51	98632	543	393064	6603185	66.95	.92	3.59	98764	354	394114	7089172	71.78
5	.31	1.55	98089	152	490024	6210121	63.31	.20	.98	98410	96	491783	6695058	68.03
10	.54	2.69	97937	263	488959	5720097	58.41	.23	1.15	98314	113	491257	6203275	63.10
15	.66	3.29	97674	321	487483	5231138	53.56	.44	2.20	98201	216	490409	5712018	58.17
20	1.55	7.72	97353	752	484687	4743655	48.73	.54	2.69	97985	264	489195	5221609	53.29
25	1.89	9.41	96601	909	480493	4258968	44.09	1.19	5.94	97721	580	487002	4732414	48.43
30	2.16	10.75	95692	1029	475616	3778475	39.49	1.12	5.59	97141	543	484204	4245412	43.70
35	1.91	9.51	94663	900	470827	3302859	34.89	1.15	5.74	96598	554	481459	3761208	38.94
40	3.22	15.98	93763	1498	464677	2832032	30.20	3.04	15.09	96044	1449	476218	3279749	34.15
45	5.79	28.57	92265	2636	454043	2367355	25.66	3.74	18.54	94595	1754	468128	2803531	29.64
50	10.11	49.39	89629	4427	435914	1913312	21.35	6.02	29.69	92841	2756	456591	2335403	25.15
55	17.56	84.34	85202	7186	406156	1477398	17.34	8.43	41.34	90085	3724	440117	1878812	20.86
60	28.96	135.53	78016	10574	360863	1071242	13.73	16.05	77.35	86361	6680	413350	1438695	16.66
65	51.93	230.77	67442	15564	294206	717379	10.64	21.56	126.07	79681	10045	370651	1025345	12.87
70	80.77	336.60	51878	17462	211131	416173	8.02	60.20	262.60	69636	18286	297662	654694	9.40
75	139.69	512.25	34416	17630	123351	205042	5.96	103.72	410.91	51350	21100	198438	357032	6.95
80	207.73	661.01	16786	11096	53241	81691	4.87	182.98	612.69	30250	18534	100014	158594	5.24
85	1000.00	1000.00	5690	5690	28450	28450	5.00	1000.00	1000.00	11716	11716	58580	58580	5.00

Mx is observed mortality rate.
Qx is the probability of a person of exact age x dying within the interval x to x + n.
lx is the number surviving to exact age x out of 100,000 born alive.
dx is the number dying in interval x to x + n.
Lx is the number of years lived by cohort between age x and age x + h.
Tx is the total years of life remaining to survivors at age x.
e°x is the complete expectation of life, or mean after lifetime at age x.

TABLE 3–III

EXPECTATION OF LIFE AT BIRTH AND AT AGE 65 FOR
SELECTED POPULATIONS

	Males			Females		
	Birth	Age 0–64	Age 65–74	Birth	Age 0–64	Age 65–74
Circa 1960						
Jewish Populations						
American Jewish	67.0	56.4	10.6	71.9	59.0	12.9
Detroit	66.6	56.4	10.2	71.6	58.8	12.8
Milwaukee (1963)	67.5	56.6	11.0	72.0	59.8	12.2
Providence (1963)	70.8	59.2	11.6	73.4	60.0	13.4
Israel (1965)	70.7	56.3	14.4	73.5	57.8	15.7
Canadian Jewish (1961)	68.4	57.0	11.4	72.2	59.3	12.9
Relevant Non Jewish Populations						
U.S. white (1963)	67.5	54.7	12.8	74.4	58.4	16.0
Michigan white (1959–61)	67.7	55.0	12.7	74.0	58.4	15.6
Rhode Island white (1959–61)	67.8	55.2	12.6	73.7	58.4	15.3
Wisconsin white (1959–61)	68.5	55.2	13.3	74.6	58.7	15.9
Canada (1961)	68.4	54.8	13.6	74.3	58.1	16.2
Sweden (1961–65)	71.6	57.7	13.9	75.7	59.9	15.8
Circa 1950						
Jewish Populations						
Detroit Jewish (1956)	66.6	56.6	10.0	71.6	59.3	12.3
Israel (1951)	67.3	53.8	13.5	70.1	55.5	14.6
Relevant Non Jewish Populations						
U.S. white (1959)	66.3	53.5	12.8	72.0	57.0	15.0
Canada (1951)	66.3	53.0	13.3	70.8	55.8	15.0
Sweden (1946–50)	69.0	55.5	13.5	71.6	57.3	14.3
Circa 1940						
Jewish Populations						
Detroit Jewish	67.1	54.5	12.6	70.2	56.7	13.5
Canadian Jewish	67.5	55.5	12.0	69.9	57.0	12.9
Non Jewish Populations						
U.S. white (1940)	62.8	50.7	12.1	67.3	53.7	13.6
Canada (1941)	63.0	50.2	12.8	66.3	52.2	14.1
Sweden (1941–45)	67.1	53.4	13.7	69.7	55.4	14.3

Source: Data for Canadian non-Jews, Sweden, U.S. white and Israel are from United Nations Demographic Yearbook, 1948–1966. New York, Statistical Office of the U.N., Department of Economic and Social Affairs. Data for Detroit and Milwaukee collected by the authors, data for Providence see Goldstein, *op. cit.* Canadian Jewish data for 1961 are unpublished data generously furnished by Mr. H. G. Page, Chief Vital Statistics Section, Dominion Bureau of Statistics, Ottawa, Canada. Canadian Jewish data for 1940 are from Spiegelman, *op. cit.* Michigan, Rhode Island and Wisconsin data are from: Vital Statistics of the U.S. 1965 Vol. II Section 5, Life Tables.

TABLE 3-IV
NUMBER OF LIFE TABLE SURVIVORS TO SELECTED AGES

Age	Male								Female							
	0	1	15	25	45	55	65	75	0	1	15	25	45	55	65	75
Circa 1960																
Jewish Populations																
U.S. Jewish (1963)	1000	986	977	966	923	852	674	344	1000	988	982	977	946	901	797	514
Detroit (1963)	1000	984	973	960	922	849	662	326	1000	987	981	976	944	895	793	508
Milwaukee (1963)	1000	990	981	972	932	843	668	352	1000	991	986	985	950	905	813	516
Providence (1963)	1000	989	984	984	955	912	768	433	1000	986	984	976	969	938	822	528
Israel (1965)	1000	973	965	956	924	876	747	477	1000	981	974	970	946	904	795	557
Canadian Jewish (1960–62)	1000	987	976	972	935	867	688	384	1000	992	986	983	959	907	786	510
Relevant Non Jewish Populations																
U.S. White (1963)	1000	975	966	953	906	826	657	394	1000	981	975	969	943	900	809	611
Canada (1961–63)	1000	969	959	946	905	839	688	438	1000	976	969	964	940	901	811	615
Sweden (1961–65)	1000	983	976	966	934	887	766	513	1000	987	982	978	958	925	847	643
Circa 1950																
Jewish Populations																
Detroit Jewish	1000	980	971	966	932	853	651	279	1000	985	979	973	950	911	799	466
Israel (1951)	1000	958	939	920	883	828	695	441	1000	964	944	936	903	858	752	512
Relevant Non Jewish Populations																
U.S. White (1950)	1000	969	957	943	890	805	635	381	1000	976	968	961	927	877	767	544
Canada (1951)	1000	957	940	926	879	808	658	418	1000	966	954	945	910	860	755	540
Sweden (1946–50)	1000	973	960	945	903	847	722	477	1000	979	970	960	924	877	773	538
Circa 1940																
Jewish Populations																
Detroit Jewish	1000	973	959	950	901	820	664	406	1000	973	962	956	921	872	754	508
Canadian Jewish	1000	975	961	951	916	847	675	385	1000	980	971	966	933	873	723	445
Israel (1942–44)	1000	—	920	902	856	791	652	414	1000	—	926	913	866	813	697	466
Non Jewish Populations																
U.S. White (1940)	1000	952	931	912	843	752	583	334	1000	962	945	932	879	815	687	447
Canada (1941)	1000	938	909	889	828	759	619	381	1000	951	927	911	854	796	682	462
Sweden (1941–48)	1000	966	946	923	868	809	689	459	1000	964	943	926	847	817	697	444

Source: Table 3.

PART TWO
BLOOD GROUPING

The concept of "blood" has often been used as a term of relationship without closer definition or investigation. That relatives do, indeed, tend to have more similarities in their blood types than do strangers is a fact that has long influenced the search for blood donors. More recently, the study of blood group systems has been used by geneticists and anthropologists to demonstrate relationships which span great distances and periods of time.

Israel, especially, where there are Jews from all over the world, has become a living laboratory for the study of such relationships. Margolis, Gurevitch, and Hermoni (chaps. 4 and 5) describe their analyses of the blood of two of Israel's communities: the Sephardic Jews and the Ashkenazic Jews. Most American Jews are considered Ashkenazim, although there is a small Sephardic group.

Margolis *et al.* finds certain resemblances between the ABO and MN systems of Jews and those of the local populations where they have lived for many generations. However, Jews tend to have lower frequencies of RH negative individuals than American whites or Europeans. There is also a comparatively high frequency for the "Mediterranean chromosome" in all Jewish communities, suggesting a common Mediterranean origin of the Jewish people.

Other components of human plasma, such as the haptoglobins, also vary in their frequencies according to geography. Extensive studies have been made mapping the haptoglobin frequencies in most of the major ethnic groups of the world. In Chapter 6 Goldschmidt, Bayani-Sioson, Sutton, Fried, Sandor and Bloch compare the haptoglobin frequencies of the various Jewish communities of Israel with what is known about the haptoglobin frequencies of non-Jewish groups from the same geographic areas. Some of these comparisons between Ashkenazic and Oriental Jews show no significant differences, indicating a common genetic origin.

Chapter 4

BLOOD GROUPS IN SEPHARDIC JEWS

E. Margolis, J. Gurevitch and D. Hermoni

Sephardic Jews are the descendants of the Jews who were expelled from Spain in 1492 and from Portugal in 1497, and who settled in all parts of the Ottoman Empire.

There is no definite proof of the existence of Jews in Spain in the early centuries of the Christian Era.[1] From the official prohibition proclaimed at Illiberis in A.D. 306, it may be deduced, that in the time of the Vandal and Visigothic rule there were already Jewish settlers in Spain, who lived in peace with the Gentiles and even intermarried.

Later, after the Arab conquest, many Jews of Asia and Africa, who had served in the Arab armies, settled in Spain. Part of Castile, for example, was conquered by Berber Jews of Morocco, under the leadership of Kaulan al-Yahudi.[9]

There was also emigration. The frequent persecution of the Jews in Spain during the Arab rule often ended with part of them emigrating to North Africa. Large scale migration commenced with the massacres and persecutions of 1391, which were followed by forcible mass conversions in 1412 to 1415.

The total expulsion of Spanish Jewry in 1492 followed by those from Portugal in 1497, caused an overflow of Jewish migration into southern France, Holland, Italy, North Africa, Turkey and Asia Minor.

With such extensive geographical and political distribution, with "their thirst for knowledge together with the fact that they

Reprinted with permission from the *Am J Phys Anthropol*, *18*:197–199, 1960.

Thanks are due to Dr. R. Moab, Department of Botany, the Hebrew University, Jerusalem, for the statistical work-up of the data. We are greatly indebted to Dr. Ada C. Kopec, of the Nuffield Blood Group Centre, for checking the results of the statistical calculations.

associated freely with the outer world"[7] it was only natural that the character of the cultural economic and social life of the Sephardic Jews developed great heterogeneity.[11]

Nevertheless there were certain common traits of language, religious customs and general demeanor. In all parts of the world they retained "Ladino" (Judaeo-Spanish) as the language of speech and as a literary medium. Wherever they settled they retained their own customs and religious traditions, which often differed from the practices of the indigenous Jewish communities. They founded their own congregations and communal organizations. Social prestige and intense self-consciousness caused the Sephardim to keep aloof from their fellow Jews of German or Polish origin and there was little intermarriage with them.

The present study is concerned with Sephardic Jews from the Balkan countries who came to Israel between the years 1949–1957.

METHODS

The methods of blood group typing and the antisera used are as previously described.[4]

RESULTS AND DISCUSSION

The distribution of the ABO phenotypes and the respective genes are summarized in Table 4-I.

An interesting feature is the high frequency of the phenotype A (45%) which is the highest figure so far found in the Jewish communities studies by us. It is of interest that a frequency of about 42% A was also found in some populations of the Balkan peninsula, e.g. Turks, Serbians and Bulgarians.[10]

TABLE 4–I
ABO BLOOD GROUPS IN SEPHARDIC JEWS

Blood group	No. obs.	Frequency observed	Frequency expected	No. expected	Gene frequency
O	59	29.50	29.34	58.68	p = 32.15
A	90	45.00	45.17	90.34	q = 13.68
B	33	16.50	16.69	33.38	r = 54.17
AB	18	9.00	8.80	17.60	
Total	200	100.00	100.00	200.00	100.00

In a previous study[3] the percentage of the O group in Sephardic Jews was found to be 40.5. This result may have been affected by the fact that the group studied was heterogeneous, including Jews from North Africa (Algiers, Tunis, Morocco), southern Europe (Bulgaria, Greece) and an indigenous group from Israel.

In the present study the frequency of the O phenotype is rather low (29.5%), in comparison with the figures obtained for Moroccan (37.7%) and Tunisian Jews (39.5%). If it is assumed that the high group O frequency indicates a Berber influx in these Jewish communities, it may be that this North African component has penetrated only to a limited extent, in spite of the frequent contact over the centuries.

The phenotype B was found in Sephardic Jews at a frequency of 16.0 percent which is lower than that encountered in the population of North Africa—Berber and Arab. This, too, might be taken as an indication of less than average North African admixture.

The M and N genes are evenly distributed in the Sephardic Jews (Table 4-II). The phenotype distribution, however, shows

TABLE 4–II
MN BLOOD GROUPS IN SEPHARDIC JEWS

Blood group	No. obs.	Frequency observed	Frequency expected	No. expected	Gene frequency
MM	20	15.00	25.00	50.00	M = 50.00
MN	140	70.00	50.00	100.00	N = 50.00
NN	30	15.00	25.00	50.00	
Total	200	100.00	100.00	200.00	

an interesting phenomenon, namely the unusually high percentage of 70 for the MN phenotype. These results are confirmed by separate examination of the two main subgroups. As may be seen from Table 4-III, the percentage for the MN phenotype was

TABLE 4–III
MN BLOOD GROUPS IN TWO SEPHARDIC SUBGROUPS

	No. obs.	Phenotypes (no.)			Phenotypes (%)		
		MM	MN	NN	MM	MN	NN
From Turkey	112	13	82	17	11.60	73.20	15.20
From Bulgaria	70	10	48	12	14.30	68.60	17.10

73.20 in Sephardic Jews from Turkey and 68.60 in Sephardic Jews from Bulgaria. In this respect the Sephardim stand out from the other Jewish communities so far studied. Whether this is heterosis and thus a reflection on the herterogeneity of the Sephardic Jews developed in their cultural, economic and social life, remains a problem open to speculation.

Table 4-IV shows the distribution of the blood groups of the Rh-Hr system.

TABLE 4–IV
Rh–Hr BLOOD GROUPS IN SEPHARDIC JEWS

Blood group	No. obs.	Frequency observed	Frequency expected	No. expected	Chromosome frequency
CCDE	2	1.00	0.96	1.92	
CCDee	54	27.00	26.03	52.06	
CCddE	—	—	—	—	CDE 0.93
CCddee	—	—	0.31	0.62	CDe 45.75
CcDE	21	10.50	11.22	22.44	Cde 5.57
CcDee	70	35.00	35.61	71.22	cDE 9.23
CcddE	—	—	0.10	0.20	cdE 0.94
Ccddee	6	3.00	2.96	5.92	cDe 11.01
ccDE	18	9.00	8.19	16.38	cde 26.57
ccDee	14	7.00	7.06	14.12	
ccddE	1	0.50	0.51	1.02	
ccddee	14	7.00	7.06	14.12	
Total	200	100.00	100.01	200.02	100.00

The highest figure was obtained for the CDe, the so-called "Mediterranean chromosome" (45.75), which was characteristically high in all Jewish communities studied by us.[8] The same observation was stressed by Mourant[10] and suggests the common Mediterranean origin of the Jewish people.

The chromosome cde follows with a high frequency of 26.57 percent. This chromosome is found more in the heterozygous state, while the homozygous ccddee phenotype is infrequent (7%) as found in some Oriental Jewish communities, e.g. Baghdadi, Kurdistani and Persian Jews.[4,5] The high level of cde may be due to the acquisition of a Basque component or of a Berber component from North Africa.[10]

The chromosome cDe, characteristically high in all populations of Africa,[10] was found in the Sephardic Jews to be 11 percent. This is somewhat higher than that encountered in Moroccan and Tunisian Jews.[8] How has this chromosome penetrated the Sephardic stock? According to Mourant this component was presumably acquired mainly in Egypt and elsewhere in North Africa, but some may have come through Spain, where raised cDe frequencies are found in several regions. The latter seems most probable, as no other indications were found to suggest the permeation of considerable North African elements in Sephardic Jews.

SUMMARY

ABO, MN and Rh-Hr blood group frequencies in 200 Sephardic Jews from the Balkan States are reported and compared with findings in other Jewish communities in Israel.

REFERENCES

1. Baer, F.: *The Universal Jewish Encyclopedia.* New York, *9*:684, 1943.

2. Brzezinsky, A., J. Gurevitch, D. Hermoni and G. Mundel: Blood groups in Jews from the Yemen. *Ann Eugen, 16*:335, 1952.

3. Gurevitch, J., D. Hermoni and Z. Polishuk: Rh blood types in Jerusalem Jews. *Ibid., 16*:129, 1951.

4. Gurevitch, J., and E. Margolis: Blood groups in Jews from Iraq. *Ann Hum Genet, 19*:257, 1955.

5. Gurevitch, J., E. Hasson, E. Margolis and C. Poliakoff: Blood groups in Jews from Cochin, India. *Ibid., 19*:254, 1955.

6. Gurevitch, J., E. Hasson and E. Margolis: Blood groups in Persian Jews. *Ibid., 21*:135, 1956.

7. Kayserling, M.: *The Jewish Encyclopedia.* New York, *11*:199, 1905.

8. Margolis, E., J. Gurevitch and E. Hasson: Blood groups in Jews from Morocco and Tunisia. *Ann Hum Genet, 22*:65, 1957.

9. Mezan, S.: *The Universal Jewish Encyclopedia.* New York, *9*:683, 1943.

10. Mourant, A.E.: *The Distribution of the Human Blood Groups.* Oxford, Blackwell Scientific Publications, 1954, pp. 72–74.

11. Neuman, A.: *The Universal Jewish Encyclopedia.* New York, *9*:477, 1943.

Chapter 5

BLOOD GROUPS IN ASHKENAZI JEWS

E. MARGOLIS, J. GUREVITCH AND D. HERMONI

The term Ashkenazim is used to denote one of the great divisions of Jewry in contradistinction to the Sephardim (Spanish Jews) and the Oriental Jews, from whom they differ in many respects.

The Ashkenazim include the descendants of the German and French Jews, who, after the crusades and subsequent persecutions in Germany and after the expulsions from France, migrated into Prussia, Poland, and other countries of northern, central and eastern Europe, as well as the majority of Jews now residing in the Americas, England and South Africa.

Anthropologically the Ashkenazim differ from the Sephardim and their oriental brethren: they have a larger proportion of blonds, have rounded faces and heads and are shorter, especially in comparison with the Sephardim.

Ashkenazim originally spoke middle-high German, which later remained exclusively with the Jews who were shut up in the Ghetto, and was afterwards carried by migratory Jews into Poland, Russia and eastern Europe. In course of time this Judaeo-German became interspersed with Hebrew and Slavonic words, and it survives to this day in the form of Yiddish.[11]

The present study is concerned with Ashkenazim from Europe who immigrated into Israel during the years 1949–1957.

Reprinted with permission from *Am J Phys Anthropol, 18*:201–203, 1969.

Thanks are due to Dr. R. Moab, Department of Botany, the Hebrew University, Jerusalem, for the statistical work-up of the data. We are greatly indebted to Dr. Ada C. Kopec, of the Nuffield Blood Group Centre, for checking the results of the statistical calculations.

METHODS

The methods of blood group typing and antisera used in the present study were the same as previously described.[3]

RESULTS AND DISCUSSION

The distribution of the ABO blood groups found in Ashkenazim is given in Table 5-I. These results are very similar to figures obtained in a previous study.[4]

The Ashkenazi Jews are characterized by a very high frequency of the phenotype A—40.22 percent. Of the eight oriental Jewish communities already examined by us, none reached this high level. In the Yemenite Jews, for example, only 30 percent of A group has been found. In the Cochin region of India, the so-called "black Jews" have a very low A group percentage, 14.9 percent. On the other hand, a 45 percent frequency of A group has been recorded in Sephardic Jews which is close to the figure found in Ashkenazim.

The Jews examined in Canada[2] probably mainly Ashkenazim, have A and B gene percentages of 29 and 11, which are also close to the figures cited in Table 5-I. Raised A and B levels are considered characteristic for the European Jews.[10]

TABLE 5–I
ABO BLOOD GROUPS IN ASHKENAZI JEWS

Blood group	No. obs.	Frequency observed	Frequency expected	No. expected	Gene frequency
O	177	38.06	38.32	178.19	p = 26.57
A	187	40.22	39.95	185.77	q = 11.53
B	74	15.91	15.60	72.54	r = 61.90
AB	27	5.81	6.13	28.50	
Total	465	100.00	100.00	465.00	100.00

The frequency of the O gene in Ashkenazim was found to be 61.70 percent and thus they should be included in the 60–65 percent zone, to which large parts of Europe belong.[8,10]

The figures for the M and N genes (Table 5-II) are 53.55 and 46.45 respectively, and are similar to those found in many European populations.[10]

On the other hand, our figures are also close to the results

TABLE 5–II
MN BLOOD GROUPS IN ASHKENAZI JEWS

Blood group	No. obs.	Frequency observed	Frequency expected	No. expected	Gene frequency
MM	126	27.10	28.68	133.36	M = 53.55
MN	246	52.90	49.75	231.34	N = 46.45
NN	93	20.00	21.58	100.35	
Total	465	100.00	100.01	465.05	

encountered in Moroccan and Tunisian Jews[9] but differ from those found in most oriental Jewish communities.[3,6,7]

The distribution of the Rh-Hr chromosomes are listed in Table 5-III. The figure for the so-called Mediterranean chromosome

TABLE 5–III
Rh–Hr BLOOD GROUPS IN ASHKENAZI JEWS

Blood group	No. obs.	Frequency observed	Frequency expected	No. expected	Chromosome frequency
CCDE	2	0.43	0.44	2.05	
CCDee	125	26.88	27.66	128.62	
CCddE	—	—	—	—	CDE 0.42
CCddee	—	—	—	—	CDe 52.23
CcDE	59	12.69	12.07	56.13	Cde 0.36
CcDee	179	38.49	37.52	174.47	cDE 11.10
CcddE	—	—	—	—	cDe 5.25
Ccddee	1	0.22	0.22	1.00	cde 30.64
ccDE	40	8.60	9.20	42.78	
ccDee	16	3.44	3.49	16.23	
ccddE	—	—	—	—	
ccddee	43	9.25	9.39	43.66	
Total	465	100.00	99.99	464.94	

CDe is high, 52.23 percent, and close to the levels encountered in other Jewish communities living in the Mediterranean zone. In Moroccan and Tunisian Jews, for example, the frequency of this chromosome was found to be 53.40 and 56.09 percent respectively.[9] The Ashkenazim, however, have a much higher frequency of the so-called "North Eureopean" chromosome, cDE (11.10%). According to Mourant this is what would be expected in a Mediterranean population which has acquired a considerable local component during residence in central and northern Europe. Interestingly enough, high figures for this chromosome were found also in some oriental Jewish communities, and the question was then raised as to the origin of this chromosome in these communities.[7]

The frequency of the cde chromosome is 30.64 percent. This

is higher than the frequencies encountered in most, although not in all, oriental Jewish communities.[7] The cde chromosome is relatively rare in its homozygous combination, the frequency of the Rh negative phenotype in the Ashkenazim being 9.39 percent, lower than the percentage found in the European countries which fall mostly in the 12–16 percent zone.

The Ashkenazim, with 5.25 percent cDe differ considerably from their Sephardic (11%), Moroccan (9.45%), Tunisian (8.47%) and Tripolitanian (9.46%) brethren. This is not surprising if it is recalled that the cDe chromosome comes from African or Spanish sources.[10]

SUMMARY

ABO, MN and Rh-Hr blood group frequencies in 465 Ashkenazi Jews from European countries are reported and compared with findings in other Jewish communities in Israel.

REFERENCES

1. Brzezinsky, A., Gurevitch, D. Hermoni and G. Mundel: Blood groups in Jews from Yemen. *Ann Eugen, 16*:335, 1952.

2. Chown, B., R.F. Peterson, M. Lewis and A. Hall: On the ABO gene and Rh chromosome distribution in the white population of Manitoba. *Can J Res, E27*:214, 1949.

3. Gurevitch, J., and E. Margolis: Blood groups in Jews from Iraq. *Ann Hum Genet, 19*:257, 1955.

4. Gurevitch, J., D. Hermoni and Z. Polishuk: Rh blood types in Jerusalem Jews. *Ann Eugen, 16*:129, 1951.

5. Gurevitch, J., E. Hasson, E. Margolis and C. Poliakoff: Blood groups in Jews from Cochin, India. *Ann Hum Genet, 19*:254, 1955.

6. —— Blood groups in Jews from Tripolitania. *Ibid., 19*:260, 1955.

7. Gurevitch, J., E. Hasson and E. Margolis: Blood groups in Persian Jews. *Ibid., 21*:135, 1956.

8. Manuila, A.: Distribution of ABO gene in eastern Europe. *Am J Phys Anthrop, 14*:577, 1956.

9. Margolis, E., J. Gurevitch and E. Hasson: Blood groups in Jews from Morocco and Tunisia. *Ann Hum Genet, 22*:65, 1957.

10. Mourant, A.E.: *The Distribution of the Human Blood Groups.* Oxford, Blackwell Scientific Publications, 1954, pp. 72–74.

11. Revel, H.: *The Universal Jewish Encyclopedia.* New York, *1*:541, 1939.

Chapter 6

HAPTOGLOBIN FREQUENCIES IN
JEWISH COMMUNITIES

E. Goldschmidt, P. Bayani-sioson, H. E. Sutton, K. Fried,
A. Sandor and N. Bloch

The different Jewish groups, which have been scattered for at least 80 to 90 generations over numerous countries in three continents were doubtlessly exposed to different selective agents by their diverse environments. From time to time these Jewish groups must have experienced admixtures of various types and amounts of genes from the autochthonous populations surrounding them. However, the strict observance over long periods of a religious code forbidding intermarriage with gentiles and granting proselytism only as a comparatively rare favour appears to have ensured a large measure of reproductive isolation to each one of these communities. Wherever population size dwindled, gene frequencies may have responded with rapid drift, and inbreeding tendencies[4] may have created an "isolate effect" in large congregations. The differences as well as the affinities between the Jewish groups have aroused considerable interest.[9,13,20,16,23,24,12]

The present study of the haptoglobin frequencies in some of the Jewish communities may add further material to this discussion.

Reprinted in edited version with permission from *Ann Hum Gen, 26*:39–46, 1962.

We are greatly obliged to Dr. Tirzah Cohen for collecting the bloods of the Kurdish family sample. We are also much indebted to Dr. J. V. Neel for his encouragement throughout this study and for his criticism during the preparation of the manuscript.

METHODS

The blood samples were all collected in Israel, mainly from voluntary blood donors among healthy male army recruits, most of whom were in the age range 18 to 20 years. The subjects were questioned about the countries of origin of both their parents and also about their community affiliation in cases where geographic origin alone is insufficient for classification. Nearly all the bloods of Kurdish Jews were collected in an immigrant village which was studied simultaneously for the incidence of "glutathione instabilty" (deficiency of the enzyme glucose-6-phosphate dehydrogenase) and of thalassaemia.[1,2] These bloods came from males and females of all ages. This was a family study and the majority of the subjects investigated were therefore lost for the gene count and only a minority were chosen for this purpose. The subjects included are the oldest investigated of their kinships. Sibs, children and grandchildren of these subjects were excluded from the gene count, but the high consanguinity rate of this community made the elimination of first cousins unfeasible.

Venous blood was collected in oxalate and centrifuged and deep-frozen in Jerusalem. The frozen samples were packed in ice and shipped by air to Ann Arbor where they were subjected to electrophoresis according to the vertical starch-gel method of Smithies[29] for ascertainment of the haptoglobin and transferrin types. When necessary, cyanmethaemoglobin was added to ensure complete saturation of the haptoglobins. After the gels were sliced one half of each was stained for protein with amido black, the other half was stained for peroxidase activity (haemoglobin) with dianisidine.[19]

RESULTS

Among the 929 individuals investigated, no transferrins other than C were found.

The Hp^1 frequencies of the Jewish communities are lower, on the whole, than those reported for West Europeans.[3,11] The Oriental Jews from different countries range close to the Hp^1 frequency of 0.25 reported by Harris *et al.*[11] for a small sample of autochthonous Persians. All European Jews (Ashkenazim) originating from different areas of Central and Eastern Europe do not differ signficantly in this respect from all Oriental Jews.

It is somewhat surprising to find the Ashkenazic Jews, who are expected to exhibit some "Mediterranean features"[17] possessing slightly *lower* Hp^1 rates than the various Italian and Sardinian groups reported in the literature (Harris *et al.* 1959). The haptoglobin frequencies of gentiles in Middle and Western Europe resemble the Italian pattern, but there is a tendency to higher Hp^1 rates, especially in Switzerland, Austria, Germany and France. While the data on Slavic groups are extremely scanty, it is of interest to note that the Polish Jews have significantly less Hp^1 ($X^2 = 5.61$; $P = 0.02–0.01$) than the 0.36 found in Polish gentiles by Murawski & Miszczak.[18]

Only two small groups in the present sample show excellent agreement with non-Jews from Italy and from some Central European countries. These are the Sephardim (Spanish Jews) and the mixed group. The Spanish Jews of our sample were mostly settled in Bulgaria, Greece, Italy and Yugoslavia before their immigration into Israel and it so happens that the mixed group includes many subjects related to this community through one parent. The higher Hp^1 values of these two samples are responsible for the heterogeneity between the four major groups. But since this heterogeneity is significant only at the 5 percent level, it hardly justifies any far reaching conclusions.

The modified 2–1 phenotype appears to be very rare among Jews and was found only once in a subject from Iraq. Ahaptoglobinaemia is likewise very uncommon, in both Ashkenazim and Orientals. If phenotypic ahaptoglobiaemia may occur as a result of haemolytic conditions, a higher frequency of it might have been expected in the Oriental communities, in many of which the inherited deficiency of glucose-6-phosphate dehydrogenase (G-6-P-D) is very common.[24] It may be argued that the subjects were young army recruits selected for good physical condition by previous medical examination. Thus although they would possess the trait for enzyme deficency they would not be likely to suffer from acute haemolysis when voluntarily donating blood.

These considerations do not apply to the family sample of Jews from Kurdistan, who were unselected for physical fitness.

Especial interest attaches to the search for ahaptoglobinaemia in this community, which, apart from G–6–P–D deficiency, exhibits also a high frequency of one of the inherited anaemias–thalassaemia.[1,2,14,15]

The settlers of the village under study stem from the mountains of Kurdistan in Northern Iraq, near the boundaries of Turkey, Syria and Persia. The bloods investigated revealed a high frequency of thalassaemia minor while over 70 percent of the males as well as numerous females exhibited the enzyme deficiency.

If ahaptoglobinaemia can be temporarily produced by haemolytic conditions, the two erythrocyte defects might jointly or separately be responsible for such an effect in some individuals of this group. However, in the family sample of 91 individuals from the settlement no ahaptoglobinaemia was observed. Seventy-one persons with G–6–P–D deficiency had normal haptoglobin patterns and eight of these were also classified as suffering from thalassaemia minor. Two additional thalassaemic individuals without enzyme deficiency were also not ahaptoglobinaemic.

DISCUSSION

The blood group frequencies of the various Jewish communities have been carefully analyzed by Mourant.[16,17] The ABO system indicates a more marked diversity among the Jews from various countries than do the *Rhesus* chromosomes. It is generally held that *ABO* frequencies change rapidly under the impact of selection while the more conservative *Rhesus* group yields better historical information. Although the Jewish communities differ quite markedly in the concentrations of the *C–D–E*–chromosomes, Mourant has drawn attention to certain characteristics which are shared to some extent by all the Jews including even the Ashkenazim. The high frequencies of both the *CDe* and the *cDE* chromosomes may be interpreted as "Mediterranean" or "Asiatic" features. Moreover, in all Jewish groups, including Ashkenazim, the *cDe* chromosome is somewhat more frequent than in gentile Europeans. This characteristic, which is shared by Moslems of the Near East, is taken by Mourant as indicative of some African admixture.

The low Hp^1 frequencies observed by us in Oriental Jews furnish some complementary evidence. By this criterion the Jews resemble other nations of the Near East and are set off more distinctly from the western Mediterranean peoples. The tribes of Western Africa which have been studied have mostly Hp^1 frequencies that are much higher than those of Mediterraneans, but large areas of Africa, including the Nile valley, remain to be studied. It is not impossible that the *cDe* chromosome with its striking gradient from Africa to the Mediterranean may be a much more delicate indicator of ancient African admixture than the haptoglobins. However, the extreme rareness of the modied 2– phenotype as well as the absence of any transferrin types other than C in the Jewish groups also testify against African affinities.

The haptoglobin frequencies of the small sample of Sephardic Jews are in good agreement with those of other Mediterraneans. But it came as a surprise to find the Ashkenazim so similar to Oriental Jews with regard to this polymorphic system. In many other respects the Ashkenazim are rather set apart from the Oriental groups by characters, which they share with the gentile populations of Central and Western Europe. Thus, in a recent survey, Kalmus *et al.*[12] found the rate of colour blindness in European Jews similar to that of other Europeans and nearly twice as high as that of most other Jewish populations. The virtual absence in Ashkenazim of G–6–P–D deficiency, which is present with variable frequencies in all the other Jewish communities[23,24] is also regarded as a Central European feature.

While it is plausible that the "Asiatic" haptoglobin frequencies of European Jews may indeed reflect their origin from the Middle East, the key to their convergence, in this respect, towards the pattern of Oriental Jewry cannot be offered before the completion of the East European map of haptoglobin distributions. The Slavic peoples resemble those of the Near East in the frequency of the B antigen. The same may well apply to the haptoglobin concentrations.

Before resorting to the panacea of "drift" in order to account for all conflicting tendencies, we should weigh carefully how much ethnic information each system can supply in *large* populations. For statistical reasons "low frequency genes" like colour blindness and *cDe* in Europe may be more informative than "high frequency genes" like *Hp¹* and *CDe*. The haptoglobins do not show much geographic variation from north to south over Western Europe. Their clines in the east of Eurasia remain to be studied.

SUMMARY

Haptoglobin and transferrin types have been determined by starch gel electrophoresis on blood from 929 subjects belonging to various Jewish communities.

The frequency of the Hp^1 gene in 499 Ashkenazic Jews is 0.29 and does not differ significantly from the value of 9.26 found in 345 Jews of Oriental origin. The Hp^1 frequency of Ashkenazic Jews is significantly lower than that reported for the autochthonous populations of Central and Western Europe. Two small samples collected among Sephardic Jews and among the offspring of intercommunity marriages exhibit somewhat higher frequencies of the Hp^1 gene.

The modified 2–1 phenotype was found in a single subject from Baghdad. There were three cases of ahaptoglobinaemia among Ashkenazic Jews and three among the Oriental groups. No ahaptoglobinaemia was discovered in a family sample of 92 Jews from Kurdistan among whom thalassaemia minor was common and the majority of whom were affected with G–6–P–D deficiency.

All transferrins were of type C.

REFERENCES

1. Cohen, T., Bloch, N., Goldschmidt, E., Matoth, Y. and Adam, A.: High frequency of G6PD deficiency and thalassemia in Jews from Kurdistan. *Proc Conf Human Popul Genet Israel* (in press).

2. Cohen, T., Goldschmidt, E., Adam, A., Theodor, E. and Szabo, M.A.: The frequency of rhumatic heart disease, glutathione instability and thalassaemia in children of Kurdish Jews. (Hebrew). *J Med Ass Israel*, 57:233–6, 1959.

3. Galatius-Jensen, F.: *The Haptoglobins, A Genetical Study*. Copenhagen, Dansk Videnskabs Forlag, 1960.

4. Goldschmidt, E., Ronen, A. and Ronen, I.: Changing marriage systems in the Jewish communities of Israel. *Ann Hum Genet, Lond., 24:*191–204, 1960.

5. Gurevitch, J., Hasson, E. and Margolis, E.: Blood groups in Persian Jews. *Ann Hum Genet, Lond, 21,* 135–8.

6. Gurevitch, J., Hasson, E., Margolis, E. and Poliakoff, C.: Blood groups in Jews from Tripolitania. *Ann Hum Genet, 19:*260–1, 1955.

7. Gurevitch, J., Hasson, E., Margolis, E. and Poliakoff, C.: Blood groups in Jews from Cochin, India. *Ann Hum Genet, Lond, 19:*254–6, 1955.

8. Gurevitch, J., Hermoni, D. and Margolis, E.: Blood groups in Kurdistani Jews. *Ann Eugen, 18:*94–5, 1953.

9. Gurevitch, J., Hermoni, D. and Polishuk, Z.: *Rh* blood types in Jerusalem Jews. *Ann Eugen, 16:*129–30, 1951.

10. Gurevitch, J. and Margolis, E.: Blood groups in Jews from Iraq. *Ann Hum Genet, 19:*257–9, 1955.

11. Harris, H., Robson, E.B. and Siniscalco, M.: Genetics of the plasma protein variants. Is *Biochemistry of Human Genetics. Ciba Found. Symp.* pp. 151–77, 1959.

12. Kalmus, H., Amir, A., Levine, O., Barak, E. and Goldschmidt, E.: The frequency of inherited defects of colour vision in some Israeli populations. *Ann Hum Genet, Lond, 25:*51–5, 1961.

13. Margolis, E., Gurevitch, J. and Hasson, E.: Blood groups in Jews from Morocco and Tunisia. *Ann Hum Genet, Lond, 22:*65–8, 1957.

14. Matoth, Y., Shamir, Z. and Freudlich, E.: Thalassaemia in Jews from Kurdistan. *Blood, 10:*176–89, 1955.

15. Matoth, Y. and Pinhas, J.: Thalassaemia in Jews from Kurdistan. *Bull Res Count, Israel,* 7B, 215, 1958.

16. Mourant, A.E.: *The Distribution of Human Blood Groups.* Oxford, Blackwell Scientific Publications, 1954.

17. Mourant, A.E.: The blood groups of the Jews. *Jewish J Sociol,* 1:155–76, 1959.

18. Murawski, K. and Miszczak, T.: Haptoglobin types in Poland. *Science, 133:*1427, 1961.

19. Owen, J.A., Silberman, H.J. and Got, C.: Detection of haemoglobin, haemoglobin-haptoglobin complexes and other substances with peroxidase activity after zone electrophoresis. *Nature, Lond, 182:*1373, 1958.

20. Sachs, and Bat-Miriam, M.: The genetics of Jewish populations. I. Finger print patterns in Jewish populations in Israel. *Am J Hum Genet,* 9:117, 1957.

21. Smithies, O.: An improved procedure for starch-gel electrophoresis: further variations in the serum proteins of normal individuals. *Biochem J,* 71:585, 1959.

22. Sutton, H.E., Neel, J.V., Binson, G. and Zuelzer, W.W.: Serum protein differences between Africans and Caucasians. *Nature, Lond., 178:*1287, 1956.

23. Szeinberg, A. and Sheba, C.: Hemolytic trait in Oriental Jews connected with an hereditary enzymatic abnormality of erythrocytes. *Israel Med J 17:*158–68, 1958.

24. Szeinberg, A., Sheba, C. and Adam, A.: Selective occurrence of glutathione instability in red blood corpuscles of the various Jewish tribes. *Blood, 13:*1043–53, 1958.

PART THREE
GENETIC DISORDERS

For many years it has been evident to medical practitioners that certain disorders occur with greater frequency in specific ethnic groups compared with others. In the past quarter century there has been growing research devoted to the deleterious genes which may trigger these disorders.

In Chapter 7 Post reviews the literature on "Jewish diseases," concentrating on 12 hereditary diseases of Ashkenazic Jews, all of which are rare metabolic defects, usually appearing in infancy, and often leading to early death. He then offers some explanations for the higher frequencies of these diseases among Jews.

In a detailed letter to the *Lancet*, Sheba (Chap. 8) gives a short historic account of the Jewish dispersion and he provides a table of gene frequencies in several Israeli population groups. He also lists, very briefly, various disorders found more frequently among these groups.

In Chapter 9 Yaacov Rotem adds a note to Sheba's letter in a succeeding issue of the *Lancet* with more information on familial dysautonomia, the "most Jewish of all diseases."

Familial dysautonomia (also called the Riley Day Syndrome after the doctors who first observed and described it) is investigated by McKusick, Norum, Farkas, Brunt, and Mahloudji in Chapter 10. Its clinical features are described and an estimate is made of its frequency in American Jews as between one in 10,000 and one in 20,000.

This is less than the frequency of Tay-Sachs Disease (TSD), recently much in the news. Myrianthopoulos and Aronson estimate in Chapter 11 that TSD occurs once in approximately 6,000 Jewish births and once in approximately 500,000 non-Jewish births. They too, attempt to explain this differential frequency.

Gaucher's Disease is another genetic disorder with a very high frequency among Ashkenazi Jews. Groen, who had treated patients afflicted with this disease in the Netherlands before World War II, and subsequently in Israel, in Chapter 12 studies it and comments upon a remarkable characteristic of this disease: patients with active Gaucher's Disease produce only healthy offspring.

Chapter 7

JEWS, GENETICS AND DISEASE

R.H. POST

A paper of this title appeared in *Harofé Haiviri,* the Hebrew Medical Journal, for 1962 (pp. 261–275) by Louis B. Brinn of New York, discussing twelve hereditary diseases that appear to be more frequent among Ashkenazi Jewish populations of Western Europe and the United States than in neighboring populations. Eight are rare, monomeric entities of fairly reliable diagnosis. The author considers the probability of more thorough reporting among Jews; the many environmental differences between them and neighboring Gentiles—in diet, exercise, personal hygiene, mode of life, and so forth; the possibilities of the environment altering or modifying the chemical bases of these diseases. He leaves one with the impression that at least eight of these diseases represent bona fide cases of gene frequency differences between populations.

All are rare metabolic defects, with onsets usually during infancy or childhood, generally appearing in pedigrees as recessives with high penetrance and constant expressivity but occasionally appearing as dominants with low penetrance and variable expression of symptoms. Exceptions to these statements are noted below, together with references (in parentheses) to reviews citing reports of particular association with Ashkenazi populations and other points relevant to the present discussion:

1. *Dystonia musculorum deformans.*[2,4] (torsion dystonia, etc.) Dominant in most pedigrees, with variable expressivity.

2. *Familial autonomic dysfunction.*[2,5] (Riley-Day Syndrome) Usually recessive but occasionally dominant.

3. *Gaucher's disease.*[2,6,7,8,9] (familial splenic anemia). Perhaps

Reprinted with permission from *Eugenics Q, 12:*162–164, 1965.

not a single entity. Recessive in most pedigrees but dominant in some. Onsets from infancy to early adult life.

4. *Infantile amaurotic idiocy.*[2,6,7,8,9] (Tay-Sachs disease)

5. *Niemann-Picks disease.*[2,6,9] (lipoid histiocytosis)

6. *Pemphigus vulgaris.*[1,2] Genetic basis not clear. Onset age range 19–82, average about 55. Reported among Negroes as well as Caucasians.

7. *Pentosuria, essential or idiopathic.*[2,6,7,9] Benign: selective disadvantage very slight. Onsets at all ages.

8. *Polycythemia vera.*[2,6,9] (erythremia)

Genetic basis not clear; probably not a single entity.

Brinn[2] mentions four additional "genetic" diseases that have been reported more frequently among Ashkenazi Jewish populations than among other Caucasians: idopathic hypercholesterolemia, diabetes mellitus, regional enteritis, and thrombosis obliterans. The list might be extended to include Wilson's disease and plasma thromboplastic antecedent deficiency,[9] phenylketonuria,[6,7,9,] and Karposi's dermatosis. Since these diseases are not particularly uncommon among non-Jewish Caucasian populations, they will not be included in the considerations which follow.

Students of human evolution are immediately challenged to explain a marked difference between populations in the frequency of any genetic trait, whether it be normal or pathological. Brinn[2] mentions inbreeding and genetic isolation of Ashkenzi Jews as possible explanations for their allegedly higher frequencies. Since the effect of consanguineous marriage in increasing the frequency of a recessive trait is eliminated by a single generation of random marriage and since the rate of cousin marriage in the last generation or two in Western Europe and the United States has not been high, inbreeding must be largely discounted. Genetic isolation per se can serve only to maintain a high or low gene frequency that has been previously established in a population, but not to create it. The fundamental cause, assuming no differences in mutation rates, must be sought in differential rates of natural selection between Jews and Gentiles operating over many generations and based upon differences in ecological habitat or environment.

Three suggested explanations come to mind. Since they lie

beyond the qualifications of the present writer for detailed discussion, they will be merely mentioned. They concern contrasts between Jews and Gentiles with respect to demographic, sociological, and epidemiological situations, respectively. The first two depend on the assumption that both of the heterozygous parents of a patient with a recessive disease, or one of the parents of a patient with a dominant disease, has been under a slight selective *disadvantage,* such as would decrease the likelihood of biological survival (normal rate of reproduction) in the environment of Gentiles in recent centuries, but to a lesser degree in the environment of Ashkenazi Jews. In the third suggested explanation a selective *advantage* of the heterozygous carrier is assumed, under the special environmental conditions of Jewish populations.

The environmental contrasts in the three suggested explanations are, in brief:

Demographic situation. Continuous habitat of most Jewish populations for several millenia in cities or towns, more rarely in villages, but almost never "on the land," whereas Gentiles have been essestially rural, since town and city death rates have been so high until almost up to the turn of the past century that Gentile urban populations have been maintained only through a continuous recruiting of migrants from the surrounding countryside. Genetic carriers of these diseases might be at a selective disadvantage in rural habitats.

Sociological situation. Greater tolerance and concern of Jews for illness, handicaps, and all types of afflictions; religious customs and taboos that have effectively provided greater protection to persons handicapped or afflicted in various ways, such as is assumed (but not established) is the heterozygote "carriers" of the genetic diseases here considered; complete absence of what might be called the "Spartan Complex," referring to the ancient Greek custom of subjecting infants to rigorous tests aimed to eliminate "weaklings," echoes of which are recognizable in former Gentile medical practices such as purging, leeching, sweat-bathing followed by a cold plunge, etc. Such customs might have eliminated Gentile carriers of these diseases more frequently than Jewish carriers, who were rarely subjected to them.

Epidemiological situation. Greater exposure of urban populations than of rural populations to infectious and contagious diseases, particularly to epidemics such as of plague and smallpox. Heterozygous carriers might have a selective advantage under the stress of these diseases, against which the genes might confer protection. Jewish populations have probably been subjected more intensively than Gentile populations to contagious diseases during the past two millenia.

The weakest point in these hypotheses is that the allegedly heterozygous "carrier" is not determinable in any of these diseases, and no information is available as to whether it is an advantage or disadvantage in natural selection. Secondly, the evidence of higher frequencies among Jews can hardly be accepted in full when only a few hundred cases of any of these diseases have been reported, since the sampling may easily be biased, particularly in large cities where most of the cases have been found. Nevertheless, the assumption of mild heterozygote disadvantage is not unreasonable, and the numbers of reports of higher frequencies among Jewish patients are impressive, as indicated by the authors listed in the bibliography.

Since Gentiles today are rapidly changing their ways of life in the direction of the traditional Jewish environment—with rapidly growing towns and cities, rapidly increasing protection of slightly handicapped or afflicted persons through modern public health and individual health facilities—it seems reasonable to consider the question of whether the frequencies of these eight diseases—indeed, perhaps of all genetic diseases—might become progressively greater among all modern populations in future generations. This trend would be accentuated as medical examinations, therapies, preventives, and public health facilities become further improved, producing lower juvenile and adolescent death rates and higher rates of marriage and reproduction for carriers of genetic disease.

REFERENCES

1. Adair, H., and J. Owens: Pemphigus vulgaris. *South Med J,* 55:1034–1039, 1962.

2. Brinn, L.B.: Jews, Genetics and disease. *Harofé Haivri,* 261–275, 1962.

3. Goldschmidt, E. (Ed.): *The Genetics of Migrant and Isolate Populations.* Baltimore, Williams and Wilkins, 1963.

4. Johnson, W., G. Schwartz, and A. Barbeau: Studies on Dystonia Musculorum deformans. *Arch Neurol,* 7:301–313, 1962.

5. Hould, F.: La Dysautonomie Familiale. *Laval Méd,* 33:225–227, 1962.

6. Hsia, D.Y.: *Inborn Errors of Metabolism.* Chicago, Yearbook Publishers, 1959.

7. Sheba, C., A. Szeinberg, B. Ramot, A. Adam, and I. Ashkenazi: Epidemiologic surveys of deleterious genes in different populations in Israel. *Am J Pub Health,* 52:1101–1106, 1962.

8. Sorsby, A.: *Clinical Genetics.* London, Metheuen, 1956.

9. Stanbury, J.B., *et al.,* (Eds.): *The Metabolic Basis of Inherited Disease.* New York, McGraw-Hill, 1960.

Chapter 8

GENE–FREQUENCIES IN JEWS

Chaim Sheba

During the past 25 years I have been investigating gene-frequencies in exiles returning to Israel. It seems to me that some genetic studies of conditions in Jews have been based on an oversimplified concept—that of a simple division of Jews into Ashkenazim and non-Ashkenazim. It may be that I was partly responsible for this oversimplification when, in 1945, I showed that constitutional haemolytic anaemia is found only in non-Ashkenazim.[1] I should like to present a short account of the genetic distribution of Jews, and of the gene frequencies of some conditions found in the different groups.

The Ashkenazim were the Jews who lived in Europe, and later in the United States and Israel. They spoke Yiddish—a sort of mittelhoch-deutsch-cockney written in Hebrew characters—and could also be identified by the setting of the liturgy in their prayer books.

The non-Ashkenazim come under the group heading, Sepharadim (sepharad = sunset). The common language of the Sepharadim is the Ladino—ancient Castilian Spanish written in Hebrew characters of the kind used in Southern France by Rashi, the Bible commentator of the eleventh century. These Jews provided all Jewry with the bitter lemon, the "ethrog," for the feast of the tabernacle. Splinter groups of Jews lived as far away

Reprinted with permission from *Lancet*, June 6, 1970, pp. 1230–1231.

These data were assembled from material in the Tel-Hashomer Institute of Human Genetics, and with the help of Avinoam Adam, Israel Ashkenazy, Mariassa Bat-Miriam, Bathsheba Bonné, Bernie Cohen, Joseph Gafni, Eliahu Gilon, Harry Heller, Nehammah Kossover, Amira Mani, Baruch Padeh, Mordechai Pras, Bracha Ramot, Yecheskiel Samra, Uri Seligsohn, Mordecai Shani, Ezra Sohar. I am especially grateful to Aryeh Szeinberg, of Tel-Hashomer and Elisabeth Goldschmidt, of Jerusalem.

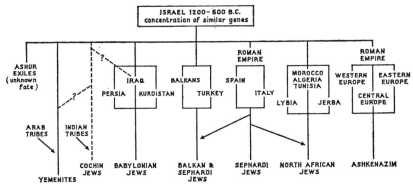

Figure 8–1. Ethnic distribution of Jews from Israel between 1200 B.C. and A.D. 1970.

as Cochin, on the southwestern tip of India, and the Yemen, on the southwestern tip of Arabia. Another isolated group of Jews lived in Hadramaut (Court of Death), six weeks' camel distance from Aden. There were also, of course, large Jewish congregations in Morocco, Algiers, Tunis, Libya, and Egypt, and very small remnants in Pakeen, in Upper Gallilee, and Sichem, in Samaria. There was a flourishing independent community in Babylon (now Iraq), with satellites in Iran, Kurdistan, the Caucasus mountains, Afghanistan, Syria, the Lebanon, and Asia Minor. The Balkan Jews of Greece, Bulgaria, Yugoslavia, and Italy really belonged to the Sephardic group (with the possible exception of Stephen Dunn's 200 families). The accompanying figure shows a scheme of the distribution of the various groups, designed for me by Dr. Israel Ashkenazy, of Tel Aviv University.

Now a brief account of some of the gene frequencies. Rough estimates for some of the most extensively studied conditions are shown in the accompanying table. In addition, the following conditions are almost exclusively found in Ashkenazi as opposed to non-Ashkenazi Jews: Tay-Sachs disease, Gaucher's disease, Buerger's disease, pentosuria, and dysautonomia. (Congenital pyloric stenosis is also about three times more prevalent than among non-Ashkenazim.)

The following conditions are *almost* exclusively found in non-Ashkenazim: glycogen-storage disease, pituitary dwarfism (with high growth-hormone levels), vitamin-B_{12} malabsorption, and Wolman's disease (familial xanthomatosis). Libyan Jews, with the highest gene-frequency of familial Mediterranean fever, must have been a special isolate, as were the Jews of Ispahan (Iran), with the highest frequency of Dubin-Johnson syndrome.

REFERENCES

1. Schieber, C.: *Lancet,* 2:851, 1945.

TABLE 8-I
ROUGH ESTIMATES OF GENE-FREQUENCIES IN SEVEN ISRAELI COMMUNITIES

	Place of origin						
	Morocco Algeria Tunisia	Libya	Yemen	Iraq	Kurdi-stan	Iran	Europe U.S.A.
Population (thousands):	415	60	140	210	30	80	1100
Conditions*:							
G.-6P.D. def.	0.006	0.01	0.05	0.25	0.58	0.15	0.003
-thalassæmia	0.005	(?) 0	Rare	0.01	0.10	0.015	0
F.M.F.	0.02	0.04	0	0.015	9 cases	0	10 cases
D.J.S.	9 cases	0	0	5 cases	4 cases	64 cases	7 cases
P.K.U.	0.005	0	0.019	0.009	0	0.015	0
Atyp. pseudochol.	0.003	—	0.036	0.05	—	(?) 0.05	0.017
Color blindness	0.06	0.06	0.04	0.05	0.05	0.06	0.09

* Gene frequencies unless otherwise stated. G.-6P.D. def. = glucose-6-phosphate dehydrogenase deficiency. F.M.F. = familial Mediterranean fever. D.J.S. = Dubin-Johnson syndrome. P.K.U. = phenylketonuria. Atyp. pseudochol. = atypical pseudocholinesterase.

Chapter 9

GENE—FREQUENCIES IN JEWS

Yaacov Rotem

D
r. Sheba's instructive contribution to this subject[1] makes only passing reference to the disease familial dysautonomia. Inasmuch as this disorder is confined not merely to Jews, but to a particular ethnic subsection of the Jewish community, I thought it might be of interest to complement the data in Dr. Sheba's note.

Thirty-four cases of familial dysautonomia—this "most Jewish of all diseases"—have been diagnosed in Israel up to 1970. The age-distribution ranged between seven months and 24 years. The gene-frequency calculated by our group[2] approaches the remarkably high level of 1 percent in the Ashkenazi population. All the patients in Israel came from Jewish families of Eastern European (Ashkenazi) origin. Not a single case has been found so far amongst Sephardic Jews, an ethnic group comprising over 50 percent of the population here. The restriction of this disease to Ashkenazi Jews raises the possibility that genetic mutation occurred in central and eastern Europe after the expulsion of the Jews from Spain in 1492.

REFERENCES

1. Sheba, C.: Gene-frequencies in Jews. *Lancet,* June 6, 1970, p. 1230.
2. Moses, S.W., Rotem, Y., Jagoda, N., Talmor, N., Eichhorn, F., Levin, S.: *Israel J Med Sci,* 3:358, 1967.

Reprinted with permission from *Lancet,* August 8, 1970, p. 315.

Chapter 10

THE RILEY-DAY SYNDROME—OBSERVATIONS
ON GENETICS AND SURVIVORSHIP

V. A. McKusick, R. A. Norum, H. J. Farkas,
P. W. Brunt, and M. Mahloudji

Familial dysautonomia, as it has subsequently become known, was first clearly described in 1949 by Riley, Day and their colleagues[1] working in the Pediatrics Department at Columbia University College of Physicians and Surgeons. During the years since 1949, the entity as an ailment of the pediatric age group has become reasonably well known.[2]

In the present study an attempt has been made to identify and analyze all families with one or more cases of dysautonomia known in the United States and Canada, for the following purposes: (1) of determining its frequency, mode of inheritance and ethnic distribution; (2) of determining the overall clinical picture on the basis of a large number of cases, particularly the prognosis and behavior of the disorder in late adolescence and adulthood; and (3) from the clinical and pathologic material available, hopefully to get clues as to the nature of the basic defect.

Ascertainment was accomplished through the Dysautonomia Association (a voluntary health agency with headquarters in New York City), through parents who often knew of other cases and through pediatricians and pediatric neurologists in many parts of the country.

Over 220 affected families are now known to us. The present interim report is concerned primarily with the genetics

Reprinted in edited version with permission from Isr J Med Sci, 3:(no. 3) 1967.

We gratefully acknowledge the assistance of Mrs. Myra Harris, R.N., and Mrs. Kathryn Smith who have been responsible for much of the data collection.

We are indebted to the Dysautonomia Foundation, Inc. of New York City, for both financial and moral assistance. The cooperation of parents and patients is also gratefully acknowledged.

of the disorder and survivorship and is based on the findings in 164 families on which studies have been completed.

CLINICAL FEATURES

Based on the reports in the literature and personal observations by the writers of over 100 cases, the clinical features can be summarized as follows:

Beginning in early infancy, indeed usually evident soon after birth, the major features are difficulty in feeding and swallowing with frequent regurgitation the aspiration of which appears to be the source of their recurrent bronchopneumonia. Lack of tearing, relative insensitivity to pain, emotional lability, breath holding attacks with loss of consciousness, episodic vomiting, unexplained high fever, skin blotching, excessive sweating, and motor incoordination are noted in the first two or three years. Somewhat later, postural hypotension and paroxysmal hypertension appear, the latter sometimes requiring differentiation from that characterizing pheochromocytoma. By the age of eight or nine most patients show kyphoscoliosis which steadily progresses in severity. Death, especially from pulmonary infection, takes a heavy toll in the first decade.

Most of the patients are undersized. Because of absence of tearing and corneal hypalgesia, corneal ulceration is a recurrent and serious problem in many. A characteristic facial appearance has often been commented on. The mouth is transverse with a tendency to symmetrical facial drooping.

Probably all patients with this disorder have blunting of taste and in all cases, the fungiform and probably circumvallate papillae are missing from the tongue although filiform papillae are normal. This consistent feature of dysautonomia probably occurs in no other condition.

Sexual development is essentially normal and there is no evidence of endocrine dysfunction.

The defect in swallowing has two components, although both may not be present in the same patient: (1) an abnormality in the behavior of the pharyngeal musculature (constriction in the hypopharynx) characteristic of that seen in brain stem lesions; and (2) a dilated and aperistaltic esophagus, typical of that seen in achalasia, i.e. with defect in the ganglia of the esophageal wall. Aspiration leads to repeated bronchopneumonia and pulmonary fibrosis. An additional feature is relative insensitivity of the respiratory control mechanism to carbon dioxide excess and to oxygen deficit. Intermittently cold hands and a whittling of the terminal phalanges are presumably related to vasoconstriction.

The impressive features of the neurologic examination are reduced sensitivity to pain, absent gag reflex in some, absent deep tendon reflexes, rombergism, and in most, ataxia evident if the patient attempts to walk on a straight line. The voice often has a monotonous and nasal quality. One new feature of the clinical picture we can add on the basis of the study of older patients is that of Charcot neuropathic joints. Severe involvement of the knees with effusion and subluxation has been observed in teen-age patients. Similar changes, though milder, were observed in the shoulders and elbows of some patients. Because the Charcot joint develops before closure of the epiphyses, the x-ray changes differ from those in adults in respect to the added feature of epiphyseal damage.

By all indications mental retardation is not a primary feature of dysautonomia. Any retardation observed may be due to anoxia in breath holding attacks, effects of high fever or dehydration. Emotional instability is a striking feature.

SURVIVORSHIP

The 164 families studied to date contain 200 affected persons. Over a fourth of patients are dead by the age of ten years. As the study is carried further, the figures on prognosis will probably get worse rather than better because proportionately more families in which all affected persons are deceased will probably be interviewed. Furthermore, affected infants dying very early may not have been recognized as affected and so not included in our series. Thus, this is a minimal estimate of the gravity of the condition.

GENETICS

In this series, 91 males and 109 females were affected; the sex difference is not significant. Riley and Day early recognized that dysautonomia is a disease of Jews and the present study confirms this. In two families the mother apparently has no Jewish ancestry, although the father is Jewish. In all the other 164 families, both parents are Ashkenazi Jews. Furthermore, 326 of the 328 Jewish parents have ancestry derived from the area of the Jewish Pale in eastern Europe.

The presumption has been that dysautonomia is autosomal recessive. In all cases both parents are normal and there are nine instances of parental consanguinity. Of these nine, five are first cousin marriages. A segregation analysis by the Lenz-Hogben method (which assumes that all affected families have been ascertained or, if not all, that those ascertained are a random sample of the whole) yields results closely consistent with the idea that dysautonomia is indeed autosomal recessive.

The families provide some suggestion that the occurrence of the Riley-Day syndrome plays a role in family planning. Of 61 two-child families in which only one was affected, in 42 the affected child was the latter born. Of 30 three-child families with one sib affected, in 16 the affected child was last born. Both of these figures differ significantly from one-half and one-third, respectively.

We estimate that the frequency of dysautonomia in American Jews is between 1 in 10,000 and 1 in 20,000 births. (The frequency of the gene in American Jews is 0.01 at the highest and one in 50 may carry the gene.) This is somewhat less than in the frequency of Tay-Sachs' disease, which also has a high frequency in Jews of this same extraction, but Tay-Sachs' disease is not so strictly limited to Jews.[3] It is also less frequent than pentosuria, which like dysautonomia occurs almost only in Jews.

Many rare recessive genes tend to show inhomogeneity in global distribution. Particular groups tend to have a high frequency of some genes and a low frequency of others. Among Ashkenazi Jews, for example, phenylketonuria is almost completely unknown. Inbreeding per se cannot be responsible for the high frequency of the Tay-Sachs, pentosuria and dysautonomia genes in Jews. A role of selective advantage of the heterozygote or of random genetic drift can only be speculated.

THE BASIC DEFECT

Observations of others[4] bearing on the nature of the basic defect include the following:

Physiology. Pain and flare are absent on histamine skin test. The response to infused norepinephrine, mecholyl and related drugs is greatly exaggerated. Taste, deep tendon reflexes and histamine flare have been temporarily restored in some patients by administration of mecholyl.

Neuropathology. Cytologic changes have been observed in the hypothalamus, brain stem and autonomic ganglia including those of the gastrointestinal tract. Many of the manifestations of dysautonomia may be accounted for by a defect (functional or anatomical or both) in the autonomic nervous system, including its central connections. Other features suggest a defect in sensing mechanisms: defect in taste, hypalgesia, absent axon reflex, absent deep tendon reflexes, respiratory control insensitivity, Charcot joints. The scoliosis and incoordination might also be due to a kinesthetic deficiency: The postural hypotension and paroxysma hypertension may be due to a baroceptor defect.

Chemistry. Urinary excretion of 3-methoxy, 4-hydroxy mandelic acid is relatively low and of homovanillic acid relatively high. Recessive inheritance suggests an enzyme defect. Although this leaves a rather wide-open field, a defect in an enzyme involved in the metabolism of acetylcholine seems, in the present state of ignorance, especially worthy of investigation.

REFERENCES

1. Riley, C.M., Day, R.L., Greeley, D. McL. and Langford, W.S.: Central autonomic dysfunction with defective lacrimation. I. Report of five cases. *Pediatrics, 3:*468, 1949.

2. Riley, C.M. and Moore, R.H.: Familial dysautonomia differentiated from related disorders. Case reports and discussion of current concepts. *Pediatrics, 37:*435, 1966.

3. Myrianthopoulos, N.C. and Aronson, S.M.: Population dynamics of Tay-Sachs disease. I. Reproductive fitness and selection. *Am J Hum Genet, 18:*313, 1966.

4. Dancis, J. and Smith, A.A.: Familial dysautonomia. *New Engl J Med, 274:*207, 1966.

Chapter 11

POPULATION DYNAMICS OF TAY-SACHS DISEASE.

I. REPRODUCTIVE FITNESS AND SELECTION

N. C. MYRIANTHOPOULOS AND S. M. ARONSON[2]

INTRODUCTION

Tay-Sachs disease (TSD) or infantile amaurotic familial idiocy is a hereditary disease of lipid storage in which the sphingolipid ganglioside accumulates in the cytoplasm of the neurons of the brain. It is characterized by progressive degeneration of cerebral function which commences soon after birth and ends in death usually within the first or second year of life. The disease has been demonstrated to be due to the homozygous condition of an autosomal recessive gene, apparently with complete penetrance.[2,10,12,16] When the disease was first recognized, it was thought to be an exclusively Jewish disorder, but verified cases in non-Jewish infants were reported later. These cases have become increasingly numerous in the literature in recent years, and Myrianthopoulos[13] showed that fully one-third of cases in the United States are of non-Jewish origin.

It is further well established that TSD is more frequent among the Ashkenazi Jews than among other Jewish (Sephardi) groups and non-Jewish populations. (See above references as well as Ref. 5, 6, 7.) Although considerable literature has recently been devoted to the genetics, epidemiology, and demography of the disease, the major problem of why the TSD gene, despite its

Reprinted in edited version with permission from *Am J Hum Genet* 18:(no. 4) July, 1966.

We would like to express our thanks to Dr. Alfred Naylor for his advice and help in the analysis of the material and to Dr. Jerry D. Niswander for reading and criticizing the manuscript.

mass elimination, is found in such high frequency among the Ashkenazi Jews is still unresolved. The purpose of this paper is to examine the mechanisms by which the frequency of so lethal a gene could have become elevated and then maintained at the present high level and to present evidence which suggests that one such mechanism may have been responsible for this phenomenon.

Estimates of the frequency of the TSD gene among Jews and among non-Jews are in rather close agreement (Table 11-I). In the United States, the disease occurs once in approximately 6,000 Jewish births and once in approximately 500,000 non-Jewish births. On the basis of this birth incidence, it is estimated that one of 40 Jewish persons and one of 380 non-Jewish persons is heterozygous for the TSD gene. Thus, the gene frequency is about ten times higher and the birth incidence 100 times higher among Ashkenazi Jews than among non-Jews. A difference of the same magnitude apparently exists between the Ashkenazi Jews and the other Jewish groups in Israel and the Eastern Mediterranean. The birth incidence of TSD among the Sephardic and Oriental communities of the Middle East and North Africa appears to be even lower than that found in non-Jewish Europeans and Americans.

TABLE 11-I

ESTIMATES OF THE FREQUENCY OF THE TSD GENE AMONG JEWS AND NON-JEWS

Source	Region	Years surveyed	Birth incidence of TSD	TSD gene frequency	Carrier frequency
Among Jews					
Goldschmidt *et al.* (1956)	Israel	1948–1952	0.00020	0.014	0.028
Kozinn, Wiener, and Cohen (1957)	New York City	1944–1955	0.00012	0.011	0.022
Myrianthopoulos (1962)	United States	1954–1957	0.00016	0.013	0.025
Aronson (1964)	New York City	1951–1962	0.00023	0.015	0.030
Among non-Jews					
Kozinn, Wiener, and Cohen (1957)	New York City	1944–1955	0.0000022	0.0015	0.003
Myrianthopoulos (1962)	United States	1954–1957	0.0000017	0.0013	0.0026
Aronson (1964)	New York City	1951–1960	0.0000026	0.0016	0.0032

The following mechanisms can be invoked to explain the differential frequency of TSD and the gene responsible for it in the two population groups: (1) differential breeding pattern; (2) genetic drift; (3) differential mutation rate; (4) differential fertility of the heterozygote, and (5) a combination of any of these mechanisms.

Differential breeding pattern would involve such socially conditioned forces as intermarriage between genetically different groups and close inbreeding within a group. It may be argued that the high frequency of TSD among the Ashkenazi Jews represents a repeated introduction of genes through local intermarriage with non-Jews which was subsequently abetted by inbreeding and genetic drift. This is improbable since we have no evidence that TSD was present in any appreciable frequency in the non-Jewish Polish, Lithuanian, and Russian populations among whom the Jews settled after the diaspora. It is from these areas that most of the ancestors of the Jewish TSD cases in the United States appear to have come.[3]

Consanguinity data are not helpful and merely reflect gene frequency levels in the two groups. In general, with rare recessive genes, the consanguinity rate among parents of affected children bears an inverse relationship to the gene frequency. This is precisely what we find in our data.[13] In a series of 83 TSD families, the first-cousin marriage rate among parents of Jewish infants was 1.78 percent, while among the parents of non-Jewish infants it was 7.70 percent. Consanguinity of varying degrees was found in 5.26 percent of parents of Jewish infants and in 11.12 percent of parents of non-Jewish infants. First-cousin marriages among the Ashkenazi population of Israel range between 1 percent and 2 percent which is not significantly different than the rate for the Jewish population in the United States,[7] while that of the Sephardic and Oriental communities is extraordinarily high, ranging from 7 percent to 29 percent.[5] Yet, the birth incidence of TSD in these latter communities is very low, perhaps even lower than that found in non-Jewish European populations. It might be argued that the high consanguinity rate of the Sephardic Jews has served to deplete the gene from this population rather rapidly and the process must be continuing. However, this cannot account for the low frequency of the gene in non-Jewish populations.

The argument for genetic drift is weak enough at the outset, for drift, in the strict sense, is supposed to have its random effect on the frequencies of near neutral genes or slightly unfavorable ones. It is, perhaps, permissible to stretch the operational definition of drift to include lethal genes, such as the TSD gene, although we do not know of a precedent.

Genetic drift could be held partly accountable for the rise of the TSD gene at a very high frequency if it could be shown that the Jewish isolates of Europe, especially of northeastern Poland and the surrounding areas, were composed of very small marriageable populations without social contact with neighboring communities. There is sufficient historical commentary, however, to indicate a fertile intercommunication between these religious-cultural communities. In a review of the places of birth of the foreign-born Jewish grandparents and great-grandparents of a large number of TSD cases, Aronson[1] found that about 40 percent of the grandparent marriages were between coreligionists born in different countries, 49 percent were between individuals born in the same East European country but in separate cities, and only 11 percent of the marriages were between individuals born in the same community. These figures indicate that the grandparents and great-grandparents of children with TSD, at least as far back as 1850, were sufficiently mobile to choose marriage partners in centers beyond their own immediate communities. Further, from our demographic studies of these areas, it appears that the Jewish communities were large enough to support synagogues and schools and to engage in active social life. Many thousands of Jews lived in northeastern Europe for many generations. We can find no evidence for circumstances which theoretically might favor drift, such as migration of small groups, famine, disease, or war, affecting all or a large number of these Jewish communities simultaneously. No doubt, such circumstances existed at one time or another, within one community or another. But even under conditions of complete genetic isolation, random fluctuation of the TSD gene in some communities must have been balanced in other communities. And our demographic data show that the Jews of the United States, among whom our observations were made, emigrated not from a few selected communities but from hundreds of cities, towns, and villages of northeastern Europe (S. M. Aronson and N. C. Myrianthopoulos, unpublished data). On the basis, then, of what is known, it is unreasonable to hold genetic drift as the predominant factor responsible for the elevation of the TSD gene frequency among the Ashkenazi Jews.

The possibility of differential mutation rate is equally unlikely. The mutation rate needed to account for the estimated frequencies of the TSD gene would be equal to the frequency of the trait in the population, i.e. about one mutation per 6,000 gametes per generation among Jews and one mutation per 500,000 gametes per generation among non-Jews, which is absurb. All available evidence indicates that mutation rates of specific loci tend to be rather constant within species.

THE POSSIBILITY OF HETEROZYGOTE ADVANTAGE

The possibility of heterozygote advantage was considered earlier[13] but not pursued because of lack of adequate control data to test it. Heterozygote advantage would provide an adequate explanation for the differential increase of the TSD gene if it could be shown that Jewish heterozygotes were more fertile than the Jewish homozygous normal and thus were able to transmit the mutant gene to the next generation differentially.

The magnitude of the selective advantage required by heterozygotes in order to maintain the frequency of the lethal TSD gene at such a high level among the Ashkenazi Jewish population is given by the following equation:

$$S = q / (1 - q)$$

S is the selection coefficient against the normal homozygote. Substituting the estimated frequency of the TSD gene among the Ashkenazi Jews of 0.0126,

$$S = 0.0126 / (1 - 0.0126) = 0.0128$$

and the fitness of the three genotypes is

$$TT = 1 - S = 0.9872$$
$$Tt = 1$$
$$tt = 0$$

which means that a selective advantage of about 1¼ percent on the part of heterozygotes is sufficient to maintain the gene at equilibrium despite its mass elimination via the TSD homozygotes. In order to determine if this is the case in the TSD population, it is necessary to collect and examine information on the fertility of Jewish women, particularly those known to be carriers of the TSD gene.

Our study population could, of course, be the parents of children with TSD, since these are both known to be heterozygous. But their total reproductive performance is almost certain to be biased by the birth of a child with a lethal hereditary disease and by the knowledge that there is a high probability of repeating this misfortune in subsequent pregnancies. This bias is quite evident from birth order analysis of 188 Jewish TSD cases in 150 sibships of two or more, shown in Table 11-II, calculated by the method of Haldane and Smith.[9] In theory, the test makes use of A, the sum of birth ranks of all affected sibs, and compares it with its theoretical mean value, calculated on the assumption that there is no birth rank effect. In practice, the arithmetic is simplified if $6A$ is tested in place of A. Both $6A$ and its variance are integers and are given in table form in the article by Haldane and Smith. Among the Jewish TSD cases, $6A$ exceeds its mean by almost six standard deviations. A similar birth rank effect, although not as striking, is found among non-Jewish TSD cases, where $6A$ exceeds its mean by almost three standard deviations.

TABLE 11–II
EFFECT OF BIRTH RANK AMONG TSD JEWISH CASES

Sibship size	Birth rank								Total
	1	2	3	4	5	6	7	8	
2	28	65							93
3	16	15	35						66
4	4	2	4	7					17
5	1	1			3				5
6									
7	1			1		1	1		4
8						1	1	1	3
Total	50	83	39	8	3	2	2	1	188

$6A = 2646$ $6A - m = 363$
$m = 2283$ Number of standard
$s^2 = 3721$ deviations exceeding mean $= 363/61 = 5.95$
$s = 61.0$

This finding is almost predictable and does not really indicate that birth rank effect is a phenomenon of biological significance. It merely reflects the bias which is introduced by a voluntary truncation of family size when a child with TSD has been produced. This effect is much more pronounced among the Jewish cases, since Jewish parents who have a TSD child are more aware of the social and medical consequences of such an occurrence than are non-Jews generally, and the eugenic problem concerns them more acutely.

An unbiased estimate of the fertility of the unsuspecting heterozygotes, who unknowingly perpetuate the gene, can be obtained by assessing the fertility of the grandparents of the affected children. It may be assumed that at least one maternal and one paternal grandparent of an affected child is a heterozygote. It can also be assumed that by the time the TSD homozygote (grandchild) has been identified, the fertility of the grandparents will have been completed. The fertility can be estimated by determining the number of surviving offspring, that is, the sibships containing the parents of the affected, and comparing with an appropriate control group.

SOURCE OF DATA AND METHODOLOGY

The data for this study came from two sources: from screening by one of us (N.C.M.) of death certificates from the Bureau of Vital Statistics assigned to rubic 325.5 (*mental deficiency, other and unspecified types*) of the International List of Causes of Death, for deaths which occurred in the United States during the years 1954–1957, inclusive, and from a case registry of cerebral sphingolipidoses which was begun by one of us (S.M.A.) in 1952.

The first source, which constitutes as complete ascertainment of cases as possible for the four year period, yielded 89 cases of TSD, 58 in children of Jewish parents, 29 in children of non-Jewish parents and two cases in children with one Jewish and one non-Jewish parent. The second source provided 296 cases in 242 families, mostly from the New York City area, and contains a much larger proportion of Jewish cases. From this source,

226 cases were in children of Jewish parents, 35 in children of non-Jewish parents, and 35 in children with mixed or doubtful parentage. Over 85 percent of cases recorded as having died from 1954 through 1957 were picked up independently through the second source. (For details about the method and criteria for selection of cases, see Ref. 1 and 13.)

The unit of this investigation is not the affected individual but the family, particularly the sibship of the parents of the affected child. By personal contact and mailed questionnaire, we sought to obtain from the parents precise and detailed information concerning dates of birth and death and neurological conditions of siblings, parents, aunts and uncles, grandparents, and first cousins of these cases, as well as other demographic data. We were able to collect all the required information for 194 families of Jewish cases and 47 families of non-Jewish cases.

In this paper, we are concerned exclusively with the sibships of the Jewish TSD parents, comprising 388 sibships with 1,244 total siblings. The distribution of the sibships of the parents of Jewish cases, which include the parents themselves, and the distribution of the control sibships to be described below, is given by place of birth in Table 11-III. These are separated into U.S. born and non-U.S. born for purposes of analysis, since it is conceivable that a heterozygote effect might exist in the one group and not in the other.

The ordinarily difficult task of selecting the proper control proved to be straightforward in our case. The lack of adequate demographic and fertility data for the Jewish population of the United States dictated the only logical alternative: to obtain a population sample which would be representative of United States Jewry and comparable to our own TSD sample with regard to those variables which were required for comparison and control.

The sources of the control sibships were seven synagogues (Philadelphia, Pennsylvania; White Plains, Brooklyn, and Lawrence, New York; Bridgeport and Trumbull, Connecticut; and Boston, Massachusetts) as well as some fraternal societies (not affiliated with synagogues) from the New York City area. The selected controls were married couples with children among whom Tay-Sachs disease had not occurred. Thus, the claim can be made that the control sample is representative of the urban and suburban Jewish population of the northeastern United States, corresponding approximately with the TSD sample in country of birth, age, number of children, religious-cultural background, socioeconomic level, and geographic distribution. The cooperation of these people was entirely voluntary, and it was secured after an appeal and an explanation of the general scope of the study. The specific aim, i.e. the comparison of fertility and test for heterozygote advantage, was not discussed with them. Each control was asked to complete a confidential questionnaire, giving much the same information as that obtained from the parents of the TSD cases. This information was collected from 406 couples comprising 812 sibships with 2,848 total siblings. Their distribution is shown in Table 11-III.

TABLE 11–III
TSD AND CONTROL SIBSHIPS

	Number of sibships	Total number of sibships
TSD		
U.S. born	322	1008
Non-U.S. born	66	236
Total	388	1244
Controls		
U.S. born	713	2436
Non-U.S. born	99	412
Total	812	2848

One possible bias which could weaken the power of the comparison stems from the well known correlation of family size of closely related individuals. The family size of a propositus group could be greater than that of the control group to the extent that there is a correlation between the propositus sibship size and the sibship size of the parental generation. Unfortunately, it is impossible to demonstrate presence or absence of correlation between sibship size of our index cases and that of the parents because the parents have not completed their reproduction in most instances and also because Jewish parents of TSD children tend to curb their reproduction, as was demonstrated by the birth rank test (Table 11-II). Information about the siblings of the grandparents, almost all of whom were born in Europe and most of them now dead, is very scanty; therefore, a correlation at this level cannot be attempted either. The only positive statement that can be made is that the selected controls had, on the average, no fewer children than the TSD parents and that both groups must have come from relatively large families. We feel that this bias, if it has entered at all in the selection of the control group, is not of sufficient magnitude to influence the results.

RESULTS

Selective advantage in modern genetics is expressed as a function of relative reproductive fitness. The concept of relative reproductive fitness of individuals with specific traits, or carriers of specific genes, although simple enough, has proven surprisingly difficult in practical application because the genetic situations on which the concept of fitness has a deciding bearing are often variable and subtle. Relative fitness in its simplest terms can be expressed as the ratio of the mean number of children of two groups, an affected group and a control group. In practice, such a ratio is not easy to derive. The affected group, for example, may not have completed their reproduction. There is no universal definition of the unit of fertility, neither need there be; further, there is the proverbial problem of what constitutes an adequate control group for a particular genetic situation and under a particular set of circumstances. These problems and their many ramifications have been dealt with extensively in methodological papers.[11,15]

In this study, the definition of relative fitness of the heterozygous carriers for the TSD gene is reduced to its simplest terms because the grandparents whose fertility is assessed have completed their reproduction at the time of the study. The unit of fertility is defined as a livebirth who has survived to reproductive age, for which 21 years is considered a reasonable lower limit: the analysis, however, will also include all livebirths.

The competed reproductive performance of the TSD heterozygotes, represented by the sibships of parents of TSD children and that of the controls, is shown in Table 11-IV. The number of

TABLE 11-IV

FERTILITY OF JEWISH TSD AND CONTROL FAMILIES

Decade of birth:	1890–1899		1900–1909		1910–1919		1920–1929		1930–1939		1940–1949	
	TSD	Control	TSD	Control	TSD	Control	TSD	Control	TSD	Control	TSD	Control
U.S. born												
Number of sibships	2	45	13	71	81	210	136	249	84	127	6	11
Total siblings	7	217	58	338	326	803	382	732	215	322	20	24
Number dying before age 21	0	25	2	31	11	43	4	37	2	15	0	0
Number surviving to age 21	7	192	56	307	315	760	378	695	213	307	20	24
Average total	3.50	4.82	4.46	4.76	4.02	3.82	2.81	2.94	2.56	2.54	3.33	2.18
Average surviving to age 21	3.50	4.26	4.31	4.32	3.88	3.62	2.78	2.79	2.54	2.42	3.33	2.18
Non-U.S. born												
Number of sibships	2	20	5	22	14	25	30	23	15	8	0	1
Total siblings	13	121	27	118	49	84	103	66	44	21		2
Number dying before age 21	0	5	2	14	5	4	3	11	4	0		0
Number surviving to age 21	13	116	25	104	44	80	100	55	40	21		2
Average total	6.50	6.05	5.40	5.36	3.50	3.36	3.43	2.87	2.93	2.62		
Average surviving to age 21	6.50	5.80	5.00	4.72	3.14	3.20	3.33	2.39	2.67	2.62		

sibships, total number of siblings, number of siblings surviving through age 21, and average number of total and surviving siblings are given by decade of birth of each "proband" TSD and control parent. These are further subdivided according to the U.S. born versus non-U.S. born dichotomy. The "proband" parents are distributed by decade of birth so that the effects of fertility trends over a span of half a century would not obscure the over-all heterozygote effect, if any, and the contribution of each decade may be properly evaluated and weighted.

From a cursory inspection of Table 11-IV, it becomes evident that there are some rather consistent differences between the TSD and control sibships, especially among the non-U.S. born, favoring the TSD sibships. These differences are clearly seen when the mean number of total and surviving siblings is adjusted for sample size. Table 11-V shows the ratio of adjusted reproductive performance of TSD heterozygotes and controls. The adjustment was made by multiplying the number of control sibships by the average number of TSD siblings in each decade, and vice versa, and summing up over all decades. This represents a simple but true measure of fertility, and it shows that in all four categories the ratio is in favor of the TSD heterozygote. Its highest deviation from unity, about 16 percent, is in the category of non-U.S. born who survive to age 21; it decreases in the two following categories and becomes negligible among the total U.S. born siblings.

The differences which resulted after adjustment for sample size are, as expected, small and not statistically significant.

TABLE 11–V
RATIO OF ADJUSTED FERTILITIES OF TSD GRANDPARENTS
AND CONTROLS

U.S. born			
Total siblings	TSD / Controls	= 1010.30 / 1007.22	= 1.0031
Siblings surviving to age 21	TSD / Controls	= 991.25 / 953.70	= 1.0394
Non-U.S. born			
Total siblings	TSD / Controls	= 235.85 / 211.34	= 1.1160
Siblings surviving to age 21	TSD / Controls	= 221.91 / 191.00	= 1.1618

DISCUSSION

The failure to find statistically significant differences in fertility between TSD heterozygotes and controls does not invalidate the argument of heterozygote advantage. The predicament here is that in order to be statistically significant, the differences in fertility would have to be huge and thus entirely out of line with the hypothesis which requires that only a small increase be present and operating in order to maintain the gene frequencies of a pair of alleles in polymorphic balance. The observed differences are of the right magnitude and all in the same direction and therefore compatible with the hypothesis that the TSD heterozygote has a selective advantage over the presumed homozygous normal. But, unless either the fitness differential or the study sample is large enough to produce statistically significant differences, the probability of sampling variation must be kept in mind.

By this approach, then, the evidence cannot be considered as decisive and at best is only suggestive. But, since no reasonable support has been found for all the other logical hypotheses, including that of genetic drift, it is, perhaps, not idle to examine how ancillary and indirect evidence may bear on the hypothesis of heterozygote advantage.

Some evidence in favor of the heterozygote advantage theory is offered by the demonstration that, on the whole, the TSD sibships have significantly better survival than the control sibships. It appears that this advantage is largely due to the contribution of the U.S. born. This is surprising, especially since the fertility differential, although not significant, showed a definite gradient (Table 11-V), being highest for siblings born outside the United States who survived to reproductive age, and becoming negligible when total siblings born in the United States were considered. One possible explanation for this is that the data for the non-U.S. born group are not as reliable as those for the U.S. born, or perhaps a number of unknown factors are at play. Be that as it may, it is not unreasonable to attribute differential survival to resistance to some adverse situation, e.g. disease, conferred by the TSD gene. Such an explanation is compatible with the hypothesis of heterozygote advantage.

Historical perspective may also furnish some helpful information. At least three culturally and ethnically distinct Jewish groups are recognized in our times. These date back to the first century A.D., if not earlier. One group, known as the Ashkenazi, are those Jews who, after having left Palestine, dispersed in central, eastern, and western Europe, and includes their descendants who emigrated from there to North and South America, South Africa, and Australia. Another group, the Sephardi, lived in the countries around the Mediterranean, including the European part of Turkey. A third group, the Oriental Jews, live in Asia Minor, Iraq, Iran, and Yemen. It is generally agreed that the three Jewish groups achieved cultural and perhaps genetic individuality during the two thousand years of the diaspora. The rise of the frequency of the TSD gene in one of these groups can also be assumed to have been a part of the same process.

The conquest of Jerusalem by Titus during the first century A.D. is a historical landmark which altered fundamentally the course of life and cultural activity of the Jewish people. Although there were large numbers of dispersed Jews before the Roman conquest of Jerusalem, it is only since then that the mass exodus began. One may argue that the Jewish people who immigrated to central, eastern, and western Europe, especially those who ultimately settled in Poland and the Baltic States, developed a way of life subject to certain selective pressures which favored the rise of the TSD gene, while those who stayed around the Mediterranean and in the Oriental part of Palestine pursued a life which did not favor any appreciable change of the status quo. Post[14] suggests that the continuous habitat of most Jewish populations for several millennia in cities which have greater exposure to infectious and contagious diseases than rural populations, along with greater tolerance and concern of Jews for illness, may have provided an ecological environment different enough from that of the Gentiles to result in differential rates of natural selection between Jews and Gentiles.

It should be noted that TSD is not the only genetic disorder which has a uniquely high frequency among the Ashkenazi Jews. Gaucher's disease, Niemann-Pick disease, and possibly other rare metabolic disorders are known also to have a very high frequency among them and a much lower frequency among the other Jewish groups and non-Jewish populations. It is interesting that the antecedents of the majority of Jewish cases of both Gaucher's disease and Niemann-Pick disease in the United States are also traced to the north-eastern provinces of Poland and the Baltic States. This may be explained on the grounds that all three lipid storage diseases are subject to the same unknown selective force and share the same polymorphic properties.

The historical argument can be carried one step further by estimating the magnitude of a presumed selective advantage required to raise the TSD gene frequency from 0.0013 at the end of the first century A.D., when the mass emigration of the Jews began, through 50 generations to the late nineteenth century, when TDS was recognized as occurring chiefly among the Ashkenazi Jews with a gene frequency of 0.0126.

Although the differences in fertility are not significant, the apparent definite fertility gradient in the four categories suggests that differential survival might be an important component. Indeed, when the percentage loss in each decade is calculated (Table 11-VI), the loss among controls, with only two exceptions, is higher—and survival to age 21 lower—than that among the TSD sibships.

The over-all difference in survival to age 21 between the TSD and control sibships is statistically significant.

It appears, then, that a selective advantage of about 4½ percent would suffice, under the assumptions, to raise the gene frequency to its present level among the Ashkenazi Jews. This is not too different from the over-all advantage of about 6 percent estimated from our data and, therefore, compatible with the hypothesis of heterozygote advantage.

TABLE 11–VI
LOSS OF SIBLINGS NOT SURVIVING TO AGE 21, PER DECADE

Decade of birth	1890–1899	1900–1909	1910–1919	1920–1929	1930–1939	1940–1949
U.S. born						
TSD	0.00	0.03	0.03	0.01	0.01	0.00
Controls	0.11	0.09	0.05	0.05	0.05	0.00
Non-U.S. born						
TSD	0.00	0.07	0.10	0.03	0.09	0.00
Controls	0.04	0.12	0.05	0.17	0.00	0.00

The most promising approach is, of course, through demographic studies of the east European Ashkenazi communities in the areas where the antecedents of the TSD cases lived for many generations. If a selective agent is involved, its identification may possibly be achieved through an analysis of the political, social, ecologic, and epidemiologic forces uniquely influencing these communities. The recent genocide of the Jewish peoples during World War II, the destruction of records, and the rapidly changing traditional Jewish way of life make this undertaking extremely difficult. But in another generation, whatever evidence still remains will disappear altogether. Demographic studies of the type mentioned above have been initiated by us and are now in progress.

SUMMARY

It is now well established that the birth incidence of Tay-Sachs disease (TSD) is a hundred times higher (and the gene frequency ten times higher) among the Ashkenazi Jews than among other Jewish groups and non-Jewish populations. There is no evidence that differential breeding pattern, genetic drift, or differential mutation rate can explain the difference in gene frequency distribution. The possibility of differential fertility of the heterozygote is examined at length. The reproductive performance of the grandparents of Jewish infants affected with TSD is compared with that of an appropriate control group. Although the differences in reproductive performance between the two groups are not statistically significant, the results suggest, but do not prove that the Jewish heterozygote enjoys an over-all reproductive advantage of about 6 percent over the presumed homozygous normal. The advantage appears to be greatest for offspring born outside the United States and surviving to reproductive age, diminishes for offspring born in the United States and surviving to reproductive age, and becomes negligible when total offspring born in the United States is considered. Survival to age 21, however, is significantly higher among TSD sibships than among control sibships, and this finding corroborates the heterozygote advantage hypothesis. Historical evidence also appears to corroborate the hypothesis and to place the rise of the TSD gene among the Ashkenazi Jews in historical times, perhaps during the early centuries of the diaspora.

REFERENCES

1. Aronson, S.M.: Epidemiology. In B.W. Volk (Ed.): *Tay-Sachs' Disease.* New York, Grune and Stratton, 1964, pp. 118–153.

2. Aronson, S.M., Aronson, B.E., and Volk, B.W.: A genetic profile of infantile amaurotic family idiocy. *Am Med Assoc J Dis Child,* 98:50–65, 1959.

3. Aronson, S.M., and Volk, B.W.: Genetic and demographic considerations concerning Tay-Sachs' disease: In S.M. Aronson and B.W. Volk, (Eds.): *Cerebral Sphingolipidoses: A Symposium on Tay-Sachs' Disease and Allied Disorders.* New York, Academic Press, 1962, pp. 375–394.

4. Cochran, W.G.: Some methods for strengthening the common X^2 test. *Biometrics, 10*:417–451, 1954.

5. Goldschmidt, E., and Cohen, T.: Inter-ethnic mixture among the communities of Israel. *Cold Spring Harbor Symp Quant Biol,* 24:115–120, 1964.

6. Goldschmidt, E., Lenz, R., Merin, S., Ronen, A., and Ronen I.: The frequency of the Tay-Sachs gene in the Jewish communities of Israel. Presented at 25th Annual Meeting of Genetics Society of America, Storrs, Connecticut, 1956.

7. Goldschmidt, E., Ronen, A., and Ronen, I.: Changing marriage systems in the Jewish communities of Israel. *Ann Hum Genet, (Lond.) 24*:191–204, 1960.

8. Hald, A.: *Statistical Theory with Engineering Applications.* New York, Wiley and Sons, 1952, pp. 407–408.

9. Haldane, J.B.S., and Smith, C.A.B.: A simple exact test for birth-order effect. *Ann Eugen (Lond.), 14*:117–124, 1948.

10. Kozinn, P.J., Wiener, H., and Cohen, P.: Infantile amaurotic family idiocy. *J Pediat, 51*:58–64, 1957.

11. Krooth, R.S.: The use of fertilities of affected individuals and their unaffected sibs in the estimation of fitness. *Am J Hum Genet, 7*:325–360, 1955.

12. Ktenidés, M.: Au subjet de l'hérédité de l'iodotie amaurotique infantile (Tay-Sachs'). Thesis no. 2264, University of Geneva, 1954.

13. Myrianthopoulos, N.C.: Some epidemiologic and genetic aspects of Tay-Sachs' disease. In S.M. Aronson and B.W. Volk (Eds.): *Cerebral Sphingolipidoses: A Symposium on Tay-Sachs' Disease and Allied Disorders.* New York, Academic Press, 1962, pp. 359–374.

14. Post, R.H.: Jews, genetics and disease. *Eugen. Quart.* 12:162–164.

15. Reed, T.E.: The definition of relative fitness of individuals with specific genetic traits. *Am J Hum Genet, 11*:137–155, 1959.

16. Slome, D.: The genetic basis of amaurotic family idiocy. *J Genet, 27*:363–376, 1933.

Chapter 12

GAUCHER'S DISEASE
HEREDITARY TRANSMISSION AND
RACIAL DISTRIBUTION

J. J. GROEN

INTRODUCTION

More and more cases of Gaucher's disease are being observed and published. On the basis of this accumulating experience it becomes possible to trace the mechanism of inheritance of this condition with more accuracy.[1-4] It is the purpose of this paper to review some of the newer evidence within the framework of previous knowledge and to draw attention to the importance of the new data for eugenic counseling in medical practice and for the light which the hereditary occurrence of this disease may shed on the history and racial composition of the Jewish people.

REVIEW OF DATA

1. The observation that Gaucher's disease occurs in so called "horizontal spread"[1] has been abundantly confirmed. In the large majority of the families which have been described so far, the disease affected brothers and sisters or cousins, whereas only very occasionally a (usually mild) case has been found among the parent or grandparents of the patients.[4]

2. In a few cases a parent developed the disease in a mild degree only late in life; in other cases it was possible to demonstrate by bone marrow biopsy that a seemingly healthy parent was actually suffering from the condition but in a subclinical form without symptoms or signs.[1,5,7]

Reprinted with permission from *Arch Intern Med*, 113:543–549, 1964.

Supported by a grant from the foundation for the scientific cooperation between the Netherlands and Israel.

TABLE 12–I
OFFSPRING OF 8 MARRIED PATIENTS WITH MANIFEST
GAUCHER'S DISEASE

Case No.	No. and ages of children in 1962	Abortions	Gaucher cases among offspring
1	—	1	—
2	—	—	—
3	—	1 (?)	—
4	One: 24	—	—
5	Twins: 17, 17	—	—
6	Five: 13, 11, 7, 4, 2	2 (?)	—
7	Three: 12, 10, 1	—	—
8	One: 2	—	—

3. The equal occurrence in both sexes, the approximate 50 percent frequency among the siblings of the affected generation, and the rarity of consanguinity in the parents[1,4] confirmed the previous assumption that Gaucher's disease is inherited as a single dominant non-sex-linked characteristic, although a recessive mechanism cannot be excluded.[2]

4. Since my previous paper was published 15 years ago, the observation that patients who suffer from clinically manifest Gaucher's disease produce only healthy offspring or none at all has been confirmed by others[4] and by a follow-up study and the observation of new families by me. Unfortunately most of the patients and their families who were described in the previous paper perished in the gas chambers of Auschwitz and Birkenau concentration camps. But a few survivors and newly observed families illustrated in Table 12-I demonstrate the conspicuous feature with sufficient frequency to regard it as a characteristic element in the transmission pattern of the condition: Not a single case of Gaucher's disease has been observed among 12 children of eight patients. Some of these children have now been followed up into adolescence, and none has developed even a suspicious sign.

HEREDITARY MECHANISM

Considering the available evidence the hypothesis appears justified that the metabolic defect of Gaucher's disease occurs as a mutation, at first in such a mild degree that the affected individual does not suffer from any manifest disturbance or suffers only late in life. By an unknown mechanism the defect is transferred to a second generation (and sometimes even to a third) in increasing severity ("penetrance"), until it produces clinical disease in 50 percent of the offspring. Once present in such a degree, half of the next generation is so severely affected that the disease becomes incompatible with life. As a result 50 percent of the offspring die in utero (or 50 percent of the spermatozoa or ova may not even be viable); only the 50 percent of the offspring which are unaffected are born and remain healthy.

As a possible substrate of this peculiar mechanism of inheritance by "enhanced penetrance" in succeeding generations, it may be supposed that in the first mutation the abnormal glucose moiety of the cerebroside kerasine[3] is produced in such small amount that the individual does not suffer from the accumulation of the abnormal substance in a demonstrable degree. In succeeding generations the amount of abnormal kerasine which is produced and stored increases so much that its accumulation in liver, spleen, and bone marrow causes clinical symptoms and signs. In the next generation the metabolic disturbance interferes so seriously with the metabolism of the spermatozoa or ova as to be incompatible with life. Most geneticists nowadays conceive a mutation as a fixed metabolic or structural entity, but there is no reason why the facts should not teach us to modify this standpoint.

IMPORTANCE FOR EUGENIC COUNSELING

Whatever the underlying mechanism and the postulated theory, the observation that patients with manifest Gaucher's disease produce only healthy offspring is of great importance for the counseling of these patients and their future marriage partners. It means that whatever risks the marriage with a Gaucher patient may involve from the point of view of future sickness, we can put the marriage candidates at ease about the possibility of transferring the disease. In other words, in such counseling we need not advise against the marriage for reasons of eugenics. The problem is a purely human one, viz, whether the love between the marriage candidates is strong and understanding enough to accept the risk of future ill health of one of the partners. It may be pointed out, *inter alia,* that due to the fact that the literature describes the more severe cases preferentially, there exists in the minds of the lay public and of many doctors an exaggerated picture of the severity of the disease. The majority of the patients I have been able to follow are leading successful, if moderately active, lives and have required medical treatment only intermittently. Whereas it is true that only a few of the patients reach old age, most of them, if properly taken care of, have reached middle age in comparatively good health.

It may also be worth mentioning in this connection that the marriages of these patients have certainly not been more unhappy than the average; among my cases the reverse seems the rule. There were no divorces, and in all cases the marriage partner stood the stresses of the illness of the patient extremely well. In a few cases where I had occasion for a confidential question, the marriage partner unhesitatingly stated that she had never been sorry for her decision to marry the patient.

The only eugenic problem that can occur in Gaucher's disease would be the case of parents, who are clinically unaffected, but who have already produced a child with the disease. Such a couple may expect more cases among its offspring with a 50 percent chance, and it is the task of the counselor to help them in forming a decision. Here again I would like to point out as my personal opinion that one need not regard the life of a patient with Gaucher's disease as so unbearable that one has to prevent the birth of such an individual at all cost. Adult Gaucher's disease is a condition which does not affect the central nervous system, and this has been quite obvious in my patients, the majority of whom were and are valuable men and women, who fulfilled their tasks as husband or wife, fathers or mothers, and in their respective professions at least as well as the average healthy individual. It seems as if the decision whether such a couple should decide to practice contraception depends more on their capability of giving enough love and understanding to a handicapped child than on the handicap for the child itself.

RACIAL DISTRIBUTION

It has been known for some time that Gaucher's disease occurs preferentially among Jews. Of the 31 cases described by me[1] from

Amsterdam, only one, a "sporadic" case, was non-Jewish. In 1950 another, seemingly non-Jewish child was seen, but the mother told me confidentially that she had once loved a Jew very much . . . This high proportion of Jews among the cases was in striking contrast to the proportion of Jews in Holland, who before World War II constituted less than 2 percent of the population of the Netherlands and less than 10 percent of the population of the city of Amsterdam. It is no wonder, therefore, that the disease is not rare in Israel where several papers have already appeared on the condition, and where I have seen in four years six new cases, four of which belong to families in which more cases are known.

All cases observed so far (including those seen by me) occurred in so called Ashkenazi Jews who had been born in Russia, Poland, Germany, Western Europe, North America, and South Africa. Ashkenazi Jews are generally understood to be those that have lived during the centuries of the Diaspora in Central, Eastern, and Western Europe and their descendants who have emigrated from there to North and South America, South Africa, and Australia. Other Jews, whose ancestors have lived during the past centuries in the countries round the Mediterranean, including the European part of Turkey, are generally designated as Sephardim, while the groups that have lived since historical times in Asia Minor, Iraq, Iran, and Yemen are usually called Oriental Jews. No cases of Gaucher's disease have been reported from any of these last-named countries so far.

In Israel the preferential occurrence of Gaucher's disease among the Ashkenazim is even more striking. Whereas almost half of the two million Jewish population of Israel consists of Jews who returned from Mediterranean countries, the Near East, North Africa, Yemen, and of their offspring, not a single case of Gaucher's disease has been observed among them, against at least 30 cases among the Ashkenazi Jews. This fact first mentioned by Franco[6] and confirmed by Fried[8,4] was found to be equally true for my new cases. In the records of the Hadassah University Hospital in Jerusalem 26 cases of Gaucher's disease are filed; all of them are Ashkenazim.

Such an outspoken preference for the occurrence of a specific mutation (a labile gene) is in itself a racial characteristic, like physical anthropological criteria or blood group frequencies. It is clear that such a characteristic cannot be ascribed to the cultural habits and ways of life which the Ashkenazi Jews adopted from their environment during the exile; it must be due to a hereditary chromosomal characteristic, which distinguishes the Ashkenazim from other Jews and all other races.

Two possibilities can be considered as the cause of such a chromosomal difference. In the first place it might be presumed that by intermarriage certain hereditary traits have become incorporated into the Ashkenazi Jewish group but not in the Sephardi.[9] This seems to be the case for the blood groups, but for Gaucher's disease the explanation cannot hold because, if this were so, Gaucher's disease would be expected to be at least equally frequent among certain non-Jews in Western, Central, or Eastern Europe, which is not the case. In all these countries, Gaucher's disease among non-Jews is extremely rare.

The alternative explanation would be that the Jewish people, already before its dispersal from its country, about 2,000 years ago, was not so homogeneous genetically and racially as it is often supposed and *that the present distinction between Ashkenazim, Sephardim, and Orientals corresponds to ethnic and genetic differences which existed already before the exile.* This conclusion supports the hypothesis held already by historians, who base their opinion on archeological and biblical sources. The Bible describes extensively[10-14] a 12-fold tribal heterogenicity of the ancient Jews.* Even when one doubts the tradition that the tribes represented the descendants of the 12 sons of Jacob, there is no reason to reject the hypothesis that the tribes actually existed during the earliest times of the Jewish nation, within which each occupied its own area. This hypothesis, now enforced by the differential distribution of Gaucher's disease, leads us on an interesting sidetrack to pursue once more the old question of what happened to the tribes in later times and especially in how far the present differentiation of Jews into Ashkenazim, Sephardim, and Orientals still represents their former tribal heterogenicity.

Our knowledge, partly biblical, partly historical, about the

---

* Biblical references are from the original Hebrew text which in the references quoted corresponds to the Authorized King James Version.

further fate of the tribes is incomplete. According to the Scriptures, the 12 tribes, which had been united under David and Solomon, separated after the death of the latter into the kingdoms of Judea (encompassing the tribes and territories of Juda and Benjamin) and Israel (the other ten tribes and the regions they occupied).[15,16] The separation lasted for many centuries, and, although there was contact between the two states, we may assume that while intermarriage between Juda and Benjamin took place on one hand, and between the ten other tribes on the other, a gross genetic separation remained between what had now become the two national or ethnic groups. The assumption that a certain degree of genetic separation remained is the more justified, as it was a religious tradition in the Middle East to marry as much as possible inside one's own family.[17]

After the conquest of the kingdoms of Israel (722 B.C.) and Judea (587 B.C.), a large number of the inhabitants were deported to Assyria[18,19] and Babylon,[20] respectively. There they were separated in space, and it is not likely that they had mixed intensively when, in 538 B.C. Cyrus, after having conquered Assyria and Babylon, permitted both groups to return.[21] Not all Jews made use of this opportunity, and the communities in Kurdistan, Iraq, and Persia are generally considered as remnants of the exiles.[22] The problem of which exiles returned and where they (re)settled is unsolved by official history, but, according to an emphatic statement in the Bible,[23-25] those that originally came from Judea returned there.

We know nothing about those that had been deported from the kingdom of Israel more than a hundred years earlier. Considering the tenacity with which Jews (and monotheistic populations in general) have maintained themselves within pagan communities in historical times, the assumption seems warranted that they still existed and that a certain number of them also made use of Cyrus' permission to return. Who exactly were the ones that returned and who stayed (and partly preserved their Jewish identity until recent times[22]), we know practically nothing about. Neither do we know whether the return took place in a group, and so we have no possibility even to speculate whether some of the ten tribes came home and others did not, or whether they had completely mixed and the part of them that returned was just a fraction of that mixture. It should also not be forgotten that, again according to the Scriptures,[25,27] a not inconsiderable number of the inhabitants of the kingdom of Israel had never left the country.

However that may be, we are told that those who came back to Judea and Jerusalem took strong measures against intermarriages with other groups around them, whether Jews, Samaritans, or otherwise.[28-30] We may suppose that they did not exactly encourage any others who returned from exile to settle in Judea. As a result the separation between the populations of Juda and Israel was more or less continued after the Babylonian exile, the first again settling mainly in Judea, the others joining those who had never left, in Galilee and the coastal plain of "Palestine" (Philistine).

During the following centuries (the period of the Second Temple) the country, although mainly Jewish in its population, was consecutively under Persian, Greek, Egyptian, and Roman rule or influence. Almost all information we have about this time concerns the inhabitants of Judea and Jerusalem, who apparently kept their religious and national identity and, (so long as we do not hear the contrary) we may assume, in the main also their mixed Juda-Benjamin ethnic composition, although some mixture with the Jews living in Galilee and the coastal plain probably took place. The inhabitants apparently lost all knowledge about what happened to the tribes (an accurate historian like Flavius Josephus does not give us any information on this point), but it is interesting that in the first century Paul still designates himself as a descendant of the tribe of Benjamin.[31]

We have historical evidence that during this period of the Second Temple important groups of Jews emigrated from their country to settle in the important cultural centers round the Mediterranean like Alexandria and Rome. There are much vaguer stories about Jewish migration to Ethiopia, Yemen, and Armenia.[22] In neither case do we know when or from where these groups left or who their tribal ancestors were.

In the heroic revolts against the Romans which took place during the first centuries A.D. several Jews from Galilee and some from the coastal plain participated, but the majority of the insur-

gents were inhabitants of Judea and Jerusalem. They offered the
most tenacious resistance against the Romans, so that when Jerusalem and the Second Temple were destroyed by Titus' soldiers,
the fighters from Judea were the ones that were taken as slaves
to Rome. The same happened after the revolt of Bar Kochba
(132–135 A.D.). It can safely be assumed that once in Rome these
exiles received support from the Jews who already lived there,
who helped them to migrate further into the countries that were
during the first centuries of the Christian era under Roman rule
(similarly to what we know to have happened during later centuries of Jewish migration!). The tolerance of Charlemagne
furthered the dispersion of their descendants through the whole of
his empire during the early Middle Ages, so that when the Dark
Centuries of the Crusades and the other persecutions began, the
descendants of these Jews were settled in communities all over
Western and Central Europe. According to this concept, therefore, the Judean Jews (still mainly descendants of Juda and Benjamin) were the ancestors of the Jews of Western, Eastern, and
Central Europe, and thereby also of those who later migrated to
North and South America, South Africa, and Australia; in short,
of those who have since then become designated as Ashkenazim.
It is interesting that skull measurements recently carried out on a
number of skeletons of the fighters under Bar Kochba revealed
them to be predominantly brachycephalic like the Ashkenazim
of our days.[32]

The Jews who had been living in the late biblical and early
Christian era in the coastal plain of Palestine and in Galilee, left
their country much later, presumably only after the fifth century
when the Roman empire collapsed and was unable to defend the
region against the attacks by nomadic robbers. They spread to
Asia Minor and along the Mediterranean where they also found
refuge with and support from the Jews that had already settled
there before; they probably moved into Spain after its conquest
by the Arabs. Most of their descendants remained round the Mediterranean for centuries; later a considerable number who were
driven out of Spain and Portugal by the Inquisition settled in
Italy, Holland, and England. These groups are continued in the
Sephardim of our time.

The hypothesis underlying these considerations is therefore two-fold: In the first place, that the original tribal heterogenicity of the Jewish people, although modified by a preferential mixing of some tribes, was never completely lost; it continued via the kingdoms of Juda and Israel and after the return of a part of the Syrian and Babylonian exiles during the period of the Second Temple. In the second place, that when the great Diaspora during the first centuries of the Christian era took place, the by now two ethnic groups emigrated at different times and along different ways to different areas. Once in these different areas they preserved their ethnic and cultural heterogenicity which is still maintained in their present differentiation into Ashkenazim versus Sephardim and Orientals. However scanty the archeological and historical data at our disposal may be,[22,33,34] the remarkable predilection of Gaucher's disease for Ashkenazi Jews supports the hypothesis that the Ashkenazim differ from other Jews not only in the way they pronounce the Hebrew language and in their synagogal rites and rabbinical customs, but that there also exists genetic differences between them and the other groups of Jews, more particularly that they might be the continuation of the tribal (genetic) group of Juda and Benjamin, which dates back to long before the exile. This does not mean that the Ashkenazim (or Sephardim or Orientals are racial entities; they are also racial mixtures, but they are mixtures of different composition. To the Ashkenazi mixture one tribal or racial group (the origin of which one cannot even guess) contributed the labile gene of the Gaucher mutation.

It is a fascinating thought that the modern study of hereditary traits and diseases can contribute towards the elucidation of what happened during times of historical twilight. The above hypothesis may serve as an example, illustrating how the predilection for the Gaucher's mutation may throw light on the genetic roots, racial composition, and historical wanderings of the Jewish people.

SUMMARY

Although Gaucher's disease is clearly a hereditary disorder, the mechanism of its transmission has not yet been elucidated with certainty. I have drawn special attention to the remarkable fact that patients who have the disease in a clinically manifest degree produce only healthy offspring. A hypothesis is offered to explain this, and the consequences of the phenomenon for genetic counseling are pointed out.

Gaucher's disease is much more frequent among Jews than non-Jews. Among the Jews it has been observed among the Ashkenazim only. This observation supports the hypothesis that the Jews were ethnically already heterogeneous before their Diaspora and that the present Ashkenazim are decendants of a group, which existed already as such in biblical times. The present paper gives reasons for believing that the Ashkenazim are the continuation of the inhabitants of the kingdom of Judea, comprising the tribes of Juda and Benjamin, whereas the Sephardim and Oriental Jews can be considered as descendants of the inhabitants of the kingdom of Israel, which comprised most of the other tribes.

REFERENCES

1. Groen, J.: The hereditary mechanism of Gaucher's disease. *Blood*, 3:1238, 1948.

2. Hsia, D.Y.; Naylor, J.; and Bigler, J.A.: Gaucher's disease: Report of two cases in father and son, and review of the literature. *N Engl J Med*, 261:164, 1959.

3. Fredrickson, D.S., and Hoffman, A.F.: Gaucher's Disease. In J.B. Stanbury, D.S. Fredrickson, and J.B. Wyrgurk (Eds.): *The Metabolic Basis of Inherited Disease*. New York, McGraw Hill Book Company, 1960, p. 603.

4. Fried, K.; Goldschmidt, E.; and Matoth, Y.: In E. Goldschmidt (Ed.): *Genetics of Migrant and Isolate Populations*. Baltimore, Williams & Wilkins Company, 1962, p. 292.

5. Stransky, E., and Dauis-Lawas, D.F.: Heredity in the infantile type of Gaucher's disease. *Am J Dis Child*, 78:694, 1949.

6. Franco, S.: Studies in Gaucher's disease. *Harefuah*, 25:143, 1943.

7. Stransky, E., and Conchu, T.L.: Heredity in the infantile type of Gaucher's disease. *Ann Paediat*, 177:319, 1955.

8. Fried, K.: Gaucher's disease among the Jews in Israel. *Bull Res Counc Israel*, 7B:213, 1958.

9. Leibowitz, J.O.: The history of gene flow into Jewish groups. *Bull Res Counc Israel*, 7B:220, 1958.

9a. Groen, J.: Historical and genetic studies of the twelve tribes of

Israel and their relation to the present ethnic composition of the Jewish people. *Jewish Quarterly Review, 158*:1, July, 1967.

10. Genesis 49:1–28.

11. Numbers 1:17–54.

12. Deuteronomy 33:6–25.

13. Joshua 13:8–33; 14:1–15; 15:1–63; 16:1–10; 17:1–18; 18:11–28; 19:1–51.

14. I Chronicles, chap. 2–8.

15. I Kings 11:29–41.

16. I Kings 12:16–24.

17. Numbers 36:5–10.

18. II Kings 17:23.

19. II Kings 17:23.

20. II Chronicles 36:20.

21. Ezra 1:1–4.

22. Ben-Zvi, I.: *The Exiled and the Redeemed.* Philadelphia, The Jewish Publication Foundation, 1961.

23. Ezra 1:5.

24. Ezra 2:1–2.

25. Nehemia 11:1–36.

26. II Chronicles 30:6, 11, 18, 21, 25.

27. II Chronicles 31:1.

28. II Kings 17:24.

29. Ezra 4:2–3.

30. Nehemia 13:23–25.

31. Romans 11:1.

32. Nathan, H., and Haas, N.: Anthropological data on the Judean desert skeletons, in *Genetics of Migrant and Isolate Populations,*[4] p. 284.

33. Reubeni, A.: *The Antiquity of the Hebrews.* Jerusalem, Rubin Mass, 1962.

34. Shapira, H.L.: *The Jewish People: A Biological History.* Paris, UNESCO, 1961.

PART FOUR
CARCINOMA

There are complicated interrelationships between environmental factors and possible genetic factors in cancer morbidity. Many studies have been made and are continuing to be made of this interrelationship. Most studies of ethnic group membership as a factor in cancer incidence are done in those cities where it is possible to identify the patients by hospital and death records. In investigating the incidence of cancers among Jews, the preponderant research sites have apparently been in the state of Israel and the city of New York.

Jewish women tend to have a very low incidence of cancer of the cervix. Casper finds this to be true both in New York City and in Israel and discusses this in Chapter 13. This may suggest the involvement of a genetic factor. Ashkenazic women have a much higher incidence for endometrial cancer than do non-Ashkenazic women in Israel. Furthermore, Jewish women in New York seem to have an even higher incidence for endometrial cancer than does the general white female population in the United States.

In Chapter 14 Dunham, Thomas, Edgcomb, and Stewart investigate the environmental factors which may influence these differences. They consider such items as the age of the woman at the time of her first intercourse, the number of sex partners she had, and the possible role of circumcision of her male partners. Incidentally, there seems to be no association between circumcision of the male partner and rates of cervical cancer.

The influence of environmental factors on breast cancer is studied by Bertini and Ber in Chapter 15 in an extensive survey of the ethnological and endocrinological aspects of benign and malignant breast lesions in Israel. Ashkenazic women tend to have an incidence of breast cancer approaching the high rate found in the United States and some European countries.

Women of Oriental Jewish background, however, have a low incidence, approaching that of Japanese women. Yemenite women have remarkably few breast cancers. Bertini and Ber relate these findings to the hormonal activity of the members of these groups.

An overall survey of studies of cancers of uterine cervix and corpus, breast, and ovary, done in Israel and New York City over a period of years, is summarized by Stewart, Dunham, Casper,

112

Dorn, Thomas, Edgcomb, and Symeonides (Chap. 16). They show that environmental factors and constitutional traits enhance susceptibility to these diseases. They do not draw conclusions on the role of ethnicity.

Penile carcinoma is so rare among Jews that its absence has often been attributed to the Jewish religious practice of circumcising male infants at eight days of age. Margolis discusses the question of whether there is also an inherited characteristic of immunity in Chapter 17. After reviewing the literature, Margolis comes to the conclusion that the causes of penile cancer are still obscure, and that there may be forces of both heredity and environment interacting in its etiology.

Seidman (Chap. 18) compares the incidence of lung cancer mortality of Jewish males in New York City to those of Catholic and Protestant males. Some decades ago Jewish men had a much higher lung cancer death rate. Now their lung cancer death rate is lower than that of Catholics and Protestants. Siedman discusses the possible roles of cigarette smoking and exposure to gas, dust, or fumes, in influencing this low death rate.

A study done in Pittsburgh by Herman and Enterline compares the lung cancer rates among Jews and non-Jews, males and females, and relates them to cigarette smoking behavior and is reported in Chapter 19. While Jewish men have relatively lower lung cancer mortality rates compared to non-Jewish men, Jewish women have surprisingly higher rates as compared to non-Jewish women. An attempt is made to find possible explanations for this seeming paradox.

Leukemia is also included in this section. It has been found that there is a higher mortality from leukemia among Jews than among non-Jews in New York City. In an attempt to investigate the factors involved, Graham, Gibson, Lilienfeld, Schuman, and Levin (Chap. 20) exclude New York City from the population they study. Although child victims of leukemia show no significant difference along ethnic lines, Jewish adults do show a higher risk. Non-Jewish Russians also show a higher than average incidence of leukemia. The highest risk group, however, is that of Jews born in Russia. Further research along genetic and sociological lines is suggested.

Chapter 13

RATES OF UTERINE CANCERS IN JEWISH WOMEN IN ISRAEL AND NEW YORK CITY

J. Casper

The various research projects which have been undertaken during a period of two years in Israel and New York for the purpose of elucidating the as yet mysterious reason for low incidence rate of cervical cancer in Jewish women, even if they have not resulted in a complete understanding of the facts and figures obtained, have nevertheless produced several interesting observations hitherto unknown.

The most astonishing fact revealed through these observations and investigations was the almost identical incidence of cervical cancer in Jewish women in Israel and in New York. Age-adjusted rates—adjusted to the total population of the continental United States in 1950—show a figure for cervical cancer in Israel as low as 4.63 per 100,000 and in New York 4.66 per 100,000 (Fig. 13-I).

These figures, we assume, cannot be regarded as merely coincidental or accidental. At first sight, at least, this coincidence in figures means that Jews living under various and different conditions show the same low tumour incidence. It means that there is the same incidence of cervical cancer among Jews living in New York, under generally more or less satisfactory economic conditions, as there is among the Jews in Israel under economic conditions which are, on the average often of a lower standard.

In Israel the population includes, apart from a middle-class, a large number of skilled and unskilled workers, small artisans and hard-working farmers.

In Israel, there is a large percentage of immigrant Jews from oriental countries with a standard of living which is sometimes

Reprinted with permission from Int J Cancer, 16:1686–1688, 1960.

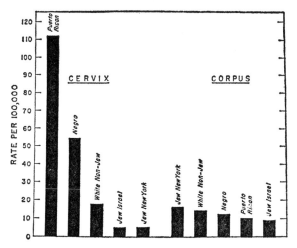

Figure 13–1. Incidence of uterine cancer in New York and Israel.

very primitive, and, on the other hand, a percentage of Jews originating from Central and Eastern Europe with much higher living standard which is more comparable to American standards. The much higher incidence rate figures for cervical cancer in the white, non-Jewish population of New York, as well as the much higher figures in the colored population and particularly amongst the Puerto Ricans, living in New York, was to be expected.

In contrast to the divergent figures for cervical cancer obtained in the various ethnic groups investigated in our project, the figures for endometrial cancer do not seem, at first sight, to differ to this extent. The deviations are, statistically at least, not very significant. But we found that we have to analyze the incidence for endometrial cancer more exactly in Israel with its mixed Western and Oriental Jewish population.

The incidence for endometrial cancer, age-adjusted, in Jews in New York is 14.57 per 100,000, in Israel 7.71 per 100,000. The rate of endometrial cancer in the white female population in selected metropolitan areas of the United States in 1947 was 10.31 per 100,000 slightly lower than the figure for Jews in New York. The Israeli figure for endometrial cancer is lower.

Among the Jewish population one large group (about 60%) includes Jews originating from Central and Eastern Europe and who are termed Ashkenazi Jews. The other groups (about 40%) comprise Oriental Jews as well as descendants of Jews who lived for hundreds of years around the shores of the Mediterranean, and who are in habits and customs much nearer to the Oriental Jews.

Whilst the figures for cervical cancer are identical in both Jewish groups in Israel, we found that Ashkenazi Jews have an age-adjusted incidence for endometrial cancer of 11.24 per 100,000, corresponding with the figure for the white population in the U.S.A. (Fig. 13-2).

However, the incidence for endometrial cancer in non-Ashkenazi Jews is much lower, only 3.19 per 100,000. The rate is Puerto Ricans living in New York is also lower than the white population in New York—8.31 per 100,000. In this connection, the low incidence figure for endometrial cancer found by Segi in Japan seems to be interesting.

In Israel, cancer of the corpus uteri with regard to various ethnic groups, behaves like ovarian and mammary cancer, and both these tumours show a much higher incidence rate in the Western Ashkenazi Jews. The high frequency rate of mammary cancer among Ashkenazi Jews in Israel is comparable to figures obtained for the White American population. The incidence rates

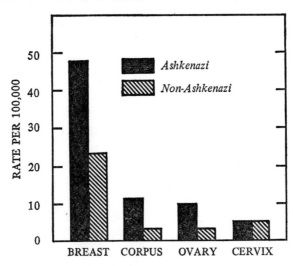

Figure 13–2. Incidence of female genital cancer among Ashkenazi and non-Ashkenazi Jewesses in Israel.

for the latter tumour obtained for non-Ashkenazi Jews are about half of those observed in Ashkenazi Jews.

The almost identically low figures for cervical cancer in both Jewish groups—in New York the majority of Jews are Ashkenazi Jews—in contrast to the much higher figures in other peoples, would suggest that a genetic factor could be involved. Religious laws do not seem to play a part as a decisive factor in the low incidence rates. We found particularly that the abstinence after menstrual bleeding and following delivery which is demanded by the Jewish religious laws, is not observed by a large proportion of the Jewish population, and noted especially that there is no significant difference in the proportion of non-observance in our cervical cancer group and in control groups.

Fertility and parity do not seem to have any influence in our cervical cancer cases, but it is remarkable that the cervical carcinoma patients gave a history of first intercourse and first pregnancy at a median age which was found to be more than three years earlier than that obtained in other genital cancers which were investigated by us and in the control group (Table 13-I).

TABLE 13–I
ISRAEL STUDY: MEDIAN AGES IN YEARS

	First intercourse	*First pregnancy*
Cervix	19.7	21.5
Corpus	22.8	24.6
Breast	23.9	25.6
Ovary	24.4	26.9
Control	23.0	24.8

The criterion which is often used in measuring the incidence of cervical cancer, by comparing the ratio between cervical cancer occurrence and that of corpus cancer, does not seem to be of particular value. The incidence of corpus cancer in various countries is so divergent that a low figure for this ratio sometimes means only a higher incidence of corpus cancer and not a lower incidence of cervical cancer. But, nevertheless, in the table which follows we may clearly recognize three different groups (Table 13-II).

The first group: The white population of the U.S.A. and the population of Denmark as a typical representative of Western and Central European population with a ratio of 1.2–2.9. The

TABLE 13–II
AGE-ADJUSTED INCIDENCE RATES

	Cervix	*Corpus*
White:		
Selected urban U.S.A.	39.1	16.8
Connecticut U.S.A.	26.0	15.5
Denmark	28.6	10.0
Non-white:		
Selected urban U.S.A.	78.6	16.2
South African Bantu	59.1	—

second group comprises the non-white population in the U.S.A. with a ratio of 4.4. The Jews in New York and in Israel (not mentioned in Table 13-II) occupy a special position with a ratio of less than 1.0 and in this also present a unique and peculiar group.

SUMMARY

Jewish women in Israel and in New York, i.e. Jewish women from different community groups, with different cultural backgrounds, descendants from Western and Oriental ancestors, with different customs and habits, show absolutely identical low-incidence figures for cervical cancer.

On the contrary, incidence figures of endometrial cancer in Jewish women of Western descent in New York and in Israel correspond with the figures for the white Western population. In Oriental and Mediterranean Jewish women, endometrial cancer is less frequent. Mammary and ovarian cancer rates in Israel resemble endometrial cancer.

It is to be noted that there is a correlation between behaviour of mammary and ovarian cancer and of endometrium cancer, in that both show a relatively lower incidence among Oriental and Mediterranean Jews as compared with Western Jews.

Chapter 14

SOME ENVIRONMENTAL FACTORS AND THE DEVELOPMENT OF UTERINE CANCERS IN ISRAEL AND NEW YORK CITY

L. J. DUNHAM, L. B. THOMAS, J. H. EDGCOMB, AND H. L. STEWART

The study of cancer of the uterus in New York City and Israel was designed to investigate the low frequency of cancer of the uterine cervix in Jewish women compared to its frequency in non-Jewish white women. It is part of a larger study of environmental features and cancer of the uterus which will include a comparison with Negro women in the United States, a group known to have a high frequency of cancer of the cervix.

The wide variations in rates of cervix cancer shown in Fig. 14–1 in the five bars on the left may be contrasted to the much smaller differences in corpus cancer shown in the corresponding bars on the right. The rates for cervix cancer in Jewish women are low, less than a third of the rate for non-Jewish white women. The rates are approximately equal for Jewish women in Israel and New York City. Past reports on the low frequency of cancer of the uterine cervix in Jewish women have been based mainly on relative frequency data from hospitals. Since hospitals vary in the proportions of male and female patients of various ages, races, and socio economic levels and with various types of disease, data from hospitals cannot be meaningfully compared. The incidence rates shown were collected for this study from New York City and Israel by Dr. Harold F. Dorn and his associates. They represent the number of newly diagnosed cases per year per 100,000 resident women. The figures are age-adjusted and permit valid

Reprinted with permission from *Int J Cancer*, *16*:1689–1692, 1960.

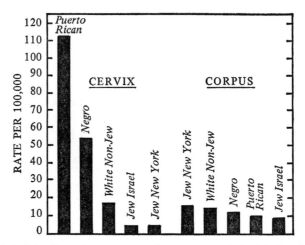

Figure 14–1. Number of new cases of cancer per 100,000 female population in New York City (1952) and Israel (1952–53). Age adjusted using total population of continental USA, 1950.

comparisons. They are the first rates established for Jewish as contrasted to non-Jewish women.

The three parts of the study were the determination of rates already described, the review of pathologic diagnoses in cancer cases by Dr. Harold L. Stewart and his associates, and the study by interview of certain features of patients' histories. Replies were recorded on a prepared questionnaire. Individual questions related to environmental features inherent in marriage and intercourse, pregnancy, menstruation, and gynecologic and endocrine disease. In this report, the role of the circumcision status of male partners of women with and without cancer is discussed. Special interest in this feature of patients' histories has been expressed by investigators of the epidemiology of cancer of the uterine cervix. Most of the partners of Jewish women are Jewish men who have been circumcised in infancy while the majority of the partners of non-Jewish women are uncircumcised men. Here is a clear-cut difference between Jews and non-Jews. If it were proved that uncircumcised partners are strongly associated with cases of cancer of the uterine cervix this finding would assist in explaining the low incidence of cervix cancer in Jewish women and might also offer a practical means of reducing the disease in non-Jewish women.

Fig. 14-2 illustrates the percentages of women with uncircumcised partners in the New York City study. The three bars on the left represent percentages of uncircumcised partners of non-Jewish patients with cervix cancer, corpus cancer and the control group, free of any form of cancer. The corresponding three groups of New York City Jewish patients are represented by the three bars on the right. It was the opinion of the interviewers that the data obtained relative to the circumcision status of the male partners were reliable. However, Lilienfeld reports, in an unpublished study, disagreement in more than 30 percent of cases between the findings on physical examination by a physician and the statement by males of their own circumcision status. The data obtained from female partners may even be less dependable. In addition there is at present no basis for any statement concerning differences in reliability of data obtained from cervix cancer and control patients.

The points which I wish to make about the data presented are these:

First, non-Jewish cervix cancer patients had a lower proportion

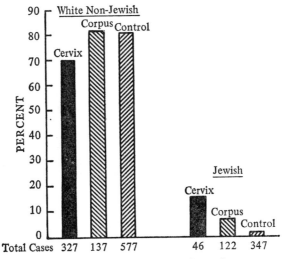

Figure 14-2. Percent uncircumcised partners by ethnic group and diagnosis in New York City.

of uncircumcised partners than either corpus cancer or control patients. From this evidence no support is afforded to the assumption that uncircumcised partners are associated with cases of cervix cancer. The groups of non-Jewish patients are useful for determining the importance of the circumcision status of the male partners, since considerable numbers of patients with uncircumcised partners and patients with circumcised partners both exist in this population group.

Second, it is less revealing to study features associated with circumcision status of partners of the Jewish women since uncircumcised partners are infrequent in this population group. In Israel the number of uncircumcised partners was so few that it had no statistical value and graphic representation was not included in Fig. 14–1. What findings there are for the Jewish patients in New York City are not conclusive. Seven of 46 cervix cancer patients or 15.2 percent, gave a history of intercourse with uncircumcised partners. Compared with the control patients the difference is statistically significant at the 5 percent level. However, compared with corpus cancer patients, the difference fails to be significant at the 5 percent level. No suggestion has been made that the development of corpus cancer is in any way related to uncircumcised partners.

Age standardization of cases may be mentioned. The percentages of uncircumcised partners of Jewish and non-Jewish cervix cancer patients by age of the patients were standardized for the age distribution of the corresponding control patients. No appreciable changes in percentages of uncircumcised partners were evident for either ethnic group as a result of the standardization.

Last, it will be remembered that incidence rates of cervix cancer in Jewish patients in New York City and Israel are almost identical. However, uncircumcised partners of Israel patients are very few. The figure shown here for New York City Jewish cervix cancer patients exceeds the low figure for cervix cancer patients in Israel. On the basis of a postulated influence of the greater proportion of uncircumcised partners in New York City Jews with cervix cancer, a difference in rates in the two areas, New York City and Israel, would be expected. If this influence exists, rates of cervix cancer in New York City Jews would be higher

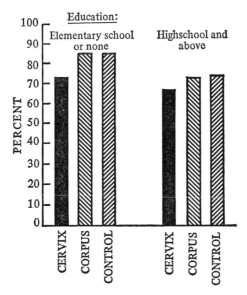

Figure 14–3. Percent uncircumcised partners of white non-Jewish patients by diagnosis and education level.

than in Israel Jews. As you have seen, no such difference was found.

The study of non-Jewish patients with and without cervix cancer may be carried beyond the analysis shown. One question is whether cancer patients and control patients are of equivalent socioeconomic status. Fig 14–3 illustrates the findings if education level of the patient is taken as an index of socioeconomic level. Proportions of uncircumcised partners are illustrated for cervix cancer, corpus cancer and control patients at two levels of education. Cervix cancer patients have fewer uncircumcised partners than corpus cancer and control patients, when the education level is elementary school or none. The same relationship is evident for patients with any high school or other advanced education. Associations with circumcision status in this study do not appear to be changed when adjustment is made for differences in socioeconomic level.

It is known that, in general, age at first intercourse is somewhat younger for cervix cancer patients. It seems useful as in Fig. 14–4, to compare cervix cancer and control cases by categories of age

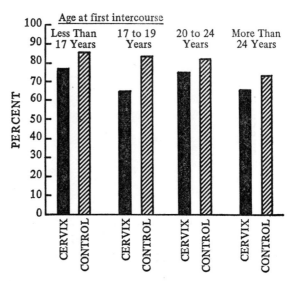

Figure 14–4. Percent uncircumcised partners of white non-Jewish patients by diagnosis and age at first intercourse.

at first intercourse. The relationship of cervix cancer and control patients with respect to proportions of uncircumcised partners remains similar for various ages at first intercourse, whether early or late. The proportions are slightly lower for cervix cancer than for control cases in each category of age at first intercourse.

Patients having a history of more than one marriage are more frequent among cervix cancer than among control cases. It seemed possible that a separate study of one time married patients and patients married more than once would have some bearing on the study of circumcision status of partners. The graph shown in Fig. 14–5 illustrates the analysis of uncircumcised partners of non-Jewish cervix cancer and control patients one time married contrasted to those married more than once. Although proportions of uncircumcised male partners are higher for those patients married more than once, even in this group the cervix cancer patients do not have as large a percentage of uncircumcised partners as do the control patients. Investigations of this feature fails to change the findings.

In conclusion it may be stated that there is no evidence of an association of uncircumcised male partners with a diagnosis of

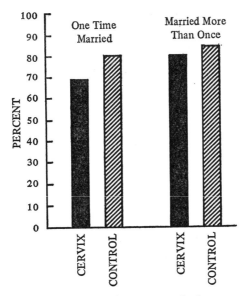

Figure 14–5. Percent uncircumcised partners of white non-Jewish patients by one time married and married more than once. Cervix cancer and control cases.

cancer of the uterine cervix. The different risks of cervix cancer for Jewish and non-Jewish women are not explained by a history of different frequencies of uncircumcised partners in the two ethnic groups.

SUMMARY

Studies on cancer of the uterine cervix and corpus in Israel and New York City were described. The three parts of the study were the determination of rates, the review of pathologic diagnoses of cancer cases and the study by interview of certain features of patients' histories. Replies to questions about environmental features associated with marriage, intercourse, pregnancy, menstruation and gynecologic disease were recorded on a prepared questionnaire. The circumcision status of male partners of Jewish and non-Jewish white women with and without cancers was analyzed. The information presented included the percentage of uncircumcised partners by diagnosis, and for non-Jewish patients an analysis of uncircumcised partners by diagnosis at different education levels, different ages at first intercourse and for one time married as contrasted to more than once married patients. There was no evidence of an association of uncircumcised male partners with a diagnosis of cancer of the uterine cervix.

Chapter 15

THE ETHNOLOGIC AND ENDOCRINOLOGICAL ASPECTS OF BREAST CANCER AND CYSTIC MASTOPATHY IN ISRAEL

B. Bertini and A. Ber

It has often been noted that there is some relationship between the incidence of various kinds of cancer and the standard of living of the population. At present, the highest breast cancer incidence is in Denmark; the disease is very rare in Asia.[23] At the same time, primary cancer of the liver is very rare in Europe and North America, while it is very common in Africa.[16]

In countries with a high living standard, breast tumors are the most common of all malignant tumors affecting women. According to O'Donnell et al.,[16] 1 out of every 20 women in the United States is apt to contract breast cancer: 24.8 percent of all malignant tumors among American women are breast cancers, and there are 62,500 new cases every year. The breast cancer mortality is 19.3 percent of the total cancer mortality of American women (23,900 cases annually).[16] In 1960, there were 25.6 breast cancer deaths per 100,000 women, with a breast cancer incidence of 67.8 per 100,000.[16]

Within a country there are also differences in cancer incidence

Reprinted in edited version with permission from *Cancer*, A Journal of the American Cancer Society, Inc., 17:(no. 4) April, 1964.

This study was supported in part by a grant from the Labour Sick Fund. The authors wish to express their appreciation to Mrs. S. Seligson-Singer, Head of the Labour Sick Fund Statistical Dept. and to Mr. D. Strasberg for their excellent assistance in the statistical analysis. The authors also wish to thank all the doctors of the Labour Sick Fund hospitals and outpatient clinics and of the Hospital Poriah, Tiberias, for their cooperation.

between the various ethnic and social groups. Wynder *et al.*[32] pointed out that in the United States the incidence of breast cancer among Negro women is 60 percent lower than among white women.

Segi[22,23] arrived at the same conclusions for Japan, where the breast cancer incidence is one of the lowest in the world. Even the few breast cancer cases in that country are found among the population with a higher living standard. The same phenomenon holds for India,[32] where the highest incidence is found among Parsies, who are considered a well-to-do segment of the population, and the lowest among Hindus and Moslems, a low population stratum from the social and economic point of view. Stocks[28] and Schwartz *et al.*[21] have reached the same conclusions for France. Steiner[26] has shown the difference in incidence between the various ethnic groups to be due to a greater extent to environmental than to genetic factors. The difference depends more on the various cultural habits and demographic factors than on race per se.

It has been suggested that earlier marriage, larger number of children, and longer nursing periods in women of the lower social strata may be responsible for the lower incidence of breast cancer. Japanese women, particularly peasant women, until recently nursed their children up to the age of three years. Segi[22,23] suggested that this long period of nursing may be the cause of atrophy of the ovaries that, in itself, serves as a protection against the development of mammary gland tumors. He also found that Japanese women affected by breast cancer had married later, had had fewer children, and had nursed them for shorter periods than had the women from the control group.

Wynder *et al.*[32] in their research on the incidence of breast cancer in the United States (Negro and white women), England, India, and Japan, arrived at a similar conclusion, i.e., that factors changing endocrinological activities, such as breast feeding or early castration, are apt to reduce breast cancer incidence.

As far back as 1844, Stern[27] showed that the frequency of the disease among unmarried women is higher than among married ones; in recent years, Olch[18] as well as Wynder *et al.*[32] maintained the same. Many authors have drawn attention to a similar difference between married women who have borne many children and childless women, the latter showing a higher incidence of the disease. In England, for instance, in 1948–1949 the breast cancer incidence was 52.6 per 100,000 married women with children, 69.7 for childless women, and 74.6 for unmarried ones.[12]

Trushnikova[30] concluded that the breast cancer incidence is higher among women starting sexual relations at a more advanced age. In this group, the frequency of hormonal disturbances was found to be three times higher than in the control group.[30]

In spite of considerable research, opinion on the role of hormones in carcinogenesis is still divided. Some authors claim that the relation between the appearance of tumors and hormonal imbalance is genetic. Others assume that endogenous disturbances, particularly in the metabolism of steroid hormones, are responsible for the start of the tumors. Green[5] and Lathrop and Loeb[7] affirm that breast tumors are chiefly acompanied by changes in the mucosa of the uterus and in the hypophysis and adrenals. This suggests that the endocrinological imbalance is a factor favorable to breast disease. There may be a direct relation between the severity of hormonal disturbances and the appearance of the tumor.

These conclusions are not yet firmly established and are far from being unanimously accepted. The role played by hyperestrogenism in the development of breast tumors and chronic mastopathy is especially debatable. Sometimes quite opposite opinions have been given. For instance, Schubert and Schröder[20] and Sicard and Marsan[24] have found a specific steroid metabolism in women with breast cancer different from that in normal women. On the other hand, Liu,[11] Yamamoto,[33] Smith and Emerson,[25] and Bertini et al.[1] were unable to establish any relation between estrogenic secretion and the disease. However, it is generally accepted that hormonal, particularly estrogenic, stimulation is required for the initiation of the tumor; the tumor then becomes independent of external hormonal influence. Pullinger[19] thinks that once the tumor is formed it is capable of producing an intercellular hormone, which stimulates further growth of the tumor. Therefore, in his opinion, no increased ovarian hormonal secretion is usually found in breast cancer patients. This hypothesis needs further verification.

Although there has been extensive research in developed countries on the epidemiological aspect of breast cancer, in small and underdeveloped countries epidemiological data are almost completely lacking. Even the registration of cancer cases is insufficient because of inadequate medical facilities and lack of suitable medical personnel. It is exactly in these countries that special research and an exact survey might be of decisive importance in determining the relation between the development of the cancer and the economic, cultural, and demographic conditions of the population.

In Israel, little epidemiological data are available. Apart from the work of Kallner[6] relating to the death rate from malignant growths (including breast cancer) between 1950–1957, no other work of importance has appeared on the epidemiological aspect of the disease and on the relation between carcinogenesis of the breast and environmental conditions.

Israel is a country of mass immigration of many ethnic groups from different parts of the world. The newcomers continue their own particular way of life long after their arrival in the country. The problem of whether there are differences in breast cancer incidence between the various communities is, therefore, very important, and research on the possible relation between this incidence and environmental and hormonal factors seemed to us to be timely.

Up till now, only partial research on breast cancer in Israel has been done. No work has been published on the ethnologic and endocrinological aspects of cystic mastopathy and breast cancer and on the connection between them. It should be mentioned, however, that in 1960 a monograph was published by Laurent and Leguerinais[8] on breast diseases in the Middle East (Israel and Iran) based on a survey made by one of the authors. The survey was particularly concerned with the cancer incidence and mortality rate in these two countries. According to the data quoted, there were 15 cancer cases per 100 deaths in Israel and only 3 per 100 in Teheran. There was also a considerable difference between the two countries in the frequency of the various kinds of cancer. The authors[8] arrived at the conclusion that the epidemiological aspect of cancer in these two countries was also different from that of Western European countries.

Our own research, presented in this paper, was pursued along two lines: (1) general ethnologic and (2) endocrinological. The aim was to determine (1) the difference in breast cancer incidence between Jewish Israeli women of European and American origin, on the one hand, and those of Oriental origin (in particular Yemen and Iraq), on the other; and (2) the age group most affected by mastopathy and breast cancer in Israel.

MATERIALS AND METHODS

Research was carried out on 833 women belonging to six ethnologic communities and different age groups. The data were collected from patients at Breast Cancer Centers of the Labour Sick Fund throughout the country.

The women were divided into three disease groups: (1) breast diseases other than cancer, (2) breast cancer, and (3) other medical problems (control). Every group was divided by community and by age. In a small number of Oriental women it was difficult to determine the age, and, therefore, they were grouped under the heading of age unknown.

For endocrinological research purposes, the ovarian activities of each of the 833 women were examined by three methods: (1) The Allen-Doisy bioassay method for determining the total estrogenic content of the urine. The diagnostic criteria were: up to 50 m.u., hypofunction; from 50 to 250 m.u., normal levels; 250 m.u. and more, hyperfunction. (2) The Papanicolaou cytohormonal method for determining estrogenic activity from vaginal smears. The diagnostic criteria were up to 20 percent superficial acidophilic cells, hypofunction; from 20 to 50 percent, normal levels; 50 percent and more, hyperfunction. (3) The Aschheim-Zondek method, with small modifications, for determining the total gonadotropins in the urine.

In accordance with the results of the hormonal examinations, the patients of the different ethnologic and age groups were classified into three main categories: (1) ovarian hypofunction, (2) normal ovarian function, and (3) ovarian hyperfunction. The cytological method brought about the addition of a fourth category, atrophy.

All examinations, a total of 4,000, were made at the Central Endocrinological Laboratory of the Labour Sick Fund Zamenhof Clinic, Tel Aviv.

RESULTS

Among 833 women, 428 had breast diseases; 298 had cystic mastopathy and 130 had breast cancer. The control group contained 405 women without breast disease who were sent for tests for the following gynecologic reasons: hormonal disturbances, childlessness, vaginal hemorrhages, and various infections.

Ethnic Group. According to the distribution of women by disease group and geographical area of origin, P was found to be lower than 0.001 ($x^2 = 165.3$, 4 *df*). In testing the significance between the breast cancer and cystic mastopathy groups in relation to area of origin, it was found that P was higher than 0.02 but less than 0.05 ($x^2 = 7.8$). In comparing the breast cancer and control groups and the cystic mastopathy and control groups in relation to area of origin, it was found that in both cases P was less than 0.001 ($x^2 = 82.5$ and $x^2 = 136.6$, respectively).

Estrogen and Gonadotropin Levels. In testing the significance in relation to estrogen activity in both groups of diseases combined and between each of the two groups, P was found to be less than 0.001 (4 *df*). This proves that there is a significant dependence of breast disease on estrogen level. (The results were identical in both biological and cytological tests.) In contrast, no significant interdependence was found between the disease groups and gonadotropin level (the lowest P is 0.10 and the highest is 0.80).

Ethnic Group and Estrogen Level. On the basis of geographical area of origin, no interdependence was found between breast disease and estrogen level ($0.50 > P > 0.30$, 4 *df*). On the contrary, when testing the significance in the control group according to the same criterion, interdependence was found between ethnic group and estrogen level ($0.02 > P > 0.01$, 4 *df*).

Age Group and Estrogen Level. Strong interdependence was found between disease groups in the age groups 20 to 39 and

40 to 54 in relation to estrogen level. In both of these groups, P was less than 0.001.

DISCUSSION

The six ethnic groups studied were divided, according to breast disease incidence, into two clearly defined groups: (1) women of European and American origin and Israeli-born women (the breast cancer incidence approaches that of countries with a high rate, e.g. Denmark, Scotland, and the United States[23]) and (2) women from Islamic countries (whose breast disease incidence is low and, according to the results of our preliminary research and an on-the-spot survey, approaches that in Japanese women,[23] whose breast cancer incidence is among the lowest in the world). In Yemenite women in particular, no breast cancer had been found hitherto. This phenomenon, though it pertains to only a small number of cases and requires a comprehensive investigation of all relating factors, seems to be very significant.

Of all the women from Islamic countries studied, only 7.5 percent had breast cancer and 9.7 percent had cystic mastopathy, while the remaining 82.8 percent were in the control group and free of breast disease. In contrast to this, out of all women from Western countries together with those born in Israel, 43.3 percent had cystic mastitis, 17.9 percent had breast cancer, and only 38.8 percent were free of breast disease.

Within the Oriental communities themselves, there were also differences in breast cancer incidence. For instance, Yemenite women were exceptional, in that out of a total of 428 women with breast disease, there was not one of Yemenite origin. This raised the question whether this phenomenon pertains to all women of Yemenite origin in Israel or whether the negligible number of women sent to Breast Cancer Centers and clinics is due to a specific reluctance on the part of Oriental women to undergo medical examination. In order to clear up this point, Labour Sick Fund institutions in different parts of the country and a few government hospitals in the vicinity of Yemenite settlements were visited, and many physicians (surgeons, pathologists, oncologists) were interviewed. All corroborated that not a single case of mastopathy in Yemenite women was registered during a period of several years. However, during a period of 15 years, two Yemenite women with breast carcinoma were patients at the Hasharon Hospital, Petah Tikva, where a special Breast Cancer Center exists. At the Labour Sick Fund Central Clinic for Breast Diseases in Tel Aviv, where an average of 500 to 600 women affected by breast diseases are examined every month, in more than 10 years there were also two cases of breast cancer in Yemenite women.

All physicians interviewed believed that the cause does not lie in the reluctance of these women to submit to medical examination, because the percentage of consultations with these women in regard to other diseases is not lower than that for other communities. In the present study, European and American women comprised 39.3 percent of the control group and those from Islamic countries comprised 38 percent of this group; of the latter, 13 percent were Yemenite women.

It deserves special mention that, according to the data obtained in our study, cystic mastopathy and breast cancer incidence is already different in Israeli-born women from that of their mothers born outside the country. The incidence in this category begins to approach that of European and American women, particularly in regard to cystic mastopathy.[23]

These findings confirm the theory that environmental factors play an important role in carcinogenesis of the breast. We know, for instance, that there is a marked difference between Yemenite women who immigrated from Yemen and those born and educated in Israel. The latter marry at a later age, do not bear as many children, and nurse for shorter periods; their living standard is higher, and their emotional life is more intense. The same phenomenon is observed even in women from Iraq, whose environmental habits are different and whose living standard is, in general, higher than that of Yemenite women. The incidence of breast disease in these women is higher than that in Yemenite women.

It is supposed that in addition to environmental factors, there is a relation between the development of cystic and cancerous breast diseases and ovarian activity. This supposition is based on the rarity of these diseases in early age and in castrated women and on the lower incidence in women nursing their children for protracted periods. For instance, the low breast cancer incidence in Japanese women is related mostly to the long duration of nursing.[32]

The conclusions arrived at by Copeland,[2] Degrell and Kádas,[3] and Okada,[17] based on clinical and pathological data, underline the relation between breast cancer and benign breast diseases. Their experimental work on animals has also shown the correlation between the two categories of breast disease, confirming the supposition that basic endocrinological factors are essential for the development of both diseases. Wang et al.[31] found cancerous developments in 19 percent of 32 patients with cystic mastopathy who were observed for five years. In 159 breast cancer cases, previous cystic mastopathy was found in the anamnesis in 21 percent.

In the opinion of Taylor[29] and Nathan and Rosner,[14] determination of the estrogenic level makes follow-up of the development of breast diseases, particularly cancerous diseases, possible. They believe that breast cancer recidivism is often accompanied by increased estrogenic activity, and, in cases of metastases, hyperestrogenism may sometimes also be noted.

In our determinations of gonadotropin and estrogen levels in all control women, a greater hormonal imbalance was, in general, found among women of European and American origin than among those from Oriental communities. From the hormonal aspect, Israeli-born women are like women of the Western sector. Among women of Asian origin without breast disease, more hormonal fluctuations were observed in Iraqi than in Yemenite women.

Nevertheless, we were unable to find marked differences in the estrogenic level between Western and Eastern women affected by breast disease. In general, the results reveal greater estrogenic activity among women affected by breast diseases, particularly by cystic mastopathy, than among women not so affected. This estrogenic activity was also reflected by later appearance of the menopause than in the control group. A large percentage of these patients continued to menstruate after the age of 50, while in women from the control group with normal estrogenic activity the menopause occurred between the ages of 40 and 48.

Most breast cancer and cystic mastopathy patients were concentrated in the groups with normal and hyperestrogenic activity, only a small percentage being in the hypoestrogenic group. Of the women affected by breast cancer between the ages of 20 to 39, 65.4 percent were in the estrogenic hyperfunction or normal groups and only 34.6 percent were in the hypofunction group. In contrast, of control women in the same age group, only 38 percent were in the hyperfunction or normal groups, and the majority of the women (62%) were in the hypofunction group.

In most breast disease patients we found an inclination to hyperestrogenism, but, as it was not noted in every case, no conclusion can be drawn concerning specific estrogenic metabolism characteristics in women affected by breast disease. We were able to determine with certainty a considerable and persistent hyperestrogenism only in a number of breast cancer patients resistant to hormonal treatment.

The division of our patients into age groups revealed that until the age of 19 there was not a single case of cancer, mastopathy constituting only 1 percent. The age most affected by mastopathy was lower than that for breast cancer, the majority of mastopathy cases (45.3%) occurring in the 20- to 39-year age group, in contrast to 20 percent of the breast cancer cases. The opposite was true with regard to breast cancer. The majority of women affected were in the 40- to 54-year age group (68.5%), in contrast to 48.3 percent of mastopathy patients. Of women in the control group affected by various hormonal disturbances, 82.9 percent were up to 39 years of age and only 15.3 percent were between 40 and 54 years of age.

Experimental work on breast diseases by Dilman,[4] Lazarev,[9] and others has shown that the hyperplastic process of the mammary gland depends on the simultaneous influence of estrogens and hypophyseal hormones (follicle-stimulating hormone, mammogenic hormone, and somatotropic hormone), but opinion is divided on the levels of gonadotropin in the urine and blood of patients with cystic breast disease and breast cancer.

Lemon[10] and Loraine[13] have found normal or low levels of urine follicle-stimulating hormone in postmenopausal breast cancer patients. Netter and Gorins[15] and Dilman[4] have noted imbalances in gonadotropic metabolism, but these were inconsistent.

The results obtained by us in gonadotropic investigations in all women without breast disease have shown greater gonadotropic imbalances in women from Europe and the United States (28.9%) than in women from Islamic countries (10 to 17.9%). Normal gonadotropic activity was noted in the vast majority of the Oriental women (82.1 to 90%), as against 71.1 percent of Western women.

Greater gonadotropic activity was present in patients with breast cancer and cystic mastopathy than in the control group, though the difference was not statistically significant. The majority of breast disease patients with hypergonadotropic activity was concentrated in the 40- to 54-year age group (62.7 to 64.1%), while women in the control group with a hypergonadotropic level constituted only 6.4 percent of the same age group (most of them were in the lower range of this age group and had not had the climacteric).

In spite of these results, it is difficult to relate the hypergonadotropism of this age group to breast disease only, this being the menopause age, when fluctuations in gonadotropic secretion may physiologically occur.

SUMMARY

A total of 428 women with cystic mastopathy or breast cancer and 405 controls with various gynecologic disturbances but without breast disease were studied from the ethnologic and endocrinological aspects. They represented 6 ethnic groups: Israeli-born women of different ethnic groups and immigrants from Yemen, Iraq, other Asian countries, North Africa, and Europe and the United States of America.

Urine estrogen and gonadotropin levels were determined in all patients. A statistical evaluation of the influence of ethnic group and age on the incidence of breast diseases was performed.

From the ethnologic aspect, the results revealed that the incidence of breast disease, particularly breast cancer, is high among immigrants of European and American origin and very low among immigrants from Eastern countries, especially among Yemenite women. However, no marked difference was found in the incidence of breast disease between Israeli-born women of different ethnic groups. This points to the importance of demographic factors in carcinogenesis of the breast.

The endocrinological investigations in the control group revealed a more pronounced hormonal imbalance among European and American women than among women from Oriental countries. However, in the group of patients with breast cancer, there was no marked difference in the urine estrogen level between the two sectors. Though a tendency to hypergonadism has been noted in patients with breast diseases, no characteristic hormonal disturbances could be detected in this group.

Most patients with breast cancer were in the 40- to 54-year age group, and those with cystic mastopathy were in the 20- to 39-year age group.

REFERENCES

1. Bertini, B.; Saposhnik, A., and Rosner, D.: L'examen cyto-vaginal dans le cancer du sein; son importance dans l'interprétation clinique et thérapeutique. In Wied, G.L. (Ed.): *Proceedings of the First International Congress on Exfoliative Cytology.* Philadelphia, J.B. Lippincott Company, 1961, pp. 56–61.

2. Copeland, M.M.: Precancerous lesions of breast; how to treat them. *Postgrad Med,* 27:332–336, 1960.

3. Degrell, I., and Kádas, I.: Die Beziehungen der Matstopathia cystica zum Brustdrüsenkarzinom. *Zentralbl allg Path,* 100:398-401, 1959–1960: abstr. in *Excerpta med sect 16,* 9:75–76, 1961.

4. Dilman, V.M.: [Gonadotropin secretion increase in breast cancer as indication of diencephalohypophysis activity augmentation.] *Vopr onkol,* 6 (1): 105–108, 1960.

5. Green, H.N.: Immunological concept of cancer; preliminary report. *Br Med J* 2:1374–1380, 1954.

6. Kallner, G.: Cancer mortality in Israel (1950–57). Special Series

Publication No. 107. Jerusalem, Israel. Central Bureau of Statistics, 1961.

7. Lathrop, A.E.C., and Loeb, L.: Further investigations on origin of tumors in mice; III, on part played by internal secretion in spontaneous development of tumors. *J Cancer Res 1*:1–20, 1916.

8. Laurent, C., and Leguerinais, J.: *Le cancer au Moyen-Orient (Israël et Iran); données épidémiologiques. Monographie de l'Institut National d'Hygiène.* Paris, France. J. & R. Sennac, 1960, p. 19.

9. Lazarev, N.I.: [Theoretical basis of hormone therapy of breast cancer.] *Ark Patol, 22* (2): 3–18, 1960.

10. Lemon, H.M.: Cortisone-thyroid therapy of metastatic mammary cancer. *Ann Int Med, 46*:457–484, 1957.

11. Liu, W.: Vaginal cytology in breast cancer patients. *Surg Gynec Obst, 105*:421–426, 1957.

12. Logan, W.P.D.: Marriage and childbearing in relation to concer of breast and uterus. *Lancet, 2*:1199–1202, 1953.

13. Loraine, J.A.: *Clinical Application of Hormone Assay.* Edinburgh, Scotland, E. & S. Livingstone Ltd., 1958.

14. Nathan, P., and Rosner, D.: [Cancer of breast.] *Dapim Refuim, 19*:185–191, 1960; English summary, p. VIII.

15. Netter, A., and Gorins, A.: Cancer mammaire et hormones. In *Les facteurs hormonaux de la croisance; la grand mammaire. Rapports de la VI° Réunion des Endocrinologistes de Langue Française,* Bruxelles, 1961. Paris, France. Masson et Cie. 1961; pp. 185–230.

16. O'Donnell, W.E.; Day, E., and Venet, L.: *Early Detection and Diagnosis of Cancer.* St. Louis, Mo., The C.V. Mosby Company, 1962, pp. 137–140.

17. Okada, T.: Relationship between mastopathia and breast cancer. *Jap J Clin Path,* 7:122, 1959; abstr. in *Excerpta Med Sect 16,* 9:333, 1961.

18. Olch, I.Y.: Menopausal age in women with cancer of breast. *Am J Cancer, 30*:563–566, 1937.

19. Pullinger, B.D.: Significance of functional differentiation in mammary tumours. *Lancet* 2:823–828, 1949.

20. Schubert, K., and Schröder, H.: Steroidstoffwechsel bei Brustkrebs; vie Mitteilung, die Differenzanalyse der Harnsteroide beim Testosterontest zur Charakter isierung Unterschiedlicher Stoffwechselleistungen. *Arch Geschwulstforsch, 16*:105–113, 1960.

21. Schwartz, D.; Denoix, P.F., and Rouquette, C.: Enquête sur l'étiologie des cancers génitaux de la femme; I, cancer du sein. *Bull Assoc franç étude cancer, 45*:476–493, 1958.

22. Segi, M.: Geographical and racial distribution of cancer of breast. *Schweiz Ztschr allg Path, 18*:668–685, 1955.

23. Segi, M.: Cancer Mortality for Selected Sites in 24 Countries (1950–1957). Sendai, Japan. Department of Public Health, Tohoku University School of Medicine. 1960. Cited by O'Donnell, W.E.; Day, E., and Venet, L.[16]

24. Sicard, A., and Marsan, C.: Renseignements fournis par la cytologie dans le diagnostic des tumeurs du sein. *Mém Acad chir, 83:*71–75, 1957.

25. Smith, O.W., and Emeron, K., Jr.: Urinary estrogens and related compounds in postmenopausal women with mammary cancer; effect of cortisone treatment. *Proc Soc Exper Biol Med, 85:*264–277, 1954.

26. Steiner, P.E.: *Cancer, Race and Geography; Some Etiological, Environmental, Ethnological, Epidemiological, and Statistical Aspects in Caucasoids, Mongoloids, Negroids, and Mexicans.* Baltimore, Md., The Williams & Wilkins Company, 1954.

27. Stern, R.: Nota sulle ricerche de dottor Tanchou intorno la frequenza de cancro. *Ann univ med, 110:*484–503, 1844.

28. Stocks, P.: Social status in relation to carcinoma of breast. *Schweiz Ztschr allg Path 18:*706–717, 1955. Cited by Wynder, E.L.; Bross, I.J., and Hirayama, T.[32]

29. Taylor, S.G.: Hormonal modification in treatment of disseminated cancer of breast. *Am J Med, 21:*688–696, 1956.

30. Trushnikova, F.V.: [Functional disturbances in patients with cancer of breast]. *Vopr onkol 4:*702–707, 1958; abstr. in *Excerpta med sect, 16, 7:*941, 1959.

31. Wang, T.Y.; Wang, T.T., and Chang, T.C.: [Cystic hyperplasia of breast and its early stage of malignant changes.] *Chinese J Surg, 7:*1162–1167, 1959; abstr. in *Excerpta med sect 16, 8:*1332, 1960.

32. Wynder, E.L.; Bross, I.J., and Hirayama, T.: Study of epidemiology of cancer of breast. *Cancer, 13:*559–601, 1960.

33. Yamamoto, T.: Endocrinological studies on tumors of breast. *Nagoya M J, 4* (1):25–44, 1957–1958. Cited by Netter, A., and Gorins, A.[15]

Chapter 16

PENILE CARCINOMA AMONG JEWS

EMMANUEL MARGOLIS

E stimates of the incidence of penile carcinoma in Great Britain, Western Europe and the United States range from 1 percent to 5 percent of all cancers in males.[2,13] Sanjurjo and Gonzalez[17] found an even lower frequency in Puerto Rico. Sporadic reports from institutions of Asia indicate that the percentage of patients with cancer of the penis is much higher in that area, namely 21.9 percent in India, 18.3 percent in China, and 18.9 percent in other Far Eastern countries.[11]

It is maintained that cancer of the penis occurs relatively frequently in Negroes.[18] Lenowitz and Graham[9] found that in the United States cancer of the penis was five times more common in Negroes than in Whites.

The occurrence of carcinoma of the penis in Jews and persons who perform circumcision after birth is so exceedingly rare that isolated cases are widely quoted in the literature.[1,2,3,8,10,12,16]

Cancer of the penis occurs more often among Moslems, who circumcise their males at a later date, usually between six and 14 years, than among Jews who perform circumcision on the eighth day after birth. This might indicate that the precancerous changes can become well established at an early age and may progress to definite carcinoma formation even when the preputium has been removed comparatively early in life.[4]

The fact that carcinoma of the penis occurs relatively frequently in Negroes, is infrequent in white non-Jewish men, and is practically unknown in Jews raises the question of racial susceptibility and immunity.

Reprinted with permission from *Eugenics Q*, 8:(no. 3) September 1961. Published by American Eugenics Society, 230 Park Ave., N.Y.C.

Is this distribution really due to inherited racial characteristics or is it dependent on environmental factors? According to Sorsby[19] the immunity of the Jews should be attributed to circumcision and not to racial factors.

In a comprehensive study on the etiologic factors in carcinoma of the penis, Schrek and Lenowitz[18] obtained positive correlations for the factors carcinoma of the penis, syphilis, gonorrhea, and the colored race. The authors believe the common denominator in these four factors to be poor sex hygiene. According to them, circumcision possibly lessens the accumulations of smegma and dirt, and in this way inhibits cancer.

Omitting the still inconclusive studies on the carcinogenic[14] or carcinostimulatory[15] effects of the human smegma, we nevertheless feel that the hypothesis proposed by Schrek and Lenowitz[18] is far from being indubitable. If this hypothesis were correct, one would expect circumcision during boyhood to also protect against cancer of the penis; and then it might be reasonable to present once more the question proposed by the Editors of *Lancet* (1932) 28 years ago, namely: If cancer of the penis might be prevented by the hygiene of circumcision, it is thus demonstrated that cancer is a preventable disease, and if it can be prevented in one organ by appropriate hygienic care, why can it not be prevented in other organs by similar hygienic measures appropriate to those respective organs?

Schrek and Lenowitz[18] are aware of this. They therefore admit that the "individuals circumcised early in life are protected against cancer of the penis not by cleanliness but by some other process, the nature of which is not known."

The causes of penile cancer, being a part of the fundamental problem of cancer etiology, are still obscure. It seems therefore justifiable to concentrate our efforts on a thorough evaluation of the different characteristics and peculiarities of the patients and the possible causative factors. The correct answer might be detected in the interaction between them.

The possibility of racial susceptibility, or at least of racial predisposition, deserves due consideration. It is of interest, for example, that in the Hottentots a rather tight and elongated prepuce appears to be a racial characteristic; at the same time it was found that epithelioma of the penis is the commonest malignant tumor in male Hottentots.[7]

Up to the present time the evidence of circumcision as an effective measure against penile cancer is based upon negative rather than positive findings.

Positive data of confirmative value could be added if the cases of noncircumcised Jews developing penile carcinoma were collected and studied. If such a study then showed that, on the one hand, the incidence of cancer of the penis among noncircumcised Jews and noncircumcised Gentiles was the same and that, on the other hand, so was the incidence among circumcised Jews and circumcised Gentiles, it would then be possible to evaluate with certainty the protective importance of circumcision early in life.

However, cases of noncircumcised Jews are very rare, circumcision being a universal practice, a part of the religious rite of the Jews. Wollbarst (cited in 4) did report finding one noncircumcised Jew with penile cancer. In the Tumour and Radium Institute of the Rothschild Hadassah University Hospital in Jerusalem, Israel, only one case of penile carcinoma in a noncircumcised Jew has so far been recorded. Recently, two instances have been reported of carcinoma in Gentile patients circumcised in infancy.[3] In both cases, an injury seemed to be an apparent factor in the etiology.

It might be helpful if contact could be established with physicians in the U.S.S.R. in order to obtain more authoritative information concerning the incidence of penile carcinoma among the Jews of Russia, who, since the Revolution, probably have not circumcised their newborns.

It will be of utmost interest to collect and study such cases. These data when analyzed might become valuable contributions to the problem of penile cancer and the etiology of cancer in general.

REFERENCES

1. Amelar, R.D.: Carcinoma of penis due to trauma occurring in a male patient circumcised at birth. *J Urol, 75*:728, 1956.

2. Bleich, A.R.: Prophylaxis of penile carcinoma. *JAMA, 143*:1054, 1950.

3. *The Cancer Bulletin. Circumcision.* 10:5, 158.

4. Dean, A.L., Jr.: Epithelioma of the penis. *J Urol,* 33:252, 1935.

5. Dean, A.L., Jr.: Epithelioma of the penis in a Jew who was circumcised in early infancy. *Tr Am Assoc Genito-Urin Surg,* 29:493, 1936.

6. Editorial Annotation. Cancer preventable? *Lancet,* 222:146, 1932.

7. Hellman, J.: Circumcision and penile cancer. *Lancet,* 269:349, 1955.

8. Ledlie, R.C.B., and D.W. Smithers: Carcinoma of penis in a man circumcised in infancy. *J Urol,* 76:756, 1956.

9. Lenowitz, H., and A.P. Graham: Carcinoma of the penis. *J Urol,* 56:458, 1946.

10. Marshall, V.F.: Typical carcinoma of the penis in a male circumcised in infancy. *Cancer,* 6:1044, 1953.

11. Ngai, S.K.: Etiological and pathological aspects of squamous-cell carcinoma of penis among Chinese. *Am J Cancer,* 19:259, 1933.

12. Paquin, A.J., Jr., and J.M. Pearce: Carcinoma of the penis in a man circumcised in infancy. *J Urol,* 74:626, 1955.

13. Paul, M.: Cancer of the penis in Ceylon. *Ann Roy Coll Surg Eng,* 20:50, 1957.

14. Plaut, A., and A.C. Kohn-Speyer: Carcinogenic action of smegma. *Science,* 105:391, 1947.

15. Pratt-Thomas, H.R., and E. Heins: Carcinogenic effect of human smegma. *Cancer,* 9:671, 1956.

16. Reitman, P.H.: An unusual case of penile carcinoma. *J Urol,* 69:547, 1953.

17. Sanjurjo, L.A., and F.B. Gonzalez: Carcinoma of the penis. *J Urol,* 83:433, 1960.

18. Schrek, R., and H. Lenowitz: Etiologic factors in carcinoma of penis. *Cancer Res,* 7:180, 1947.

19. Sorsby, M.: *Cancer and Race.* London, John Bale, Sons and Danielson, 1931, p. 120.

Chapter 17

EPIDEMIOLOGY OF CANCER OF UTERINE CERVIX AND CORPUS, BREAST AND OVARY IN ISRAEL AND NEW YORK CITY

H.L. Stewart, L.J. Dunham, J. Casper, H.F. Dorn,
L.B. Thomas, J.H. Edgcomb and A. Symeonides

SUMMARY AND CONCLUSIONS

This issue presents an incidence, interview, and pathology study of cancer of the uterine cervix and corpus in Puerto Rican, Negro, Jewish and non-Jewish white women in New York City and of uterine cervix, uterine corpus, breast, and ovary in women in Israel. Interviewers queried women with these cancers to elicit information about factors that might have influenced their disease. The incidence rates were compared and the data from the interviews analyzed.

The physicians in practice in New York City and Israel initially diagnosed the cancers of the patients in this study. Insofar as possible the pathologists associated with this study reviewed these initial diagnoses. The reviewers aimed to make as certain as possible the diagnosis of the neoplastic lesion, the site of its origin, and its histologic type.

Six percent of the total number of patients interviewed were eliminated from the study, mostly because the reviewing pathologists could not confirm the diagnosis of cancer. Another 3 percent of the total number of patients interviewed were retained, but their initial diagnoses were changed by the reviewing pathologists. In the instance of carcinoma *in situ* of the cervix the reviewers admitted into the study 56 patients with this diag-

Summary and Conclusions reprinted with permission from *Journal of the National Cancer Institute*, 37:(no. 1) July, 1966.

nosis, after they had changed the diagnosis of 17 lesions initially listed as carcinoma *in situ* to non-neoplastic proliferative lesions of the cervix. They changed 24 diagnoses from invasive carcinoma of the cervix to carcinoma *in situ* and four other diagnoses from carcinoma *in situ* to invasive carcinoma.

The patients were divided into the *Total Cancer Group* and the *Selected Cancer Group*. The Selected Cancer Group consisted of 337 patients with invasive squamous cell, transitional cell, or undifferentiated cell carcinoma of the uterine cervix; 366 cases of adenocarcinoma, adenoacanthoma or undifferentiated cell carcinoma of the uterine corpus and, from Israel only, 393 patients with carcinoma of the breast and 53 patients with carcinoma of the ovary. The Total Cancer Group contained an additional 188 patients. These patients included all of those with relatively uncommon histologic types of uterine cancer, and cancer occurring in the cervical stump after a previous subtotal hysterectomy; they also included all the patients with carcinoma *in situ,* and the 59 Israeli patients whose lesion either had not been biopsied or, had been biopsied, but not reviewed by the National Cancer Institute pathologists.

There are differences and similarities in the incidence rates of cancer of the cervix among the Puerto Rican, Negro, non-Jewish white, and Jewish women in New York City and the two groups of Jewish women in Israel. In the two localities, New York City and Israel, the rates for the Jewish women were virtually identical, 4.1 and 4.8, respectively. The two subgroups of Jewish women in Israel, the Ashkenazi and Sephardi-Oriental, also had virtually identical rates of cancer of the cervix, 4.7 and 4.9, respectively. Moreover, the incidence rates by age for cancer of the cervix for the Ashkenazi Jews and the Sephardi-Oriental Jews of Israel and the Jews of New York City agreed closely one with another. The incidence rate for Jews was less than that for non-Jewish white women in each group. The peak incidence for the non-Jewish white women coincided approximately with age at menopause, while that for Jews was about 15 years later. A comparison of the incidence of cancer of the cervix for non-Jewish white women in New York City with that reported for white women from selected urban areas of the United States revealed that the incidence rate in New York City was about one half that in the other areas, 15.0 in comparison with the average of 39.1. The rate for cancer of the cervix for New York City non-Jewish white women was also low in comparison with the rates reported for women in Iowa, Connecticut, New York State, and Denmark but was close to the rate for women in Saskatchewan, Canada. For the Negro, the rate of 49.6 from New York City was lower than the rate of 78.6 from selected urban areas of the United States and was closer to the rate of 59.1 for the Bantu women from South Africa. The extraordinarily high incidence rate of cancer of the cervix for Puerto Rican women in New York City, 105.7, was about twice the rate, 49.5, reported for this neoplasm in the female population of Puerto Rico.

Cancer of the corpus showed no such wide variation in incidence rates as did cancer of the cervix. The rates were 7.3 for Puerto Rican, 10.0 for Negro, 13.1 for non-Jewish white, and 15.6 for Jewish women in New York City and 8.6 for Jewish women in Israel. Within the range of variation, the difference in the rate of cancer of the corpus was actually greater between Jewish women in New York City and Jewish women in Israel than between the Jewish women of New York City and the women of the other three groups, the Negro, Puerto Rican, and non-Jewish white women in New York City. The rate for corpus cancer was nearly as high for Jewish women in New York City, 15.6, as that reported for any other group of women in the United States. In Israel there was also a pronounced difference in the incidence rate of cancer of the corpus between Ashkenazi and Sephardi-Oriental Jews, 11.2 as compared with 3.2. Ratios of cancer of the cervix to cancer of the corpus for Jewish women were low, 0.3 for New York City and 0.6 for Israel. By contrast, the ratio of cancer of the cervix to cancer of the corpus was greater than 1.0 for every group of non-Jewish women; the ratios varied from 1.1 to 14.5.

The incidence rate of cancer of the breast for Israeli women was 40 and of cancer of the ovary was 7.4; for the subgroups these were for the breast and ovary, respectively, 23.5 and 3.0 for Sephardi-Oriental and 47.9 and 9.5 for Ashkenazi.

The rates were not calculated for choriocarcinoma; the 20 patients with this lesion are tabulated by age, geographic area, group, and subgroup.

The relationship of the circumcision status of the male partner to cancer of the cervix was evaluated in Jewish patients in New York City. The difference between patients with cancer of the cervix and controls was statistically significant ($P < 0.05$), but the difference between patients with cancer of the cervix and patients with cancer of the corpus was not significant.

Of the non-Jewish white women in New York City, 69.7 percent with cancer of the cervix, 81 percent with cancer of the corpus, and 80.6 percent that were controls gave a history of intercourse with one or more uncircumcised partners. The differences between these figures are not statistically significant even after the age of patients with cancer of the cervix was standardized for the age distribution of the control patients. Furthermore, classification of the patients according to educational grade level, occupational status, age at first intercourse, frequency of intercourse, number of marriages, and age at diagnosis yielded no support for a relationship between uncircumcised partners and cancer of the cervix.

Other environmental factors or cultural traits that were either not significantly or not consistently associated with cancer of the cervix were abstinence from intercourse after menses, dissolution of marriage by widowhood, divorce, or separation, more than one marriage (when adjusted to the age at marriage), semipermanent extramarital sexual relations, intercourse five and more times per week, contraception, pregnancy, a total of three or more pregnancies, the trimester at termination of pregnancy, the method of delivery, crowding of pregnancies, a particular age at menarche or menopause, characteristics of the menstrual cycle, and certain diseases, surgical operations, and treatments in the medical history.

The median age at first intercourse was lower for each group of Jewish and non-Jewish white patients with cancer of the cervix than for the corresponding control patients. The interval from the age at first intercourse or the age at first marriage until the age at which cancer was diagnosed was no shorter when the age at first intercourse or age at first marriage was under

20 years than when it was 20 and more years. Moreover, cancer of the cervix did not develop any earlier in patients who had uncircumcised partners, more than one marriage, a comparatively large number of pregnancies under age 30, or a relatively early age at menarche.

A comparison of specific environmental factors related to marriage and pregnancy in the three groups of Jewish women in whom the incidence of cancer of the cervix was similar revealed wide differences. These were for New York City Jews, Israeli Ashkenazi Jews, and Israeli Sephardi-Oriental Jews, respectively, as follows: (1) the median age at first intercourse 22, 22.4, and 16 years; (2) for marriage before age 20 years, 23, 17, and 47 percent; (3) for first pregnancy before age 25 years, 56, 46, and 73 percent; (4) for five or more pregnancies, 21, 30, and 58 percent; (5) for average number of pregnancies, 3.4, 3.5, and 5.6 pregnancies.

There were, respectively, the following differences between the Israeli Ashkenazi Jews and the Israeli Sephardi-Oriental Jews in their practices of the laws of Niddah[1] and their socioeconomic status as judged by education: (1) for nonpractice of the laws of Niddah, 68 and 48 percent; (2) for no formal education, 15 and 62 percent; and (3) for education through grade 9 or above, 39 and 13 percent. These results would, of course, be consistent with the hypothesis that circumcision of the male partner has removed the carcinogenic factor from Jews and hence these differences are without significance.

The observations on patients with cancer of the corpus, breast, and ovary are consistent with the hypothesis that a proportion of women who develop these cancers have environmental factors and constitutional traits that enhance their susceptibility to these diseases. For patients with cancer of the corpus there was an association with irregular menses, natural menopause at age 53 and over, excess weight, age at first marriage and age at first intercourse of 20 years and over, the never-pregnant state, relatively few pregnancies, and, except for the Israeli Ashkenazi, the never-married state. Israeli women with cancer of the breast and ovary in comparison with the controls showed: a higher proportion who had never married; more whose ages were greater than 20 years at first intercourse, marriage, and pregnancy; more whose pregnancy terminated during the first trimester; fewer who had ever been pregnant; fewer who had a total of 5 or more pregnancies.

The group of carcinoma *in situ* patients is small and their age and socioeconomic status differ from those of the patients with invasive carcinoma of the cervix. The patients with carcinoma *in situ* had a lower median age at menarche. Their median age at the time the diagnosis was made was for the New York City non-Jews 41.4 years and for New York City Jews 42 years. These figures are, respectively, 9.3 and 5.2 years less than the median age of the patients at the time the diagnosis of invasive carcinoma of the cervix was made. The patients with carcinoma *in situ* were from a higher socioeconomic level than the controls and the patients with invasive carcinoma of the cervix.

1. In accordance with the laws of Niddah, the menses are defined as the entire period of bleeding, including both regular bleeding. The laws forbid husband and wife to cohabit or to come into physical contact during the menses and for 7 days thereafter, amounting to a total period averaging about 12 days of abstinence from intercourse.

Chapter 18

LUNG CANCER AMONG JEWISH, CATHOLIC AND PROTESTANT MALES IN NEW YORK CITY

H. Seidman

The differences in lung cancer mortality among Jewish, Catholic and Protestant Caucasian males in New York City for 1940, 1949 to 1951 and 1959 to 1961 are presented in this paper. The mortality data are shown by age as a proportion of total deaths and, in some instances, as death rates per 100,000 population. We do not have any direct information on smoking habits in New York City. However, unpublished data from Hammond and Garfinkel[2] on smoking practices among the Jewish, Catholic and Protestant Caucasian males enrolled in other large cities of the United States are given. Also given are some unpublished data on occupational exposures.

Wynder and Mantel[13] found that admissions for lung cancer at a New York City hospital relative to total admissions in a recent period were lower for Jewish males than for Catholic or Protestant males. They found much more cigarette smoking among patients with epidermoid and anaplastic lung cancer than among controls for males of each religious group. The Jewish male controls smoked cigarettes less than the Catholic

Reprinted in edited version with permission from Cancer, A Journal of the American Cancer Society, Inc., 19:(no. 2) February, 1966.

I thank Dr. E. Cuyler Hammond for his helpful suggestions and for the unpublished data on smoking habits and occupational exposures, Mr. H. Stephen Victor for his assistance in processing the data, Mr. Louis Weiner and Dr. Carl Erhardt of the New York City Department of Health and Dr. Vincent H. Handy of the New York State Department of Health for providing death records and Mr. Howard G. Brunsman of the United States Bureau of the Census for furnishing unpublished population data.

or Protestant males. In addition, Wynder and Mantel found some differences among religious groups in the proportion of men with occupational exposures to substances which have been considered to relate to lung cancer but the differences did not seem large enough to account for the magnitude of the differences in the rates of lung cancer. They concluded that the lower rate of epidermoid and anaplastic lung cancer among Jewish males appeared to be consistent with their smoking history.

In studies of cancer death rates in the Caucasian population of New York City who were 45 years and over and who were treated as one age group MacMahon[3] for 1955 and Newill[5] for the more extensive period of 1953 to 1958 found that lung cancer death rates for Jewish males were much lower than for Catholic or Protestant males. In an earlier study in New York City Bolduan and Weiner[1] for 1931 showed that deaths from cancer of the respiratory system (most of which were lung cancer) comprised a considerably higher proportion of deaths from all causes in the Jewish as compared with non-Jewish Caucasian male decedents throughout almost all age groups.

MATERIALS

The New York City Department of Health has furnished us with a coded record for each death which occurred in New York City in 1940, 1949 to 1951 and 1959 to 1961 and for each cancer death which occurred in 1958 and 1962. We resorted to the death certificates of the 1958 to 1962 foreign-born cancer victims to code further detail on the country of birth. The New York State Department of Health has provided us with an IBM card For that part of our analysis which deals with lung cancer and for cancer deaths in 1958–1962.

For that part of our analysis which deals with lung cancer deaths as a proportion of total deaths we have used only Caucasian males dying in New York City (exclusive of nonresidents) who were buried in Jewish, Catholic and Protestant (including nonsectarian) cemeteries. These comprise most of the Caucasian male deaths in New York City. We have included the nonsectarian cemeteries with the Protestant cemeteries since the Protestants comprise most of these interments.[4] For the computation of lung cancer death rates—the number of lung cancer deaths annually relative to the population at risk—the "specified" denomination deaths were supplemented with the cremations, City Cemetery and out-of-town burials and the deaths in upstate New York of New York City residents. These "unspecified denomination" deaths were allocated as Jewish, Catholic and Protestant in proportion to those "specified" within age and socioeconomic class groups.

Population denominators for the computation of death rates were based upon data from the 1940,[7,8] 1950[9,12] and 1960[10,11] censuses of population of the United States Bureau of the Census.

In a previous study[6] we estimated the 1950 New York City Caucasian male population, Jewish and non-Jewish, by age and socioeconomic class. These estimates were used in computation of the 1949–1951 Jewish, Catholic and Protestant death rates. Separate Catholic and Protestant population figures were derived from the non-Jewish total under the assumption that the Caucasion Catholic and Protestant death rates for all causes of death were equal within age and socioeconomic class groups. We have not tried to make population estimates by religious groups for the 1960 period.

Lung cancer deaths in this paper are the deaths classified under list numbers 162 and 163 of the seventh revision of the International List for 1958–1962 and of the sixth revision for 1949–1951. For 1940 they are the deaths in the New York City subdivisions of list number 47 of the fifth revision covering cancers of the lung, bronchus, pleura and trachea. Analysis of the 1949–1951 New York City deaths classified under both the fifth and sixth revisions showed about 6 percent more male deaths attributed to lung cancer under the fifth revision than under the sixth. We have made no adjustment for these differences in this paper.

The data presented on smoking habits and occupational exposures come from the original questionnaires of men enrolled by volunteer workers of the American Cancer Society between October 1959 and February 1960. We have given the data for

Caucasian Jewish, Catholic and Protestant men living in cities which in 1960 had a population of more than 250,000 persons. Among the cities from which these subjects were drawn were Chicago, Los Angeles, Philadelphia, Detroit, Baltimore, Houston, Cleveland, St. Louis, San Francisco, Boston, Dallas, New Orleans, Pittsburgh, San Antonio, San Diego, Buffalo and Cincinnati.

RESULTS

In 1959 to 1961 the overall percentages of lung cancer deaths of total deaths for both Catholics and Protestants were more than 50 percent in relative excess of the Jewish. In the younger age groups the excess was even greater. The excess persisted throughout all age groups until there was a sharp reversal in age group 80 to 84. The Catholic percentages were much the same as the Protestant.

In the period ten years earlier, the overall percentages, Jewish, Catholic and Protestant, were not very different. However, there was the pattern of lower Jewish percentages in the younger age groups and higher percentages in the older age groups. In this period the reversal started in age groups 70 to 74.

Comparisons based on the percentage that a particular cause of death is of total deaths are subject to the disadvantages that differences in the death rate from all causes of death are ignored. It is therefore worthwhile to check the percentage of total death findings against death rate findings. We are able to do this for the 1949 to 1951 period. Among New York City Caucasian males in this period non-Jewish death rates from all causes of death were higher, and in some instances much higher, in all age groups except 75 and over, compared with the Jewish.[6] Consequently, the excess in lung cancer death rates in Catholic and Protestant males relative to the Jewish males in 1949 to 1951 at ages 35 to 64 was substantially greater than the corresponding excess shown by the percentages of total deaths.

Unpublished data are available on smoking habits, both on a lifetime basis and on a current basis for Caucasian Jewish, Catholic and Protestant men in cities of 250,000 or more population from Hammond and Garfinkel.[2] Most of the men had a history of regular smoking—83 percent of the Catholics, 80 percent of the Protestants and 79 percent of the Jews. However, the Jews showed more pipe or cigar smokers who never smoked cigarettes regularly than did the Catholics or Protestants. Thereby, either on a lifetime basis or on a current basis, Jewish males showed the lowest percentage of regular cigarette smokers; Catholics showed the highest percentage of cigarette smokers and Protestants were intermediate to Catholics and Jews. Among the current regular cigarette smokers, there were proportionately as many Jewish as Catholic or Protestant men who smoked more than a pack a day. However, on the average, Jewish cigarette smokers smoked fewer cigarettes because of the larger percentage of less than half-a-pack-a-day smokers and the smaller percentage of one-pack-a-day smokers.

In addition, a definitely smaller percentage of Jewish men than of Catholic or Protestant men had had occupational exposure to inhalants such as gas, dust or fumes. The percentages of men subject to other suspected exposures such as chemicals, solvents, oil, x-ray and radioactive materials did not differ much among the three religious groups.

It is evident that among the Caucasian male population of New York City a decided reversal has taken place with time in the frequency of lung cancer in Jews compared with either Catholics or Protestants. Twenty and 30 years ago the Jewish lung cancer mortality was much higher than the Catholic or Protestant, up to double or more, throughout a wide range of age groups. However, the Jewish percentages of lung cancer deaths out of total deaths increased little with time (in data not presented here, U.S. born Jews showed a marked increase though not as sharp as the non-Jews) as compared with the substantial increase among Catholics and Protestants. By 1959 to 1961 disadvantageous Jewish figures are to be seen only in those 80 years or older. In almost all of the other age groups it is now the non-Jewish which show considerable lung cancer excess.

The data for males give the impression that a relatively high risk lung cancer Jewish group passed in wavelife fashion with time and was followed by a relatively low risk group. That this pattern was not entirely an artifact of changes in the native-foreign-born composition of the Jewish population may be inferred from the trends in the Russian-born lung cancer death rates (the Russian born in New York City being almost entirely Jewish). The lung cancer death rates in the Russian-born population are higher than in the native Jewish population. However, it is apparent that the same kind of changes with time are evident in this entirely foreign-born group as in the total Jewish population.

A finding of interest is that the Jewish males show lung cancer death rates which continue to increase with advancing age instead of the much more usual pattern in "cross-sectional" data of rising to a peak and then decreasing.

COMMENT

The main purpose of this paper was to provide some additional data on differences in lung cancer frequency and smoking practices among religious groups to supplement the findings at a New York City hospital by Wynder and Mantel.[13] It is evident that the results of the two studies are in good agreement.

The recent mortality data from this study, and from Mac-Mahon[3] and Newill[5] are all consistent with the hospital data in showing decidedly lower lung cancer rates for Jewish compared with Catholic or Protestant males. For lung cancer rates in Catholic compared with Protestant males the situation is not quite clear but, at present, there can be at most only a small difference.

The differences in smoking habits among religious groups which were found in the study subject who lived in large cities of the United States other than New York City are not necessarily representative of the differences in New York City. They are not even necessarily representative of the differences among religious groups in the cities from which the subjects were drawn. However, there is considerable internal consistency in these smoking data in subclassifications by age and educational attainment such that the differences among the religious groups cannot be dismissed as artifacts of selection factors. Taken at face value, the smoking data of this study and of Wynder's and Mantel's control cases are consistent in indicating that the proportion of men smoking cigarettes was lowest in Jews, highest in Catholics and intermediate in Protestants. A larger proportion of Jewish than of Catholic or Protestant men smoked pipes or cigars only.

This study and the control cases of the hospital study agree in showing a smaller proportion of Jewish than of Catholic or Protestant men subject to occupational exposures. In this study the proportion of Protestant men subject to occupational exposures was much like the Catholic whereas in the hospital data it was intermediate to the Catholic and the Jewish. We do not have any data on the occupational exposures or the smoking habits of the lung cancer cases.

We do not have any direct information on the classification of the lung cancer deaths in New York City according to histologic type. However, at least in the recent years the bulk of the lung cancer cases in males must have been epidermoid or anaplastic carcinomas. Thus, in males it is difficult to see how the lung cancer mortality patterns for the epidermoid and anaplastic carcinomas could be very different from the patterns for total lung cancer in 1960 and 1950. Data for the various religious groups on the trends with time in histologic type certainly would be of interest with respect to the trends in the lung cancer mortality.

The Russian-born males showed surprisingly high (in an absolute sense) lung cancer death rates in New York City for 1940. In data for 1940 not presented here other foreign-born groups which in New York City are predominantly Jewish—the Austrian born, the Polish born and the Hungarian born—showed similarly high rates but the predominantly non-Jewish foreign-born groups did not.

REFERENCES

1. Bolduan, C., and Weiner, L.: Causes of death among Jews in New York City. *N Engl J Med, 208*:407–416, 1933.

2. Hammond, E.C., and Garfinkel, L.: Smoking habits of men and women. *J Nat Cancer Inst, 27*:419–442, 1961.

3. MacMahon, B.: The ethnic distribution of cancer mortality in New York City. *Acta Un Int Cancr, 16*:1716–1724, 1960.

4. MacMahon, B. and Koller, E.K.: Ethnic differences in the incidence of leukemia. *Blood, 12*:1–10, 1957.

5. Newill, V.A.: Distribution of cancer mortality among ethnic subgroups of the white population of New York City, 1953–58. *J Nat Cancer Inst, 26*:405–417, 1961.

6. Seidman, H., Garfinkel, L., and Craig, L.: Death rates in New York City by socio-economic class and religious group and by country of birth, 1949–1951. *Jewish J Soc, 4*:254–273, 1962.

7. U.S. Bureau of the Census: Population, nativity and parentage of the white population, general characteristics. Sixteenth Census of the U.S. —1940. Washington, D.C., U.S. Government Printing Office, 1943.

8. U.S. Bureau of the Census: Unpublished tabulation from third count (card B) mother tongue, value rent by tenure, age, citizenship for white population of foreign origin by nativity, country of birth of parents, and sex—New York City, 1940. *Ibid.*

9. U.S. Bureau of the Census: Special reports, part 3, chapter A, nativity and parentage. U.S. Census of Population—1950, vol. 4. Washington, D.C., U.S. Government Printing Office, 1954.

10. U.S. Bureau of the Census: Final report PC(1)-34D—Detailed characteristics, New York. U.S. Census of Population—1960. Washington, D.C., U.S. Government Printing Office, 1962.

11. U.S. Bureau of the Census: Unpublished tabulations, nativity and parentage—New York City, 1960. *Ibid.*

12. Welfare and Health Council of New York City: Characteristics of the population by Health Areas, New York City, 1950, part I and part II (Manhattan, Bronx, Brooklyn, Queens, Richmond). New York, Research Bureau, Welfare and Health Council of New York City, 1953.

13. Wynder, E.L., and Mantel, N.: Some epidemiological features of lung cancer among Jewish males. *Cancer, 19*:191–195, 1966.

Chapter 19

LUNG CANCER AMONG THE JEWS AND NON-JEWS OF PITTSBURGH, PENNSYLVANIA, 1953–1967: MORTALITY RATES AND CIGARETTE SMOKING BEHAVIOR

B. Herman and P.E. Enterline

There is at present a growing literature related to the study of cancer frequency among the various racial, ethnic and religious subgroups of North America. These investigations have been helpful in the consideration of possible etiology of such disease.

Investigations of the religious distribution of cancer have emerged due, in large part, to the impetus of the finding of low Jewish and high non-Jewish rates of cervical cancer.[4,8,12,46] Differences for these two groups have been reported for hematopoietic, colon, kidney, pancreatic, and lung cancer.

LUNG CANCER STUDIES BY RELIGION

Due to the lack of any information on religion in the official census and vital statistics reports of the United States, early studies of the religious distribution of lung cancer utilized proportionate mortality rates as indices of mortality differentials. In 1931, Bolduan and Weiner[2] conducted a study of the causes of death among the Jews and non-Jews of New York City.

Reprinted in edited version with permission from the Am J Epidemiol, 91: (no. 4) 1970.

This article is based upon the dissertation submitted by the senior author for his Doctor of Science degree at the Graduate School of Public Health of the University of Pittsburgh. This research was supported by the United States Public Health Service Training Grant No. 5–T01–GM–00010–12.

More recently, localities within the United States have utilized sample surveys or other means in order to arrive at population estimates of religious sub-groups. This has led to a more accurate appraisal of lung cancer mortality by religion through the computation of age-standardized mortality rates for such sub-groups. Three such mortality rate studies have been conducted in New York City.

MacMahon[21] studied cancer mortality for the year 1955 among the Caucasian population age 45 years and over. The results with regard to lung cancer (International Statistical Classification (ISC) Nos. 162–163) were as follows: (1) the Jews were significantly lower for mortality due to this site than were the Catholics and Protestants; (2) the Jewish male rate was considerably lower than that for the Catholic or Protestant male; and (3) the Jewish female had a higher rate than did the females of the other two religious groups. Although noting significant differences in rare single-gene diseases and thus obvious genetic differences between the Jew and non-Jew, MacMahon stressed the need to first examine possible environmental differences, i.e. smoking, drinking and attitudes toward medical care as determinants of the cancer variation noted.

Newill[27] extended the work of MacMahon in New York City to include six years (1953–1958) of cancer mortality rather than the one year originally examined. The methods of the earlier work were used and average annual death rates for cancer at various sites were estimated. The results related to lung cancer were identical to those cited by MacMahon, i.e., the lower mortality for both the Jews in general compared to other religions and the Jewish male relative to the non-Jewish male, and the higher mortality for the Jewish female compared with her non-Jewish peers. The rates (per 100,000 population) for Catholic, Protestant and Jewish males were 136.2, 159.9 and 107.5, respectively, and 19.0, 21.1, and 30.4 for Catholic, Protestant, and Jewish females, respectively. The mortality differences noted between Catholics and Protestants were small in comparison with those noted between the Jews and non-Jews regardless of sex. The investigator speculates that characteristics related to religious affiliation such as diet, recreation, occupation, and socio economic status were responsible.

Seidman[34] studied the lung cancer (ISC Nos. 162–163) mortality experience among male Caucasians of the three major religious groups of New York City for 1940, 1949–1951, and 1959–1961.

A recent study of lung cancer admissions to New York's Memorial-Sloan-Kettering Medical Center has been conducted by Wynder and Mantel.[44] It supports the findings of previous studies regarding the low lung cancer mortality among Jewish males relative to other males.

A study of cancer mortality was conducted by King *et al.*[15] in Baltimore City and Baltimore County for the year 1959. Mortality differentials for various sites by religious preference were expressed for each sex as ratios of age-adjusted death rates to the corresponding rates for all faiths combined. Cancer of the lung (ISC Nos. 162–163) was relatively rare in Jewish males. Their ratio was 0.41 as compared to 0.91 and 1.42 for the Protestant and Catholic males, respectively. However, the Jewish female had a ratio of 1.54 compared with her Protestant and Catholic peers' figures of 0.99 and 0.80, respectively. These findings further support the evidence presented in the work of New York City investigators.

The most recent reports of cancer mortality by religion are those from Canada where religious enumeration is part of the official census. Segall[33] examined the average annual age-adjusted death rates and sex-ratios of such rates for selected sites of cancer in Montreal for the period 1959-1963. Comparisons were drawn between persons ethnically Jewish, French, and British. The average annual age adjusted lung cancer (ISC Nos. 162–163) mortality rates per 100,000 population were found to differ among these groups. The Jewish male had the lowest lung cancer mortality rate among males while the Jewish female had a rate more than two times that of either the French or British female. As a result, the Jewish sex-mortality ratio was very low.

Horowitz and Enterline[13] studied lung cancer (ISC Nos. 162–163) death rates for the 28 census tracts in the City of Montreal which were most heavily Jewish for the period of 1956–1966, both by ethnic origin and by religion with results similar to those noted by Segall. They found that the Jewish male and female lung cancer cases smoked less than their non-Jewish counterparts. Furthermore, both the Jewish males and females had a lower proportion of epidermoid and anaplastic carcinomas (carcinomas usually associated with cigarette smoking) than did the non-Jewish males and females. The authors further conducted a two percent random sample survey of smoking behavior among the Jews and non-Jews in the area of Montreal (28 census tracts) for which death rates were calculated. Jewish males and females were not only found less frequently to be cigarette smokers, but also to smoke less heavily, if they did smoke, than their non-Jewish counterparts. The Jewish male's cigarette smoking behavior seemed to explain his low rate of lung cancer relative to other males. The high lung cancer death rate among Jewish females relative to non-Jewish females could not be explained.

The present study endeavored to see whether the Jewish male's low lung cancer mortality rate compared to that of the non-Jewish male; and whether the high Jewish female mortality rate for lung cancer relative to non-Jewish females noted in other cities existed in the City of Pittsburgh during the period of 1953–1967, and to what extent cigarette smoking behavior seemed to be related to the overall male and female inter-religious pattern of lung cancer mortality.

MATERIALS AND METHODS

Sample Selection

All of the certificates of death covering the years 1953–1967 on which was recorded lung cancer (ISC Nos. 162–163) as the underlying cause of death for white residents of the City of Pittsburgh were reviewed. Of these deaths, only those males and females who had resided within a 40 census tract area, economically homogeneous and with a large Jewish population, prior to their death were included as study subjects. In addition, appropriate corrections were made for major differences noted between assigned (death certificate) cause and verified cause (hospital records). Because the number of cases below 45 years of age* was very small, it was decided to study the mortality experiences of only those 45 years and above as was done by MacMahon and Newill in their studies in New York City. There were 572 lung cancer deaths at ages 45 and over from the 40 census tracts. Death certificates, and hospital, pathological and cancer registry records served as the principal sources of information regarding each subject.

Determination of Decedent Religious Group

Comparisons were made solely between *Jewish* and *non-Jewish* populations as defined by this study. The religion of each decedent was determined by combining information from four sources: *Place of burial* and *funeral director* as listed on the certificate of death, the *obituary column* of the *Jewish Chronicle* (the Jewish weekly newspaper of Pittsburgh) and *hospital records*. Previous studies[8,21,27,34] have shown that place of burial identifies the religious Jew and non-Jew quite adequately, apparently because those individuals buried in Jewish cemeteries are almost exclusively Jewish. Funeral homes were categorized as being either Jewish or non-Jewish. In general, Jewish funeral directors bury only the Jewish deceased. Furthermore, the number of Jews that might be misclassified because of being buried in non-Jewish or non-sectarian cemeteries and/or by non-Jewish funeral directors apparently is too small to be of any significance.†

The obituary column of the Jewish newspaper served to further increase the validity of the Jewish designations based upon the information from certificates of death. Hospital records were lastly scrutinized and served to strengthen the final judgment of the investigator as to the religion of the deceased. Such records con-

---

*Fourteen (Jewish males: 2; non-Jewish males: 11; Jewish females: 0; and non-Jewish females: 1).

† The present study demonstrated 100 percent agreement between the Jewish designation of the deceased based upon death certificate information (place of burial and funeral director) and that reported upon the hospital record; furthermore, no cases were found buried in non-Jewish and non-sectarian cemeteries or by non-Jewish funeral directors while having the Jewish designation on their hospital charts.

tain religious preference as stated by the patient himself or other confidant at the time of hospital admission. In the few instances when charts were not available, the Allegheny Cancer Registry abstracts supplied the needed information regarding religion.

As a result, 78 Jewish male, 37 Jewish female, 380 non-Jewish male and 77 non-Jewish female cases were identified.

The Descriptive Study

Populations at risk. Those Jewish and non-Jewish white individuals 45 years of age and over, residing in the 40 census tract area* as defined for this study during the period 1953–1967, served as the populations at risk for the various death rates computed. The average total population at risk for the period 1953–1967 was 52,362 of which 13,240 were Jews and 39,122 were non-Jews. These 40 census tracts contained approximately 95 percent of the Jewish population, 45 years of age and over, in Pittsburgh.

Estimates of the Jewish and non-Jewish age and sex distributions, for the various years under study, were derived from data from the City of Pittsburgh censuses for the years 1950[33] and 1960,[39] and the population studies of Pittsburgh Jewry conducted by the United Jewish Federation of Pittsburgh during 1953 and 1963.[3] Average annual age-adjusted mortality rates by sex for the period of 1953–1967 were calculated. Sex mortality ratios were calculated utilizing the above mortality rates.

Smoking behavior information was obtained for most cases using hospital charts. In order to test the validity of hosiptal chart information regarding smoking, comparisons were made of such information for a small number of randomly chosen cases with that obtained by telephone calls to relatives and friends of the deceased. There was a high consistency of smoking information reported from hospital records and telephone calls. Knowledge of the decedents' smoking behavior was therefore derived, for the most part, from hospital chart reviews. Only when information was not available on such records were telephone calls to relatives or friends of the deceased made. Agreement was found to be high

*An area of high socioeconomic rank, based upon median income, median school years completed and percent of sound housing.[6]

for smoking information recorded on multiple charts from the same hospital or when more than one hospital was attended by the deceased. For a few cases, smoking habits were not obtained because neither records nor relatives or friends were available.

RESULTS

Lung-Cancer Mortality Rates Among the Jews and Non-Jews

Some striking differences are noted among the religious groups. The Jewish male was found to have a lower lung cancer death rate (92.5) than his non-Jewish equal (148.6). The Jewish female, however, had a lung cancer death rate (41.8) approximately twice that for the non-Jewish female (21.7). As a result, the ratio of male to female lung cancer death rates among the Jews (2.2) was notably low when compared with the ratio for the non-Jews (6.8).

Cigarette Smoking Behavior

The various histological types of lung cancer are known to differ in both incidence and etiology.[6,16-18,20,42] The epidermoid and anaplastic lung cancers have been shown to be more strongly related to cigarette smoking than the glandular types of lung neoplasm (i.e. adenocarcinoma and terminal bronchiolar carcinoma). The proportion of epidermoid and anaplastic carcinomas was found to be slightly lower among Jewish males relative to non-Jewish males. The category made up 82.4 percent of the Jewish males' lung pathology as opposed to 88.7 percent of those among non-Jewish males. Consequently, glandular tumors comprised a greater proportion of Jewish male histological types than was the case for non-Jewish males. The Jewish female also had a lower proportion of epidermoid and anaplastic neoplasms (63.3 percent versus 73.1 percent) and thus a higher percentage of glandular tumors contributing to her total lung pathologies compared with her non-Jewish equal. Although females tended to differ by religion in their percentage of known histopathology, it is highly unlikely that under-reporting or over-reporting of pathology in one religious group would lead to a bias referable to a specific type of pathology.

The proportion of cigarette smokers was smaller among Jews (75.3% versus 91.8%). They also tended more to pipe and/or cigar only smoking than did the non-Jewish male (8.2% versus 3.4%). The findings for Jewish females relative to other females were similar to those found for Jewish males. They showed a greater proportion of non-smokers of cigarettes (56.8%), than did the non-Jewish females (34.2%).

Of those male cases who smoked cigarettes, the Jews had both higher and lower proportions of light (5.5% versus 3.4%) and heavy (54.5% versus 59.0%) smoking categories, respectively. Although among female cigarette smokers, the percentage of heavy smokers by religion was basically similar (about 50%), the Jews, nevertheless, smoked less heavily, having a higher proportion of the one-to-10-cigarette per day category (25.0% versus 10.4%) comprising their total cigarette smoking.

The Jewish male tended to have a slightly shorter duration of cigarette smoking than was the case for his non-Jewish peer. The Jewish female, however, appeared to have smoked for a far shorter time than did the non-Jewish female; i.e. 62.5 percent of Jewish females smoked less than 25 years while only 20 percent of the non-Jewish females did likewise. Because of the rather large discrepancy in the percentage of unknown information among the females by religion (50.0% for Jewish smokers versus 79.2% for non-Jewish smokers) and its possible effect on the accuracy of the above findings, it was decided to estimate what the extreme effect of adding 29.2 percent more non-Jewish female cases to the one to 25 years category would be. It was interesting to find that, even with all of these cases placed in the shorter duration category, the new non-Jewish female value of 61.9 percent remained below that for the Jewish female. This suggests that the initial findings represented true differences between the groups.

DISCUSSION

It appears that the similar pattern of lung cancer mortality noted among the Jews and non-Jews in other places existed as well in the City of Pittsburgh during the period 1953–1967. Thus, the Jewish male was found low in lung cancer mortality relative to his non-Jewish equal while the Jewish female experienced approximately twice the lung cancer mortality rate of the non-Jewish female. These differentials resulted in the lower sex ratio of rates among the Jews.

The purpose of this study, however, was not merely to determine whether the above findings existed in the City of Pittsburgh, but to further see whether such patterns observed could be explained on the basis of cigarette smoking behavior.

The present investigation demonstrated that, during the 15-year period from 1953–1967, the Jewish male had a low proportion of epidermoid and anaplastic carcinomas comprising his lung histologies relative to his non-Jewish equal. This finding suggests that the low lung cancer death rate among Jewish males might be due to their low rate of cigarette smoking. In support of such an assumption are the results regarding type, amount, and duration of smoking among the Jewish and non-Jewish male lung cancer deceased. The proportion of cigarette smokers was low for the Jews relative to the non-Jews. Furthermore, those Jewish males who did smoke tended to smoke less heavily and for a shorter duration of time than other males. The Jews also had a higher proportion of pipe and/or cigar only smokers than did the non-Jews.

Among females who died of lung cancer during the aforementioned 15-year period, the proportion of epidermoid and anaplastic carcinomas was found lower for the Jews than for the non-Jews. This implies that cigarette smoking may not be the reason for the high death rate of the Jewish females relative to other females. This was supported by data on type, amount, and duration of smoking. Jewish females had a proportion of non-smokers in excess of that found for non-Jewish females. In addition, if the Jewish female smoked, she tended to do so less heavily and for a shorter period of time than did the non-Jewish female.

These findings, regarding religious differences in lung cancer mortality rates and the smoking behavior that characterized the lung cancer cases comprising the numerators for such rates, are highly consistent with those presented by Horowitz and Enterline.[13]

Apparently what one has identified here among Jewish females in Pittsburgh, as was the case in Montreal, is a paradoxically high lung cancer mortality rate group tending to consume few cigarettes, relative to other females. As a result, further studies by religion are warranted in order to identify the factors contributing to this peculiar relative difference of lung cancer mortality.

Some investigations have shown both the greater preoccupation of the Jew, particularly the female, with matters of health and a greater reception to physician care than other religious groups.[19,22,25,30] The non-Jew, in not receiving such handling, may then have a greater degree of misdiagnosis as regards lung cancer. Consequently, the lower rates for the non-Jew among females may be in part the result of missed cases stemming from under-diagnosis on their death certificates.

In addition to the possibility of better diagnosis among Jewish females, there is evidence that a fair number of genetically determined diseases (i.e. diabetes mellitus, Gaucher's disease and Tay-Sachs disease, among others) appear more frequently among the Jews than the non-Jews.[9,11,26,28,46] This is particularly the case within Ashkenazi Jewish populations of Europe and the United States, i.e. the Jews comprising the sample considered in this study. Important also is the fact that the Jews have lower mortality rates (from all causes) at early ages and higher mortality rates at later ages relative to the non-Jews. The reversal in mortality experience tends to occur sooner (i.e. at ages 55–64) among the Jewish females than the Jewish males (at ages 65–74) when comparing each group with their non-Jewish peers.[8] It is hypothesized by Spiegelman[36] that the higher Jewish death rates at older ages may arise from the effect, in later life, of their low mortality in early life. The better living conditions that may account for the lower rates of Jewish mortality in infancy, childhood, and through middle age may result in proportionally more physically impaired persons living until the ages when the chronic diseases take their effect. In support of such an assumption, Goldstein[8] reported both higher and lower chronic disease death rates for the Jews 65 years of age and over and 45–64 years of age, respectively, when compared to the non-Jews of similar ages. The above results appear to reflect actual differences in physiological resistance or constitutional make-up by religion, sex, and age. If such underlying biological differences in terms of heredity, constitution, and other innate influences do exist, regarding the disease and mortality patterns noted, by religion, they may likewise exist in the case of lung cancer. If this is so, it is further safe to assume that these can in turn affect differences by religion in the anatomy of and prognosis for the lung disease.

Finally, there may be a religious differential in frequency of metastatic (secondary) adenocarcinomas of the lung, which results in an apparently high lung cancer mortality rate among Jewish females relative to other females (i.e. a high proportion of lung cancers coded as primary or not stated are actually secondary). The Jewish female has a higher risk for breast, colon, and ovarian tumors,[15,21,27,29,41,43,45] which readily metastasize to the lung[24,32] than does the non-Jewish female. Such tumors are known to "masquerade," in many instances, as primary lung cancer at the time of diagnosis.[31,32] Whether the tumor found in the lung is primary at that site or the result of metastases from another organ is often very difficult to ascertain. In this regard, Wynder[40] recently mentioned that even at Memorial Hospital in New York City, which specializes in cancer diagnosis and treatment, hospital-diagnosed primary adenocarcinomas of the lung were erroneously made due to difficulty in detecting the actual primary site prior to death. The errors were found at the time of autopsy.

The above errors are obviously still more difficult to detect among the Jews because of their greater reluctance to undergo autopsy examination than is the case for the non-Jews.[1,14] In support of such unwillingness on the part of the Jew are the findings of the present study. The Jews, both males and females, had lower proportions of cases undergoing autopsy. Among females, in the present study, the Jew had the higher proportion of ISC 163, i.e. malignant neoplasms of lung unspecified as to whether primary or secondary.

It is quite possible that the Jewish male is also affected by similar metastases from glandular primaries at other sites. The Jewish male has a higher risk for colon, kidney and other cancers[15,21,27,43,45] than does the non-Jewish male. These neo-plasms are known to have a strong predilection for the lung as a metastatic site.[24] The mortality rates among the Jews and non-Jews should be computed with adequate control for cigarette smoking behavior so as to see if the Jews of both sexes might have higher rates than their non-Jewish equals without the con-founding influence of smoking. Furthermore, it is apparent that, until more autopsies are performed on the Jew, one will not be able to determine adequately the extent of the possible contri-bution of the metastatic glandular lesion to the rates of the Jewish male and female.

The Jewish cases, irrespective of sex, were predominantly from Eastern Europe while the non-Jews were, for the most part, na-tive-born. These findings are in line with MacMahon's[23] statement that "in most American communities the Jewish group is pre-dominantly Eastern European in ancestral background." It is difficult to determine with the data available whether being foreign (and of Eastern Europe) was important for the mortality experience of the Jew during the present investigation.

CONCLUSIONS

The following inferences seem to be indicated by the results and rationale of this investigation:

1. Lung cancer mortality among the Jews and non-Jews existed in a pattern similar to that in other places in the City of Pittsburgh from at least 1953 until 1967.

2. Among males, the histology and smoking behavior of the Jewish lung cancer cases suggest that the low lung cancer death rate of the Jewish male relative to other males can be explained by his low rate of cigarette smoking.

3. Among females, the histology and less pronounced smoking behavior of the Jewish lung cancer cases intimate that *cigarette smoking may not be the reason for the Jewish female's high lung cancer death rate relative to other females.* A survey of the smok-ing behavior characterizing the Jews and non-Jews, living within the 40 census tracts of the City of Pittsburgh, should be conducted in order to lend further support to the preceding assumptions.

Such a survey by religion should also include consideration of other environmental factors, for example, differences in kitchen environment.

4. Religious differences in diagnostic handling, death certificate reporting, and biological processes should be considered as possible factors influencing the lung cancer mortality patterns observed. There is also the possibility that a religious differential in frequency of metastatic (secondary) adenocarcinomas of the lung can explain the lung cancer differential between the Jewish and non-Jewish female. Finally, studies are justified regarding the effect of place of birth on the phenomenon under study.

REFERENCES

1. Berkowitz, P. and Berkowitz, N.S.: The Jewish patient in the hospital. *Am J Nurs*, *67*:2335–2337, 1967.
2. Bolduan, C. and Weiner, L.: Causes of death among Jews in New York City. *N Engl J Med*, *208*:407–416, 1933.
3. Bronner, J.D.: The Jewish Community of Pittsburgh: A population study, 1963. The United Jewish Federation of Pittsburgh.
4. Casper, J.: Rates of uterine cancers in Jewish women in Israel and New York City. *Acta Un Int Cancr*, *16*:1686–1688, 1960.
5. Chiazze, L., Jr. and Ciocco, A.: Intracommunity variation in cancer incidence for Pittsburgh. *Public Health Rep*, *82*:759–770, 1967.
6. Doll, R., Hill, A.B. and Kreyberg, L.: The significance of cell type in relation to the aetiology of lung cancer. *Br J Cancer*, *11*:43–48, 1957.
7. Dunham, L.J., Thomas, L.B., Edgcomb, J.H. and Stewart, H.L.: Some environmental factors in the development of uterine cancer in Israel and New York City. *Acta Un Int Cancr*, *16*:1689–1692, 1960.
8. Goldstein, S.: Jewish mortality and survival patterns: Providence, Rhode Island, 1962–1964. *Eugen Q*, *13*:48–61, 1966.
9. Goodman, R.M., Elian, B., Mozes, M. and Deutsch, V.: Buerger's disease in Israel. *Am. J Med*, *39*:601–615, 1965.
10. Graham, S.: Social factors in cancer epidemiology. *Ann NY Acad Sci*, *84*:807–815, 1960.
11. Groen, J.J.: Gaucher's disease. Hereditary transmission and racial distribution. *Arch Intern Med*, *113*:543–549, 1964.
12. Hammond, E.C. and Garfinkel, L.: Smoking habits of men and women. *J Nat Cancer Inst*, *27*:419–442, 1961.
13. Horowitz, I. and Enterline, P.E.: Lung cancer among the Jewish. Presented at the Ninety-Sixth Annual Meeting of the American Public Health Assoc., Detroit, Nov. 14, 1968 (Section on Cancer Epidemiology). *Public Health Rep*, *84*:226–227, 1969.

172 *Ethnic Groups of America*

14. Jakobovits, I.: The religious problem of autopsies in New York Jewish hospitals. *Hebrew Med J, 2*:233–238, 1961.

15. King, H., Diamond, E. and Bailar, J.C., III.: Cancer mortality and religious preference. A suggested method in research. *Milbank Mem Fund Quart, 43*:349–358.

16. Kreyberg, L.: Main histological types of primary epithelial lung tumors. *Br J Cancer, 15*:206–210, 1961.

17. Kreyberg, L.: Histological lung cancer types—A morphological and biological correlation. *Acta Path Microbiol Scand,* (suppl), *157*:1–92, 1962.

18. Kreyberg, L.: Histological classification of lung cancer. *Nat Cancer Inst Monogr, 15*:43–45, 1964.

19. Lilienfeld, A.M.: Diagnostic and therapeutic x-radiation in an urban population. *Public Health Rep, 74*:29–35, 1959.

20. Lombard, H.L. and Huyck, E.P.: An epidemiological study of lung cancer among females. *Growth, 32*:41–56, 1968.

21. MacMahon, B.: The ethnic distribution of cancer mortality in New York City, 1955. *Acta Un Int Cancr, 16*:1716–1724, 1960.

22. MacMahon, B. and Koller, E.K.: Ethnic differences in the incidence of leukemia. *Blood, 12*:1–10, 1957.

23. MacMahon, B., Pugh, T.F. and Ipsen, J.: *Epidemiologic Methods.* Boston, Little Brown and Co., 1960, p. 114.

24. Marcus, E. and Zimmerman, L.M.: *Principles of Surgical Practice.* New York, McGraw-Hill Book Co., Inc. (The Blakiston Division), 1960, chapter 18.

25. Mechanic, D.: Religion, religiosity, and illness behavior: The special case of the Jews. *Hum Org, 22*:202–208, 1963.

26. Myrianthopoulos, N.C. and Aronson, S.M.: Population dynamics of Tay-Sachs disease. I. Reproductive fitness and selection. *Am. J Hum Genet, 18*:313–327, 1966.

27. Newill, V.A.: Distribution of cancer, mortality among ethnic subgroups of the white population of New York City, 1953–58. *J Nat Cancer Inst, 26*:405–417, 1961.

28. Post, R.H. Jews, genetics and disease. *Eugen Q, 12*:162–164, 1965.

29. Post, R.H.: Breast cancer, lactation, and genetics. *Eugen Q, 13*:1–29, 1966.

30. Rinder, I.D.: Mental health of American Jewish urbanites: A review of literature and predictions. *Int. J. Soc. Psychiat.* 1963, *9*:104–109.

31. Rosenblatt, M.B., Lisa, J.R. and Trinidad, S.: Metastatic lung cancer masquerading as bronchogenic carcinoma. *Geriatrics, 21*:139–145, 1966.

32. Rosenblatt, M.B. and Lisa, J.R.: Simulation of lung cancer by metastases. *J Am. Geriat Soc, 15*:921–930, 1967.

33. Segall, A.J.: Distribution of cancer mortality among ethnic subgroups of Montreal, 1959–63. Presented at the 57th annual meeting of the Canadian Public Health Association, Quebec City, June 2, 1966.

34. Seidman, H.: Lung Cancer among Jewish, Catholic and Protestant males in New York City. *Cancer, 19*:185–190, 1966.

35. Seidman, H., Garfinkel, L. and Craig, L.: Death rates in New York City by socioeconomic class and religious group and by country of birth, 1949–1951. *Jew J Sociol, 4*:254–273, 1962.

36. Spiegelman, M.: The longevity of Jews in Canada, 1940–1942. *Popul Stud, 2*:292–304, 1948.

37. Treusch, J.V., Hunt, A.B. and Rousuck, A.A.: Infrequency of carcinoma of uterine cervix among Jewish women. *Am J Obstet Gynec, 52*: 162, 1946.

38. U.S. Bureau of the Census. U.S. Census of Population: 1950, Vol. III, Census Tract Statistics. Chapter 43: Pittsburgh, Pa., 1952.

39. U.S. Bureau of the Census. Census, Pittsburgh, Pa., 1960. Final report PHC (1) -118, 1962.

40. Wynder, E.L. personal communication, March, 1969.

41. Wynder, E.L., Bross, I.J., and Hirayama, T.: A Study of the epidemiology of cancer of the breast. *Cancer, 13*:559–601, 1960.

42. Wynder, E.L. and Graham, E.A.: Tobacco smoking as a possible etiologic factor in bronchiogenic carcinoma: A study for six hundred and eighty-four proved cases. *JAMA, 143*:329–336, 1950.

43. Wynder, E., Graham, S. and Eisenberg, H.: Conference on the etiology of cancer of the gastro-intestinal tract. Report of the Research Committee, World Health Organization on Gastroenterology, New York, N.Y., June 10–11, 1965. *Cancer, 19*:1561–1565, 1966.

44. Wynder, E.L. and Mantel, N.: Some epidemiological features of lung cancer among Jewish males. *Cancer, 19*:191–195, 1966.

45. Wynder, E.L. and Shigematsu, T.: Environmental factors of cancer of the colon and rectum. *Cancer, 20*:1520–1561, 1967.

46. Zakon, S.J.: Hebrew Medicine and Hebrews in Medicine, 1200 B.C. to 1961 A.D. *Quart Bull Northw Univ Med Sch, 36*:74–80, 1962.

Chapter 20

RELIGION AND ETHNICITY IN LEUKEMIA

S. Graham, R. Gibson, A. Lilienfeld, L. Schuman
and M. Levin

The finding of a relationship between such social factors as religion and ethnic background and disease is useful in suggesting avenues for future research which may identify factors more directly related to the disease. For example, Smith found that Japanese-Americans have an unusually high risk of carcinoma of the stomach, that this risk is even higher among the Japanese of Hawaii, and higher still among Japanese of Japan.[6] This has stimulated the intensive investigation of Japanese with and without disease to identify a cultural or genetic factor more closely associated with the development of gastric cancer.

Brian MacMahon, studying death certificates and burial records for evidence of religious background, found a higher mortality from leukemia among Jews than among non-Jews who died in New York City.[5] His data did not allow him to examine the relationship for childhood as opposed to adult leukemia, and leukemia of the various cell types. Subsequent writers such as Lilienfeld[4] speculated that the high rate among Jews may have been related to the fact that this religious group may as a whole have had better medical care and a consequent greater exposure to irradiation. The research reported here undertakes to examine further some of these questions.

METHOD

The population under investigation is that of the Tri-State Leukemia Study. Cases consisted of all leukemia patients re-

Reprinted in edited version with permission from *Am J Public Health, 60:* (no. 2) February 1970.

ported from 1959 to 1962 in all the metropolitan districts and their surrounding counties in New York State, exclusive of New York City, and the metropolitan areas of Minneapolis and Baltimore.[2] Reporting of cases in New York State was via the State Tumor Registry supplemented by an ancillary reporting system, and that in Maryland and Minnesota by special registries set up by Drs. Lilienfeld and Schuman especially for the purpose. Controls consisted of a random sample of the same populations from which patients were drawn. Ascertainment of previous medical history—including physicians seen, hospitals at which treatment was received, and sociological characteristics—was through interviews by trained interviewers in the homes of cases and controls. Reliability was investigated by a reinterview of a 7 percent sample and was found to be acceptable for the factors to be discussed here. Ascertainment of previous irradiation experience was through examination of medical records in possession of physicians, dentists, and hospitals in which the subjects had been treated. It is significant that irradiation experience of subjects as reflected in these records was about twice that reported by them in interviews.

FINDINGS

Examination of the 319 child subjects under 15 years of age and the 884 control children showed no differences in their religious or ethnic (nationality) backgrounds or in those of their parents. Analysis of the same question among adults, however, showed that Jews born in the United States had a higher risk of leukemia than other religious groups, that persons born in Russia had a higher risk than persons born in either the United States or other European countries, and that individuals who were Jewish as well as being born in Russia had a higher risk than any of the above-mentioned groups. No differences in irradiation, we were left with somewhat fewer cases and controls. It is difficult to speculate as to the effects of these eliminations.

A total of 1,414 adult cases and 1,370 controls in the same age groups were available for study. After eliminating persons for whom no information was available as to age, religion, and irradiation, we were left with somewhat fewer cases and controls. It is difficult to speculate as to the effects of these eliminations.

The risk among Jews in our total population is 2.4 times that of non-Jews, and the risk among the foreign born is 1.4 times that of the native born. Data are adjusted for age differences between cases and controls, using techniques of Cochran.[1] The relative risk figures were developed using Sheehe's adaptation of techniques suggested by Woolf[7] and Haldane.[3] Investigation of differences in distribution of cases and controls by individual European country of birth showed no significant differences except for the Russian born. The Russian born had 2.93 times the risk of other foreign born.

Relative risks of leukemia adjusted for age, for persons born in Russia as compared to individuals born in the United States whose parents were *not* born in Eastern Europe, show a risk 3.81 times that of native-born individuals (p<.001). The native born of Eastern European parentage are genetically and sociologically more similar to the Russian born. It is interesting that although the Russian-born risk was 2.91 times that of this group, the risk was less than that for the genetically and socially less closely related population, the native born of non-Eastern European parents. Thus, as would be expected, when the comparison is with a group more similar to the Russian born, the size of the Russian excess risk is lower. The Russian-Americans had a significantly higher risk (p = .008) than those born in a foreign country outside Eastern Europe. It should be pointed out that all foreign born in these studies derived from Europe. It would thus appear that Russian birth carries with it some higher risk of leukemia among adults than does birth in other areas.

Having noted this, together with the higher Jewish risk, it would be interesting to be able to separate out the Jews in this Russian population to determine whether they have risks different from those of persons of other ethnic background of either Jewish or non-Jewish faith.

Russian Jews had a risk of 5.29 times that of United States-born non-Jews whose parents were born in countries outside Eastern Europe (p < .001). Again, the Russian Jews had a risk 4.3 times that of U.S.-born non-Jews of Eastern European parents, a group ethnically somewhat more similar to themselves (p = .001). Despite small numbers, their risk also was significantly higher than those of native-born Jews of non-Eastern European parentage, non-Jews born in other than Eastern European countries, and even Russian-born non-Jews. The Russian Jews, of course, are ethnically and religiously more similar to these groups than to the native-born non-Jews. And it is interesting that their risks exceeded those of the more similar culture groups in smaller degree than those of the culturally more distant groups. The Russian Jews, in brief, had a risk that exceeded that of either the Russians or Jews considered separately. Although small numbers give us less confidence in these findings, there is some suspicion that there is a decline in risk as the comparison moves to groups which are ethnically and religiously more similar. The smallest excess of all is encountered in comparing the Russian Jews with native-born Jews of parents born in Eastern Europe, and foreign-born Jews from countries outside Eastern Europe, both groups culturally most similar to the Russian Jews.

In considering the findings of MacMahon's earlier paper, Lilienfeld suggested that a possible explanation of the higher risk of Jews for leukemia is their better medical care and their consequent larger exposure to irradiation.[4] A number of investigators have suggested that the type of leukemia most related to irradiation is myeloid, and for this reason we examined the histology of the leukemia in our nationality and religious populations. The histologic distribution of Jewish cases did not differ in any important way from that of the non-Jewish cases in this population. The various foreign-born ethnic groups did not greatly differ in histology of their leukemia.

A more direct examination of this question was afforded by this study. It will be recalled that irradiation exposure information was sought from subjects via interview, by inspection of the records in all hospitals which had treated the subjects, and by correspondence with the physicians who had treated them. When Jews were considered alone a smaller proportion of cases than controls were irradiated. The same was true of non-Jews, when considered separately. The latter result was expected. It will be recalled that in our earlier paper adult cases had less exposure to irradiation than controls when all irradiation was considered. It was only when cases were considered histologically that a relationship was discovered. Only the myeloid leukemias were significantly related to postnatal irradiation among adults.

We have been unable to establish that irradiation can account for the higher risk of leukemia found among Jews and Russians.

In view of our finding of a high risk of leukemia among persons derived from Russia, and especially for Russian Jews, we were concerned as to the possibility that this was a pan-slavic phenomenon. An examination of the Polish-Americans in our population revealed 47 cases and 15 controls. This was 15.5 percent of the foreign-born cases and 9.0 percent of the foreign-born controls (p. < .05). Only seven of the cases and two of the controls were Jewish, rendering examination of the Polish Jewish risk impossible. The risk of the Polish-born was 3.9 times that of native-born subjects of Polish parents (p = .005), and 2.12 times that of native-born subjects of native parents (p = .007). These findings would suggest the need to examine the risk of Polish-Americans in series large enough to make more meaningful comparisons.

DISCUSSION

We have attempted to investigate further MacMahon's finding of an enhanced risk of leukemia among Jews. We discovered that no higher risk existed for leukemia of childhood, but that among adult Jews and Russians, considered separately, the risks were higher. Furthermore, it appeared that Poles, regardless of the fact that there are few Jews among them, have a higher risk of adult leukemia. There was no convincing evidence that Jews of non-Eastern European background had higher risks than other populations. On the other hand, however, it was rather clear that Russian Jews had a risk higher even than that of Russians in general or of Jews in general. There was some implication in these data that the excess risk of Russian Jews over other groups was less among those groups culturally more similar to themselves. Thus, the Russian Jewish risk was 5.3 times that of United States-born non-Jews of non-Eastern European parentage but only 3.9 times that of foreign-born non-Jews.

Jewish leukemias were not concentrated in any particular histologic category more than those of non-Jews, as might have been the case had their risk been a function of more exposure to irradiation. Neither did any nationality group differ significantly from the others in histology. Furthermore, irradiation did *not* appear to carry any excess risk among either Jews or non-Jews in this population. This was to be expected because in our earlier study of this same population, irradiation exposure enhanced risk for myeloid leukemias only. On the other hand, the high risk for Jews appeared in both the irradiated and non-irradiated populations, ranging from about 2 to 3.4. It is interesting that the Poles carried a somewhat higher risk of leukemia than other populations, despite the fact that there were few Jews among them.

It would thus appear that, in this population, Russians, Jews, and Poles all had higher risks of leukemia than other ethnic and religious groups, and that Russian Jews had particularly high risks. One could posit a genetic characteristic of this population which could produce these risks. On the other hand, the finding—that the degree to which their risk exceeds those of other populations appears to decline among populations culturally more similar to themselves—suggests the importance of either a social or a genetic trait or both. These data urge the importance of searching further into the possibility that sociological as well as genetic characteristics of this ethnoreligious group may in some way be related to leukemia of adults.

Such studies could be rewarding carried out both in the United States and abroad. Research comparing adult leukemias with controls in both Russia and Poland is certainly indicated. This might be particularly fruitful in comparisons involving Jews and non-Jews in the two populations. Variables studied might with profit include history of irradiation and illness, particularly with viral diseases and occupational carcinogens. Familial aggregation studies comparing leukemia in the kin of cases and controls also should be undertaken. Research among larger leukemia populations in the United States is much needed, replicating the present research but using substantially larger numbers. Geographical areas chosen for study should be those likely to yield proportions of various nationality and religious groups of size sufficient to provide analyses more reliable than those attempted here. Familial aggregation, irradiation, viral illnesses, animal contacts, diet, and occupational exposures would again be of interest.

SUMMARY

Research on the Tri-State Leukemia Study population showed no difference among child cases and controls in religious and ethnic background, nor indeed on any demographic parameter. Among the over 1,200 adult cases and 1,200 adult controls, however, Jews, Russians, and Poles all had significantly elevated risks. For Russian-Jews, the risk was over five times that of non-Jews born in the United States. They exceeded other groups which were culturally similar to themselves in smaller degree than those which were more dissimilar culturally. There was no difference histologically in the distribution of Jewish and non-Jewish cases, and the Russian and Jewish relationship appeared to persist in both the irradiated and nonirradiated populations.

REFERENCES

1. Cochran, W.G.: Some methods for strengthening the common X^2 tests. *Biometrics, 10*:417–451, 1954.

2. Graham, S.; Levin, M.L.; Lillienfeld, A.M.; Dowd, J.E.; Schuman, L.M.; Gibson, R.; Hempelmann, L.H.; and Gerhardt, P.: Methodological problems and design of the tri-state leukemia survey. *Ann NY Acad Sci, 107*:557–569, 1963.

3. Haldane, J.B.S.: The estimation and significance of the logarithm of a ratio of frequencies. *Ann Human Genet, 20*:309–311, 1955.

4. Lilienfeld, A.M.: Diagnostic and therapeutic x-radiation in an urban population. *Pub Health Rep, 74*:29–35, 1959.

5. MacMahon, B., and Koller, E.K.: Ethnic differences in the incidence of leukemia. *Blood, 12*:1–10, 1957.

6. Smith, R.L.: Recorded and expected mortality among the Japanese of the U.S. and Hawaii with special reference to cancer. *J Nat Cancer Inst, 17*:459–473, 1956.

7. Woolf, B.: On estimating the relation between blood group and disease. *Ann Human Genet, 19*:251–253, 1954.

PART FIVE
MORBIDITY PATTERNS

A number of diseases of internal organs have been related to ethnic factors by medical researchers, either because Jews seem to have higher incidences of such diseases or because, generally, Jewish morbidity rates are lower than those of their non-Jewish neighbors. Jews seem to be especially susceptible to ulcerative colitis, atherosclerosis, hypertension, and Buerger's Disease. They have lower rates of incidence of tuberculosis. There are conflicting views on their susceptibility to diabetes.

Using a sample of U.S. veterans, where ethnic group is known, Acheson (Chap. 21) investigates the distribution of ulcerative colitis and regional enteritis. The proportion of Jews is four times as high as in a sample of general medical and surgical patients. Acheson draws no conclusion as to whether hereditary or environmental factors are involved.

"Atherosclerotic heart disease is recognized. . . . as the chief cause of morbidity and mortality of man at the peak of his mental and social activity," say Toor, Katchalsky, Agmon and Allalouf in Chapter 22. They evaluate the incidence of atherosclerosis among different immigrant groups in Israel finding that its incidence is highest among Jews from western countries. These findings are then correlated with facts about diet and cholesterol level of the blood. Toor et al. suggest that the rise in cholesterol is dependent upon diet.

Using a large medical student population, Ross and Thomas divide them up according to ethnic group in order to compare the incidence of hypertension and coronary disease among them and their parents. Male parents of Jewish European ancestry have the highest rate of coronary disease, as reported in Chapter 23.

Buerger's Disease, once thought to occur mainly among Jews, but more recently described as existing among a number of ethnic groups, is a vascular disease similar to atherosclerosis. A study by Goodman, Elian, Mozes, and Deutsch in Israel, comparing the incidence of Buerger's Disease among the various Jewish population groups, shows a significantly higher incidence among Ashkenazim and is summarized in Chapter 24.

Diabetes has often been considered a disease to which Jews

as an ethnic group are disposed by heredity. In Chapter 25 research by Cohen in which the prevalence of diabetes among various Jewish groups in Israel is compared, shows the highest incidence of diabetes among Jews of Ashkenazic orgin. However, this is no higher than diabetes rates in other population groups. In his conclusion, Cohen stresses the important influence of environmental conditions in determining the appearance of the disease.

Although records of a century ago seem to show a relatively high frequency of tuberculosis among Jews, more recent studies show a strikingly lower tuberculosis death rate among Jews than among non-Jews in the same location. In Chapter 26 Rackower assembles a great deal of the literature on this subject and uses the results of studies in Israel to show why this resistance of Jews is true in some cases but not true in others. In Israel, where the mortality rate for tuberculosis is one of the lowest in the world, the Yemenite Jews are the most susceptible to infection.

Chapter 21

THE DISTRIBUTION OF ULCERATIVE COLITIS AND REGIONAL ENTERITIS IN UNITED STATES VETERANS WITH PARTICULAR REFERENCE TO THE JEWISH RELIGION

E. D. Acheson

In the course of a study of the distribution of ulcerative colitis and regional enteritis in U.S. veterans an apparent excess of patients professing the Jewish religion was noted. In view of the differences of opinion expressed in the literature as to whether or not these diseases are unduly prevalent in Jews this point was examined in detail.

MATERIAL

Data were obtained for all 2,320 male veterans discharged from the 174 hospitals of the Veterans Administration with a diagnosis of regional enteritis (572.0) or chronic colitis or enteritis not specified as ulcerative (572.3) from 1953 to 1957, and for ulcerative colitis (572.2) for 1956 and 1957.[13] The patients were then classified according to the words used in the discharge diagnosis into five groups. A detailed study of the clinical records of 81 of these patients in a related investigation[1] had demonstrated a

Reprinted in edited version with permission from GUT, Vol. 1, December, 1960.

Begun while the author was Radcliffe Travelling Fellow of University College, Oxford.

Dr. M.T. Musser and Dr. C.A. Bachrach offered valuable criticisms. I wish to thank Mrs. H. Bickley for her help in preparing the tables and manuscript.

high standard of investigation and diagnosis in the ulcerative colitis and regional enteritis groups. No further records were examined in this study.

METHOD

The distribution of the 2,320 patients in terms of religion, race, and birth place was compared with that of a 12.5 percent sample of all patients discharged in October, 1956, with general medical and surgical conditions. This sample consisted of 4,072 veterans. A 25 percent sample of all such discharges (7,705 patients) in February, 1956, was also used to confirm the overall proportion of Jews.

RESULTS

Approximately four times as many Jews were found among veterans with regional enteritis and ulcerative colitis as among the sample of all discharges for general medical and surgical conditions. A similar excess of Jews was found in the group of patients suffering from enterocolitis and various combinations (mixed forms) of the two diseases. On the other hand, in the ill-defined conditions described as "chronic enteritis" and "chronic colitis" the proportion of Jews was similar to that in the control group.

The proportion of Negroes discharged with any of the diagnoses under study except chronic enteritis was materially smaller than the proportion in the sample of all discharges. However, even when this is taken into account and the number of Jews in each diagnostic group is expressed as a proportion of all whites, the striking excess of Jews with ulcerative colitis, regional enteritis, or mixed forms remains. This excess could also be demonstrated when World War I veterans, and veterans of World War II and the Korean conflict were compared separately with the corresponding groups in the control sample. This analysis was necessary because the control group as a whole was older than the test group. It permitted comparable age groups to be studied.

As the Jewish population of the United States is concentrated in the north-eastern part of the country, it was important to determine whether the apparent excess of Jews suffering from the diseases under study was due to a localization of these diseases in the north east. A suggestion of such a distribution had been found by Acheson[2,3] in studies of the deaths attributed to these diseases in the United States. A higher proportion of veterans with ulcerative colitis and regional enteritis are Jewish than in the control group regardless of the region of birth within the United States: this generalization extends to foreign born veterans. The single exception (patients with regional enteritis born in the west) may be due to the small numbers involved.

DISCUSSION OF RESULTS

The differences in the proportions of Jews with ulcerative colitis, regional enteritis, or mixed forms of these diseases as compared with a sample of all discharges of general medical and surgical cases might be explained by (1) a bias in the sample of such discharges resulting in a decrease in the proportion of Jews contained in it; (2) a tendency for Jews with ulcerative colitis or regional enteritis to seek hospital treatment in veterans' hospitals to a greater extent than those suffering from other general medical and surgical conditions; (3) a real excess of Jewish sufferers from these conditions, or a form of the disease requiring more frequent admission to hospital in these people. In case the October general medical and surgical discharges were not representative of the period under study, a count was also taken of all Jewish patients discharged in February, 1956. The proportion of 2.2 percent (167 of 7,705 patients) found was almost identical to that in the October sample and disposes of the first objection. The second argument, while difficult to refute, seems highly unlikely. It therefore seems probable that the results reported here indicate either that these diseases are more prevalent or are more severe among Jews than among other whites. A certain amount of support can be obtained for the former view from the literature. Sloan, Bargen, and Gage[11] found that 9.4 percent of 2,000 ulcerative colitis patients treated at the Mayo Clinic were Jewish. Paulley[9] compared the proportion of Jewish patients with ulcerative colitis in two London hospitals with the proportion of Jews found among all patients discharged. He found twice as many Jews among the ulcerative colitis patients.

In the original description of regional enteritis by Crohn, Ginzburg, and Oppenheimer[5] all 14 patients were Jewish. However, when reflecting on the developments which had occurred over the next 20 years, Crohn and Janowitz[6] felt that "no ethnic group preponderates." Boyce[4] in his monograph, disagrees and states that the disease is more prevalent in Jews. Van Patter, Bargen, Dockerty, Feldman, Mayo, and Waugh[12] reporting 600 cases from the Mayo Clinic found 153 Jews (25.5%). The figure mentioned by Ruble, Meyers, and Ashley[10] is even higher; they found that 43 of 100 patients at the Harper Hospital were Jews. In view of the fact that neither of these institutions are Jewish foundations these figures are remarkable even in the absence of information about the ethnic structure of the overall hospital populations.

It is not known whether the apparently increased susceptibility of Jewish persons to ulcerative colitis and regional enteritis demonstrated here is due to an hereditary or an environmental influence. It would be interesting to know the relative prevalence of the diseases in Ashkenazic and Sephardi-Oriental Jews, and among those who do and do not adhere strictly to the dietary law.[7,8]

CONCLUSIONS

The proportion of Jews in samples of patients discharged from Veterans Administration hospitals with ulcerative colitis, regional enteritis, and mixed forms of these diseases was about four times higher than in samples of all general medical and surgical patients.

No excess was found in the proportions of Jews with chronic colitis not specified as ulcerative, or with chronic enteritis, not specified as regional.

When the cases of ulcerative colitis and regional enteritis were distributed by geographical region of birth a higher proportion of Jews with ulcerative colitis or regional enteritis than in the control group was noted in every region except one.

REFERENCES

1. Acheson, E.D.: *Q J Med,* 29:489, 1960.
2. Acheson, E.D.: *J Chronic Dis,* 10:469, 1960.
3. Acheson, E.D.: *J Chronic Dis,* 10:481, 1960.

4. Boyce, F.F.: *Regional Enteritis, Diagnostic and Therapeutic Considerations.* Philadelphia, J.B. Lippincott, 1955.

5. Crohn, B.B., Ginzburg, L., and Oppenheimer, G.D.:*JAMA* 99:1323, 1932.

6. Crohn, B.B. and Janowitz, H.D.: *JAMA, 156:*1221, 1954.

7. Dorn, H.F.: *N Engl J Med, 261:*571, 1959.

8. Kallner, G.: *Lancet, 1:*1155, 1958.

9. Paulley, J.W.: *Gastroenterology, 16:*566, 1950.

10. Ruble, P.E., Meyers, S.G., and Ashley, L.B.: *Harper Hosp Bull,* 15:142, 1957.

11. Sloane, W.P., Bargen, J.A., and Gage, R.P.: *Gastroenterology, 16:* 25, 1950.

12. Van Patter, W.N., Bargen, J.A., Dockerty, M.B., Feldman, W.H., Mayo, C.W., and Waugh, J.M.: *Gastroenterology, 26:*347, 1954.

13. World Health Organization. *Manual of the International Statistical Classification of Diseases, Injuries and Causes of Death (sixth revision).* Geneva, 1948–49.

Chapter 22

ATHEROSCLEROSIS AND RELATED FACTORS IN IMMIGRANTS TO ISRAEL

M. TOOR, A. KATCHALSKY-KATZIR, J. AGMON, AND D. ALLALOUF

I mmigrant groups to Israel from western and eastern countries differ widely in morbidity and mortality from coronary disease. They provide, therefore, an opportunity for epidemiologic study of atherosclerosis. The influence of socioeconomic conditions and diet upon blood lipids and proteins was investigated in 2,200 subjects belonging to different immigrant groups and social classes. These findings were correlated with morbidity and mortality rates of the equivalent groups in the whole population.

Atherosclerotic heart disease is recognized in the western world as the chief cause of morbidity and mortality of man at the peak of his mental and social activity. In the search for clues of the etiology of atherosclerosis in man, different workers[1-4] and in particular, Keys,[5] established a positive correlation between the amount of fat in the diet, the level of serum cholesterol, and the frequency of atherosclerosis. Nevertheless, other workers express the opinion that genetic factors might influence the incidence of atherosclerosis.[6,7] Further epidemiologic research is therefore

Reprinted in edited version by permission of the American Heart Association, Inc. *Circulation,* 22:(no. 2) August 1960.

Supported by grants of the Research Fund of the Executive Committee of the General Federation of Labour of Israel and the "Solel Boneh" Company.

The authors are grateful to Dr. G. Kalner, Head of the Department of Health of the Central Bureau of Statistics of the Israel Government for the statistical data on the mortality from cardiovascular diseases for the years 1953 to 1957, and to Professor J. Casper, Head of the Pathological Department of the Beilinson Hospital, for the postmortem findings of 385 cases of myocardial infarction. The authors wish to thank Mrs. S. Seligson, Head of the Statistical Medical Department of the Workers' Sick Fund of Israel, for the statistical analyses and to Mrs. A. Heicht, B.Sc., for her assistance in the dietary survey.

189

necessary to clarify the effects of the different environmental factors in the pathogenesis of atherosclerosis.

A study of atherosclerosis in different immigrant groups in Israel revealed that its frequency is significantly higher in the groups from western countries than in those from eastern ones. The lowest incidence was found in the group that had arrived most recently from Yemen.[8-11]

In order to clarify the causes for these differences, socioeconomic conditions, diet, and the blood lipids of the various immigrant groups in Israel were examined. The group of immigrants from Yemen, composed of "early" immigrants living in Israel over 20 years and "recent" immigrants living in the country for about five years, was of special interest as this genetically pure group made it possible to observe the effect of changing environment on the morbidity and mortality of atherosclerosis.

CHARACTERIZATION OF THE HUMAN MATERIAL

In 1953 and 1954 we examined the following groups of manual workers: 274 "recent" and 254 "early" Yemenite immigrants,[11] 146 Iraqi immigrants, and 262 European immigrants. In addition, the following groups of immigrants were examined: 400 European white-collar workers, professionals, and middle-class persons and 400 atherosclerotic Europeans with clinically proved myocardial infarction.

In 1957 and 1958 we reinvestigated a group of 182 "recent" Yemenites who had by then been resident in Israel for 9 to 10 years (henceforth called "semi-recent") as well as an additional 144 "early" Yemenites and 138 manual workers of European origin.

All subjects were selected at random and underwent a thorough physical examination by one of us with the help of their local physicians. Persons with a history of cardiovascular disease or other pathology liable to affect the serum cholesterol level were rejected. The following were also rejected: subjects with blood pressure higher than 140/90, subjects considerably underweight, subjects with enlargement of the spleen or liver, subjects presenting low blood cholesterol levels in the presence of impaired liver function, and pregnant and lactating women.

Social Conditions

The "recent" Yemenites examined in 1953 and 1954 lived in transit camps under poor conditions and were mostly unskilled and partly unemployed manual workers. Their income compared to that of other groups investigated was the lowest (I.L.19.* per person per month). The economic condition of the "early" Yemenites examined in 1953 and 1954, who were in the main skilled laborers and farmers, was better with an income of I.L.38. per person per month. In 1957 and 1958 the social conditions of these two groups were restudied. Although there was no significant change in the economic conditions of the "early" group, the economic conditions of the "recent" Yemenites were considerably ameliorated. Their monthly income per person had risen to I.L.30.

The income of manual workers of European origin was higher (I.L.68. per person per month) whereas the average income of European white-collar workers, professionals, and middle class reached I.L.90. per person per month.

Diet

A dietary survey was conducted in two stages by a dietitian with the help of a "recent" Yemenite trained for the purpose. In 1953 and 1954, 55 "recent" and 21 "early" Yemenite families were surveyed. In 1957 and 1958, 30 "semi-recent" and 20 "early" Yemenite families were included in the dietary survey. Some of the "semi-recent" Yemenites had formerly belonged to the "recent" group investigated in 1953 and 1954. The daily composition of food of the whole family and the quantity of food consumed by each member of the family was weighed and recorded for seven consecutive days. The particular method of food preparation as well as types and quantities of spices, which are abundantly in use by these groups, was noted.

The dietary survey of 1953 and 1954 showed that the "recent" Yemenites consumed mainly "Pita," a type of flat, yeastless bread; large quantities of vegetables; very little meat (once weekly), and very little fat—mainly in the form of "samne" (boiled butter with

* I.L.1. 800 = $1.00

"hilbe"*. Since the socioeconomic conditions of the "early" Yemenites were better, their caloric intake and the percentage of calories derived from fats were higher than those of the "recent" Yemenites. Both groups made abundant use of sunflower seeds, chickpeas, nuts, and almonds.

The dietary survey of the group of "semi-recent" Yemenites examined in 1957 and 1958 revealed that with the improvement in the socioeconomic conditions there was a considerable increase in the total caloric intake as well as in the percentage of calories derived from fats, whereas in "early" Yemenites the increase in total caloric and fat intake was moderate.

CLINICAL AND LABORATORY METHODS

Each subject was weighed and measured nude. Blood pressure was measured in the sitting position; blood samples were collected in the morning from fasting subjects, and the serum was removed three to four hours later. Every blood examination was performed in duplicate and results diverging by more than 5 percent were discarded. A detailed description of our methods appeared previously.[10] For the additional determinations of protein,[12] lipoprotein,[13] and cholesterol[14] fractions carried out in 1957 and 1958, paper electrophoretic methods were used. Total blood proteins were determined by a modification of the biuret method. (Globulins were precipitated with solution of sodium sulfate 22.2 percent.)

RESULTS

Nutritional Status Expressed by the Weight:Height Ratio

Men: The lowest weight:height ratio was found among the "recent" Yemenites resident in Israel for about five years. After nine to ten years residence in Israel, the average weight of the "semi-recent" Yemenites in the age group 45 to 64 increased significantly and reached the weight:height ratio of the "early" Yemenites. The weight:height ratio of the "early" Yemenites approached that of the manual workers of European origin al-

* The seed of fenugreek, Trigonella foenumgraecum.

though it was still significantly lower. A significant difference in all age groups was found between middle-class Europeans and European patients with myocardial infarction.

Women: The lowest weight:height ratio was found in "recent" and "semi-recent" Yemenites. A significant difference between the "early" Yemenites and "semi-recent" Yemenites remained even after nine years in Israel. In the 35 to 54 age groups, a higher value of the weight:height ratio was observed in the middle-class European immigrants than in the manual workers of the same origin. In the age group 45 to 64, the weight:height ratio of the European group with myocardial infarction was significantly higher than that of the middle-class European immigrants.

Hemoglobin

The mean hemoglobin values in all groups were slightly lower than those accepted in western countries.[15] In women these values were lower than in men for all groups. In men of the 45 to 64 group the hemoglobin values were significantly higher in manual workers of European origin than in "early" Yemenites, whereas in women it was higher in all age groups.

Blood Pressure

The lowest mean systolic and diastolic pressures were found in the "recent" Yemenite group. Higher blood pressures were found in the "early" Yemenites, still higher in the Iraqis, increasing with the European manual workers, middle-class, and professional Europeans with myocardial infarction. As cases with elevated blood pressure were excluded from our study, no definite conclusions were drawn from these data.

Blood Proteins and Protein Fractions

In general, no significant differences in total proteins, albumin, and globulin fractions were found in any of the groups, regardless of age. A significant difference, however, in albumin, alpha 1 and alpha 2, was found between European manual workers and Europeans with myocardial infarction only in the 55 to 64 age groups.

Cholesterol

The mean serum cholesterol value was lowest for "recent" Yemenites examined in 1953 and 1954 in men of all age groups.

Values for "early" Yemenites were significantly higher statistically (men: t = 7.99 — 6.96 — 7.53; women: t = 3.77 — 6.07 — 4.62). Four years later the group of "semi-recent" Yemenites examined showed a significant rise in their mean cholesterol values—for men in the 45 to 54 and 55 to 64 age groups (t = 4.23 to 6.21) and women in the 45 to 54 age group (t = 2.7). These values, however, were still significantly lower than the mean cholesterol values of the "early" Yemenites in men of all age groups.

There was no significant difference in the mean serum cholesterol values among the "early" Yemenites, the Iraqi, and European manual workers. A highly significant difference was found between the European manual workers and the European middle class in both sexes and in all age groups (men: t = 4.85 — 14.1 — 8.13; women: t = 5.77 — 5.3 — 5.05). The highest cholesterol values were found in the group of European patients with myocardial infarction.

Alpha and Beta Cholesterol

Comparison of "semi-recent" Yemenites and "early" Yemenites showed a significant increase in beta cholesterol values in milligrams percent for "early" Yemenite men 35 to 64 years old (t= 2.57, 3.4, 2.7) and women 55 to 64 years old (t = 3.86). A highly significant difference in beta cholesterol was found between European manual workers and men with myocardial infarction of all three age groups (t = 6.02, 7.87, 3.11). No significant difference was found in alpha cholesterol between these two groups.

The outstanding results were the constancy of alpha cholesterol in milligrams percent and the variability of beta cholesterol in all groups examined.

Lipoproteins

Comparisons between "semi-recent" Yemenites and "early" Yemenites showed significantly lower alpha lipoprotein and higher beta lipoprotein values in men 55 to 64 years old. Significantly higher values for beta lipoproteins were found in European men, manual workers, 35 to 44 years old (t = 3.37).

Phospholipids

Significant differences in phospholipid values were found between "recent" Yemenites and "semi-recent" Yemenites between men 35 to 44 and women 35 to 44 and 55 to 64 years old. A comparison between the "semi-recent" and "early" Yemenites showed significant difference in all age groups of both sexes.

Cholesterol:Phospholipid Ratio

The cholesterol:phospholipid ratio followed the general pattern of differences in cholesterol levels among the various groups.

MORBIDITY FROM MYOCARDIAL INFARCTION

In order to evaluate the incidence of morbidity from atherosclerosis in the different groups, we reviewed 5,000 cases of myocardial infarction from all but one of the leading hospitals in Israel over the period 1947 to 1957. On the basis of this material we calculated the incidence of myocardial infarction in "early" and "recent" Yemenites and eastern and western immigrants. The relative difference in morbidity from myocardial infarction in the various groups is expressed as rates per 1,000 persons of the same sex and age group in the whole population. The respective rates were *men*: "recent" Yemenites, 0.1; "early" Yemenites, 1.6; immigrants of eastern origin, 5.2; immigrants of western origin, 17.7; *women*: "recent" Yemenites, 0; "early" Yemenites, 0.2; immigrants of eastern origin, 1.4; immigrants of western origin, 4.4. It is to be stressed that members of all immigrant groups had the same access to all hospitals concerned.

MORTALITY RATES FROM ATHEROSCLEROSIS

Data concerning atherosclerosis mortality rates for the various immigrant groups covered the period 1953 to 1957 for the whole population of Israel.

The atherosclerotic mortality rate for 1953 to 1957 of the "early" Yemenites in the 45 to 64 age group was about four times the mortality rate of "recent" Yemenites in men and three times in women. The mortality rate of the European Jews was considerably higher.

The mortality from all other diseases in men of both Yemenite groups is practically the same.

CORONARY ATHEROSCLEROSIS AND MYOCARDIAL INFARCTION

In order to obtain a quantitative correlation between the extent of coronary atherosclerosis and myocardial infarction, we summarized the results of 385 postmortem examinations performed in our hospital on patients who had died of myocardial infarction. In about 80 percent of the autopsies performed, severe atherosclerotic changes in the coronary arteries were found; in the other 20 percent moderate atherosclerotic changes were observed.

SERUM CHOLESTEROL AND MORTALITY FROM ATHEROSCLEROSIS

Comparison of serum cholesterol levels and mortality rates from atherosclerosis shows that the "recent" Yemenites with the lowest serum cholesterol values also have the lowest mortality rates from atherosclerosis; the "early" Yemenites with higher cholesterol values have a higher mortality rate from atherosclerosis.

DISCUSSION

This epidemiologic study shows that atherosclerosis was lowest in the group of "recent" immigrants from Yemen, the poorest among the groups investigated. In 1953 and 1954, after five years in Israel, their nutritional status and blood cholesterol levels were lower than that of any other group of Israeli inhabitants.

A follow-up study of this group in 1957 and 1958, after nine to ten years in Israel, showed that their socioeconomic condition had improved and that there was a rise of 43 percent in their total caloric intake as well as a rise of 7 percent in their percentage of calories derived from fats. In men 45 to 64 years old there was a highly significant increase in their nutritional status as well as in serum cholesterol level. These findings demonstrate the gradual transition of the poorest group of "recent" Yemenites with the lowest cholesterol level to the economically better-off group of "early" Yemenites with higher cholesterol levels.

Dietary survey of the "early" Yemenites showed that although the composition of their food remained essentially similar to that of the "recent" Yemenites, their total caloric and fat intake increased and approached that of the European manual workers.[16]

It can be assumed that the rise in serum cholesterol level in the "semi-recent" and "early" Yemenites is due to over-all higher caloric and fat intake. Another factor to be considered is a possible change in the ratio of saturated to unsaturated fatty acids[2,17-20] or a shift to a less bulky diet poorer in vegetables. These possibilities are now under investigation.

The morbidity and mortality from atherosclerosis of the "early" Yemenites is higher than that of the "recent" Yemenites, but the mortality from other diseases is practically the same in both groups. As the "recent" and "early" Yemenites belong to the same genetic group, the difference in their serum cholesterol values can be mainly attributed to the differences in diet consequent to changing socioeconomic conditions. This increase in serum cholesterol values in "early" Yemenites may cause the increase in the morbidity and mortality from atherosclerosis.

Another indication that the caloric imbalance is an important factor in determining the group incidence of atherosclerosis is that during World War I and particularly World War II, when food was scanty, the over-all mortality from atherosclerosis was considerably diminished.[21-24] Likewise, physicians who survived the Nazi concentration camps reported that during the years of their imprisonment, they never encountered patients with myocardial infarctions or patients with anginal syndrome, even in persons over 50 years of age. Moreover, persons who were previously known to them as patients with atherosclerotic heart disease became free of clinical manifestations of their disease after losing considerable weight due to the conditions prevailing in the concentration camps.[25-27]

Cholesterol as an Atherogenic Index

Comparison of the incidence of atherosclerosis with the results of clinical and laboratory investigations shows that only the total and beta cholesterol levels give a direct correlation with the epidemiologic data. Neither the other blood lipids nor the protein fractions show any significant differences among the various groups examined.

As the alpha cholesterol was found to be constant in both sexes and all ages of the various population groups while the variability was localized in the beta cholesterol, determination of total cholesterol alone can serve as an atherogenic index.

In the different population groups examined, it was found that an improvement in the socioeconomic status is accompanied by an increase in the cholesterol content of the blood. It can, consequently, be stated that the mean cholesterol level is a socioeconomic characteristic of a population group and can be allotted varying values for different social groups of the same age, sex, and ethnic origin. This fact is seen not only among the Yemenites but also among the various classes of western immigrants. This corresponds to similar findings in different social classes in Spain,[28] Italy,[29] and India[30] as well as in Japanese in Japan and Japanese in Hawaii.[31] The so-called cholesterol norms of the western or westernized countries are "simply standards for preclinical coronary disease,"[31] as pointed out by Keys, and should be substituted by a mean value obtained from population groups nearly free of atherosclerosis found in underdeveloped countries.

On the basis of our available data, it seems that the value of a normal cholesterol level in adults is about 160 mg percent in men and 180 mg percent in women, as found in "recent" Yemenites. These values were also confirmed by other workers.[32]

The cholesterol level of blood withdrawn from the umbilical cord of newborn infants of different population groups throughout the world showed no dissimilarity due to race or class and, in almost all cases, was about 80 mg percent.[33-35] The rise of cholesterol occurs at an early age and is dependent upon the composition of diet.[35]

Prevention of Atherosclerosis

Since myocardial infarction is the main cause of morbidity and mortality in western civilization, its prevention is a major problem of public health. Although multiple factors, such as changes in blood coagulability, physical activity, stress, and hormones as well as local factors in the coronary arteries are implicated in the pathogenesis of myocardial infarction, atherosclerosis is generally accepted as being its underlying cause. In our material no case of myocardial infarction without atherosclerosis was found, and about 80 percent of the cases had severe coronary atherosclerosis. The present observations on 2,200 subjects of western and eastern origin and of different socioeconomic groups corroborate the investigations carried out in underdeveloped countries which show that, in populations with low serum cholesterol values, the mortality rate from myocardial infarction is correspondingly low.[2,36-38] With amelioration of the socioeconomic status, along with an increase in the total caloric intake, a decrease in consumption of bulky vegetable food and an increase in percentage of calories derived from fats, blood cholesterol and atherosclerotic mortality rate rises. These observations suggest that the appearance of atherosclerosis in any population group may be retarded or prevented by maintaining a balanced caloric intake of a bulky diet with no more than 15 to 20 percent of calories derived from fats.

SUMMARY

Clinical experience in Israel, supported by statistical surveys, showed a low incidence of atherosclerosis among immigrants from eastern countries as compared to immigrants from western countries. In particular, the incidence of atherosclerosis among immigrants from Yemen was found to be strikingly low.

An investigation of the socioeconomic condition, diet, and nutritional status of 2,200 immigrants from western and eastern countries belonging to different social groups was carried out. Determinations of serum total lipids, total cholesterol, alpha and beta cholesterol, phospholipids, lipoproteins, proteins, and protein fractions were performed.

Significantly the lowest serum cholesterol and beta cholesterol values were found among the "recent" Yemenites (after five years in Israel), the poorest economically, and with an imbalanced caloric intake of the lowest fat content. Higher cholesterol and beta cholesterol values were found among "early" (after 20 years in Israel) Yemenites, Iraqi, and European manual workers with no significant differences among them, whereas in Europeans of higher economic level these values were even higher.

Review of 5,000 hospitalized cases of myocardial infarction showed a very low incidence for Yemenites, higher for immigrants from other eastern countries, and considerably higher for European immigrants.

A statistical survey of the entire population for the years 1953 to 1957 showed that the mortality rate from atherosclerosis was extremely low for "recent" Yemenites, considerably higher for "early" Yemenites, and still higher for European immigrants.

These results suggest the influence of socioeconomic conditions, diet, and total caloric balance on serum cholesterol values and atherosclerosis morbidity and mortality. They support the assumption that atherosclerosis is a disease of lipid metabolism influenced by phenotypic factors and therefore can be prevented.

REFERENCES

1. Rosenthal, S.R.: Studies in atherosclerosis, chemical experimental and morphologic. *Arch Path, 18*:473, 660, 1934.

2. Snapper, I.: *Chinese Lessons to Western Medicine.* New York, Interscience Publishers Inc., 1941.

3. Dock, W.: Prophylaxis and Therapy of Atherosclerosis. Fifty-ninth Annual Meeting of the Association of Life Insurance Medical Directors of America, October 19–20, 1950.

4. Katz, L.N., and Stamler, J.: *Experimental Atherosclerosis.* Springfield, Ill., Charles C Thomas, 1953.

5. Keys, A.: Diet and the incidence of heart disease. *Bull Univ Minnesota Hosp, 24*:376, 1953.

6. Adlesberg, D.: Hypercholesteremia with predisposition to atherosclerosis. *Am J Med, 11*:600, 1951.

7. Page, J.H., Lewis, L.A., and Gilbert, J.: Plasma lipids and proteins and their relationship in coronary disease among Navajo Indians. *Circulation, 13*:675, 1956.

8. Asher, G.: Myocardial infarction in Israel. *Dapim Refuiim, 7*:199, 1948.

9. Dreyfus, F.: The incidence of myocardial infarction in various communities in Israel. *Am Heart J, 45*:749, 1953.

10. Toor, M., Agmon, J., and Allalouf, D.: Changes of serum total lipids, total cholesterol and lipid phosphorus in Jewish Yemenite immigrants after 20 years in Israel. *Bull Res Counc Israel, 4*:202, 1954.

11. —, Katchalsky, A., Agmon, J., and Allalouf, D.: Serum lipids and

atherosclerosis among Yemenite immigrants in Israel. *Lancet, 1:*1270, 1957.

12. Kunkel, H., and Tiselius, A.: Electrophoresis of proteins on filter paper. *J Gen Physiol, 35:*89, 1951.

13. Swahn, B.: A method for localisation and determination of serum lipids after electrophoretical separation on filter paper. *Scand J Clin Lab Invest, 4:*98, 1952.

14. Nikkila, E.: Lipid protein relations in normal and pathological serums. *Scandinav J Clin Lab Invest,* (suppl. 8) 5:5, 1953.

15. Berry, W.T.C., Cowin, P.J., and Magee, H.E.: Haemoglobin levels in adults and children. *Br Med J, 1:*410, 1952.

16. Strauss, W., Shatan-Herzberg, M., and Borten, E.: Nutritional Survey in Israel. Department of Hygiene, Hadassah Medical School, Hebrew University Jerusalem, 1954.

17. Groen, J., Tjiong, B.K., Kamminga, C.E., and Willebrands, A.F.: The influence of nutrition, individuality and some other factors, including various forms of stress on the serum cholesterol; an experiment of nine months' duration in 60 normal human volunteers. *Voeding, 13:*556, 1952.

18. Kinsell, L.W., Michales, G.D., Partridge, J.W., Boling, L.A., Balch, H.E., and Cochrane, G.C.: Effect upon serum cholesterol and phospholipids of diets containing large amounts of vegetable fat. *J Clin Nutrition, 1:*224, 295, 1953.

19. Bronte-Stewart, B., Antonis, A., and Eales, L.: Effects of feeding different fats on serum cholesterol level. *Lancet, 1:*521, 1956.

20. Gordon, H., Lewis, B., Eales, L., and Brock, J.F.: Dietary Fat and Cholesterol Metabolism. *Lancet, 2:*1299, 1957.

21. Ashoff, L.: *Lectures in Pathology.* New York, Paul B. Hoeber, 1924.

22. Beitzke, H.: Zur Entstehung der Atherosklerose. *Virchows Arch, 267:*625, 1928.

23. Brozek, J., Wells, S., and Keys, A.: Medical aspects of semistarvation in Leningrad. *Am Rev Soviet Med, 4:*70, 1946.

24. Biörck, G.: *Wartime Lessons on Arteriosclerotic Heart Disease from Northern Europe. Cardiovascular Epidemiology.* New York, Paul B. Hoeber, 1956, p. 8.

25. Dvorjetski, M.: The cardiac pathology of ghettos and concentration camps. *Dapim Refuiim, 17:*200, 1958.

26. Serr, I.: Personal Communication.

27. Rudich, A.: Personal Communication.

28. Keys, A., Vivanco, F., Rodriguez Minon, J.L., Keys, M.H., and Castro Mendosa, H.: Studies on diet, body fatness and serum cholesterol in Madrid, Spain. *Metabolism, 3:*195, 1954.

29. —, Fidanza, F., Scardi, V., Bergami, G., Keys, M.H., and Di Lorenzo, F.: Studies on serum cholesterol and other characteristics of clinically healthy men in Naples. *Arch Int Med, 93:*328, 1954.

30. Wahi, P.N.: Incidence of heart disease in India. Presented to W.H.O. Expert Group Meeting on Atherosclerosis. Washington, D.C., 1958.

31. Keys, A., Kimura, N., Kusukawa, A., Bronte-Stewart, B., Larsen, N., and Keys, M.H.: Lessons from serum cholesterol studies in Japan, Hawaii and Los Angeles. *Ann Int Med, 48*:83, 1958.

32. Brunner, D., Loebl, K., Fischer, M., and Schick, G.: Cholesterol, phospholipids, total lipids and cholesterol-phospholipid ratio in males of various origin in Israel. *Harefuah, 48*:1, 1955.

33. Halbrecht, J.: Les effects de l'alimentation pauvre en proteins d'origine animale sur la gestante et le foetus, "La phophylaxie en gynecologie et obstetrique." Conferences et rapports du Congres international de gynecologie et d'obstetrique. Tome I, Geneva, 1954.

34. Rafstedt, S.: Studies on serum lipids and lipoproteins in infancy and childhood. *Acta Paediat,* (suppl.) 1955.

35. Bersohn, J., and Waybrune, S.: Serum cholesterol concentration in new-born African and European infants and their mothers. *Am J Clin Nutrition, 4*:117, 1956.

36. Walker, A.R.P., and Arvidsson, K.B.: Fat intake, serum cholesterol concentration, and atherosclerosis in the South African Bantu. Part I. *J Clin Invest, 33*:1358, 1954.

37. Higginson, J., and Pepler, W.J.: Fat intake, serum cholesterol concentration, and atherosclerosis in the South African Bantu. Part II. *J Clin Invest, 33*:1366, 1954.

38. Tejada, C., and Gore, J.: Comparison of atherosclerosis in Guatemala City and New Orleans. *Am J Path, 23*:887 1957.

Chapter 23

PRECURSORS OF HYPERTENSION AND CORONARY DISEASE AMONG HEALTHY MEDICAL STUDENTS: DISCRIMINANT FUNCTION ANALYSIS

III. Using Ethnic Origin as the Criterion, with Observations on Parental Hypertension and Coronary Disease and on Religion

D.C. Ross and C.B. Thomas

There is a considerable body of evidence to support the thesis that familial factors are involved in the etiology of hypertension and of coronary disease.[1-11] Whether the familial aggregation found by a number of observers is due to genetic or to environmental factors, or both, has not been clearly established, however. While the importance of the genetic contribution has been supported by a number of studies, including our own, final proof is lacking, and there are those who still consider that dietary habits or some other factor related to the style of life in these families may play the more significant role.[12]

Not only are hypertension and coronary disease more prevalent in some families than in others, but they have been found to be differently distributed among various ethnic groups.[13-19] That factors operating to a different extent from family to family would also operate to a varying degree in populations with different

Reprinted in edited version with permission from *Bull Johns Hopkins Hosp*, 117:37–57, July 1965.

This study was supported by Research Grant HE-01891, National Heart Institute. The computations in this paper were done in the Computing Center of the Johns Hopkins Medical Institutions, which is supported by Research Grant FR-00004 from the National Institutes of Health and by Educational Contributions from the International Business Machines Corporation.

203

racial backgrounds seems logical, since, in a sense, ethnic groups may be thought of as much larger, more complex families. Many of the epidemiological comparisons which have been made, however, involve groups which differ so widely in socioeconomic, cultural and, indeed, in almost every life pattern that the difficulty of assessing the role of each factor is enormously increased. Nevertheless, both genetic and environmental factors have been cited as being responsible for ethnic differences in the prevalence of hypertension or of coronary disease.[20-24]

Epidemiological investigations of the causes of hypertension and coronary disease have included not only the prevalence and incidence rates of the diseases themselves, but also the distribution in the study populations of factors which are precursors of the disorders in question.[25-32] In both familial and ethnic surveys, differences in respect to the distribution of such single variables as blood pressure and total serum cholesterol have been reported; higher levels of blood pressure or of cholesterol have usually been associated with an increased prevalence or incidence of hypertension or coronary disease respectively.[33-36]

In prospective studies, the predictive value of precursor factors may be heightened by including multiple variables in the statistical analysis.[28-32] In our own studies of healthy medical students, discriminant function scores based on a number of variables have been found to be significantly different for groups of subjects classified according to a history of hypertension and/or coronary disease affecting both, one or neither parent.[37]

The present study is a parallel one; its object is to determine whether significant differences in discriminant function scores based on the same nine variables can be demonstrated when subjects from the same population are grouped by ethnic origin. In addition, the relationships of differences in ethnic origin and of religious background to the prevalence of hypertension or coronary disease among the subjects' parents were also examined.

METHOD

The 1272 Johns Hopkins medical students in the classes of 1948–1964 who participated in the Study of Precursors of Hypertension and Coronary Disease[38,39] were the subjects of the present study, together with their parents. Where the subjects' own characteristics were the variables for discriminatory analysis, only male subjects were included for the sake of homogeneity. Elsewhere, both male and female subjects were used as propositi, to increase the size of the parental population.

Ethnic Groups

The ethnic groupings are based on the subject's written statements in a form filled out on registration in the Study. In addition to questions about the name, birthplace and birth date of each parent, the subject was asked to specify the "chief ancestral countries (before U.S.)" of his father and of his mother.

When the relative sizes of the groups thus defined are considered, it will be seen that those with Northwestern European ancestry formed by far the largest specific group, with the Jewish European group next in size. Although the remaining ethnic groups were small, three of them, those with Southern European, Central European and Far Eastern (Oriental) ancestry respectively, were of sufficient size to be used in statistical studies. The remaining specific groupings, those with mixed European, Near and Middle Eastern, Latin American, or "other" ancestry, were too small to be used.

Religion

Classification of religion was based on the subject's written answers to specific questions. On the personal data sheet, the following question is asked, "What church do you attend?", and on the front sheet (identifying and general information), the subject is asked to check one of the following items: "*Religion:* none/ Protestant/Catholic/Jewish/other _____." When more than one religious affiliation was recorded, the earliest one in the subject's life was used here as being the one most likely to be the same as that of the parent. The answers of many subjects to a question about Sunday School attendance gave supplemental information concerning the religion in which the subject was raised. While it is recognized that this was not necessarily the religion of the parent, it is thought that discrepancies in this regard are not an important source of error.

The 39 different specific religious affiliations recorded were grouped under the following major headings:

	N		N
1. None	77	6. Protestant (major	
2. Non-Christian Eastern	7	denominations)	668
3. Jewish	162	7. Protestant (minor	
4. Roman Catholic	163	denominations)	55
5. Eastern Orthodox	9	8. Modern doctrines	11
		9. Unknown	120

Of these, only three religious groups, Protestant (major denominations), Roman Catholic, and Jewish, were large enough to be suitable for analysis here.

Relationship of Hypertension and of Coronary Disease to Ethnic Origin

The prevalence of hypertension and of coronary disease among the parents of subjects in different ethnic groups was next examined. Here the medical student subjects are the propositi only, while the comparisons are entirely concerned with their parents—their parents' ethnic origin and status in regard to the cardiovascular disorders specified. Prevalence rates for hypertension were calculated for parents of each sex, but for coronary disease they were calculated for fathers only; there was too little coronary disease among the mothers to make that analysis meaningful. Only the four specific ethnic groups of European origin were considered here.

There was little difference in the prevalence of hypertension among the four ethnic groups; this was true for parents of both sexes. On the other hand, prevalence rates for coronary disease ranged from 75 per 1000 among Southern European fathers to 301 per 1000 among Jewish fathers. The rate of coronary disease for fathers of Northwestern European origin was intermediate (188 per 1000), while that for Central European fathers more nearly resembled that for Jewish fathers (273 per 1000).

Relationship of Hypertension and of Coronary Disease to Religion

Possible relationships between religion and the prevalence of hypertension and coronary disease were also explored. In order to avoid the difficulties which could arise from the differential distribution of ethnic groups among Protestants and Roman Catholics, only Protestants and Catholics of Northwestern European origin were compared. No significant differences were found between these two religious groups in any of the comparisons. The prevalence rates for parents of persons who stated that they were Jewish by religion (excluding parents of subjects who were Jewish by ethnic origin but not by religion) are not much different from the rates for all Jews, and showed a high prevalence rate for coronary disease similar to that noted previously.

DISCUSSION

Our results indicate that, when medical students are grouped by ethnic background, significant intergroup differences in respect to both physiological and psychological traits may be demonstrated. Through the use of discriminant function analysis, five ethnic groups of students have been characterized. Of these groups, those of Far Eastern origin (Orientals) and those of Southern European origin are the most different from each other. Physiologically, the group of Orientals is the shortest, weighs the least and has a relatively high ponderal index, while the group of Southern Europeans is the heaviest and has the lowest ponderal index, despite being relatively tall. These findings fit very well with the generally recognized differences in physique of these two racial groups. Psychologically, the Orientals have next to the lowest anger score and the Southern Europeans have the highest, which again seems to agree with the popular notion that Chinese are likely to be philosophical and do not show anger, while Spaniards, Italians and Greeks tend to be quick-tempered.[40]

It is interesting to note that the relationships of the ethnic groups, if considered in mirror image, roughly correspond to their geographic positions on the European-Asian land mass. The Far

Easterners, Northwesterners and Southern Europeans are at the corners of a triangle, with the Central and Eastern European group located inside the triangle. The Jewish Europeans, who, as a group, consist of a mixture of various European and Near Eastern strains, are also located inside the triangle, but further removed from the Northwestern corner than are the Central and Eastern Europeans. The discovery of such geographical relationships lends support to the hypothesis that these ethnic differences are genetically determined; they resemble those found in the distribution of the ABO blood groups, for example, traits which are, without much doubt, genetically controlled.

The observations on cholesterol level in these ethnic groups are of particular interest in view of the extensive literature on differences in cholesterol level between people living in different countries.[35,41-43] It is noteworthy that the mean cholesterol level of the 17 Americanized Oriental students is significantly higher than that of the pooled European groups—252.76 versus 224.95 mg per ml (p < .01).* The findings of Adamson, who studied the cholesterol levels of groups of Honolulu men of different ethnic origins, are pertinent here.[44] In her studies, the mean cholesterol level of the young Chinese men was significantly higher than that of the young Caucasian group, and the mean cholesterol for the young Japanese men was also somewhat higher than the Caucasian average. Many of these three groups of young men were university students, whose dietary fat intake resembled the American pattern.

The mean cholesterol level of the Southern Europeans in our study, on the other hand, is similar to that of the other European groups. This finding resembles that of a survey carried out in Roseto, Pennsylvania, an Italian-American community with an

---

* These data permit us to speculate as to whether there may be genetically-controlled ethnic patterns of cholesterol regulation that tend to conserve or elevate cholesterol levels in countries low in dietary fats and to moderate or depress cholesterol levels in countries where the dietary fat intake is high. Thus Orientals in Japan or China would have low cholesterol levels because of the small amount of saturated fats in the diet despite the lack of an efficient moderator mechanism. When Orientals eat the relatively high fat American diet, however, the fact that their moderator mechanisms are weaker than those of European ancestry would permit their cholesterol levels to rise to greater heights.

unusually low death rate from coronary heart disease, in which the mean serum cholesterol values of the 171 men examined corresponded closely to those reported in the Framingham Study where the study population consists of mixed ethnic groups.[45,46]

Compared with the Oriental and the Southern European groups, the Jewish, Central and Northwestern European groups were more alike and held an intermediate position. Nevertheless, two of these three intermediate groups were significantly different from each other—the Northwestern group, who were the tallest of the five groups and had the highest mean ponderal index, and the Jewish group, who were the shortest European group and reported more anger than any other group except the Southern Europeans.

In a previous paper, we considered the discriminating power of the same nine variables with respect to the same population of medical students grouped by parental history of hypertension and coronary disease, with the hypothesis that these disorders are primarily hereditary, multifactorial and interrelated.[37] In that analysis, significant differences between the offspring of affected and unaffected parents were reported for each disorder. In the present paper, we have shown that there are ethnic differences in regard to the occurrence of coronary disease within the same population of parents. Hence, one might argue that the differences previously found with respect to parental coronary disease were due to differences in the ethnic composition of the groups. However, the sets of variables which discriminated most powerfully between groups were different in each case, so that it seems unlikely that ethnic differences account for a major part of the differences between subjects grouped by parental coronary disease. Moreover, no significant ethnic differences were found in regard to parental hypertension.

Although the people used for the discriminant function analysis and for the prevalence rates for hypertension and coronary disease were drawn from two successive generations, both parents and children should be equally representative of their ethnic groups. It is of interest to note that although, on the average, the Southern European subjects exhibit somewhat higher weight, cholesterol, heart rate, systolic and diastolic pressure and the most anger and anxiety of all the European groups, their fathers have the lowest prevalence of coronary disease.

In any consideration of the multifactorial nature of hypertension and/or coronary disease, it is important to establish the degree of correlation between the variables studied. We have shown that the nine variables used here have relatively low, sometimes zero or near zero, correlations, and there was little difference between the correlation coefficients of the Northwestern and Jewish Europeans. Although Deming and his associates found a suggestive relationship between *changes* in blood pressure and cholesterol in treated hypertensive patients, Dawber, Moore and Mann found no significant correlation between systolic or diastolic pressure and cholesterol in the Framingham Study of men of 45–62 who were free from coronary disease (although some had hypertension).[46,47]* The Framingham Study findings and ours are in agreement as to the low degree of correlation between blood pressure and relative weight, and between relative weight and cholesterol.

Our prevalence studies point to the conclusion that there is a higher rate of coronary disease among Jewish men than among men of Northwestern European origin. There are also suggestively high rates of coronary disease for persons of Central and Eastern European origin and low rates for persons of Southern European origin. However, these latter rates are based on small numbers and cannot be taken as seriously as the other two rates. The objection might be raised that since these data were collected by means of questionnaires filled out by the children of those whose prevalence rates we are calculating, numerous factors other than the actual prevalence of the disease might affect the reported prevalence rates. Members of some ethnic groups might be less accurate in filling out the forms than others; there might be a greater concern or awareness of disease in one group than in another; one group might have older parents and hence more illness than another, or perhaps persons with ill parents might be more likely to report themselves to be members

*Our analysis of the control values published by Deming *et al.* shows no significant correlation between mean blood pressure and cholesterol levels in hypertensive patients.[47]

of one particular group than of another.* But, if any of these were the case, one would expect that it would influence the rates for hypertension as well as the rates for coronary disease. As a matter of fact, while there are large differences in the coronary disease rates, there is no suggestion of any differences in the rates for hypertension. This lends weight to the conclusion that there are real differences between ethnic groups in the incidence of coronary disease, which is further supported by the fact that the difference between the prevalence of coronary disease among Jewish men and Southern European men found in our analysis resembles that found between Jewish and Italian clothing workers in New York, where Jewish men had twice as much coronary heart disease as Italian men after the rates were age-adjusted.[48]

Recently, Wardwell, Hyman and Bahnson summarized the findings of two field studies regarding the relationship of ethnic background and of religion to coronary heart disease.[49] In both the Middlesex County Heart Study and the Midtown Manhattan Study, coronary disease was more prevalent among those of Northwestern European and Old Yankee stock than among those of Southern European, Eastern European and French Canadian stock. Their ethnic groupings are not entirely comparable to ours, since we did not pool Southern Europeans and Eastern Europeans as they did, and we considered France as part of Northwest Europe. Nevertheless, our results bear some resemblance to theirs, in that our Northwestern European coronary disease rates were higher than our Southern European rates.

Our results fail to substantiate their findings in regard to religion, however. Whereas we found no difference between Catholics and Protestants in the prevalence of coronary disease among the students' parents, they found a twofold increase in prevalence among Protestants as compared with Catholics. The difference they found was attributed to certain aspects of a supposed Prot-

---

* We have looked at the only one of these possible sources of bias which is readily measurable. The median birth years for four ethnic groups of fathers were: Northwestern Europeans 1891.1, Southern Europeans 1896.6, Central and Eastern Europeans 1900.0 and Jewish Europeans 1900.6. Thus the highest prevalence of coronary disease was found in the two youngest groups of fathers, which is just the opposite of what would be expected if the observed differences in prevalence were due to age differences.

estant *Weltanschauung*. However, it must be remembered that the ethnic composition of these two religions is not the same. There are very few Protestants in Southern Europe; and while there are relatively few Slavic Protestants, there are many Protestants of other ethnic backgrounds in Central and Eastern Europe. Hence, it is clear that simply taking a random selection of Protestants and Catholics would not be a proper method of comparing these two religious groups. Thus, if our finding of high incidence of coronary disease in Central and Eastern Europeans and low rates in Southern Europeans is true, and if, for example, there happened to be large numbers of Italians and of Estonians, many of whom are Lutherans, in the area surveyed, one might expect a higher rate for Protestants on this basis alone. Certainly any study of this sort should attempt to study people whose ancestors came from the same region. Accordingly, part of the explanation for the difference between our findings and theirs may be that we confined the analysis of religion to the Northwestern European group only, excluding the Southern and the Central and Eastern Europeans, while they pooled their ethnic groups, although they had already shown a differential prevalence rate of coronary disease for those groups.

SUMMARY

1. Johns Hopkins medical students have been classified according to the ancestral countries of their parents.

2. Five specific ethnic groups—four European and one Far Eastern (Oriental)—were large enough for use in a discriminant function analysis with six somatic and three psychological characteristics of the medical student subjects as variables.

3. The single variables which are significant in differentiating the ethnic groups of students are *height, ponderal index, anger* and *diastolic pressure*.

4. The within-group correlation coefficients between pairs of variables are all quite low.

5. Discriminant function analysis shows:
   a. The Far Eastern group is significantly different from all of the European groups.

b. The Southern Europeans are significantly different from the Northwestern Europeans and from the Jewish Europeans.

c. The Northwestern and the Jewish Europeans are significantly different from each other.

d. The Central and Eastern Europeans are an intermediate group, not significantly different from the Jewish or the Northwestern Europeans, and only suggestively different from the Southern Europeans.

e. The parallelism noted between the arrangement of the different ethnic groups as a result of discriminant function analysis and the geographical relationships of the regions represented is consistent with a genetic basis for these observations.

6. In the four ethnic groups of European origin, prevalence rates of *hypertension* among the subjects' parents were quite similar.

7. On the other hand, there was a highly significant difference in the prevalence rate of *coronary disease* among fathers of different ethnic origin: those of Southern European ancestry had the lowest rate, and those of Jewish European ancestry had the highest.

8. No significant differences in prevalence rates of hypertension or of coronary disease were found between Protestants and Roman Catholics of Northwestern European origin.

REFERENCES

1. Platt, R.: Heredity in hypertension. *Q J Med, 16*:111, 1947.

2. Søbye, P.: *Heredity in Essential Hypertension and Nephrosclerosis: A Genetic-Clinical Study of 200 Propositi Suffering from Nephrosclerosis.* Copenhagen, Arnold Busck, 1948.

3. Andlersberg, D., Parets, A.D. and Boas, E.P.: Genetics of Atherosclerosis. Studies of families with xanthoma and unselected patients with coronary artery disease under the age of fifty years. *JAMA, 141*:246, 1949.

4. Thomas, C.B.: The heritage of hypertension. *Am J Med Sci, 224*:367, 1952.

5. Gertler, M.M. and White, P.D.: *Coronary Heart Disease in Young Adults. A Multidisciplinary Study.* Published for The Commonwealth Fund. Cambridge, Massachusetts, Harvard University Press, 1954.

6. Thomas, C.B. and Cohen, B.H.: The familial occurrence of hypertension and coronary artery disease, with observations concerning obesity and diabetes. *Ann Intern Med, 42:*90, 1955.

7. Pickering, G.W.: The genetic factor in essential hypertension. *Ann Intern Med, 43:*457, 1955.

8. Stanoff, H.M., Little, A., Murphy, E.A. and Rykert, H.E.: Studies of male survivors of myocardial infarction due to "essential" atherosclerosis: I. Characteristics of the patients. *Canad Med Assoc J, 84:*519, 1961.

9. Rose, G.: Familial patterns in ischaemic heart disease. *Br J Prev Soc Med, 18:*75, 1964.

10. McKusick, V.A.: Editorial: Genetics and the nature of essential hypertension. *Circulation, 22:*857, 1960.

11: Murphy, E.A.: Genetics and atherosclerosis in the Seventh Hahneman Hospital Symposium. In Likoff, W. and Moyer, J.H. (Eds.): *Coronary Heart Disease.* New York, N.Y., Grune & Stratton, 1962.

12. Chazan, J.A. and Winkelstein, W., Jr.: Household aggregation of hypertension: Report of a preliminary study. *J Chronic Dis, 17:*9, 1964.

13. Dreyfuss, F.: The incidence of myocardial infarctions in various communities in Israel. *Amer Heart J, 45:*749, 1953.

14. Comstock, G.W.: An epidemiologic study of blood pressure levels in a biracial community in the Southern United States. *Amer J Hyg, 65:*271, 1957.

15. Spain, D.M. and Bradess, V.A.: Sudden death from coronary atherosclerosis. Age, race, sex, physical activity, and alcohol. *A.M.A. Arch Intern Med, 100:*228, 1957.

16. Thomas, W.A., Blache, J.O. and Lee, K.T.: Race and the incidence of acute myocardial infarction. Incidence of acute myocardial infarction among autopsies of 9064 white and 8003 Negro patients, with special reference to age, sex and diabetes mellitus. *A.M.A. Arch Intern Med, 100:*423, 1957.

17. Toor, M., Katchalsky, A., Agmon, J. and Allalouf, D.: Serum-lipids and atherosclerosis among Yemenite immigrants in Israel. *Lancet, 1:*1270, 1957.

18. Johnson, B.C. and Remington, R.D.: A sampling study of blood pressure levels in white and Negro residents of Nassau, Bahamas. *J Chronic Dis, 13:*39, 1961.

19. Yudkin, J.: Section on racial and ethnic factors. In *Henry Ford Hospital International Symposium on The Etiology of Myocardial Infarction.* Boston, Massachusetts, Little, Brown and Co., 1963.

20. Gampel, B., Slome, C., Scotch, N. and Abramson, J.H.: Urbanization and hypertension among Zulu adults. *J Chronic Dis, 15:*67, 1962.

21. Geiger, H.J. and Scotch, N.A.: The epidemiology of essential hypertension. A review with special attention to psychologic and sociocultural factors. I: Biologic mechanisms and descriptive epidemiology. *J Chronic Dis, 16:*1151, 1963.

22. Scotch, N.A. and Geiger, H.J.: The epidemiology of essential hypertension. A review with special attention to psychologic and sociocultural factors. II: Psychologic and sociocultural factors in etiology. *J Chronic Dis, 16*:1183, 1963.

23. Epstein, F.H., Simpson, R. and Boas, E.P.: Relations between diet and atherosclerosis among a working population of different ethnic origins. *Am J Clin Nutr, 4*:10, 1956.

24. Brock, J.F. and Gordon, H.: Ischaemic heart disease in African populations. *Postgrad Med J, 35*:223, 1959.

25. Stamler, J., Berkson, D.M., Lindberg, H.A., Miller, W. and Hall, Y.: Racial patterns of coronary heart disease. Blood pressure, body weight and serum cholesterol in whites and Negroes. *Geriatrics, 16*:382, 1961.

26. Paul, O., Lepper, M.H., Phelan, W.H., Dupertuis, G.W., MacMillan, A., McKean, H. and Park, H.: A longitudinal study of coronary heart disease. *Circulation, 28*:20, 1963.

27. Rosenman, R.H., Friedman, M., Straus, R., Wurm, M., Kositchek, R., Hahn, W. and Werthessen, N.T.: A predictive study of coronary heart disease. The Western Collaborative Group Study. *JAMA, 189*:15, 1964.

28. Chapman, John M. and Massey, F.J., Jr.: The interrelationship of serum cholesterol, hypertension, body weight, and risk of coronary disease. Results of the first ten years' follow-up in the Los Angeles heart study. *J Chronic Dis, 17*:933, 1964.

29. Gertler, M.M., White, P.D., Cady, L.D. and Whiter, H.H.: Coronary heart disease. A prospective study. *Amer J Med Sci, 248*:377, 1964.

30. Epstein, F.H., Simpson, R. and Boas, E.P.: The epidemiology of atherosclerosis among a random sample of clothing workers of different ethnic origins in New York City. II. Associations between manifest atherosclerosis, serum lipid levels, blood pressure, overweight, and some other variables. *J Chronic Dis, 5*:329, 1957.

31. Kannel, W.B., Dawber, T.R., Kagan, A., Revotskie, N. and Stokes, J. III: Factors of risk in the development of coronary heart disease—six-year follow-up experience. *Ann Intern Med, 55*:33, 1961.

32. Kannel, W.B., Dawber, T.R., Friedman, G.D., Glennon, W.E. and McNamara, P.M.: Risk factors in coronary heart disease: An evaluation of several serum lipids as predictors of coronary heart disease: The Framingham Study. *Ann Intern Med, 61*:888, 1961.

33. Miall, W.E. and Oldham, P.D.: A study of arterial blood pressure and its inheritance in a sample of the general population. *Clin Sci, 14*:459, 1955.

34. The Technical Group of the Committee on Lipoproteins and Atherosclerosis, and the Committee on Lipoproteins and Atherosclerosis of the National Advisory Heart Council. Evaluation of serum lipoprotein and cholesterol measurements as predictors of clinical complications of atherosclerosis. Report of a cooperative study of lipoprotein and atherosclerosis. *Circulation, 14*:691, 1956.

35. Keys, A., Kimura, N., Kusukawa, A., Bronte-Stewart, B., Larsen, N. and Keys, M.H.: Lessons from serum cholesterol studies in Japan, Hawaii and Los Angeles. *Ann Intern Med, 48*:83, 1958.

36. Skyring, A., Modan, B., Crocetti, A. and Hammerstrom, C.: Some epidemiological and familial aspects of coronary heart disease: Report of a pilot study. *J Chronic Dis, 16*:1267, 1963.

37. Thomas, C.B., Ross, D.C. and Higinbotham, C.Q.: Precursors of hypertension and coronary disease among healthy medical students: Discriminant function analysis. II. Using parental history as the criterion. *Bull Hopkins Hosp, 115*:245, 1964.

38. Thomas, C.B., Ross, D.C. and Higinbotham, C.Q.: Precursors of hypertension and coronary disease among healthy medical students: Discriminant function analysis. I. Using smoking habits as the criterion. *Bull Hopkins Hosp, 115*:174, 1964.

39. Thomas, C.B. and Ross, D.C.: Observations on some possible precursors of essential hypertension and coronary artery disease. VIII. Relationship of cholesterol level to certain habit patterns under stress. *Bull Hopkins Hosp, 113*:225, 1963.

40. Klineberg, O.: Emotional expression in Chinese literature. *J. Abnorm Soc Psychol, 33*:517, 1938.

41. Keys, A., Fidanza, F., Scardi, V., Bergami, G., Keys, M.H. and Di Lorenzo, F.: Studies on serum cholesterol and other characteristics of clinically healthy men in Naples. *A.M.A. Arch Intern Med, 93*:328, 1954.

42. Keys, A., Vivanco, F., Minon, J.L.R., Keys, M.H. and Mendoza, H.C.: Studies on the diet, body fatness and serum cholesterol in Madrid, Spain. *Metabolism, 3*:195, 1954.

43. Gordon, H.: The regulation of serum-cholesterol level. *Postgrad Med. J, 35*:186, 1959.

44. Adamson, L.F.: Serum cholesterol concentrations of various ethnic groups in Hawaii. *J Nutr, 71*:27, 1960.

45. Stout, C., Morrow, J., Brandt, E.N. Jr. and Wolf, S.: Unusually low incidence of death from myocardial infarction. *JAMA, 188*:845, 1964.

46. Dawber, T.R., Moore, F.E. and Mann, G.V.: II. Coronary heart disease in The Framingham Study. *Am J Public Health, 47*: (no. 4), Part 2,4, 1957.

47. Deming, Q.B., Hodes, M.E., Baltazar, A., Edreira, J.G. and Torosdag, S.: The changes in concentration of cholesterol in the serum of hypertensive patients during antihypertensive therapy. *Am J Med, 24*:882, 1958.

48. Epstein, F.H., Boas, E.P. and Simpson, R.: The epidemiology of atherosclerosis among a random sample of clothing workers of different ethnic origins in New York City: I. Prevalence of atherosclerosis and some associated characteristics. *J Chronic Dis, 5*:300, 1957.

49. Wardwell, W.I., Hyman, M. and Bahnson, C.M.: Stress and coronary heart disease in three field studies. *J Chronic Dis, 17*:73, 1964.

Chapter 24

BUERGER'S DISEASE IN ISRAEL

R. M. GOODMAN, B. ELIAN, M. MOZES, AND V. DEUTSCH

Buerger in 1908 described inflammatory and occlusive changes in arteries and veins of amputated lower extremities and referred to the process responsible for these findings as thrombo-angiitis obliterans (TAO).[1] Before Buerger's description of the disorder that bears his name, von Winiwarter in 1879 had described similar occlusive changes in peripheral arteries and termed this process endoarteritis obliterans.[2]

TAO (Buerger's disease) is a peripheral vascular disease characterized by its predominant appearance in men before the age of 40 years. Most of the patients are heavy smokers and frequently have one or more episodes of migrating thrombophlebitis during the course of the disease. Symptoms of ischemia usually begin in the lower extremities but with progression of the disease may involve the upper extremities.

This disease was initially thought to occur primarily in Jews,[3] a concept fostered by the setting in which Buerger performed his studies, namely, a hospital serving a predominantly Jewish segment of the population in New York City. Further investigations have shown that Buerger's disease is not restricted to Jews, for it has been described in many ethnic groups throughout the world.[4-7]

In referring back to Buerger's description of this disease in Jewish men, it is found that his patients belong to a specific ethnic group[3] whose origin stemmed from Eastern Europe; Jews

Edited version reprinted with permission from *Am J Med*, 39: (no 4) October, 1965.

This study was supported by Research Grant M-25-2646.08 from The Council for Tobacco Research Industries of the United States of America and an Advanced Research Fellowship from the American Heart Association.

217

from this region are referred to as Ashkenazim. One purpose of the present investigation was to determine the frequency of this disorder among the various Jewish ethnic groups in Israel. Is Buerger's disease a disease of the Ashkenazim, or is it found in equal proportion among the other groups?

MATERIAL AND METHODS

Most of this study was carried out at Tel Hashomer Hospital near Tel Aviv, in the most heavily populated part of Israel, where approximately 60 percent of the country's population lives. This hospital is one of the largest (880 beds) in Israel and admits a population which is almost half Ashkenazim and half non-Ashkenazim,[8] corresponding approximately to the proportions of these groups in the country as a whole. In addition to this, peripheral vascular cases are referred to the Department of Vascular Surgery from all parts of the country.

Records from 1956 to mid-1963 on patients with Buerger's disease seen in Tel Hashomer Hospital were reviewed and a total of 82 cases were noted. Of the 82 patients, 60 responded to an invitation for evaluation of their status in the out-patient department. During the year 1963 to 1964, nine new cases of Buerger's disease were found and, in addition, ten patients were studied at Rambam Hospital in Haifa and one patient was studied at Assaf Harofeh Hospital near Tel Aviv, completing the total of 80 cases included in this study. Forty-nine of the 60 patients seen in the clinic were admitted to the hospital for further evaluation.

An extensive questionnaire was completed on all patients which included, in addition to the routine history and related peripheral vascular questions, a complete history in reference to family and smoking.

Physical examination stressed the peripheral vascular system, and the palpability of the following pulses were recorded in each case: temporal, carotid, brachial, antecubital, radial, ulnar, abdominal aorta, femoral, popliteal, posterior tibial and dorsalis pedis. Oscillometric studies were recorded in the calf, thigh and forearm regions, and the Allen test[9] was also used to evaluate the radial and ulnar arteries.

The following laboratory procedures were performed on all hospitalized patients and, when possible, on those seen as outpatients: hemogram, urinalysis, fasting blood sugar, cholesterol,[10] blood urea nitrogen, serum protein electrophoresis, latex fixation, cold agglutinins cryogobulin, serological reactions, blood culture and electrocardiogram.

Brachial arteriograms were obtained in most hospitalized patients and in selected outpatients. Femoral arteriograms were obtained only in selected hospitalized patients.

Three patients underwent biopsy of a superficial vein in the lower extremity during a bout of migrating thrombophlebitis. Further examination of histopathologic tissues came from a review of material resulting from previous amputations or biopsies.

For purposes of comparing primarily peripheral pulses, fasting serum cholesterol, latex fixation and smoking histories, each patient with Buerger's disease, with the exceptions of one Arab and two Jewish women, was matched for age and ethnic origin. These control patients were selected mainly from surgical wards where, for the most part, they were to undergo minor surgical procedures for hemorrhoids, hernias and the like. No patient in the control group had a history of perpheral vascular disease, myocardial infarction, diabetes mellitus, liver disease, hyperthyroidism, rheumatoid arthritis or positive serological tests for syphilis.

Comparative studies were made also on a group of 43 randomly selected patients with arteriosclerosis obliterans (ASO). These patients underwent the same examinations, with the exception of an electrocardiogram, as the patients with Buerger's disease. In a few selected cases, brachial arteriograms were performed.

For every patient 40 years or older with Buerger's disease who had an electrocardiogram, three control electrocardiograms were selected at random and matched for age and ethnic origin. Electrocardiograms used for these control studies had been taken previously in a larger group of civil service employees being screened for cardiac disease.

Although this study is based on 80 cases, most of the observations requiring subject response are based on 79 caes, since one patient who had the classic findings of Buerger's disease was unable to give a reliable history because of a language barrier.

Sixty-three of the 79 Jewish patients (80 percent) were Ashkenazim. This is a significant finding since, if a random distribution of Buerger's disease is assumed among the main Jewish groups, only 41 Ashkenazim would be expected in this material of 79 cases ($X^2=37.47$; $P<0001$). As for the various non-Ashkenazim groups, we have no exact data on their distribution in the population studied and the number of cases of Buerger's disease among them is small. The fact that no Yemenites were observed with this disease may be significant, since the Yemenites in Israel number some 80,000 (about 4 percent of the Jewish population in Israel).

Of the 63 Ashkenazim who make up the bulk of cases, 37, or 59 percent, were born in Poland, as were their parents. In the control group matched for age and ethnic origin (not country) 29, or 36 percent, were from Poland. The exact location of family residency was determined in each patient with Buerger's disease who came from Poland; no clustering of cases in a definite area could be established other than the fact that most of these patients came from Eastern Poland.

COMMENTS

This investigation was designed to study as many patients with Buerger's disease as were available in the most representative section of Israel. The results clearly indicate that, among Jews with Buerger's disease, the Ashkenazim are most frequently afflicted. This grouping is not surprising in view of the selective occurrence of many other traits among Jewish groups;[11] however, no definitive explanation for this segregation can be offered at present. That Buerger had made this same observation originally is usually ascribed to the fact that Jewish migration to the United States at that time was mainly from Eastern Europe. Whether predisposing factors such as exposure to cold, trauma and stress in general have been more common in the Ashkenazim, and thus have served to initiate the disease process in a more susceptible group, can be no more than an interesting speculation for the present.

The question whether this disease is more common in Ashkenazic Jews than in non-Jews cannot be answered fully, since we could not arrive at a satisfactory estimate of the incidence of the disease among Ashkenazim. A minimum estimate based on demographic data is an incidence of 1:5,000 for Ashkenazic men above the age of 25 years.[12] This estimate is far greater than the general incidence suggested by DeBakey and Cohen, who wrote, "that for all white males in the population in the age range 25 to 44, the true incidence of Buerger's disease is of the order of seven or eight per 100,000 per year."[13] In this follow-up study of Buerger's disease among World War II army men, DeBakey and Cohen found a disproportionately larger number of Jews with the disease.

In reviewing the recent literature on Buerger's disease, the number of publications appearing in the Polish and Russian literature is impressive. This only adds to the confusion since there are very few Jews living in Poland today (estimated 30,000) as compared to the estimated 2,385,000 living in Russia, comprising the second largest Jewish community in the world.[14] Although opinions vary as to the frequency of this disease in Jews and non-Jews,[15,16] our study would tend to support the concept that this disorder is more common in Jews.

Since the original description of Buerger's disease, it has been observed that it is almost invariably men who are afflicted with the disease. The observation of this disorder in women has served as a stimulus for scattered case reports.[17-20] The incidence of Buerger' disease in women has been estimated to be from 1 to as high as 10 percent.[15] In our study, two women had the disease.

Despite the difficulties in attempting to determine the frequency of Buerger's disease, most clinicians in the United States agree that they are seeing fewer cases than in the past. Whether this stems from a diagnostic problem or one of actual decline is not known presently. This decline in number of cases has not occurred in Israel to the degree observed in the United States, although the frequent surgical problems and procedures common to these patients has tended to shift these cases from the medical to the surgical services.

In the past, much effort has been devoted to factors which

might predispose a person to this disease. No occupation has been implicated[15] and our studies would tend to confirm this view. Patients with this disease have been known to be heavy cigarette smokers and detailed information regarding smoking habits was sought from subjects in all groups studied. Although one of the 80 patients with Buerger's disease in our group had never smoked, and two patients stated they began smoking after the onset of symptoms, the majority were heavy cigarette smokers in comparison to a control group without vascular disease. When quantities of cigarettes smoked per day was compared in patients with Buerger's disease and patients with arteriosclerosis obliterans, the average amounts were similar.

There is good evidence to suggest that cigarette smoking in general is not beneficial to various forms of vascular disease, and our studies tend to confirm the widely held concept that if these patients cease smoking completely, their disease, in most cases, may reach a plateau, and in some, improvement may be noted. It is important to point out that beneficial results from cessation of smoking often cannot be expected in late stages of the disease, hence smoking should be stopped early in the course of the disease.

The observation that Raynaud's phenomenon occurred in 57 percent of the cases of Buerger's disease suggests that exposure to cold and frostbite can be both an aggravating and an initiating factor in promoting vascular insufficiency. The further observation that 34 percent of the patients experienced hyperhidrosis of hands and feet, in addition to Raynaud's phenomenon, implies that these patients may have an overactive sympathetic nervous system.

It is known that Buerger's disease affects the peripheral vessels in the upper extremities.[21] McKusick and Harris,[4] in their study of Koreans with Buerger's disease, observed that the upper extremity was involved in 17 of 28 patients. The 74 percent incidence of upper extremity involvement in our cases is higher than has been stated in the literature previously. (This high incidence is not considered exceptional in this study, but merely a reflection of our prime concern to determine its frequency.) Further information regarding arterial occlusive lesions in the upper limbs came from our brachial arteriographic studies, indicating that the digital arteries were the most commonly occluded vessels, as anticipated, and that the ulnar artery seems to be the second most common site of arterial occlusion in the upper limbs in Buerger's disease. Brachial arteriographic studies in other diseases involving arteries in the forearm have suggested that there may be selective sites of arterial occlusion with differentiating patterns.[22,23]

Although 5 percent of the patients with Buerger's disease had their initial symptoms in the hands, involvement of the upper limbs is usually a later finding and should be thought of as a frequent occurrence with progression of the disease. In severe cases of the disease, the upper extremities are almost always involved. The marked difference in the number of patients with arteriosclerosis obliterans with upper limb disease (5 percent) is in sharp contrast.

The question whether Buerger's disease involves parts of the vascular system other than the peripheral vasculature of the extremities is an interesting one. Our findings of a higher frequency of myocardial infarction in cases of Buerger's disease is in agreement with the concept that these patients may be more prone to coronary artery disease.[36] Histopathologic sections of the coronary artery from patients with Buerger's disease have been reported to show changes compatible with the characteristics of Buerger's disease[25,26], but this is exceptional since most will show the changes of artherosclerosis. Other visceral vessels[25,27] and the cerebral arteries[28-30] have been reported to show changes of Buerger's disease, but most investigators do not consider thromboangiitis obliterans to be a generalized vascular disease.[29] For some unknown reason, it appears that the patient with Buerger's disease is more prone to atherosclerosis.

Our histopathologic studies were confined to extremities and in one case an ulnar artery biopsy demonstrated the occlusive process to be compatible with Buerger's disease. The difficulty in obtaining pathologic material from such patients in the early stages is well known[7] and this, together with the fact that late vascular findings are often indistinguishable from arteriosclerosis obliterans, has led some to the conclusion that there is no such entity as Buerger's disease.[31,32] Some of the histopathologic features observed in Buerger's disease, involving the peripheral venous as well as arterial system are described herein. The venous lesion of migrating thrombophlebitis occurred in 53 percent of our cases of Buerger's disease, but was not observed or known to exist in any of the cases of arteriosclerosis obliterans.

Laboratory studies showed the serum cholesterol level in patients with Buerger's disease to be within the normal range when compared to a control group without vascular disease matched for age and ethnic group. Serum cholesterol levels tended to be higher in the group of patients with arteriosclerosis obliterans. Similar observations were made also by McKusick and Harris in their Korean study.[4] Other laboratory studies, with the exception of the serum latex fixation test, failed to reveal any significant abnormality. The finding of a positive latex fixation test in 17 percent of the patients with Buerger's disease, as opposed to only 3.5 percent in the control group, was a difference significant at the 5 percent level. Singer,[33] in his review of latex fixation tests, states that a positive reaction occurs at random without known cause in 1.5 percent of a hospital population.

There have been scattered reports in the literature of familial occurrences of Buerger's disease[34-38] and in a recent study of 18 cases in the Orient two brothers were noted to have the disease.[4] Four families had Buerger's disease in the group of 80 cases we studied. The possible genetic implications are intriguing and this aspect must be evaluated further.

SUMMARY AND CONCLUSIONS

Eighty cases (78 men and two women) of Buerger's disease were studied among the various ethnic groups in Israel. Of the 79 cases in Jews, 80 percent occurred in the Ashkenazic group; the higher prevalence among the Ashkenazim is statistically significant. A control group of patients without peripheral vascular disease matched for age and ethnic origin and a group of 43 cases of arteriosclerosis obliterans were also studied.

The mean age of onset of disease in cases of Buerger's disease was approximately 30 years, as compared to 47 years in cases of arteriosclerosis obliterans. Patients with Buerger's disease in general are heavy cigarette smokers when compared to those without peripheral vascular disease, but smoke approximately the same amount as patients with arteriosclerosis obliterans.

Symptoms of arterial insufficiency or migrating thrombophlebitis in patients with Buerger's disease usually begin in one extremity and, with progression of the disease, may ultimately involve all four extremities. One or more episodes of migrating thrombophlebitis occurred in 56 percent of the cases of Buerger's disease, but not in any case of arteriosclerosis obliterans. Upper extremity involvement in Buerger's disease was observed in 74 percent of the cases as compared to 5 percent of the cases of arteriosclerosis obliterans. Brachial arteriographic studies in 34 cases of Buerger's disease involving the upper extremity revealed occlusive changes most commonly in the digital arteries followed by those in the ulnar artery.

Serum cholesterol levels were within normal limits in patients with Buerger's disease and in control patients without peripheral vascular disease, but elevated in those with arteriosclerosis obliterans. Myocardial infarction, cardiac arrythmias and conduction disturbances occurred more frequently in patients with Buerger's disease than in a control group. Of the patients with Buerger's disease 17 percent had a positive latex fixation test as compared to 3.5 percent in a control group without peripheral vascular disease.

Histopathologic changes in cases of Buerger's disease showed characteristic features in both arteries and veins.

Familial aggregation in Buerger's disease was observed in four families and the role of a possible genetic factor is suggested.

These observations therefore lead us to conclude that Buerger's disease has many distinguishing characteristics and, in Jews, it occurs most commonly in the Ashkenazim. Although the etiology of this disorder still remains to be clarified, observations regarding familial aggregation and positive serum latex tests may be helpful in further delineating the basic alteration in this disease.

ACKNOWLEDGMENT

We would like to express our thanks to the following individuals who contributed so much to this study: From Tel Hashomer

Hospital to Dr. A. Adam for statistical evaluation, Professor M. Wolman for help with the histopathology, Dr. H. Neufeld for electrocardiographic interpretations, Mr. G. Altman, Mr. I. Greenfeld and Dr. B. Bogokovsky for latex fixation studies, Dr. A. Szeinberg, Mrs. G. Taubman and Mrs. B. Rosenbaum for biochemical determinations, Dr. B. Ramot for starch gel electrophoresis and lupus erythematosus preparations, Dr. R. Adar whose early assistance aided in reviewing the medical records of cases of Buerger's disease, Dr. Y. Kalter for help in identifying various cities in Poland, to Mr. J. Eidau for medical photography, to the technicians of the x-ray department for their help with the brachial arteriograms, to the nurses of Ward 12 for aiding in the care of the patients, to Mrs. A. Goodman and Mrs. R. Ravinsky for typing many early drafts of the manuscript and to Dr. H. Heller and Dr. C. Sheba for their willingness to provide many of the things that made this study possible.

To Dr. D. Ehrlich at Rambam Hospital in Haifa, who kindly made available for study his patients with Buerger's disease and to Dr. Griffel who aided in the interpretation of the histopathology. To Dr. M. Hebner from Assaf Harofeh Hospital, who made his patients available for study and to Dr. A. Rief who aided in the review of the histopathology.

To Professor A. Albertini from the University of Zurich for his helpful comments and suggestions. To Dr. V.A. McKusick from Baltimore, Maryland, who provided inspiration and guidance during this study. To Drs. J.V. Warren and W. Harris from Columbus, Ohio, for their critical evaluation of the manuscript and to Mrs. J. Muter and Mrs. A. Defenbaugh for grammatical review and to Mrs. J. Zeidman for typing the final manuscript.

REFERENCES

1. Buerger, L.: Thrombo-angiitis obliterans: study of vascular lesions leading to presenile gangrene. *Am J M Sci,* 136:567, 1908.
2. V. Winiwarter, F.: Ueber ein eigentuemliche Form von Endarteriitis und Endophlebitis mit Gangrän des Fusses. *Arch klin Chir,* 23:202, 1879.
3. Buerger, L.: *The Circulatory Disturbances of the Extremities: Including Gangrene, Vasomotor and Trophic Disorders.* Philadelphia, W.B. Saunders Co., 1924, p. 277.

4. McKusick, V.A. and Harris, W.S.: The Buerger syndrome in the Orient. *Bull Johns Hopkins Hosp, 109:*241, 1961.

5. Ishikawa, K., Kawase, S. and Mishima, Y.: Occlusive arterial disease in extremities with special reference to Buerger's disease. *Angiology, 13:*398, 1962.

6. Noble, T.P.: Thromboangiitis obliterans in Siam. *Lancet, 1:*288, 1931.

7. McKusick, V.A., Harris, W.S., Otteson, O.E., Goodman, R.M., Shelley, W.M. and Bloodwell, R.D.: Buerger's disease: a distinct clinical and pathologic entity. *JAMA, 181:*5, 1962.

8. Tel Hashomer Hospital Statistical Records, p. 34, 1956; p. 9, 1957; p. 10, 1958, p. 7, 1959; p. 10, 1960; p. 13, 1961; p. 6, 1962. Government Printing Press, Israel.

9. Allen, E.V.: Thromboangiitis obliterans. Methods of diagnosis of chronic occlusive arterial leisons distal to the wrist. *Am J M Sc, 178:*237, 1929.

10. Van Boetzlaer, G. L. and Zondag, H.A.: A rapid modification of the Pearson reaction for total serum cholesterol. *Clin chim acta, 5:*943, 1960.

11. Sheba, C., Szeinberg, A., Ramot, B., Adam, A. and Ashkenazi, I.: Epidemiologic surveys of deleterious genes in different population groups in Israel. *Am J Pub Health, 52:*1101, 1962.

12. Statistical Abstracts 1963 (Yearly Publication), Israel, 1963, p. 23. Government Printing Press. Central Bureau of Statistics, Jerusalem, Israel.

13. DeBakey, M.E. and Cohen, B.M.: *Buerger's Disease. A Follow-up Study of World War II Army Cases.* Springfield, Thomas, 1963, p. 21.

14. Fine, M. and Himmelfarb, M. (Ed.): American Jewish Yearbook 1963, pp. 350, 360. Philadelphia, 1963. Jewish Publication Society of America.

15. Allen, E.V., Barker, N.W. and Hines, Jr., E.A.: *Peripheral Vascular Diseases, 3rd ed.* Philadelphia, W.B. Saunders Co., 1962, p. 355.

16. McPherson, J.R., Juergens, J.L. and Gifford Jr., R.W.: Thromboangiitis obliterans and arteriosclerosis obliterans, clinical and prognostic differences. *Ann Int Med, 59:*288, 1963.

17. Atlas, L. N.: Case of Buerger's disease in an old woman. *AM Heart J, 26:*120, 1943.

18. Lefevre, F.A. and Burns, J.: Thromboangiitis obliterans in women: report of two cases. *Cleveland Clin, 11:*49, 1944.

19. Kaiser, G.C., Musser, A.W. and Shumacker, Jr., H.B.: Thromboangiitis obliterans in women; report of two cases. *Surgery, 48:*733, 1960.

20. Montorsi, W. and Ghiringhelli, C.: A case of Buerger's disease in women. *Angiology, 12:*376, 1961.

21. Allen, E.V., Barker, N.W. and Hines Jr., E.A.: *op. cit.* p. 371.

22. Goodman, R.M. Unpublished observations.

23. Goodman, R.M., Smith, E.W., Paton, D., Bergman, R.A., Siegel, C.I., Ottesen, O.E., Shelley, W.M., Pusch, A.L. and McKusick, V.A.: Pseu-

doxanthoma elasticum: a clinical and histopathological study. *Medicine,* 42:297, 1963.

24. Allen, E.V, Barker, N.W. and Hines, Jr., E.A.: *op. cit.* p. 379.

25. Hausner, E. and Allen, E.V.: Vascular clinics VIII. Generalized arterial involvement in thromboangiitis obliterans including report of a case of thromboangiitis obliterans of a pulmonary artery. *Proc Staff Meet Mayo Clin, 15:7,* 1940.

26. Albertini, V.A.: Nochmals zur Pathogenese des Coronärsklerose. *Cardiologia, 7:233,* 1943.

27. Nesbit, R.M. and Hodgson, N.B.: Thromboangiitis obliterans of spermatic cord. *J Urol, 83:455,* 1960.

28. Hausner, E. and Allen, E.V.: Cerebrovascular complications in thromboangiitis obliterans. *Ann Int Med, 12:845,* 1938.

29. Scheinker, I.M.: Cerebral thromboangiitis obliterans. *Arch. Neurol. & Psychiat., 52:27,* 1944.

30. Davis, L. and Perret, G.: Cerebral thromboangiitis obliterans. *Bri J Surg, 34:307,* 1946.

31. Fisher, C.M.: Cerebral thromboangiitis obliterans. *Medicine, 36:* 169, 1957.

32. Wessler, S., Ming, S., Gurewich, V. and Freiman, D.A.: A critical evaluation of thromboangiitis obliterans. The case against Buerger's disease. *N Eng J Med, 262:1149,* 1960.

33. Singer, J.M.: The latex fixation test in rheumatic diseases. A review. *Am J Med, 31:766,* 1961.

34. Biddlestone, W.R. and Lefevre, F.A.: Thromboangiitis obliterans: occurrence in brother and a sister. *Cleveland Clin Q 21:226,* 1954.

35. Martorell, F.: Thromboangiitis obliterans in two brothers. *Angiology,* 3:271, 1952.

36. Weber, F.P.: Thromboangiitis obliterans in father and son. *Lancet,* 2:72, 1937.

37. Wilensky, N.D. and Collens, W.S.: Thromboangiitis obliterations in sisters. *JAMA, 110:1746,* 1938.

38. Samuels, S. S.: The incidence of thromboangiitis obliterans in brothers. *Am J M Sci, 183:465,* 1932.

Chapter 25

PREVALENCE OF DIABETES AMONG DIFFERENT ETHNIC JEWISH GROUPS IN ISRAEL

A. M. COHEN

Diabetes is considered a disease with an inherited predisposition.[1-4] It is accepted in the literature that the Jewish race is especially disposed towards this disease,[5,7] although no definite figures are given. Our clinical experience in Israel denies this assumption.[8-10] In order to receive a definite answer, we examined the prevalence of diabetes among the Jews in Israel by a community survey. The Jewish race, however, is not a homologous group in the purely "biologic" sense. Although they have preserved their racial type, being widely spread over the globe, each group was affected by hereditary influences on the one hand, and by environment on the other. Considering the history of immigration of Jews from their homeland, and what is known about their movement as a community from country to country, we divided the Jewish population in Israel according to the country of origin into four ethnic groups. The following division is undoubtedly arbitrary, yet each group has many common physical traits and specific modes and habits of life:

Reprinted in edited version, with permission from Metabolism, Clinical and Experimental, Editor-in-Chief, G.E. Duncan, Volume X, No. 1, January 1961, Henry M. Stratton, Inc., Publisher.

Aided by a grant from the Florina Lasker Fund for the Study of Man.

My thanks are due to Dr. G. Kallner of the Central Bureau of Statistics for her guidance in the planning of the survey, and to Mr. E. Peretz of the Statistical Department of the Hebrew University for his collaboration and preparation of the statistical material, to Mrs. Daskel of the Settlement Department of the Jewish Agency, and the Social Workers in the Settlements where the survey was performed, and to Mrs. Sternberg and the Nurses of the Social Services of the Hadassah Medical Organization for the help in this survey.

Group 1, the so-called "Sephardi," includes all those whose country of origin is in the Mediterranean Basin and the Middle East: Spain, Italy, Yugoslavia, Greece, Bulgaria, Turkey, Israel, Syria, Lebanon, Afghanistan, Egypt, Sudan, Tripoli, Algeria, Tunis, Morocco, Persia and Arabia.

The *second group,* the "Ashkenazi," includes Central, Eastern and Western Europe, the United Kingdom, the United States, Canada, South America, South Africa, Australia and New Zealand.

The *third group,* the "Yemenites," comprises the Jews coming from Yemen. The Yemenite group was taken as a separate category and not included among the Sephardis, since they represent one unit with "definite" physical features and a special way of life.

The *fourth group,* the "Kurds," were also grouped in a special category since they, too, show significant differences in their physical features and mode of life.

Since in the last two groups significant differences were found in the prevalence of diabetes among the new immigrants and the old settlers (who have been living in Israel over 30 years) and their descendants, the two latter groups were each subdivided into newcomers, i.e., those who had immigrated during the last 10 years, and old settlers, i.e. those living in the country over 25 years or who were born in Israel.

METHODS

The study was conducted during the years 1958–1959, and comprises 15,958 persons—7,881 males and 8,080 females (Table 25-I). It was made in several quarters of Jerusalem, and 23 settlements in the Jerusalem corridor as well as the Ramle and Nathanya districts. House to house preliminary registration of all the inhabitants in the settlement or quarter to be examined were carried out, recording age, sex and country of origin of the father or grandfather. Where registration was complete, labeled test tubes for each member of the family were distributed in the evening, and next morning the postprandial urine was collected and tested immediately by glucose reductase (Tes-

TABLE 25–I
NUMBER OF PERSONS IN THE DIFFERENT ETHNIC GROUPS
TESTED FOR DIABETES

	Total	M	F
Sephardi	4156	2123	2033
Ashkenazi	4344	2065	2279
Yemenite new comers	4906	2463	2443
Yemenite old settlers	751	325	426
Kurds new comers	988	505	483
Kurds old settlers	598	288	310
Kuchins*	215	111	104
Total	15958	7880	8078

* Jews from India (Eds).

Tape Lilly Co.). Ninety to 93 percent of the inhabitants of the area or settlements were examined. The rest were not examined owing to stay in hospital or military service, while a few refused to be examined for social or religious reasons. In cases with positive urine test, a blood sugar, and where necessary, glucose tolerance test was performed. Cases having glycosuria and fasting blood glucose higher than 120 mg percent were considered diabetics.

In each of these ethnic groups, males and females were grouped separately and subdivided into five age groups: 3–19 years, 20–39 years, 40–49 years, 50–59 years, and 60 years and above. The percentage of each age group was calculated and compared with official statistics for the year 1957 in the Israel population according to country of origin and age group.

The following differences are to be considered in comparing the age groups of our material with those of the official statistics:

1. The classification of the ethnic groups of the official statistics is based on the country of birth of the person, while our classification is based on the community and the country of origin of the person's father or grandfather. As a result, the age group 3–19 years cannot be compared, since in the official statistics a considerable number of these children are included under the group "Israel born" and not among the community concerned. For this reason the comparison in the tables was made for the adult population (20 years and on) only. This population was considered for the percentage purpose of comparison as 100 percent.

2. In the official statistics there is no classification as to the year of immigration. Considering the fact that the majority of the Yemenites in Israel are composed of new immigrants, we allowed ourselves to compare the age groups of "new immigrants" in our material with these of the "Yemenites" of the official statistics (which includes both "new" and "old" immigrants).

3. In the official statistics there is no data as to the Kurdish community. We could not, therefore, make comparisons of the age groups of this community in our material with the official statistics. The same holds true for Yemenite "old settlers."

RESULTS

Among the Sephardi group, the prevalence of diabetes is 1.0 percent (0.8 percent in males and 1.1 percent in females). In the Ashkenazi group the percentage is 2.5 percent (1.7 percent among males and 3.0 percent among females). The difference between the Sephardi and Ashkenazi group is not statistically significant for males, but significant for females.

Among the Yemenite newcomers to the country, the prevalence of diabetes was extremely low: 0.06 percent (0.12 percent in males and zero in females). The same low incidence of diabetes was noted in the Kurdish newcomers, though we did not examine as many cases of these as of Yemenite newcomers. A very distinct difference in the prevalence of diabetes, of statistical significance, is noted in both Kurds and Yemenites between the newcomers and old settlers. In the old settlers the prevalence of diabetes is in the Yemenites 2.9 percent—of the same order of size as in the Ashkenazi group, and among the "Kurds old settled" 2.0 percent. Among 215 Kuchins we found 1 case of diabetes (male); due to the small number examined, no definite conclusion on the prevalence of the disease in this community is drawn.

The age composition of the adult population of each group tested approximately resembles that of the total population in Israel. This is especially true for the older age groups, from 50 years and above. In the age group 20–50 years, there is an internal change in distribution, but if this group is taken as a whole and not subdivided (into two subdivisions) then the percentage is likewise very close.

Diabetes was more prevalent among females in all age groups —by +23 percent among those under 50 years of age and by +44 percent among those of 50 years and above. The difference was more pronounced in the Ashkenazi than in the Sephardi group.

Among the Yemenite old settlers the prevalence of diabetes was 2 to 3 times higher among the males than the females. A possible explanation may lie in the mode of life of this community, where the husband maintians the central position in the family, which is reflected even in the amount of food served to the husband, who is entitled to the main portion, causing possibly obesity and thus predisposition to diabetes. However, this is under study and will be reported later.

COMMENT

This study demonstrates that the prevalence of diabetes among Jews in Israel in general, and even among each of the different ethnic groups separately, is not higher than that found in various surveys conducted by the same method among non-Jews in different parts of the world, Eskimos excluded, which varies between 0.7 to 3.2 percent. The groups tested in the present survey are representative, in age group partition, of the total number of their group in the country. Furthermore, the percentage of the age groups from 40 years on in the "Sephardi" and "Ashkenazi" which compose the main population in Israel in our study, is close to the Oxford group examined by Wilkerson.[11] Thus our yardstick is adequate for comparing the prevalence of diabetes in our groups with that found among non-Jews abroad.[11-18]

This finding repudiates the statement accepted in the literature that diabetes is more common among the Jewish race.[5-7] Although there are no definite figures in the literature on the prevalence of diabetes among Jews, there is a definite statement that diabetes is more common among Jews than among non-Jews, based on the following data:

1. Statistical clinical data obtained from clinics of famous

specialists in diabetes, according to which the percentage of Jewish diabetic patients visiting these clinics is high and out of proportion to the number of the Jewish population in the area, or that the morbidity of diabetes among patients visiting a certain clinic is higher among Jews than among non-Jews.[1,5-7,19,20,21] The conclusion has thus been reached that the disease is more common among Jews than among non-Jews.

Since these figures are not based on the ratio of the number of diabetes cases to the number of Jews in the country or area from where they come, they do not represent the *real* prevalence of diabetes in the Jewish community, but only the inclination or the possibility of this group, economic or other, to visit a certain physician or clinic.

2. Positive family histories of diabetes[3,21]—i.e. more cases of diabetes are recorded in the families of Jewish diabetics than in those of non-Jews: for Jewish males 30.3 percent, and 23 percent for all males; for Jewish females 29.1 percent, compared to 26.5 percent for all females.[3]

These figures, too, cannot be significant as to the prevalence of diabetes among the community in general but for the patients' families only.

3. Mortality statistics—from the death registers it was found that registered death from diabetes is higher among Jews than among non-Jews.[22-26]

These figures again cannot be relied on regarding the prevalance of diabetes among the Jewish population since they are based on death certificates only, which in many instances do not include the entire diagnosis of the deceased, especially if the diabetes is mild or the disease is not discovered and remains unknown to the patient.[11,16] Furthermore, they do not compare the age groups of the deceased with these of the general population concerned, which is of paramount importance, since death from this disease generally occurs in the higher age groups.

The prevalence of diabetes among children in Israel among the Ashkenazi and the Sephardi groups, even if the Yemenite group, where diabetes is rare, is excluded, is not higher than that reported by Ruth Weaver[27] in a survey of 818,500 pupils in the Philadelphia Public School System during 1952–53, which is one diabetic to 1,600 pupils.

Joslin[6] is emphatic that "a Jew becomes diabetic not in virtue of his race" and he continues that "if the Jewish race were specially disposed to diabetes it should occur early in life, but the Jewish child is not more prone than the young gentile to diabetes." To this we can add that neither are the adults, at least in Israel. Whether our figures are representative for Jews in Israel only or can be held true for the diaspora as well, must be ascertained by similar surveys in the diaspora.

The Yemenites and Kurds who came to Israel recently show a very low incidence of diabetes, as low as among the Eskimos.[12] These groups, though extremely different in physical appearance, have a similar history of being isolated as a community, due to the geographical situation, and had little or no contact with other Jewish communities or with the Western mode of life and food habits. Both communities, on settling for a period of 25 years or over in a place governed by Western habits, show a very steep rise in the prevalence of diabetes. A similar change in the prevalence of diabetes was noted among the Eskimos,[12] where the disease was extremely rare until recently, when Western habits of life and food were acquired. The variance in prevalence of diabetes among different Jewish ethnic groups and the change in prevalence of diabetes in the same group as a result of a change in the environmental conditions stresses again the great effect of environment on the manifestation of this disease.

REFERENCES

1. Naunyn, B.: *Der Diabetes Mellitus.* Wein, Alfred Holder, 1906, p. 37.

2. Bauer, E., Fisher, E., and Lenz, F.: *Human Heredity.* New York, The MacMillan Co., 1931.

3. Pincus, G., and White, P.: On the inheritance of diabetes mellitus. *Am J Med Sci, 1:*186, 1933.

4. Cammidge, P.J.: Heredity as a factor in the etiology of diabetes mellitus. *Lancet, 1:*393, 1934.

5. Von Noordem, C.: *Zuckerkrankheirt und Ihre Behandlung,* ed. 6. Berlin, 1912, p. 54.

6. Joslin, E.P.: The diabetic problem of today. *JAMA,* 83:727, 1924.

7. Duncan, G.G.: *Diseases of Metabolism,* ed. 3. Philadelphia, W.B. Saunders, p. 789.

8. Zaide, J.: The incidence of diabetes mellitus in our population. *Dapim Refuiim, 10:*232, 1951.

9. Sukenik, S.: The incidence of diabetes among Kupat Holim members in Tel Aviv area. *Dapim Refuiim, 12:*151, 1953.

10. Steinitz, H.: The incidence of diabetes in Israel. *Harefuah, 50:*106, 1956.

11. Wilkerson, H.L.C., and Krall, L.P.: Diabetes in a New England town, a study of 3,516 persons in Oxford, Mass. *JAMA, 135:*209, 1947.

12. Albertson, V.: Diabetes in Iceland. *Diabetes, 2:*184, 1953.

13. Schliack, V.: Diabetesprobleme Untersuchungen über die Haüftigkeit, den Altersufban, das Manifestationsalter und Manifestationsbedingungen des Diabetes Mellitus. *Dtschr med Wchnschr, 79:*855, 1954.

14. Wright, H.B., and Taylor, B.: The incidence of diabetes in a sample of the adult population in South Trinidad. *West Indian Med J 7:*123, 1948.

15. Lawrence, R.D.: Foreign letters. *JAMA, 152:*624, 1953.

16. Kenny, A.J., and Chute, A.L.: Diabetes in two Ontario communities. *Diabetes, 2:*187, 1953.

17. Tulloch, J.A., and Johnson, H.M.: Pilot survey of the incidence of diabetes in Jamaica. *West Indian Med J 7:*134, 1958.

18. Greenberg, M., and Wasserstorm, S. S.: A pilot project for control of diabetes in New York City Health Department. *N Y State J Med, 2:*3308, 1956.

19. Frerichs: *Uber den Diabetes.* Berlin, 1884, p. 185.

20. Kulz: *Klinische Efrahrungen uber Diabetes Mellitus.* Jena, 1899, p. 2.

21. Joslin, E.P., Dublin, L. I., and Marks, H.H.: Studies in diabetes mellitus. *Am J Med Sci, 192:*1, 1936; *193:*8, 1937.

22. Heimann, G.: Zur Verbeitung der Zuckerkrankheit in preussischen Staate. *Dtschr med Wchnschr, 2:*505, 1900.

23. Benedict, J., and St. Kemény, S.: Ein Beitrag zur sozialen Pathologie des Diabetes Mellitus auf Grund 1142, klinischbeobachteter Fälle. *Wien Arch inn Med, 28:*87, 1935.

24. Bolduan, C., and Weiner, L.: Causes of death among Jews in New York City. *N Engl J Med, 208:*407, 1933.

25. Sanders: *Zeikte en Sterfte by Joden en Nietjoden te Amsterdam.* Roterdam, 1918.

26. Morrison, H.: A Statistical study of the mortality from diabetes mellitus in Boston from 1895 to 1913, with special reference to its occurrence among Jews. *Boston Med Soc J, 175:*54, 1916.

27. Weaver, R.: Recent statistics on diabetes. *Diabetes, 3:*224, 1954.

Chapter 26

TUBERCULOSIS AMONG JEWS

J. RAKOWER

INTRODUCTION

The mass immigration into Israel during the past four years provides material of special interest for the tuberculosis epidemiologist. At times entire Jewish populations have been transferred from the Diaspora to Israel from Iraq, Yemen, and Bulgaria, and have been united with different stocks of the same original extraction who have lived for the past two thousand years under entirely different conditions. Although the immigration continues, there is a mass of gathered material which has already thrown new light upon certain old epidemiologic problems.

There are now four ethnic groups in Israel:

1. *Ashkenazi* comprise 50 percent of the population and originate principally from Eastern and Central Europe.

2. *Sephardi* comprise 30 percent of the population and originate from the Mediterranean countries of North Africa, Syria, Lebanon, and Turkey.

3. *Oriental communities* comprise 15 percent of the population and originate from Iraq, Persia, Kurdistan, Afghanistan, and Bukhara.

4. *Yemenite Jews* comprise 5 percent of the population and originate from the southern part of the Arab Peninsula.

Two thousand years of life in the Diaspora have had a great influence on the anthropologic characteristics of the above-mentioned groups. The Ashkenazi Jews are of middle height, 85 percent mesocephales, are 25 percent blond, and have predomi-

Reprinted in edited version with permission from *The American Review of Tuberculosis* (*Am Rev Resp Dis*) 67: (no. 1) January, 1953.

nantly blood group A.[19] The Sephardic group are 68 percent mesocephales, 30 percent brachycephales, are 5 percent blond, and have most frequently blood group B. The Oriental Jews resemble the Sephardi with the exception of the B'nai Israel (East Indian Jews) who are completely black. The Yemenite Jews are of short stature, mostly dolicocephales, and blonds are not found in this group.

It should be emphasized that no appreciable difference in mortality or morbidity from tuberculosis has been found between the Ashkenazi, Sephardi, and Oriental groups. In striking contrast is the prevalence of tuberculosis among the Yemenite Jews. The high resistance of the first-mentioned groups to tuberculosis is an old and a well-known problem which has received considerable attention. These groups were always cited as an example of a highly immune ethnic group in contradistinction to the marked susceptibility of the non-white races. This well-known fact was confirmed once again by the first published tuberculosis mortality rate in Israel for 1949. In spite of the postwar conditions, of a tremendous influx of immigrants (the population increased 50 percent in one and one-half years), and in spite of the fact that Israel was the only country which permitted free immigration of tuberculous patients, the mortality rate in Israel was one of the lowest in the world, i.e. 14.3 per 100,000 for pulmonary tuberculosis and 19.6 per 100,000 for tuberculosis of all forms.[9] The older statistics always showed that the tuberculosis mortality rate of Ashkenazi and Sephardi Jews was one-half to one-third that of Christians, and one-fifth to one-seventh that of Moslems living in the same country.

When the population of an area consists of various ethnic groups, there are always significant relationships between tuberculosis mortality and economic status. In this respect the Jews are an exception.[2] The mortality of Jews in various towns was always lower than that of other groups, regardless of economic status. A statistical study of 25,000 Jews in Tunis,[18,29] made during a twenty-four-year period, indicates that the mortality from tuberculosis was one-half that of French and Italian, and one-seventh that of the Moslems, although the standard of living among Tunisian Jews did not differ significantly from that of the Arab masses and was much lower than that of either French or Italians. The same observations apply to the Jewish communities in New York City. There the statistics cover periods which include the difficult years of Jewish mass immigration. Nevertheless, the mortality from tuberculosis among New York Jews in comparison to other ethnic groups is shown in table 26-I.[4,11]

TABLE 26-I
TUBERCULOSIS MORTALITY IN NEW YORK AMONG
DIFFERENT ETHNIC GROUPS

Author	Period	Irish	Negroes	Germans	Americans	Jews
Billings	1884–1890	645	531	328	205	76
Drolet	1918–1921	308	398	133	108	86

These observations do not mean that the mortality of Jews from tuberculosis is independent of environmental factors. On the contrary, this dependence is shown clearly in the records of tuberculosis mortality of Polish and Jewish populations in Warsaw during the first and second World Wars.[16,17]

It is clear from the foregoing that during World War I, when the two populations suffered in the same manner, the mortality from tuberculosis rose in the same manner. During World War II, when the Jewish suffering in the Warsaw ghetto was indescribable, the mortality from tuberculosis of the Polish population increased 2.3 times, while the mortality from tuberculosis of the Jewish population increased 8.5 times and became greater than the Polish mortality value. In addition to these figures, it should be emphasized that phthisiologists observed forms of tuberculosis in the Jewish population which they had never formerly seen, i.e. frequent caseous involvement of lymph nodes, massive exudative infiltrations in the lungs, and a greater tendency to miliary spread.[20]

This influence of environmental factor was also emphasized by Drolet.[12] In his study, it is shown that, as the Jewish community moved from the crowded Lower East Side tenements to a more prosperous section of Manhattan around Mount Sinai Hospital and finally into the Tremont District in the Bronx, which was a comparatively new development in 1923, their tuberculosis death rates went down from 83 per 100,000 to 65 and 52, respectively.

According to Drolet,[13] the number of known cases of tuberculosis on January 1, 1952, in three largely Jewish districts of New York City was as follows: in the Lower East Side, the known cases of tuberculosis per 1,000 residents was 5.84; in the Tremont District in the Bronx, it was much less, namely, 1.56; in the Gravesend District of Brooklyn, which is a more prosperous neighborhood, it was the lowest of any in the city, 0.82.

MORBIDITY

The significance of the morbidity rate of tuberculosis is perhaps greater than that of the death rate. A constant relationship does not always exist between these two ratios. If under normal conditions the Jewish mortality from tuberculosis is less than the non-Jewish, it cannot be deduced that the morbidity from tuberculosis will be significantly less. Comparative studies between the morbidity of the Jewish and Polish populations may provide a good example. While the Polish mortality from tuberculosis was three times greater than the Jewish, there was not a great difference between the morbidity figures for these two groups.[1,2] There were 1,100 cases of clinical tuberculosis per 100,000 Jews, while for each 100,000 Poles there were 1,300 cases of clinical tuberculosis. It should be noted, however, that the recording of new cases of tuberculosis may again vary considerably from these figures. In 1931, there were 130 new cases of tuberculosis per 100,000 Jews in Warsaw, while there were 300 cases of tuberculosis per 100,000 Poles. This apparent contradiction will be understandable when we consider that Jews are affected with milder clinical forms of the disease and therefore live longer.

The relationship between morbidity from tuberculosis and mortality has been expressed as a coefficient. In 1920 to 1939, this coefficient was five for Poles living in Poland and nine for Jews in Poland. The statistics of MacLennan[23] in 1935 showed a morbidity among the Jewish population in Palestine of 397 and a mortality of 42.6, which resulted in a coefficient of 9.3.

Proof is lacking that the incidence of tuberculosis is decreasing in Israel. The records show that the morbidity incidence is 3 per 1,000 among the old population and from 3 to 9 per 1,000 among the new immigrants.[8,9] The general morbidity rate among Jews in Israel can be estimated as 400 per 100,000 (clinical tuberculosis). The mortality rate for 1949 having been 19.6, the coefficient of morbidity to mortality was 20. When the tuberculosis rate decreased from 42.6 to 19.6, or to 46 percent of its original value, the morbidity rate remained without change.

According to Edwards and Drolet,[14] this same increasing gap has been noticed in the United States. Between 1940 and 1947, the death rate from tuberculosis decreased 27 percent, while the registration of new cases increased 22 percent. In 1930 to 1935, Drolet estimated[11] that there were in the United States two new cases reported during a given year for each death, and a total of five cases of clinical tuberculosis. In 1950, Drolet claimed the ratio of ten clinical cases for each death. These observations are similar to those of the present writer.

TUBERCULOSIS AMONG YEMENITE JEWS

Official records regarding the morbidity and mortality among different Jewish ethnic groups do not exist. In Israel there is no registration according to the various stocks. Nevertheless, there are data available which throw considerable light upon this problem. While the Yemenite Jews represent 5 to 6 percent of the total population, 45 percent of all beds in the four wards for tuberculous children are occupied by Yemenite children. Among 1,354 children in Tel-Aviv schools who reacted positively to the tuberculin test, Brinberg[5] found 28 children with active tuberculosis, of whom 21 were Yemenites. The tuberculin index was 15.3 percent among Ashkenazi children, 16.6 percent among Sephardi, 16.7 percent in Oriental communities, and 26.4 percent among Yemenites. While the infection ratio of the Yemenite to Ashkenazi children was 1.7:1, the morbidity ratio was 5:1. The morbidity ratio of Yemenite to Ashkenazi adults was 2.5:1. The mortality ratio is certainly higher. The mortality among Yemenite Jews in the Hashed Camp in Aden in 1947 to 1948 was 350 per 100,000.[7]

In regard to the different forms of tuberculosis noted in Yemenite Jews, one must emphasize that the acute forms of tuberculosis are quite frequent.[30] The massive exudative forms so rare in other Jewish groups are not unusual among the Yemenites, and it is therefore frequently possible to guess the stock from which a patient originates by the appearance of his chest roentgenogram. In the military tuberculosis hospital in Safad with 25 percent Yemenite soldiers, it was amazing to see what extensive pulmonary lesions could develop in a short time. The known symptomatic duration of tuberculosis among the fatal cases averaged 1.7 years in the Yemenite group and 8.3 years in the Ashkenazi group. Before the era of antimicrobial drugs, a one-stage evolution of the disease was frequently observed with persistent fever and a steadily downhill course, which was terminated by death ten to 14 months after onset. Undoubtedly, the very difficult social and economic conditions under which Yemenite Jews have existed account to a large extent for the high incidence of tuberculosis among them. Under this heading their primitive way of living and the complete absence of hygiene must be considered. But at the same time the North African Jews,* mostly Moroccans, who lived under the same poor economic conditions, had the expected morbidity and mortality rate. Their children occupy 8 percent of the tuberculosis beds, while the Yemenite children occupy 45 percent.

It is believed that this situation can possibly be explained only if it be assumed that the Yemenite Jews have a diminished ability to develop acquired immunity as a result of infection. An appropriate statement might be that the outcome of tuberculous infection depends, not only upon the circumstances of the individual's life, but also upon certain inborn factors associated with the stock from which he comes.[25]

It is not possible to guess even approximately the morbidity from tuberculosis of Yemenite Jews in Yemen. Yemen was almost free of tuberculosis until the Yemenite revolution against Turkey at the beginning of the twentieth century. The military forces

---

* The emigration of North African Jews during the years 1948–1950 numbered 57,700; that of Yemenite Jews, 46,638. The North African Jews constitute from 10 to 12 percent of the population.

which Turkey sent to put down the revolution brought tuberculosis with them. In Yemen there is no medical organization in the accepted sense of the term. The treatment of each disease consists in the burning of the various parts of the body. The standard of living of Yemenite Jews in Yemen was similar to that of an Arab village in Israel. The Jews did not crowd into large villages but, rather, were peasants or laborers. There was a Jewish tribe by the name of B'nai Haban which wandered with its herds, carrying arms as in the time of patriarchs.

In Yemen there are two centers of tuberculosis, Aden and Sana and their environs; the latter city is the capital. The rest of this mountainous country is free from tuberculosis. In 1913, Much[22] ascertained that almost all of Yemenite Jewish immigrants into Palestine reacted negatively to the tuberculin test. This reaction was positive if they had spent time in Aden before immigration. This writer also stated that a positive tuberculin test in the Yemenite Jews meant active tuberculosis. It seems paradoxical that, while the Jews were considered an example of a group with high resistance to tuberculosis, this particular stock represented a group with remarkably low resistance.

There has been considerable discussion concerning the relative importance of the infection, social environment, and heredity in relation to the course of tuberculosis is a given individual. Calmette,[6] for example, who represented the infectionist trend in the development of tuberculosis, maintained that because Jews are an urban element they become more infected in childhood more frequently than in other groups. He suggests that this infection is a sort of vaccination which results in a decreased morbidity and mortality. This idea, however, was no longer tenable when it was shown that the tuberculin index of Jewish children did not exceed that of Polish or Negro children. Moreover, as noted above, the economic and social status does not explain the high resistance of Ashkenazi and Sephardi Jews, just as it does not explain the diminished resistance of Yemenite Jews.

Many authors still maintain that diminished resistance of certain races is the result of natural racial susceptibility. Pinner and Casper[26] have suggested that both the high mortality and the peculiarities of the disease suggest the likelihood of true genotypic differences between Negro and white. Long[21] also states that certain differences in the anatomic character of the tubercle in Negroes from the character of the analogous lesion in whites would seem to have significant hereditary differences. Arnould,[3] in a study of tuberculosis in Celtic populations of Brittany, Ireland, Scotland, and Wales, concluded that an important factor in the higher incidence of tuberculosis in the Celts must be attributed to a certain hereditary physico-chemical constitution.

In the tuberculosis of Yemenite Jews, the factor of racial susceptibility (genotypic differences) cannot be used to explain the observations because all Jews have the same racial origin. To be sure, during the course of two thousand years or more,* an unknown degree of racial mixture has taken place. But the mixture of Arab blood took place equally in Iraq and Morocco without reducing the resistance of these Jews to tuberculous infection.

The present writer believes that the tuberculosis in Yemenite Jews is a consequence of emigration from an agricultural section and open-air life, where tuberculosis was almost unknown, to urban communities where tuberculosis was endemic.

Presumably due to the process of natural selection, the Ashkenazi, Sephardi, and Oriental Jews, who were for centuries exposed to tuberculosis in urban communities, acquired a greater degree of resistance to this infection. The Yemenite Jews, i.e. the section of Jews who lived under the desert conditions such as are found in Yemen far from the rest of the people, are now paying the same price as any other group would pay which had been free from previous contact with the tubercle bacillus. Fishberg is correct in stating[15] that there are no races which are more vulnerable to this disease because of phylogenetic peculiarities. Each human group, after exposure to the tubercle bacillus over a period of many generations, acquired a certain degree of immunity. Although the genetic mechanism plays an important role in the dynamics of natural selection, it does not imply transmission of a constant genotype as, for example, skin color

---

* Some historians assert that the Yemenite Jews belong to the Diaspora which arose after the destruction of the first temple, 586 B. C.

or stature. The transmission of a true genotypic factor is seen in the rabbit's resistance to human tubercle bacilli and in its susceptibility to infection with bovine tubercle bacilli. But in man, in whom higher resistance results from a process of natural selection through early death of constitutionally weak or nonresistant family strains in primitive people, it is not proper to speak of natural racial susceptibility by which is meant a constant, definite, transmissible susceptibility.

Certain forms of tuberculosis, for example, massive exudative infiltration, caseation of lymph nodes, and hematogenous spread, are not therefore a peculiarity of the primitive races. In the tragic days of the Warsaw ghetto, these forms of tuberculosis were very common in the Jewish population which was highly resistant until then to tuberculous infection. The fate of the Indians, Negroes, South Sea Islanders, and other groups who were decimated in acute epidemics of tuberculosis in the nineteenth century is an illustration that the high incidence of tuberculosis in primitive peoples is due to their shorter acquaintance with this disease. With the presently available improved facilities, improved methods of diagnosis, isolation technique, antimicrobial drugs, surgical therapy, BCG, and continued improvement of social and economic factors, natural selection plays a much less dramatic role.

SUMMARY

The high resistance of Jewish people to tuberculosis has once more been confirmed by the mortality rate in Israel, which is one of the lowest in the world, despite very difficult economic conditions. The morbidity rate, however, is no less than in other countries. The estimated morbidity-to-mortality ratio is 20, while in prewar time it was 9. The increase of this coefficient is due to a decrease of the mortality rate, while the morbidity rate remained unchanged. Among the four ethnic Jewish groups which are in Israel, the Yemenite Jews are remarkable for their lack of resistance to tuberculous infection. The high susceptibility to tuberculosis in this group is probably due to its shorter acquaintance with this disease.

REFERENCES

1. Adamowicz, J.: Tuberculosis among Poles and Jews in Bialystok. *Gruzlica, 6*:37, 1926.

2. Arnould, E.: La tuberculose chez les Juifs. *Rev Phthisiol, 4*:225, 1934.

3. Arnould, E.: La tuberculose en Bretagne. *Bull Un Intern Tuberc, 13*:354, 1936.

4. Billings, J.S.: Report on vital statistics of New York and Brooklyn, Census Office, 1894.

5. Brinberg, K.: Tuberculin test in Tel-Aviv schools. *Harefuah, 15*:8, 1947.

6. Calmette, A.: *Infection Bacillaire et Tuberculose.* Paris, Masson et Cie, 1928.

7. Cochrane, S.: Personal communication, 1949.

8. Chasis, J.: Tuberculosis among the new immigrants in Israel. *Harefuah Vehachevra, 5*:12, 1948.

9. Chasis, J.: Personal communication, 1951.

10. Dublin, L.I.: The causes of the recent decline in tuberculosis. *Tubercle, 9*:22, 1927.

11. Drolet, G.J.: Epidemiology of tuberculosis. in *Goldberg* (ed.): *Clinical Tuberculosis.* Philadelphia, Davis Company, 1946.

12. Drolet, G.J.: Tuberculosis among different nationalities in New York, Bulletin of the New York Tuberculosis Association, May-June, 1923.

13. Drolet, G.J.: Personal communication.

14. Edwards, H.R., and Drolet, G.J.: The implications of changing morbidity and mortality rates from tuberculosis. *Am Rev Tuberc, 61*:39, 1950.

15. Fishberg, M.: *Pulmonary Tuberculosis.* Philadelphia, Lea and Febiger, 1932.

16. Gantz, S.: Tuberculosis mortality among Poles and Jews during the World War. *Gruzlica, 6*:151, 1926.

17. Grzegorzewski, L.: Tuberculosis in Poland during the second World War. Lekarski Instytut Nauk Wydawn, 1946.

18. Henry, C.: La tuberculose en Tunisie. *Tunisie med, 6*:28, 1933.

19. Kossovitz, N., and Benoit, M.: Les groupes sanguins. *Rev anthrop, 4*:6, 1932.

20. Krzypow, B.: Personal communication, 1947.

21. Long, E.R.: Constitution and related factors in resistance to tuberculosis, *Arch Path, 32*:122, 1941.

22. Much, H.: *Beitr Z Klin Tuberk,* (suppl), 1913.

23. MacLennan, D.: *Tuberculosis in Palestine.* Jerusalem Health Office, 1935.

24. MacDougall, J.B.: Tuberculosis: A Global Study in Social Pathology. Baltimore, Williams and Wilkins Company, 1949.

25. Miller, J.A., and Rappoport, J.: Resistance in tuberculosis. *JAMA*, *107*:471, 1936.

26. Pinner, M., and Casper, J.A.: Pathological peculiarities of tuberculosis in the American Negro. *Am Rev Tuberc*, *26*:463, 1932.

27. Rich, A.: *The Pathogenesis of Tuberculosis*. Springfield, Thomas, 1951.

28. Rakower, J.: Le Pronostic des Differentes Formes de la Tuberculose Pulmonaire. Paris, Le Francois, 1932.

29. Toistivint, A., and Remlinger, J.: La lutte antituberculeuse en Tunisie. *Rev d'hyg*, *4*:128, 1900.

30. Wayl, P., and Rakower, J.: Tuberculosis among Yemenite Jews in Israel. *Harefuah*, *36*:12, 1949.

PART SIX
BEHAVIOR DISORDERS

Various types of addiction leading to abnormal behavior, as well as the distortions of behavior concommitant with mental illness, have been classified under the heading "Behavioral Disorders." Whether or not there are genetic factors involved in these disorders has not been decided with any degree of certainty, although various hypotheses have been ventured on the subject.

Jewish nonaddiction to alcohol has been a subject of some interest for a number of decades. In Chapter 27 Keller calls this, humorously, a "mystery." He discusses the environmental factors in their history as an oppressed minority, which made it dangerous for Jews to overindulge in alcohol, as well as the cultural practices which made wine drinking an integral part of some religious ceremonies. At the same time, he does not eliminate entirely the possibility of some genetic immunity to alcoholism.

Glatt describes in Chapter 28 the cultural and historic reasons for Jewish aversion to alcoholism. He also discusses the problem of drug dependence among Jews. In the United States there seem to be relatively high proportions of Jews among drug addicts. However, this problem has not yet been studied sufficiently to permit generalizations concerning environmental or genetic factors.

Wechsler, Demone, Thum, and Kasey (Chap. 29) compare religious and ethnic differences in drinking behavior. The lowest incidences are found among Jews and Italians, and high incidences are found among Irish, Canadian, and native born Catholics and Protestants.

Malzberg has been studying the incidence of mental disease among various ethnic groups for about four decades. In Chapter 30 he finds that Jews have the lowest overall rate of first admissions to mental hospitals, and in general have the lowest rates of organically originating psychoses. However, they have higher rates with respect to manic-depressive psychoses and psychoneuroses. Cross-cultural studies of mental illness compare the etiology of certain diseases in different ethnic and racial groups. Sanua reviews the literature of investigations of schizophrenia as a function of social class and ethnic group in Chapter 31. His most striking finding is that parents of Jewish and Protestant schizophrenics show different pathological development.

A comprehensive rather than comparative approach may be seen in Chapter 32 where Rinder reviews the literature dealing specifically with the mental health of American Jews. He divides his study into three levels: epidemiology, sociocultural analysis, and clinical analysis. In conclusion, he offers an integrative interpretation with some projections for the future.

To conclude, there is Weinberg's survey of mental health research on Jews all over the world (Chap. 33). Weinberg stresses the importance for mental health of the need to belong, and how the individual relates in this need to his family and group. Intergroup interactions, he goes on, are especially crucial in their effect on Jews in the Diaspora, since they have been victims of persecutions, and may tend to develop into marginal personalities more likely to break down under stress.

Chapter 27

THE GREAT JEWISH DRINK MYSTERY

M. Keller

In the early 1940's, what was to become the famous Yale (and now is the Rutgers) Center of Alcohol Studies was just beginning to take shape. It had no name yet, but Dr. Howard W. Haggard, the Director of the Yale Laboratory of Applied Physiology, had begun to collect a staff of non-physiologists who were interested in alcohol and in the study of its problems. One day as I sat by his desk, he quite suddenly fired a surprise question at me: Suppose there was a chance to do some research on the causes of drunkenness or alcoholism. Did I have any ideas for any kind of fresh research direction? And at the moment, stimulated to make a good impression on the big boss, I succeeded in touching the right button on my unconscious computer, and out came an idea. I said: "Dr. Haggard, everybody naturally thinks the secrets of alcoholism can be learned from alcoholics, that if one studies them the right way, the mystery of why they become alcoholics will be uncovered. Maybe. But wouldn't it be a good idea to study those who don't become alcoholics? I mean such a group as the Jews. It happens that practically all Jews do drink and yet all the world knows that Jews hardly ever become alcoholics. Why? What protects them? If we could discover that, wouldn't it be a masterly clue?"

Dr. Haggard, a lightning fast thinker, replied immediately: "All right, Mr. Keller—and suppose we discover why the Jews don't become alcoholics. How are we going to convert 150 million Americans to Judaism?"

But after we finished laughing over his witticism—which was to prove astoundingly insightful—Dr. Haggard did not neglect

Reprinted with permission from *Br J Addict, 64:* 287–295, 1970.

this idea, and he raised the first substantial research money to study Jewish drinking. Out of this came a number of studies at the Yale Center, including Ruth Landman's study[1] of drinking by children attending religious schools, and especially Charles Synder's dissertation, *Drinking and Sobriety*[2]—renamed, when published, *Alcohol and the Jews*.[3]

In the meantime, at Harvard, another bright graduate student in sociology, Robert Fred Bales, had gotten interested in this subject, and long before Snyder—whose excellence is not manifested in speed—was ready to publish, Bales got his Ph.D. with a dissertation[4] based on the hypothesis of a "Fixation Factor" in alcohol addiction, derived from a comparative study of Irish and Jewish social norms and drinking behaviors.

And on the west coast, Donald Davison Glad tackled this problem from still another but closely allied angle, and produced a dissertation[5] and a publication[6] describing the attitudes toward drinking, and the practices, of Irish and Jewish boys in the United States, as compared with differences in rates of inebriety among adults in these population groups.

Undoubtedly my suggestion that Jewish drinking should be studied was founded on the repeated encounter of references to the sobriety or temperance of the Jews, the absence of drunkenness or alcoholism among them. Immanuel Kant[7] had written about it in Germany, and had even bothered to formulate an explanatory hypothesis about it—philosophically profound but psychologically naive. In England the great Dr. Norman Kerr* [8] had remarked upon the absence of inebriety among the Jews, and in the United States, Robert Hunter[9] and Morris Fishberg.[10] Cheinisse[11] and Durkheim[12] wrote about it in France. In Russia it is alluded to in a fascinating tale by the great folklorist, N. S. Leskov[13] in a story about "Immortal Golovan," a folk hero beloved among the peasantry. Mystical powers were attributed to Golovan. He was supposed to have acquired the bezoar stone, which warded off the plague. Because he used his powers only for good, his irreligiosity was tolerated. Even such "un-Christian behavior" as giving milk to the Jew Yushka for his children was

---

* The founder—in 1884—of the Society for the Study of Inebriety, now the Society for the Study of Addiction.

overlooked, since the peasants assumed his motive was to extract from the Jews their two valuable secrets: that of the Judas lips, which enable one to speak falsehood in court; and that of the hairy vegetable, which enabled the Jews to drink without getting drunk!

I will not repeat the extensive documentation[2] of the observations of Jewish sobriety in country after country after country.

Since the Jews, after all, are more likely to eat a piece of herring with their drink than a slice of mandrake—I imagine that's what the hairy vegetable was supposed to be—some other protective factor must be at work.

Bales[4] compared Irish with Jewish drinking ways on the basis of documentary evidence. He found it possible broadly to characterize the drinking of the Irish as convivial; that is, the mainly sought effect was achieved through the pharmacological action of alcohol. The Jews, by virtue of cultural practices effective from infancy, acquired a ritual attitude toward drinking, and learned to use it chiefly for communion. The pharmacological effect of alcohol was secondary and could not be allowed to become dominant, as that would frustrate the fundamental motive. Thus the Jews could not permit themselves drunkenness. They were fixated on sobriety in drinking. Obviously, people who don't get drunk can hardly acquire the condition of alcoholism. The protective culture phenomenon is inherent in the religion, in the practice of sanctifying important rites, especially the rites of passage, by drinking wine and blessing it—at circumcision, when the infant boy is given his first taste of the ceremonial wine; at the transitions from weekdays to Sabbaths and festivals, in the kiddush, and back again to the weekdays in the habdalah; at the wedding ceremony, when the man and his bride drink wine from the same cup, and on other valued occasions. The inculcated ritual attitude toward drink is carried over into everyday life, so that the abuse of drink would be unthinkable. That, very briefly, is the essence of Bales' hypothesis.

Synder[3] went out into the community to study. He surveyed a randomly formed sample of the Jews of a New England city. He also analyzed the responses of a sizable sample of Jewish students in the Straus and Bacon[14] College Drinking Survey, dividing them into four categories of religious attitude or affiliation: Orthodox, Conservative, Reform and Secular. Among the population and among the students alike, the experience of intoxication was on a continuum, with those most adhering to orthodox or religious practices experiencing the least intoxication. This in spite of the fact that the orthodox tended to drink most frequently. After considering some alternative hypotheses, Snyder concluded that Bales in essence was right. The culture of the Jews, as influenced by the religion, acted as an inhibitor of drunkenness. A drunkard was defined by Jews as alien. Synder believed he saw some indications that as acculturation proceeded, as orthodoxy waned and secularism waxed, signs of an increased rate of alcoholism among Jews were emerging.

D. D. Glad[6] studied attitudes of Jewish and Irish boys and discovered quite distinctive differences undoubtedly related to their background. The Irish boys thought of drinking as promoting fun, pleasure, conviviality; the Jewish boys thought of it as socially practical and religiously symbolic and communicative.

Always it seems to come to the same thing: the Jewish culture, dominantly influenced by the religion, evokes attitudes which inhibit drinking to drunkenness, even while it encourages frequent but controlled drinking.

In fairness I should warn that, while a variety of alternate psychological, sociological and anthropological hypotheses have been considered and sometimes tested by these and other theorists—Glad, for example, tested the parental-permissiveness hypothesis but found no support for it—one important biological hypothesis has been brushed aside rather cavalierly by the social scientists: that the Jews may have some sort of genetic immunity to alcoholism. As an observer not committed to either side I must say that the reasoning against the purely biological hypothesis is less than conclusive. Insofar as this reasoning is based on the fact that no biological necessary cause of alcoholism in anybody has yet been discovered, the position is negatively sound enough, but a door to doubt must be kept open, for biology has by no means yet spoken its last word on this subject. Insofar as the antibiological reasoning is based on the notion that Jews are not a genetic unity, it is practically on a level with superstition. Of course the Jews are not a pure "race," like laboratory stocks of mice. But they constitute a sufficiently inbred strain or group of strains to have a substantial number of genetic traits in relative frequency; and a genetic trait which could influence the chances of alcoholism—if such a thing existed at all—could well prevail among Jews. But in the present state of knowledge, it would be hardly anything but superstition to adopt a genetic hypothesis, while ignoring the powerful indications of psychology and sociology.

Now I have reviewed the state of knowledge briefly and at this point it seems appropriate to ask: What is the great mystery? After all, it seems only a question of genetic versus cultural immunity, and in due time the researchers will presumably resolve the issue.

The great Jewish drink mystery which I have in mind is not just why don't the Jews get drunk today, but how did they get this way. I refer to the historical fact that the ancestors of the Jews were a bunch of renowned topers. Somehow, at some time, they reformed, or they gave it up—I mean gave up drunkenness, for they never gave up drinking. When did this happen? And how was it accomplished? If we could know that, might it not be the masterly clue we are looking for? Anyhow, my curiosity would be gratified.

That the ancestors of the modern Jews were copious drinkers, rather like the French of recent times, is well documented in the Bible. I assume that—after the archaeological discoveries of recent years—and the discrediting of much of the pseudoscholarship of the "Higher" Bible Criticism, I need not take time to demonstate the reliability of the Biblical record. In a very old part of it, the earthly blessing of the main tribe of the Hebrews, the Judah clan, whose totem, the lion-image, survives to this day at the holiest place in every orthodox synagogue, reads in part as follows: "Binding his foal unto the vine, and his ass's colt unto the choice vine, he washes his garments in wine, and his clothes in the blood of grapes. His eyes shall be red with wine . . ."* In other words, wine should flow more freely than water. It did,

---

* *Genesis,* Chap. 49: Verses 11–12.

too, in the fruitful hills of Israel and Judaea. The much later Proverbist, too, included, among the rewards of virtue, "So shall thy barns be filled with plenty, and thy presses shall burst out with new wine."† And the inhabitants did not use the wine just for washing their garments as a primitive Murine for their eyes. In very early days we find the high priest Eli readily mistaking Hannah, as she was whispering her prayers at the holy shrine, for a common drunkard.‡ And all throughout, the Prophets inveigh against drunkenness as against a rampant evil, typified by Isaiah: "Woe unto them that rise up early in the morning that they may follow strong drink, that tarry late into the night, till wine inflame them!" And again, "Woe unto them that are mighty to drink wine, and men of strength to mingle strong drink.§ That sounds like long and hard drinking—and the Prophets were no temperance preachers in the modern sense, they never protested against drinking.

Right down to the destruction of the two kingdoms, to the exile of the Judaeans into the near lands, such as Egypt, and the farther lands, such as Babylonia, near the end of the 6th century B.C., the rich grape harvests were converted into wine, and copious drinking was the practice of many. There is a tendency to distinguish the Hebrews from the Canaanites. But this is like distinguishing the Normans from the French, or the Bulgars from the Slavs. The Hebrews were Canaanites, and multitudes of them repeatedly, as was the common practice in the ancient world, chose to honor the worship of other Canaanite gods than the One who was in the beginning the particular God of the Hebrew clan. Those other Canaanite gods, even Baal and Asherah, Dagan and Anat, and others, had interesting and attractive forms of worship—orgiastic festivals frowned upon by the peculiar Deity of the Hebrews, orgies intended to ensure the fertility of man and land, and in which drunkenness was blessed rather than rebuked.

What followed upon the first great national catastrophe, when an important segment of the population was taken captive into

† *Proverbs,* Chap. 3: Verse 10.
‡ *I Samuel,* Chap. 1: Verses 13–15.
§ *Isaiah,* Chap. 5: Verses 11, 22.

exile over 2500 years ago, is an essential part of the mystery which is my topic. The interesting fact is that from that time on we almost hear no more of drunkenness among the Jews. But it is not as simple as all that.

The Biblical account stops with the return from exile after only a few generations, and the resumption of a national form of life. We need to try to examine what happened to drinking during the first exile period and, after the restoration, during the time of the second Temple.

How did the Jews behave with respect to drinking during that first exile? I cannot give an exact answer. I emphatically call attention to that period and this question because it is possible that it was then that drunkenness vanished or began to decline among the Jews. Perhaps it was connected with the disappearance of the Canaanite gods. If so, it is obviously of the utmost importance to understand what happened and how it happened.

Actually, there is some indication that the Jews in the Babylonian exile had not lost their interest in wine. The Midrash Rabbah on the Book of Esther attributes the catastrophe of Haman's plot to the fact that 18,500 Jews attended the great feast of Emperor Ahasuerus, "and they ate and drank, and became drunk, and were corrupted."*

A Midrashic statement is not necessarily historical. It could have been invented by a rabbi several hundred years later, in approved exegetic style, for homiletic purposes. But the Midrash is full of historical as well as fanciful stories, and there is no reason to assume that a record or oral tradition did not survive which described the participation of the Perso-Median Jews in the grand Empire festival, and which included an account of their excess in drinking. Wine was apparently plentiful, and as yet we have no evidence that copious drinking and drunkenness had been given up by the exiled Jewish population. Even if the Midrash is not based on a known fact but on an assumption that the pre-exilic behavior was continued, it is a reasonable assumption. Evidently the earliest authors of the idea that the Jews got drunk at the feast of Ahasuerus did not think that the pre-exilic drunkenness was abolished by the mere fact of exile.

* Chap. VII, p. 23a, edn. Horeb, Berlin.

We have no right to think so either—not until we acquire some evidence about it. But this may be the last reference to widespread drunkenness among the Jews.

We come then to the return, beginning in 537 B.C. We know from the Biblical record that only a minority returned to the land of Israel, and under the leadership of Ezra and Nehemiah, after much hardship and delay, they succeeded in building the Temple anew and established a distinctive national-cultural life. The high point of this restoration was the formal adoption of the Bible itself, the Torah, as the national Constitution. The significant consequence was the rise of a new non-political national leadership, of unsurpassed influence: the Scribes, the Bookmen, the Men of the Great Assembly, later the Pharisees and the Talmudic rabbis.

The remarkable thing about the ensuing period is the paucity of historical record. There are so few contemporary records of the next several hundred years that a historian must weep. It seems especially grievous when one reflects that the national leadership was assumed by a class known by the name of *Soferim:* Scribes!

In my opinion, from all that I can make out—and I have not researched in depth but have only skimmed what materials came to hand—it is during this period that drunkenness really was banished from Jewish life. It is in this time span, not more than 200 years, between the establishment of the Second Temple and the reappearance of the Jews on the scene of world history, which happened with the advent of Alexander of Macedonia and the start of the Hellenistic epoch, that the basis of Jewish sobriety was firmly laid. For when the historical record becomes ample again, we no longer find any evidence of drunkenness, in a people who still cultivated the vine, still poured out libations of wine to God, drank at many ceremonies, and drank with pleasure.

In this period the Scribes, whose leaders constituted the famed Men of the Great Assembly, as successors to Ezra the Scribe, firmly established the institution of the synagogue, the "little Sanctuary" in every community, which became a center of local worship and learning so mingled that worship and study could hardly be told apart. They established popular education, education for the common people. They democratized their own class: anybody, not just a hereditary Priest or Levite, could become a Scribe and a member of the Great Assembly—later a pharisee or a rabbi. They preserved the traditions and compiled and edited the sacred texts, and fixed the ritual practices and composed liturgic formulas and benedictions. One of their embellishments was to fix the rule that the pronouncement of the advent of the Sabbath, on Friday eve—the Sanctification of the Sabbath—the *kiddush*—should be recited over a blessed cup of wine. The regular and popular ceremonial drinking of wine, apart from its continued use in sacrificial libations in the Holy Temple, was their initiative. Was it in assocation with and in consequence of these developments—the remolding of the whole culture, and the embedding in that religious culture of a particular sort of use of wine and a particular attitude toward drinking—that drunkenness declined remarkably? I think we must at least suspect this.

Not, however, that drunkenness was forgotten. Indeed, it continued to be a matter of concern, and continued to be feared—as I shall attempt to show. And if remembered, and if still feared, then we must assume that it was still sometimes manifested, as we should expect. There were still winebibbers, as the phrase in Matthew suggests.[*] But no longer was inebriety common, no longer a national trait and problem. Drinking was under control. In due time, the control was to become so well established that even the fear and all but the formal remembrance of drunkenness was to vanish, as I hope to show, and the behavior was to become an attribute of the others, the non-we's, the non-Jews—as Snyder has shown.

It is in the Midrashim and the Talmud that we find the post-Biblical indications of the disappearance of drunkenness but the survival of the fear of it.

I believe it is subtly illustrated in the rhymed toast which Rabbi Akiba (1st century) recited over each cup of wine at the grand feast he gave when his son was ordained: "Wine and

---

[*] *Matthew*, Chap. 11: Verse 19.

life in the mouth of scholars, life and wine in the mouth of students." It sounds cautionary. It says, as we drink, we must remember that for finished scholars, adults, wine may take precedence over that which is our life (the Torah, the substance of scholarship), but for younger men, life—learning—must take precedence, drinking must be secondary. Even as he offered wine he had to offer this caution.

But the survival of the fear of drunkenness seems exquisitely illustrated in the ancient formula, doubtless going back to the days of the Great Assembly, for initiating a ceremonial benediction over a cup of wine, as at *kiddush,* or *habdalah,* or for the grace after meals. We read: " . . . he [the precentor, exhibiting the cup of wine in his hand] is required to say, *sabre maranan, ha-yayin mishtaker*" (that is, By your leave, or Attention, my masters, wine causes drunkenness!); the text continues: "and he says this out of fear; but they respond, *le-haiim*" (that is, "It's for life," or "For health.")* It seems to me enormously significant that the introductory formula to the use of the cup of blessing should have been a warning of the danger of intoxication in the use of wine, and that he who was to drink it should have required the permissive toast of the company, assuring him that this use was approved, safe, for life and health.

Equally interesting is that, in due course, this cautionary formula vanished! Among western Jews, the *kiddush* begins with the *sabre,* "Attention, please," and proceeds to the benediction of the wine without waiting for any response. The danger of intoxication is not mentioned. Among the Sephardic Jews, when the precentor opens with *sabre,* the company still respond, as of yore, *le-haiim,* "To life" or "To your health"—but the warning of intoxication which necessitated this response has disappeared everywhere. I take this banishment of the warning to be the sign that not only widespread inebriety, but practically any drunkenness, and even the fear of it, had vanished.

There are other signs, in the rich rabbinic literature of the middle ages, that drunkenness was no longer feared. Best of all these I like the discussion, in a 16th century work, of the problem

---

* Beth Joseph, Sec. 167, citing Shibbale ha-Leket.

of dilution of wine. The ancient custom, well-established in the times of the Men of the Great Assembly, and repeatedly confirmed in the Talmud, required strictly that wine be drunk, diluted; surely a precaution related to the surviving fear of drunkenness. Even *kiddush* wine, which was required to be "fit for libation"—and libation wine was absolutely undiluted—had to be diluted for drinking. Indeed, anyone who drank undiluted wine was assumed to be a drunkard. Thus we find the Talmud† ruling that the accused "rebellious son," among other wrongful acts, must have drunk a given large quantity of wine in one draft before he could be found guilty; however, it had to be diluted wine. For, if he had drunk so much undiluted wine, then he must be a drunkard—and a drunkard could not be held responsible. But great medieval authorities ruled that the European wine (i.e. of France or Germany) need not be diluted: "Our wines are much better undiluted since they are not so strong" [as the wines of the ancients], one wrote;* and another: "Our wines are not strong and are better when not diluted."**

These rulings verge on the fantastic. These wise rabbinic authorities were so firmly convinced that the European wines were weaker, less intoxicating, than the wines of their ancestors, that they went so far as to reform the law fixed by the highest ancient authorities and hallowed by more than two millenia of custom. Why should they think the modern wines comparatively so weak? I can only guess it was because, on the one hand, they knew their ancestors used to get drunk on wine, and on the other hand, any Jew getting drunk on the local wines was unheard of. Perhaps it was naive that they should have failed to realize that the difference was not in the strength of the beverage but in the motivation of the drinking. Their ancestors drank for the purpose of getting drunk, and managed with diluted wine; their contemporaries did not wish to get drunk, and hence they could safely drink wine undiluted.

Along the same line, 16th century authorities discussing the use of the newly available distilled spirits for the lesser *kiddush*

† Babylonian Talmud, Tracate Sanhedrin, 68*b* ff
** Lebush ha-Hur, p. 91.
* Aruk ha-Shulhan, Sec. 272.

on the Sabbath morning (called the Great Kiddush), note the difficulty of fulfilling the requirement to quaff the quantity of a *reviit* (the displacement of 1.5 eggs) of distilled spirits. "In the case of brandy," Rabbi Jacob ben Samuel wrote, "it is not customary to drink so much at once."‡

Indeed, it is abundantly evident that it was no longer customary to drink enough of anything that would cause intoxication, and the Jewish authorities simply no longer seriously feared that anyone might.

I believe I have shown three significant developments relevant to the disappearance of inebriety among the Jews. One is the banishment of the pagan gods of Canaan, to whose worship orgiastic drinking had been attached. The second is the development of the religious culture, with the Bible, the Torah, as Constitution, along with the institution of the local synagogue as a place of popular education as much as worship. Third is the positive integration of drinking in religiously oriented ceremonials in the home and synagogue, including meals and rites of passage. The integration of moderate drinking with most religious actions, and most important activities with religion, may have gone hand in hand with the displacement of the pagan gods and their ways, including the interest in orgiastic drinking. When the alien paganism of the Greeks came upon the scene in the Hellenistic era, the bulk of the people rejected its allurements. They had no doubt their own ways were better. Sobriety was indeed fixed in Jewish culture. If we can elucidate the means by which this was effected more explicitly than I have been able to do, we might have the "answer."

REFERENCES

1. Landman, R.H.: *Q J Stud Alcohol*, 13:87, 1952.

2. Snyder, C.R.: Culture and Sobriety; A Study of Drinking Patterns and Socio-cultural Factors Related to Sobriety among Jews. Doctoral dissertation, Yale University, 1954.

3. Snyder, C.R.: *Alcohol and the Jews; A Cultural Study of Drinking and Sobriety.* (Rutgers Center of Alcohol Studies Monogr. No. 1.) New Brunswick, N.J., Rutgers Center of Alcohol Studies Publications Division 1958

‡ Responsa, Beth Jacob, No. 57.

4. Bales, R.F.: The Fixation factor. In Alcohol Addiction: An Hypothesis Derived from a Comparative Study of Irish and Jewish Social Norms. Doctoral dissertation, Harvard University, 1944.

5. Glad, D.D.: Attitudes and Experiences of American-Jewish and American-Irish Male Youths as Related to Differences in Inebriety Rates. Doctoral dissertation, Stanford University, 1947.

6. Glad, D.D.: *Q J Stud Alcohol,* 8:406, 1947.

7. Kant, I.: *Anthropologie;* Pt. I, Book 1, 1798. Cited in Jellinek: *Q J Stud Alcohol, 1:*777, 1941.

8. Kerr, N.: *Inebriety, Its Etiology, Pathology, Treatment and Jurisprudence.* London, Lewis, 1888.

9. Hunter, R.: *Poverty.* New York, Macmillan, 1904.

10. Fishberg, M.: *The Jews: A Study of Race and Environment.* Scott, New York (1911).

11. Cheinisse, L.: *Sem méd 28:*613, 1908.

12. Durkheim, E.: *Le Suicide.* Paris, Alcan, 1897.

13. Leskov, N.S.: *Nesmertel'nyi Golovan. (Deathless Golovan.)* In Leskov, (Ed.): *Complete Works,* Vol. 6, pp. 351–397. Moscow; Gos-izd-khudozh. lit., 1957. [Orig. date 1880.]

14. Straus, R.: and S.D. Bacon.: *Drinking in College.* New Haven, Yale University Press, 1953.

Chapter 28

ALCOHOLISM AND DRUG DEPENDENCE AMONGST JEWS

M.M. GLATT

ALCOHOLISM

On two of their festivals (Passover and Purim) Jews are admonished and encouraged by their religion and tradition to imbibe a great deal of alcohol. There can hardly be any other nation whose members have to be ordered to indulge in heavy drinking—if there are any laws, they are usually directed against it. Yet statistics and observations over a great many years and throughout the countries where Jews were scattered testify to the fact that Jews—not famous for their avoidance of overeating— have been well known for their relative freedom from drunkenness and alcoholism, scourges of so many other ancient and modern nations. At first glance this is the more surprising as it is uncommon to find Jews who are abstainers. In this country, for example, an investigation carried out a few years ago by the *Jewish Chronicle* showed that the great majority of its readers took alcoholic drink regularly, and similar results were obtained by American studies which demonstrated that the proportion of abstainers was considerably smaller among Jews than among other denominations. The finding that most Jews take drink should in theory make for a relatively high rate of alcoholism, seeing that on the average roughly one drinker in fifteen could be expected to develop into a problem drinker.

In theory, there would seem to be other reasons why alcoholism amongst Jews should not be uncommon. Among the causative factors involved in the aetiology in alcoholism (and drug de-

Reprinted with permission from *Br J Addict, 64:* 297–304, 1970.

pendence) two generally regarded as important are the individual's psychological make-up and his environment, the latter including—apart from availability, cultural factors, and so on— the amount of stress and strain to which he is exposed. Other factors being equal, it seems common sense to suggest that anxious, worrying, neurotic persons exposed to environmental stress and frustration might more readily tend to look for relief and oblivion in the bottle than the emotionally more stable. The proportion of neurotics and worriers amongst Jews seems certainly not lower than amongst the general population; if there is any difference it might be rather the other way round. If, as usually reported, alcoholism amongst Jewish people is rare (occasionally relief drinking amongst Jews may have taken place, e.g. amongst the poor Jewish population in Poland in the 18th century prior to the emergence of Chassidism), it would seem that there must be powerful influential counter-balancing forces at work. Thus, the suggestion was put forward in the early days of the modern scientific approach to alcoholism that investigations into the reasons for Jewish sobriety might yield important clues as regards the aetiology and the prophylaxis of alcoholism.

The finding that despite a history of widespread acceptance of alcoholic drink for thousands of years amongst Jews (coupled with their constant exposure to strain and stress), there was so little drunkenness and problem drinking among them, produced many hypotheses. For example, Kant,[1] 200 years ago, ascribed the rarity of drinking excesses among Jews to the need of small, insecure minority groups to be for ever on guard and keep a cool head in order not to attract even more unfavourable attention and avoid censure. Somewhat similarly, an American– Jewish writer[2] 60 years ago spoke of the necessity for a Jew who wanted to get anywhere to outshine his non-Jewish neighbor in virtue, in order to counterbalance the disadvantage of being born into a minority group; thus, whilst he may drink, he must do so in moderation. Quite different was a theory put forward in recent years by another American writer[3] who believes in the possibility of hereditary patterns in the various ethnic groups favouring or tending to prevent the development of alcoholism.

However, modern research in this field has concentrated chiefly on sociological thoughts and explanations. For example, the American sociologist, Ullman,[4] suggested that in groups or societies where drinking customs were well integrated and consistent with the rest of the culture, alcoholism rates will be low; conversely, in a society with not-integrated drinking patterns, and ill-defined, contradictory attitudes towards drinking, the individual drinker will be at a loss to know where he stands and how much drinking, for example, may be permitted on a given occasion. In such a society, with confused attitudes towards drinking, alcoholism rates may be expected to be high. The Irish, including the Irish–Americans, who have very high alcoholism rates,[5] are usually quoted as examples of a society with poorly integrated drinking habits. Often the purpose of drinking is to get drunk, but the reaction of the drinking environment to his drinking may vary greatly from occasion to occasion. Jews, alongside Italians and Chinese on the other hand, are quoted as examples of societies with well integrated drinking customs.[4] Italians as well as Jews are, as children, introduced to alcoholic drinks in the family home—in the case of Jews often in the form of religious rituals. By the time adolescence is reached there is no mystery attached to drinking, no promise of deep, hidden pleasures. Thus, Italians and Jews are said not to develop contradictory attitudes and guilt feelings about drinking. Irish and Jewish attitudes to drinking were compared by other American sociologists: e.g. R.F. Bales[6] contrasted Irish convivial drinking for the pharmacological effect of alcohol with the ritual Jewish drinking; D.D. Glad[7] found that Irish boys thought of drinking as aimed at getting fun, conviviality, whereas Jewish boys stressed the socially practical and religiously symbolic aspects of drinking.

The most thorough studies in this field were carried out by Snyder[5] in the United States who interviewed a sample of adult Jewish men, and investigated by the questionnaire method the drinking practices of college students of various religious denominations. He found an intrinsic connection of Jewish sobriety with Orthodox religious life, factors and influences interfering with Orthodox religious practices apparently also exercising a negative influence on sobriety. Thus, among Jewish students the

Orthodox were drunk least often, followed in the rates of drunkenness by "Conservatives," "Reform," and the "Secular" (least religious) students, the latter being drunk most often. Similarly, whilst drunkenness became more common among successive Jewish generations in the United States, sobriety among the Orthodox was not impaired in later generations. Moreover, "prodromal" (early) signs of alcoholism became more frequent among Jewish students, the more tenuous their connection with Orthodox religious tradition.

Problem Drinking in Israel

Israel has no alcoholism problem. On a visit there, the present writer nine years ago managed to unearth one old alcoholic in a hospital in Jerusalem and nobody seemed to have heard of an Alcoholics Anonymous Group which had been said abroad to have recently been formed in Tel Aviv. One of the hospitals visited at the time was Talbieh Psychiatric Hospital in Jerusalem which then had hardly any alcoholic admissions. A paper published by two of its doctors[8] three years later (1963) showed a certain increase, in that 25 Jewish male alcoholics (all over 30 years of age*) had been admitted to that hospital which serves 60 percent of the population of Israel. The number of alcoholics (out of a total population of over 2 million) was still considered as insignificant. Factors regarded as contributing to the development of alcoholism, among the European patients, were the European holocaust and disintegration of the Jewish community and its controls; among the patients from the Middle Eastern countries (who had often previously been accustomed to heavy drinking) the stresses arising from the need to adjust to a very different economic and social environment.

DRUG DEPENDENCE

The only reference to addictive drugs in the old Jewish literature—according to Louis Lewin[10] was the representation of poppies on the bronze coins of a Maccabean prince and king

---

* This is of some interest because elsewhere there seems to have been a recent increase in alcoholism among the young.[9]

(Jochanan Hyrcanos). Certainly little notice was taken in this country of drug abuse by Jews until a few years ago the *Observer* picked up the finding by two London General Practitioners—published in 1965 in *The British Journal of Addiction*[11]—that among their 100 drug addicts there were 17 Jews plus two "Half-Jews." This, of course, would be an extremely high proportion, but subsequent investigations would seem to indicate that the drug dependence rate among Jews is much less high, and that for some reason or other they were over-represented among these two G.P.s' patients, who seem also in other aspects to have formed a nonrepresentative sample (possibly containing a high proportion of older "therapeutic" addicts as against the modern, young "non-therapeutic" addict). Other sources gave the proportion of Jewish patients among their addicts as roughly 4 to 5 percent; e.g. one London G.P. treating many addicts gave a figure of 4 to 5 percent; another London practitioner found two Jewish addicts among 40 patients; the Anglican Nursing Home, Spelthorne St. Mary, had 4 percent of Jewish addicts among their female patients, and a Salvation Army report showed that of their Soho addict contacts 5 percent (15 people) were Jewish. Our own figures were of a similar order of magnitude. Thus, among patients seen outside hospital over a 20 months' period in 1966/7, nine addicts out of a total of 123 were Jews (approximately 6%, and during the recent period between February 1968 and July 1969, 10 out of 93 (9%): among the 26 males there were six Jews (23 percent), among the 65 females, four (6%). During this time (1966–1969) the proportion of Jews among addicts seen in hospital, out-patient clinics, and in prison was considerably lower. (For example, over the past 2½ years, among 56 male and female addicts seen at the Paddington Clinic and Day Hospital, there were one Jew and one "half-Jew," and at the University College Hospital Out-Patient Treatment Centre, there were two Jews and one "half-Jew" among 35 mainly male addicts.) If the proportion of Jews among addicts in the London area were to approximate 5 percent, this would be slightly above the percentage of Jews among the general population in London (3%), and it would be also higher than the proportion of Jews among alcoholics. However, it would seem that—compared with London addicts in general—among the Jewish sample there seem to be more "therapeutic" and relatively older people, and a relatively high proportion of jazz musicians (among jazz musicians the abuse of drugs seems to be more common than among other professions).

There have also been reports from the United States that there were relatively high proportions of Jews among addicts—for example, in 1965 an estimate among members of Synanon showed that among 500 addicts 100 were Jewish. Another report from New York estimated the number of Jewish addicts there as 10,000 of whom more than 5–1000 were said to be girls. There have also been some recent reports of an increase of drug abuse in Israel. In 1967[12] the number of hashish smokers in Israel was estimated to be between 3500 and 10,000. There was no evidence then of LSD, cocaine or amphetamine abuse, although there was abuse of codeine and pento-barbitone; among narcotic drugs there was abuse of morphine and opium, and much less of heroin. However, according to statements in recent months hashish smoking had become a problem not only among many American students at the Hebrew University, but was also getting a hold on the Israeli youth, including middle-class children.

It is interesting, of course, to speculate why drug abuse and dependence should be more common among Jews than alcoholism. Of the reasons given for the rarity of alcoholism among Jews, some would not apply to drug dependence—such as the fact that Jews brought up in Orthodox homes begin to know alcohol as part of the Jewish ritual. Therefore, the Jewish adolescent, wanting, for example, to show his emancipation from, or rebellion against, parental authority, might choose drugs rather than alcohol, which for him too has by that time acquired ritual connotation. Moreover, whilst drunkenness has usually been condemned by Jewish culture, use of drugs seems by no means uncommon. For example, a recent American investigation showed that tranquillizers were used more by Jews than by Protestants or Catholics. The growing-up youngster, therefore, witnessing this form of drug-taking by his parents, may feel he is still staying within the framework of parental acceptance and customs accepted by Jews.

However, both among alcoholics and drug addicts in our experience the Jewish abuser has generally moved away not only from Jewish religious orthodoxy, but also from other Jewish customs and interests. The fact mentioned by the two London General Practioners in their paper[11] that there were two half-Jews among their addicts may thus not have been a mere coincidence, but illustrating the general finding that often Jewish addicts have become alienated from Jewish religious customs, ideals and ambitions. With two exceptions there was among our Jewish alcoholic and drug addicted patients no Orthodox person, and the two exceptions were both highly neurotic people. It might seem that the more closely involved Jews are with their "in-group subculture"—religious adherence (and close family ties) perhaps being the most important factor, but a more general type of participation and interest in the work of the Jewish community being also relevant—the less likely are they to become involved in activities such as heavy drinking and drug-taking, which may be common among certain sections of non-Jewish society. Moving away from interest and participation in "Judaism" may leave such people in an emotional or social void, making it possible or attractive for them to get involved with other subcultures such as those where drugs may be easily available, and drug-taking the fashion. Having lost their old yardstick of behaviour and attitudes, they flounder in a void searching and groping possibly unconsciously for a new anchorage. They may therefore take up any new popular fad in order to be "with it"—whatever may happen to be the "it" at the moment.

Another possible point to be kept in mind in this connection is Jellinek's "vulnerability acceptance" hypothesis;[13] in this instance, possibly working in the way that among very observant Jews, and those actively involved in "Judaism," drunkenness and drug abuse are probably taboo, and therefore mainly the psychologically abnormal will expose themselves to such a risk, whereas among those who have moved out of their Jewish circle, even the psychologically less unstable may begin to share the customs of other sections of Society, including drinking and drug taking.

In congruity with the observation that it is mainly Jews moving around the fringe, rather than at the centre, of "Judaism" is our finding of a relatively high number of "half-Jewish" male and female youngsters (of whom one parent was Jewish, the other not) among the addicts. In the sample described (since February 1968) we saw six such patients, in addition to others seen at other facilities. (We saw three alcoholic "half-Jews" during the same period.) However, clearly alienation from "Judaism" is certainly not the only factor involved; professional (doctors, etc.) availability, fashionability of drug-taking in one's occupation (jazz musicians[14]), a high degree of emotional instability, a feeling of personal inadequacy, or of inability to come up to excessive parental expectations, an attempt to get away from parental domination or "sheltering" or from the "narrowness" of parents' outlook, or severe environmental stress (including a feeling of loneliness), etc., were other factors mentioned as playing a role in the history of our Jewish drug dependent patients.

Closer study of the incidence of alcoholism and drug dependence among Jews and of the factors involved should provide important lessons for students of addiction. One important point, if our previous considerations should be borne out by further studies, is the factor of close "involvement." In the rehabilitation of alcoholics and drug addicts it is obviously not sufficient just to remove the drug. It is necessary to replace it with some constructive interest, activity or ideal that is at least as important to the individual as alcohol or drugs were in the past—a new "commitment" or emotional involvement. This is also illustrated by the fact that in Alcoholics Anonymous as well as in Synanon and Daytop Lodge it seems mainly those people who get closely involved in these fellowships who seem to derive the most benefit.[15]

SUMMARY[16]

Throughout the ages alcoholism among Jews has been conspicuous by its relative absence. Among the different hypotheses put forward to explain this fact has been that of the ritual connotation of alcohol among Jews (in contrast, for example, with secular drinking among the Irish). On the other hand, two London General Practitioners found among their drug addicts a proportion of nearly 20 percent Jews. In our own experience, however, with alcoholics and drug addicts in the London area, alcoholism among Jews is not as uncommon, and addiction to other drugs not as common, as indicated in the foregoing. There may be some causal relationship betwen the fact that few of the Jewish alcoholics and drug addicts seen still had strong ties with Judaism. Research into the alleged higher incidence of drug addiction among Jews in contrast to the rarity of alcoholism should provide important clues of value for the study of the aetiology of these problems in general.

REFERENCES

1. Kant, I. Quoted from E.M. Jellinek: *Q J Stud Alcohol, 1:*777, 1941.
2. Fishberg, M.: *The Jews: A Study of Race and Environment.* New York, Scott, 1911.
3. Williams, R.J.: *Q J Stud Alcohol, 7:*567, 1947.
4. Ullman, A.D.: *Ann Am Acad Pol Soc Sci, 315:*48, 1958.
5. Snyder, C.R.: *Alcohol and the Jews.* New Haven, Yale Center Alcohol Studies, 1958.
6. Bales, R.F.: *Q J Stud Alcohol, 6:*480, 1946.
7. Glad, D.D.: *Ibid. 8:*406, 1947.
8. Shuval, R., and D. Krasilowsky: *Israel Ann Psychiat, 1:*277, 1963.
9. Glatt, M.M. and D.R. Hills: *Br J Addict, 63:*183, 1968.
10. Lewin, Louis: *Phantastica.* London, Routledge, Kegan, Paul, 1964.
11. Ollendorff, R., and J. Hewetson: *Br J Addict, 60:*109, 1964.
12. Wislicki, L.: *Ibid. 62:*367, 1967.
13. Jellinek, E.M.: *The Disease Concept of Alcoholism.* New Haven, Hillhouse Press, 1960.
14. Glatt, M.M., D.J. Pittman, D.G. Gillespie and D.R. Hills: *The Drug Scene in Great Britain.* London, Arnold, 1969, p. 31.
15. Glatt, M.M.: *Br J Addict, 64:*165, 1969.
16. Glatt, M.M.: *Second Internat Congr Social Psychiat Proceedings (Summaries).* London, Avenue, 1969, p. 35.

Chapter 29

RELIGIOUS-ETHNIC DIFFERENCES IN ALCOHOL CONSUMPTION

H. Wechsler, H.W. Demone, Jr., D. Thum and E.H. Kasey

INTRODUCTION

Many studies have reported differences in the drinking behavior of various religious and ethnic subgroups. Underlying this research is the general hypothesis that alcohol-use patterns and social systems are intimately interrelated. Bales[1] has described three ways in which rates of alcoholism can be affected by social organization and culture: (1) . . . the degree to which the culture operates to bring about acute needs for adjustment, or inner tensions, in its members, (2) . . . the sort of attitudes toward drinking which the culture produces in the members, (3) . . . the degree to which the culture provides suitable substitute means of satisfaction.

Consistent findings have been reported concerning the use of alcohol by major religious subgroups and by several ethnic groups. Previous studies have found the highest rates of problem drinking among persons of Irish extraction and the lowest rates among Jewish and Italian persons. In a study of drinking in the United States,[10] a sample of 1,515 respondents was chosen by modified random sampling procedures to represent the total noninstitutional population twenty-one years of age and older. Seventy-one percent admitted using alcoholic beverages; percentages by religious affiliation were 90 percent for Jews, 89 for Catholics, and 63 for Protestants. Similarly, an extensive national survey by Cahalan et al.[3] found that 92 percent of the Jews admitted to

This research was supported by Public Health Service Grant UI-00022.

Reprinted in edited version with permission from *J Health Soc Behav, 11:* (no. 1) March, 1970.

using alcoholic beverages, followed by 83 percent of Catholics and 60 percent of Protestants. Despite the large proportion of Jewish persons who reported drinking, only 11 percent who drank were classified as heavy drinkers, compared with 23 percent of the Catholics and 15 percent of the Protestants. Based on the self-reports of 706 New York City adults, Haberman and Sheinberg[5] concluded that the Negro, Irish, and Puerto Rican subgroups were most likely to have drinking problems, whereas Jews and Italians were least likely to have such problems. An examination of first admissions to mental hospitals in Ohio indicated that the rate for first admissions with alcoholic disorders was higher among male non-whites than whites, and among native-born white males than foreign-born.[8]

In studying college students and House of Correction inmates, Ullman[11,12] ranked the nationality groups of those with drinking problems as follows: Irish, English, Scottish, French, German, and Italian. The McCords[9] found similar frequencies of problem drinkers in their follow-up of the Cambridge-Somerville youth study: Irish, Native Americans, Western Europeans, Eastern Europeans, British West Indians, Other Latins, and, lastly, Italians.

Nine nationality groups were identified by Demone[4] in his work on male adolescents in metropolitan Boston; this is the largest number of different ethnic groups compared in a single study. Demone found that ethnic values operated as significant factors in the development of drinking patterns, despite the assimilation of the suburban population under study and its separation from the direct influence of foreign-born and first-generation Americans. In agreement with other research, Irish and French Americans had abnormally high rates of excessive alcohol use. A very high rate was also found among Canadian Americans, a specially defined subgroup within the Demone study. The Jewish males drank most frequently, but with a significantly lower rate of problem drinking than their Catholic and Protestant peers. Similarly, although Italian Americans were not ranked lowest in this study, they manifested a below-average rate of excessive drinking.

Studies relating the use of alcohol to religious or ethnic affiliation have usually based their conclusions on self-reports of drinking or on indirect indications such as rates of hospitalization for alcohol-related disorders. As described below, Breathalyzer readings as well as several other indications of alcohol involvement were obtained in the course of a large-scale investigation of the role that drinking may play in home and other accidental injuries. The collection of Breathalyzer results on a large sample of persons provided an opportunity to employ an objective measure of alcohol level in comparisons of alcohol use among persons from different cultural backgrounds.

METHOD

This study was conducted in the Emergency Service of the Massachusetts General Hospital in Boston. The design involved interviewing a sample of patients 16 years of age and older who were admitted for treatment in the Emergency Service from October 2, 1966, through September 29, 1967. Although the study focussed on accidental injuries, the sample included patients with other conditions and diseases for comparative purposes. On each of 363 consecutive days, patients were interviewed during one of three eight-hour shifts. A schedule was developed to provide an equal distribution of shifts, days of the week, and months of the year; all holidays were covered by at least one shift. When patients could not be interviewed in the Emergency Service, questionnaires were completed through follow-up procedures in the hospital.

The interviewer obtained relevant biographical material, a description of the circumstances surrounding the accident or acute symptom onset, and several measures of the patient's drinking behavior. A Breathalyzer reading taken at the time of the interview was used as the primary index of blood alcohol concentration. In those instances when a breath sample could not be procured but a blood sample had been drawn by the admitting physician, the latter was available for the determination of blood alcohol concentration. The comparability of alcohol levels obtained by direct analysis of the blood and those from breath samples has been demonstrated in several studies.[2,6]

THE SAMPLE

During the one-year period of investigation, 16,861 persons were admitted to the Emergency Service during the study shifts. Of this number, 2,392 were below the age of 16. Of the 14,469 patients 16 years of age and older, an estimated 2,825 were found ineligible for the study.* Thus, 11,644 patients were eligible for inclusion in the study. The final sample of 8,461 patients comprised 73 percent of those eligible. A total of 3,183 patients were missed by interviews in the Emergency Service.

Despite the fact that almost three out of four eligible patients were included in the study, it was important to examine the characteristics of missed patients in order to determine whether there was any bias in the inclusion procedures. Therefore, the hospital records for a 10 percent sample ($N = 313$) of missed patients were examined for indications of alcoholism or intoxication at the time of admission. A comparison of 237 randomly selected patients who were included in the sample with those patients who were missed revealed that there was no difference in the proportion with evidence of alcoholism or drinking prior to admission (6% vs. 7%, respectively; $x^2 = 0.28$, d.f. $= 1$, $p > .05$).

SOURCES OF INFORMATION AND ANALYSIS OF THE DATA

Seventy-eight percent of the questionnaires on the sample of 8,461 patients were completed during interviews with patients in the Emergency Service, 18 percent through follow-up procedures in the hospital, and the remainder through interviews with persons who accompanied the patients to the Emergency Service.

Measures of Alcohol Use. Several indices of alcohol consumption prior to admission were availiable for different yet overlap-

---

* This estimate was based on a 10 percent sample of all excluded patients. Routinely excluded from the study were persons admitted with psychiatric problems (including alcoholics without injury and cases of attempted suicide), those who received only postoperative or continuing care in the Emergency Service, and those with dental problems of non-traumatic origin. Persons dead on arrival were not included.

ping proportions of the total sample. Breathalyzer readings were obtained for 74 percent (6,266 cases) of the total,* and venous blood analyses were done on 13 percent (1,079 cases). Other measures of alcohol consumption included (1) interviewers' observations concerning the presence or absence of the smell of alcohol on the breath of the patient at the time of admisison—77 percent (6,523 cases); (2) patients' reports on their use of alcoholic beverages prior to the injury or symptom requiring treatment—69 percent (5,812 cases); (3) a composite index based on Breathalyzer results, venous blood analyses, and interviewers' reports on alcoholic breath—90 percent (7,598 cases);† and (4) self-categorization of drinking habits—82 percent of patients in the sample who were interviewed during the last six months of the study (3,557 cases).

Religious-Ethnic Subgroups. Patients were assigned to ten religious-ethnic subgroups on the basis of (1) race (white or Negro), (2) religion (Protestant, Catholic, or Jewish), and (3) the patient's place of birth and that of his parents. Persons who were identified as "white" were categorized by religion and nativity. Among white Catholics and Protestants, native-born persons of native parentage were categorized as "native." Foreign-born persons were classified according to their country of origin, while native-born persons of foreign parentage were classified according to their parents' birthplace, and native-born persons with one foreign-born parent according to the birthplace of that parent. If both parents were born in different foreign countries, the patient was categorized according to the birthplace of his father. This procedure conforms to that of the U.S. Bureau of the Census (1963). Because of their relatively small numbers, neither Negroes nor white persons of the Jewish religion were subdivided on the basis of national origin.

* Two hundred and twenty-four persons refused to take a Breathalyzer test, comprising 3 percent of the total sample.

† Patients with a positive indication of drinking based on any one of these three measures were classified as "with alcohol," and those with no positive indications and with at least one negative indication (e.g. a negative Breathalyzer reading) were classified as "without alcohol." With the exception of inclusion in the composite index, venous blood analyses were not used in comparisons of religious-ethnic subgroups, since blood samples were obtained for only 13 percent of the total sample.

Statistical Comparisons. Each of the religious-ethnic subgroups comprised over 400 patients, providing sufficiently large cell sizes for statistical purposes. The chi-square test with a .05 level of significance was used throughout in analyzing these data. With the exception of analyses of Breathalyzer results controlled on patient characteristics (sex, age, etc.), each subgroup was compared with every other. However, because of the large number of comparisons involved, discussion is restricted to those subgroups that differed significantly from most other groups.

Breathalyzer Results

Breathalyzer readings were significantly related to religious-ethnic group membership. Jews and Italian Catholics had the lowest proportions with positive Breathalyzer readings. Among native-born, Irish, and Canadian Catholics, the proportion with positive Breathalyzer readings was at least twice that found in either the Jewish or the Italian Catholic groups. Analyses of separate groups revealed that Jews differed significantly from Italian Catholics as well as from all other groups, and Italian Catholics differed from every other group, except Other Protestants.

The relationship between the presence of alcohol (as measured by the Breathalyzer) and religious-ethnic group membership was controlled on the four social variables most frequently cited as related to alcohol consumption: sex, age, marital status, and social class. For these analyses, cell sizes required the division of patients into two categories: (1) those with readings of 0.00%— "negative," and (2) those with an indication of alcohol (0.01% and over)—"positive."

Sex. Breathalyzer results were significantly related to religious-ethnic group membership for both males and females. The lowest percentage of positive readings among males was found in the Jewish group, followed by Italian Catholics; the highest occurred among Irish Catholic males. Among females, Other Protestants, Italian Catholics, and Jews had the lowest frequencies of positive readings.

Age. Breathalyzer results were significantly related to religious-ethnic group membership for three of the four age groups. A statistically significant relationship was not found for patients over 65 years of age. In the three younger groups, Jews and Italian Catholics consistently manifested the lowest frequencies of positive readings. Irish and Canadian Catholics had the highest percentages in the 26- to 45-year-old group, although native-born Catholics ranked highest in the 16- to 25- and 46- to 65-year-old groups.

Marital Status. Separate analyses were done on single persons, currently married persons, and those who had been married (widowed, divorced, or separated). For all three groups, Breathalyzer results were related to religious-ethnic group membership at statistically significant levels. Jews consistently had the lowest percentage of positive readings. Italian Catholics also had relatively low frequencies of positive readings. Irish Catholics had the highest percentage in the single and currently married groups, and native-born Catholics were highest among formerly married persons.

Social Class. Patients were divided into four social class groups according to the Hollingshead Two-Factor Index of Social Position.[7] Statistically significant relationships were found between Breathalyzer results and religious-ethnic group membership for each social class group except Class III. In all four groups, Jews had the lowest proportion of positive readings. Irish Catholics and Negroes had the highest percentages in Classes I and II, whereas native-born Catholics were ranked highest in Classes I, II, IV, and V.

Other Indices of Alcohol Consumption

Observations of Alcoholic Breath. Alcoholic breath was detected least frequently among Jews and Italian Catholics and most frequently among Irish and native-born Catholics. No significant difference was found between the Jewish and Italian Catholic groups, although each differed significantly from all other groups.

Self-Report of Drinking Before Episode. Sixty-nine percent of the patients provided information on the time interval between their last drink and the injury or onset of symptoms which brought them to the Emergency Service. In the present context, this information may be interpreted as an indication of whether or not the person consumed alcoholic beverages during a specified period of time. The proportion of those who reported having consumed alcohol within six hours before the injury or onset of symptoms was less than 10 percent among Jews, Italian and Other Catholics, and Other Protestants. In contrast, 19 percent of native-born Catholics and 15 percent of native-born Protestants reported drinking during this six-hour period. Jews, Italian and Other Catholics, and Other Protestants did not differ from each other, but each group differed significantly from all other groups. Native-born Catholics did not differ from either Canadian Catholics or native-born Protestants, although they differed at significant levels from all other groups.

Composite Index of Alcohol Consumption. The Jewish group had the lowest proportion of persons with indications of the presence of alcohol at the time of admission, followed by Italian Catholics and Other Protestants. Canadian, Irish, and native-born Catholics had the highest proportions; approximately one out of five showed some evidence of alcohol. Significant differences were found between Jews and every other group, including Italian Catholics. Italian Catholics differed from all other groups except Other Protestants, where the difference was not significant. Native-born Catholics differed from other groups, excepting Canadian and Irish Catholics and Negroes.

Self-Categorization of Drinking Behavior. During the final six months of the study, patients were asked to rate themselves, according to their usual drinking behavior as "abstainer," "very moderate drinker," or "moderate-to-heavy drinker." Self-categorizations were obtained from 82 percent of those asked.

Self-categorization was significantly associated with religious-ethnic group membership. Significant differences were found between Jews and every other group. Italian Catholics differed significantly from Other Protestants; each differed from all other groups, except in the comparison of Other Protestants with Other Catholics, where the difference was not significant. Of all those who admitted some drinking, the Jewish group had the lowest proportion with self-ratings of moderate-to-heavy (18% for Jews, compared with 32% for Italian Catholics and 45% for all other groups combined).

SUMMARY AND DISCUSSION

Differences in the drinking behavior of several religious-ethnic groups were examined within the context of a study that utilized the Breathalyzer to measure alcohol levels in a hospital emergency service population. Previous studies have found the highest rates of problem-drinking among Irish persons and the lowest rates among Jews and those of Italian descent. Unlike the present study, however, most studies have relied entirely on self-reports or on hospitalization rates rather than on direct indications of the use of alcohol.

In agreement with previous research, the proportion of patients with positive indications of alcohol consumption was consistently lower among Jews and among Catholics of Italian descent. This pattern was observed for each of four indices of the use of alcohol prior to admisison to the Emergency Service, and similar trends were evident when patients were asked to categorize their usual drinking behavior. Among persons who admitted that they drink, only 18 percent of Jews and 32 percent of Italian Catholics rated themselves as moderate-to-heavy drinkers, compared with 45 percent for all other drinkers combined.

Other investigations have reported the greatest use of alcohol among the Irish. In the present study, the Irish Catholic group was observed to include a high proportion of persons with positive alcohol indications; however, drinking among Canadian and native-born Catholics and among native-born Protestants approximated that of the Irish. The results on Canadian Catholics are in agreement with those reported by Demone,[4] who found high rates of alcohol consumption among both Canadian and Irish groups in metropolitan Boston. Also, native-born Catholics in the present study might be expected to reflect patterns of alcohol use similar to those found among Irish Catholics. Since the first large Catholic group to migrate to the Boston area came from Ireland, it is probable that those classified as native-born Catholics include a large number of persons of Irish descent.

The overall relationship between religious-ethnic group membership and alcohol consumption was maintained when controls were applied for sex, age, marital status, and social class. Nevertheless, the results should be interpreted cautiously. The sample chosen for this study was composed of patients admitted to the emergency service of a large general hospital, and the drinking patterns of people who are ill or injured may differ from those of the general population. However, the consistency of the results suggests that distortion due to this factor may have been minor.

REFERENCES

1. Bales, R.F.: Cultural differences in rates of alcoholism. *Q J Stud Alcohol*, 6:480–499, 1946.
2. Borkenstein, R.F., *et al.*: *The Role of the Drinking Driver in Traffic Accidents*. Bloomington, Indiana University, Department of Police Administration, 1964.
3. Cahalan, D., I.H. Cisin, and H.M. Crossley: *American Drinking Practices: A National Survey of Behavior and Attitudes Related to Alcoholic Beverages* (Report No. 3). Washington, George Washington University, Social Research Group, 1967.
4. Demone, H.W., Jr.: Drinking Attitudes and Practices of Male Adolescents. Unpublished Ph.D. Dissertation, Brandeis University, 1966.
5. Haberman, P.W. and J. Sheinberg: Implicative drinking reported in a household survey: a corroborative note on subgroup differences. *Q J Stud Alcohol*, 28:528–543, 1967.
6. Harger, R.N., and R.B. Forney: Aliphatic alcohols. In A. Stolman (Ed.): *Progress in Chemical Toxicology* (Vol. 1). New York, Academic Press, 1963, pp. 53–134.
7. Hollingshead, A.B.: Two-Factor Index of Social Position. New Haven, Yale University, Mimeo, 1957.
8. Locke, B.Z., and H.J. Duvall: Alcoholism among first admissions to Ohio public mental hospitals. *Q J Stud Alcohol*, 25:521–534, 1964.
9. McCord, W., J. McCord, and J. Gudeman: *Origins of Alcoholism*. Stanford, Stanford University Press, 1960.
10. Mulford, H.A.: Drinking and deviant drinking, U.S.A., 1963. *Q J Stud Alcohol*, 25:634–650, 1964.
11. Ullman, A.D.: Socio-cultural backgrounds of alcoholism. *Ann Am Acad Pol Soc Sci*, 315:48–54, 1958.
12. Ullman, A.D.: Ethnic differences in the first drinking experience. *Soc Prob*, 8:45–56, 1960.
13. U.S. Bureau of the Census. U.S. Census of Population: 1960. In *Characteristics of the Population* (Vol. I). Washington, Government Printing Office, 1960.

Chapter 30

THE DISTRIBUTION OF MENTAL DISEASE ACCORDING TO RELIGIOUS AFFILIATION IN NEW YORK STATE, 1949–1951

B. Malzberg

There are types of behavior associated with religious beliefs and practices that are recognized as falling within the scope of abnormality.

Delusions and hallucinations related to religious symbolisms are not uncommon. Mass psychopathy resulting from extreme practices, such as that associated with belief in possession, has affected untold numbers. Mass suggestion may bring waves of psychoneuroses, such as the dance manias of the Middle Ages. The most striking cases are the great mystics; there is still disagreement as to whether or not they belong within the normal range of mental health.

It is clearly possible to find individuals whose abnormalities of conduct may be ascribed to, or at least associated with, extreme expressions of religious beliefs, practices and rituals. Which is cause and which is effect cannot always be determined. Neither can one generalize from such data so as to conclude that there is a necessary relation between the extremes of religious behavior and degrees of mental abnormality.

The question may be made clearer if we express it in statistical language. Suppose that a population were classified in accordance with a scale showing degrees of religious devotion. Would the incidence and prevalence of mental disease vary in correlation with a distribution derived from such a scale?

Reprinted in edited version with permission from *Ment Hyg*, *46*: (no. 4) October, 1962.

This investigation was supported by a research grant from the National Institute of Mental Health (Grant M–1140 C4).

Insofar as religion reduces worries and tensions, it may be a factor in the maintenance of mental health. And there is some evidence that people who attend church regularly feel less distressed than those who attend infrequently.[4] But such a broad description does not provide a necesary basis for discussing the frequency of mental disease.

Obviously, there are no large bodies of graded data obtained from large populations which can answer this question at present. Small sample populations would not suffice because they could not lead to significant rates. We are therefore restricted to data which can throw only indirect light upon the relation of religion to mental disease.

We may consider formal religious affiliation as expressed by membership in church bodies, or by other expressions of preference for such relation.

If, therefore, we had a classification of the general population in terms of formal religious affiliation, we could compare such a distribution with corresponding first admissions to hospitals for mental disease. Such statistics, with respect to the general population, are usually prepared by organized churches, which list their memberships. This gives no clue to the number who are not active members, who do not affiliate but who consider themselves, nevertheless, members of such church bodies.

The decennial census of population does not provide data with respect to religious affiliations. In March, 1957 however, the Bureau of the Census carried out a sample survey in which voluntary answers were obtained from the civilian population, aged 14 years and over, to the question "What is your religion"?[1]

It was estimated on the basis of the sample that two-thirds of those aged 14 and over were Protestants, a fourth were Roman Catholics, and 3 percent were Jewish. The distribution varied throughout the country. Protestants were less numerous in the northeastern states, their percentage dropping to 42. Roman Catholics increased to 45 percent of the total, and Jews increased to 8.5 percent. Similar data are not given for individual states.

In theory, it is possible to use the distribution of the population according to religious affiliation as the base for the determination of rates of first admissions. Unfortunately, enumerations of first admissions with respect to religious affiliation are not sufficiently complete to permit computation of reasonably accurate rates for the United States. It is therefore necessary to limit such an investigation to a single state. The succeeding analysis will therefore be limited to New York State.

However, there are no official data giving the distribution of the population of New York State according to religious affiliation. A rough approximation to such relative distribution of the whole population may be made by considering the religious affiliations attributed to white first admissions to all hospitals for mental disease in New York State. There were 51,337 such first admissions from October 1, 1948, to September 30, 1951, of whom 24,422, or 47.6 percent, were Roman Catholic. Protestant denominations included 17,373, or 33.8 percent. Jews totaled 8,123, or 15.8 percent. All others, including unascertained, totaled 1,419, or 2.8 percent. A rough approximation to the general population would therefore imply that half the population of New York State was Roman Catholic, a third was Protestant, and a sixth was Jewish.

The distribution differs significantly as between New York City and the remainder of the state. First admissions from New York City were distributed as follows: Roman Catholic, 51.3 percent; Protestant, 20.0 percent; Jewish, 25.4 percent. In the remainder of the state first admissions were distributed as follows: Roman Catholic, 42.8 percent; Protestant, 51.2 percent; Jews, 3.8 percent.

It is evident, therefore, that Protestant first admissions (and Protestants in general) resided largely outside of New York City, whereas Jews were concentrated heavily in that city. Of the Protestant first admissions, a third were from New York City, and two-thirds were from the remainder of the state. Of the Jews, 90 percent were from New York City, and only 10 percent from the remainder of the state. It is probable that of the latter, a majority were from counties contiguous to the metropolis. Of the Roman Catholics, 60 percent were from New York City, and 40 percent were from the remainder of the state.

Jewish first admissions were almost completely from urban areas; only 1.6 percent were from a rural environment. Roman Catholics were also heavily urban, only 8.8 percent being of rural origin. Of the Protestants, 76.5 percent were urban, and 23.5 percent were rural in origin.

TABLE 30-I

WHITE FIRST ADMISSIONS TO ALL HOSPITALS FOR MENTAL DISEASE IN NEW YORK STATE, 1949–1951, CLASSIFIED ACCORDING TO RELIGIOUS AFFILIATION AND ENVIRONMENT

Environment	Protestant			Roman Catholic			Jewish			Other		
	Males	Females	Total	Males	Females	Total	Males	Females	Total	Males	Females	Total
Urban	6,316	6,970	13,286	11,072	11,195	22,267	3,356	4,636	7,992	741	489	1,230
New York City	2,545	3,163	5,708	7,097	7,097	14,654	3,050	4,205	7,255	563	359	922
Other	3,771	3,807	7,578	3,975	3,638	7,613	306	431	737	178	130	308
Rural	2,058	2,029	4,087	1,086	1,069	2,155	57	74	131	111	78	189
Total	8,374	8,999	17,373	12,158	12,264	24,422	3,413	4,710	8,123	852	567	1,419

White first admissions to all hospitals for mental disease in New York State during 1949–1951 are classified in Table 30-II according to mental disorders.

Of the 17,373 white Protestant first admissions, 4,005, or 23.1 percent, were psychoses with cerebral arteriosclerosis, and 3,197, or 18.4 percent, were senile psychoses. Together, they included 41.5 percent of Protestant first admissions, compared with 33.3 percent among total white first admissions. Dementia praecox included 3,930 cases, or 22.6 percent of the total, compared with 26.9 percent for all white first admissions.

Roman Catholics had a different distribution. Alcoholic psychoses represented 7.3 percent of all such first admissions, compared with 5.3 percent among all white first admissions. Psychoses with cerebral arteriosclerosis and senile psychoses together included 30 percent of the total, compared with 41.5 percent for Protestants. Dementia praecox included 28.4 percent of the total.

Jewish first admissions differed from both Protestants and Roman Catholics with respect to the distribution of mental disorders. There were only 27 first admissions with alcoholic psychoses, or 0.3 percent of total Jewish first admissions, compared with 4.9 and 7.3 percent for Protestants and Roman Catholics, respectively. The proportionate distribution of the psychoses of advanced age was less for Jews than for the other religious groups. However, the relative proportions of the functional disorders were higher for Jews.

Proportionate differences in the distribution of mental disorders are not equivalent to differences in the incidence of such disorders. The latter is obtained from the ratio of admissions to the total population, and is usually expressed as an annual rate of first admissions per 100,000 population. Since the basic populations are not available for the several religious denominations in New York State, it is not possible to compute corresponding rates of first admissions for the State.

Such a comparison is possible, however, for New York City. In 1952, the Health Insurance Plan (H.I.P.) made an area probability survey of the population of New York City, and included 13,558 persons in 4,190 households.[3] When the sample was compared with the 1950 census of population for New York City, satis-

TABLE 30-II

WHITE FIRST ADMISSIONS TO ALL HOSPITALS FOR MENTAL DISEASE IN NEW YORK STATE, 1949–1951, CLASSIFIED ACCORDING TO RELIGIOUS AFFILIATION AND MENTAL DISORDERS

Mental disorders	Protestant				Roman Catholic				Jewish			
			Total				Total				Total	
	Males	Females	No.	Percent	Males	Females	No.	Percent	Males	Females	No.	Percent
General paresis	130	71	201	1.2	260	97	357	1.4	27	6	33	0.4
Alcoholic	674	174	848	4.9	1,385	397	1,782	7.3	26	1	27	0.3
With cerebral arteriosclerosis	2,058	1,947	4,005	23.1	2,294	2,061	4,355	17.8	592	720	1,312	16.2
Senile	1,170	2,027	3,197	18.4	1,149	1,823	2,972	12.2	284	563	847	10.4
Involutional	456	976	1,432	8.2	644	1,483	2,127	8.7	352	822	1,174	14.4
Manic-depressive	232	460	692	4.0	269	595	864	3.5	251	424	675	8.3
Dementia praecox	1,701	2,229	3,930	22.6	3,608	3,316	6,924	28.4	1,156	1,316	2,472	30.4
Psychoneuroses	486	461	947	5.4	578	1,003	1,581	6.5	336	519	855	10.5
Other	1,407	654	2,121	12.2	1,971	1,489	3,460	14.2	389	339	728	9.0
Total	8,374	8,999	17,373	100.0	12,158	12,264	24,422	100.0	3,413	4,710	8,123	100.0

factory agreement was found in the relative distributions of common items. It was therefore concluded that the sample also gave a satisfactory distribution with respect to religious affiliation.

On this basis, it was found that 51.5 percent of the white population of New York City was Roman Catholic; 16.0 was Protestant; 29.7 percent was Jewish; and 2.8 percent belonged to other religious groups or were not reported.

We showed previously that the first admissions from New York City were distributed as follows: Roman Catholic, 51.3 percent; Protestant, 20.0 percent; Jewish, 25.4 percent. It therefore follows that Protestants had a higher proportion among first admissions than expected on the basis of their proportion in the general population. Roman Catholics and Jews were below their expectations, especially so in the case of Jews.

According to the census of April 1, 1950, the white population of New York City totaled 7,116,441.[2] Distributing this total in accordance with the relative proportions shown in the sample study, we estimate the religious affiliation of the general white population of New York City in 1950 as follows: Roman Catholic, 3,664,967; Protestant, 1,138,631; Jewish, 2,113,583; other, 199,260.

On this basis, Protestants had an average annual rate of 167.1 per 100,000 population, compared with 133.2 for Roman Catholics and 114.4 for Jews.

Rates of first admissions vary with age. They are at a minimum below age 15, and increase to a maximum at advanced age. Thus, the preceding crude rates are dependent in large part upon the age distributions of the several religious groups. The differences occur principally at ages 15 to 44 and ages 65 and over. Of the Protestants, 37.1 percent were aged 15 to 44, compared with 45.4 percent of Roman Catholics and 40.6 percent of Jews. On the other hand, 27.8 percent of Protestants were aged 45 to 64, compared with 19.4 percent of Roman Catholics and 24.9 percent of Jews. The corresponding percentages at age 65 and over were 9.3, 5.9 and 7.6, respectively.

The heavier weighting of the Protestants at ages 45 and over tends to raise their crude rate. Hence, it is necessary to compare corresponding age-specific rates. We find that Protestants had higher rates than Roman Catholics in three of the four age groups, and that they had higher rates than Jews in all age groups. Catholics, in turn, had higher rates than Jews in two of three age groups. It is, therefore, highly probable that Jews had the lowest average annual overall rate, and that Protestants had the highest. Catholics had an intermediate rate.

General Paresis

Of the 5,708 Protestant first admissions, 71 were diagnosed as general paresis, giving an average annual rate of 2.1 per 100,000. Roman Catholics had a corresponding rate of 1.9. The lowest rate, 0.4, occurred among Jews. The latter had lower age-specific rates than either Protestants or Roman Catholics. Catholics, in turn, had lower rates than Protestants at ages 15 to 44 and 65 and over, but the differences are small and probably not significant.

Alcoholic Psychoses

Protestants had an average annual rate of 10.4 per 100,000 with alcoholic psychoses. This was slightly higher than the rate of 9.7 per 100,000 for Roman Catholics. Jews had the significantly lower rate of 0.4.

Protestants and Catholics both had significantly higher rates than Jews at corresponding ages. Protestants had a higher rate than Catholics at ages 15 to 44, but they had lower rates at higher ages. It is possible that standardization might result in a lower rate for Protestants.

The Catholic population of New York City consists largely of Irish and Italians. The Irish had a higher rate of such psychoses than any other white group. Italians, on the other hand, had the lowest rate, next to Jews.

Psychoses with Cerebral
Arteriosclerosis

The Protestant population of New York City was older than the Catholic or Jewish population. Those aged 45 and over included 37.1 percent of Protestants, compared with 25.3 percent of Catholics and 32.5 percent of Jews. We might therefore anticipate a higher rate of first admissions with psychoses with cerebral arteriosclerosis among Protestants. In fact, they had an average annual rate of 36.7 per 100,000, compared with 24.7 for Catholics and 18.7 for Jews. That the differences are not spurious is shown by the fact that at ages 65 and over, which include the bulk of such admissions, Jews had a rate of 186.0, compared with 311.4 for Catholics and 324.9 for Protestants.

Senile Psychoses

The relative distribution of senile psychoses was similar to that for psychoses with cerebral arteriosclerosis. Jews had the lowest average annual rate, 12.2 per 100,000. Protestants had the highest rate, 36.0. Catholics were intermediate with a rate of 17.0. At ages 65 and over, the rates were 154.8 for Jews, 278.6 for Catholics, and 375.9 for Protestants.

Involutional Psychoses

In each of the preceding groups of disorders, Jews had a lower rate of first admissions than either Protestants or Catholics. This is reversed in connection with involutional psychoses. Jews had an average annual rate of 16.6 per 100,000, compared with 12.4 for Catholics and 14.6 for Protestants. The difference between the two latter populations is probably spurious, due to age selections, since Protestants had lower age-specific rates, beginning at age 45. The rate for Jews is probably significantly higher than that for Protestants. There is no such certainty with respect to the difference between Jews and Catholics.

Manic-depressive Psychoses

Jews had an average annual rate of manic-depressive psychoses of 8.8 per 100,000. Catholics had the lowest rate, 4.0, and Protestants were intermediate with 5.5. The differences are probably significant, since Jews had higher age-specific rates than Protestants, and the latter, in turn, had higher rates than Catholics.

Dementia Praecox

Jews had an average annual rate of 35.5 per 100,00 with dementia praecox, compared with 41.7 for Protestants. The difference is probably significant since Jews had lower age-specific rates, beginning at age 15. The crude rate for Catholics was 41.2, but compared with Jews the difference is probably not significant, since the age-specific rates did not differ significantly during the age interval specific to this disorder. The crude rates did not differ significantly between Catholics and Protestants. But in the significant age intervals, Protestants had a higher rate. It is therefore probable that Protestants had a higher rate of first admissions with dementia praecox than Catholics.

Psychoneuroses

Jews had an average annual rate of first admissions of 11.7 per 100,000 with respect to psychoneuroses, twice that for either Protestants or Catholics. The differences are significant since Jews had higher age-specific rates. None of the differences between Protestants and Catholics is significant.

We combined the eight major groups of mental disorders into two categories, those of organic origin, and those termed functional. We found that the overall rate of first admissions was less for Jews than for Protestants and Roman Catholics. This was due primarily to significantly lower rates for Jews among disorders of organic origin. Thus, the average annual rates per 100,000 in this category were 31.8 for Jews, 53.3 for Roman Catholics, and 85.1 for Protestants. Jews had lower age-specific rates. Roman Catholics had a higher rate than Protestants at ages 45 to 64, but had a significantly lower rate at ages 65 and over.

With respect to the four functional disorders, however, Jews had an average annual rate of 72.6, compared with 63.5 for Roman Catholics, and 67.4 for Protestants. The rate for Jews exceeded that for Roman Catholics by 14 percent, and exceeded that for Protestants by 8 percent. The rate for Protestants exceeded that for Roman Catholics by 6 percent.

SUMMARY

A comparison of the relative frequencies of mental disease among members of the major religious groups depends upon a classification of the general population according to religion and a corresponding classification of first admissions to mental hospitals. Data of this type are available only for New York City.

Thanks to a survey of a random sample of the population of New York City by Health Insurance Plan of Greater New York (H.I.P.), it was possible to estimate the distribution of the population according to religious affiliation in 1950. Corresponding data for first admissions were available from the records of the New York State Department of Mental Hygiene, including admissions to all hospitals for mental disease, public and private.

Limitation to New York City, fortunately, placed the comparisons on a roughly comparable basis with respect to size and density of population. In addition, the survey by H.I.P. made it possible to compute age-specific rates, using broad age intervals.

It thus appeared that Jews had the lowest overall rate of first admissions, Protestants the highest, and Roman Catholics were intermediate. In general, Jews had the lowest rates among those psychoses which are of organic origin. This was especially notable with respect to alcoholic psychoses and general paresis. But Jews also had relatively low rates of first admissions with respect to disorders of advanced age.

Roman Catholics and Protestants had significantly lower rates than Jews with respect to manic-depressive psychoses and psychoneuroses. The rates with respect to involutional psychoses do not differ so conclusively. It is probable that Jews had a lower rate of first admissions with dementia praecox than either Protestants or Catholics.

Protestants generally had higher rates than Catholics for those disorders which are of organic origin: for example, psychoses with cerebral arteriosclerosis and senile psychoses. The differences do not appear to be significant in the case of functional disorders, as, for example, dementia praecox.

We have thus found differences in rates of first admissions associated with formal religious affiliations. But we cannot draw from these associations inferences as to causal relations. The several religious groups differ in important social and racial respects, which have been shown elsewhere to be related to the frequency of mental disease.

Thus, Catholics have a high rate of alcoholic psychoses, because they include Irish and Polish Slavs who have long histories of addiction to heavy drinking. The low rate of such disorders among Jews is generally attributed to social traditions arising from their special history. Protestants include large representations of English and German origin, who because of their longer residence in New York State, are older and therefore more exposed to the mental hazards of old age.

Thus, more conclusive answers as to the possible relations between religion and mental disease must be sought in further investigations, employing more meaningful classifications. Among Jews, for example, there are groups recognized by intense religious devotions and ritual exercises. With adequate resources, it would be possible to determine rates of first admissions among such a group, and to make comparisons with Jews as a whole.

It is possible to isolate similar groups among Protestants, especially among isolated mountain dwellers. Roman Catholics also provide special communities which could be studied in a similar manner. This type of data, which is psychologically better defined than that resulting merely from formal church membership, may lead to more definite conclusions as to the relation of religion to mental disease.

REFERENCES

1. Bureau of the Census. *Current Population Reports. Population Characteristics.* Washington, D. C., U.S. Government Printing Office, 1957, Series P-20, No. 79.

2. Bureau of the Census. *1950, United States Census of Population. New York. General Characteristics.* Washington, D.C., U.S. Government Printing Office, 1952, Series P-B 32, p. 84.

3. Deardorff, Neva R.: The religio-cultural background of New York City's population. *Milbank Memorial Fund Q,* 33:152–160, 1955.

4. Gurin, Gerald, Joseph Veroff and Shelia Feld: *Americans View Their Mental Health.* New York, Basic Books, Inc., 1960.

Chapter 31

THE SOCIO-CULTURAL ASPECTS OF SCHIZOPHRENIA: A COMPARISON OF PROTESTANT AND JEWISH SCHIZOPHRENICS

V.D. Sanua

INTRODUCTION

The purpose of this paper is to present a critical discussion of some of the studies on parent-child relationship in schizophrenia, as well as preliminary findings on characteristics of the home environment of schizophrenic males from two religious groups—Jewish and Protestant, and from two social classes—low and high socioeconomic status. The general hypothesis is that early unfavourable home environment affects the psychological adjustment of the individual in an adverse way. One of the basic problems in etiological studies is to relate the kind of home environment to the specific illness or deviance.

One of the recurring findings is that schizophrenic patients had an unwholesome relationship with their mothers. Some mothers were found to be over-protective, rejecting, domineering and aggressive. Fromm-Reichmann[5] coined the descriptive phrase "schizophrenogenic mother." This label has rarely been applied to the father, who was usually reported as a weak and submissive individual. The inconclusiveness of the studies reported in the literature, some of which will be described here, could be attributed to the fact that in most instances the sociocultural characteristics of the samples under study were neglected variables.

Reprinted in edited version with permission from *Int J Soc Psychiatry, 9:* (no. 1) 1963.

This study was conducted by the writer while working as a Research Fellow at the Department of Social Relations, Harvard University. The paper was read at the XVth International Congress of Scientific Psychology held in Bonn, Germany, in August, 1960.

A study by Frazee[4] revealed that the fathers, in her sample of 22 schizophrenic patients, did not have the characteristics described above namely, weak and submissive. This is what she wrote about them: "Many of the fathers were severely cruel and rejecting. This finding is interesting since it failed to support expectations of the passive, ineffectual father generally assumed in the literature." While there seems to be a contradiction between her study and the earlier efforts, it is believed that one of the reasons for such differences is the fact that most of Frazee's patients came from lower-class families, while the sample in earlier studies included an over-representation of patients belonging to the middle and upper classes.

Another study which throws doubt on the generalization of the "schizophrenogenic mother" was conducted by Hotchkiss *et al.*[10] at the Massachusetts Mental Health Centre. Of the 22 mothers who were observed during their regular visits to their schizophrenic sons in the wards only three had the characteristics of the "schizophrenogenic mother." The authors suggested that the characterization by Fromm-Reichmann of the dominant mother, rather than representing a composite picture of the mother of a schizophrenic patient, probably was derived from the conspicious behaviour of a few.

SOME PROBLEMS OF METHODOLOGY

Various methods have been used to study the home background of the schizophrenic. Most of the earlier studies relied exclusively on hospital records for the source of data. Since information in such files was not collected for research purposes investigators were likely to find an uneven quality in their coverage. The tendency therefore was to select such cases which had sufficient data.

Another set of studies, to be described, pertains to data which have been collected directly from patients or close relatives for the purpose of research. As in the previous instance, however, there was still a selective factor. Only those patients who had mothers who fulfilled certain criteria (such as adequate intelligence, education, residence close to the hospital, etc.) were included. While some investigators limited their contacts to one or two interviews, others obtained their data in the course of protracted therapy with the patients and the parents.

A criticism specific to this type of research is that samples are frequently composed of middle and upper-class patients and lack control groups. Also the number of patients who can be seen by a single therapist is limited mostly to upper-class patients which would tend to slant the data. We would, therefore, obtain only a picture of parent-child relationship in higher social strata.

Investigators in another group of studies had to rely primarily upon data obtained from psychological tests such as the Thematic Apperception Test, California F-Scale, Shoben Attitude Survey Scale, etc. Controls were included in practically all instances. One serious problem, however, is to find an adequate control group. The appropriateness of comparing hospital volunteers with mothers of schizophrenics would raise some questions.

The majority of the studies concentrated on mothers, rather than fathers, of schizophrenics for the simple reason that the mothers were more accessible. This neglect would tend to minimize the father's role in the development of the illness. Only one study, conducted by Lidz *et al.*,[14] has appeared in the literature in which the fathers of adult schizophrenics received exclusive attention.

REVIEW OF THE LITERATURE

We shall first refer to three studies whose findings will be contrasted, and later mention a few of the more recent studies and developments.*

Gerard and Siegel[6] found that in 64 (91%) of the 70 schizophrenic males they had studied there was exclusive attachment to the mother. In 40 (57%) of the cases the schizophrenic child was considered to be the favourite of the mother. There was extreme overprotectiveness, babying and spoiling.

Tiedze,[23] on the basis of interviews with 25 mothers of male and female schizophrenic patients, found that 10 mothers overtly rejected their children while 15 were more subtle in their rejection.

* For a more adequate coverage of the literature, the reader is referred to as an article by the same author which appeared in *Psychiatry* (Ref. 21).

Thomas[22] limited her study to the mother-daughter relationship of 18 schizophrenics. The mothers could not tolerate any verbal expression of hostility. They were excessively restrictive and punitive after the patients had reached puberty.

While all of the above three studies tried to describe the type of relationship which existed between the mothers and their schizophrenic children their findings have little in common. There was almost no rejection by parents in the first study; the rejection was mostly covert in the second study; and there was quite open hostility in the third investigation. A closer look at the samples may give a clue to such contradictory findings.

In the Gerard and Siegel study, informants were mostly Jewish and Italians (70%) of lower and lower-middle class. Tiedze's mothers were drawn mostly from Protestant families (64%) in the professional and business class. Thomas' group was made up exclusively of Negro families. It is felt that the data reported by the author had been coloured by a preponderance of specific ethnic and religious groups in the samples. For example, it would be expected that in Jewish and Italian families there would be more babying of children in the lower-classes whereas such practices may not be considered proper in Protestant families of higher classes. Patterns of parent-child relationship in these three groups could have been influenced by the norms of the class and culture to which they belong and this was superimposed on the pathological relationship.

A pioneering work in the study of schizophrenia, across subcultural groups, was conducted in the United States by Opler and Singer[19] with Italian and Irish Catholic schizophrenic veterans. The purpose of the investigators was to present findings on cultural differentiation with respect to both content and etiology of schizophrenic disorder.

Only two of the ten hypotheses formulated by Opler and Singer will be mentioned here. The first hypothesis was that in the Irish family, the mother instills primary anxiety and the general fear of female figures, while in the Italian families the primary hostility would be particularly felt towards the more dominant father or older sibling. The second hypothesis was that the Irish, lacking firm male identification and experiencing sexual repressions which are fostered by the culture with its high celibacy rates and protracted engagements, would develop in extreme cases latent homosexuality. With the Italians, since there is acceptance of overt expression of sexuality and because of the negative identification caused by hatred against any symbolization of an adult male role, extreme cases would show overt homosexuality. The Irish would be compliant to authority and show no evidence of acting out behaviour contrary to the Italian. These hypotheses were confirmed by the data.

The investigation conducted by Lidz et al.[14,15,16] at the Yale Psychiatric Institute, is one of the most extensive studies on families with schizophrenic members. The investigators selected 16 families for intensive interviews during the course of several years and wrote approximately 20 papers. The investigators focussed their interest not so much on the mothers, as as in previous studies, but on the interaction within the family. The following summarizes their general findings:

> As the family is the primary teacher of social interaction and emotional reactivity it appears essential to scrutinize it exhaustively. There is considerable evidence that the schizophrenic's family can foster paralogic ideation, untenable emotional needs and frequently offers contradictory models for identification which cannot be integrated.

All patients seen at the Yale Psychiatric Institute came from upper or upper-middle class families with the exception of two or three families of the lower-middle class. There was some selection in favour of intact homes and ability to support a son or daughter in a private hospital for prolonged periods. With such a selected group of 16 families, with no normal controls, generalizations should be limited in scope.

A recent study on family background of the mentally ill, including schizophrenics, is the well-known investigation conducted by Myers and Roberts[18] in New Haven. The major purpose of the study was to find out whether social and psychodynamic factors in the development of psychiatric illness were related to a patient's position in the social class structure of American society. The investigators reported that the following conditions were found to occur more frequently in families of Class V than Class III schizophrenics: general disorganization of the home: lack of parental affection, guidance and control; isolation of the father from the family; heavy responsibility of the mother; and the responsibility given to siblings in the child-rearing process; harsh but inconsistent punishment.

It should be pointed out, however, that the Class III patients were not comparable to Class V patients. Class III included 73 percent of patients of North European origin, while Class V included 70 percent of patients originating from the Southern part of Italy. The mother's heavy responsibility and the responsibility imposed on siblings in the child-rearing process may only reflect the cultural mores of the nationality of the families involved in the lower-class. Opler and Singer[19] pointed out that the cultural value system of the Italian sets greater store on paternal and older sibling dominance. The question which might be raised here is whether the findings would be similar if all of Class V patients were white Protestants.

During the past few years a fresh approach has been developing within the general framework of psychotherapy which consists in the study of interaction between patients and parents on a sustained basis. In one instance Bowen[2] studied parents who were living at the hospital with their sick children and who were placed under constant observation. While previous studies have been interested in isolating past factors which could be related to schizophrenia, these investigations were concerned with the existing interactions with the family and particularly with the type of communication among family members. As a result of these investigations such labels as "pseudomutuality,"[26] "symbiotic relationship,"[17] "double-bind,"[1] "three-party interaction,"[25] "over-adequate-inadequate reciprocal functioning,"[2] "complementary functioning"[11] have been used in describing intra-family relationships.

This approach, however, considers the family group outside the context of its culture and its community and is limited to cases where both parents are living. None of these studies has presented adequate material on the socioculture background of these families. It can be safely assumed, however, that these subjects consisted primarily of middle- and upper-class individuals. Probably because of the special selection of these patients and parents we obtain a general picture of very strong mothers and very weak and ineffectual fathers.

These inquiries do not clarify whether the existence of such distorted family relationships could be considered etiological of schizophrenia. Furthermore, there is little or no discussion of the possible presence of similar distortions in other deviant families since no controls, normal or abnormal, have ever been used. To explain schizophrenia on the basis of distorted communication would make it difficult to explain the occurrence of schizophrenia in individuals where, for example, "double-bind" or "symbiotic relationships" do not exist.

This heavy emphasis on the study of patients and parents accessible to psychiatric research centres results in little information on the schizophrenic of Class V—the lowest-income class in which, according to Hollingshead and Redlich,[9] 41 percent of the children under 17 years of age live in homes which have been disrupted by death, desertion, separation or divorce and in which the incidence of schizophrenics is eight times higher than in Class I and Class II combined.

STUDIES CONDUCTED IN EUROPE

Two investigations conducted in Europe will be mentioned. Delay *et al.*[3] wrote a survey of the literature which included many of the investigations conducted in the United States. One of the first studies undertaken by a European psychiatrist (relating schizophrenia to early home environment) was conducted by a Hungarian psychoanalyst, Hadju-Gimes.[7] This paper, according to Reichard and Tillman,[20] represents a landmark since it is the first publication on parent-child relationship representing the patient's point of view. Hadju-Gimes described four female schizophrenic patients whom she psychoanalyzed. She found that the mothers of these patients were cold, rigorous, etc., while the fathers were soft and passive. Furthermore, she found that in all cases the patients had suffered during infancy a period of starvation either because of an insufficient lactation or on account of the mother's cruelty. She hypothesized that neurotics may have parents with similar characteristics as parents of schizophrenics but what may cause schizophrenia is the starvation experience. Since her generalization is based on four cases, further investigation of the pathogenic influences of this triad of conditions (a sadistic mother, a weak father and starvation in infancy) seems necessary.

Alanen Yrjo[27] interviewed mothers, fathers and siblings of schizophrenic males and females who lived in Helsinki as well as in rural areas. He found that the majority of mothers were "stiff and bitter." Very few showed real naturalness and warmth. The majority were inclined to anxiety and uncertainty and had obsessive features. In spite of their marked disturbance most of them had a domineering and aggressive pattern of behaviour. He divided his sample into those who had good prognosis and those who had poor prognosis. He found that the mothers of the more disturbed group were more severely affected.

PROCEDURE

In view of the contradictory findings, we conducted the present pilot study to determine whether religion and social class variables, which were neglected in previous studies, could make for different patterns of family relationship in schizophrenic patients, whether differences could be found in the types of social disorganization and whether the role of father and mother and the incidence of mental illness among other members of the family would differentiate the two groups. For this purpose we selected schizophrenic patients—Jewish and Protestant, belonging to two different social classes—lower and middle or upper class.

The following criteria were used in selecting the sample. All patients were betwen the ages of 18 and 55; older schizophrenics were excluded since it could be expected that they would lack adequate information on parent-child relationship. Some records contained copious information when reports from social workers, family agencies, schools and public welfare agencies were included. Some cases had information on the mother and not on the father and vice-versa, but they were still included in the study. All patients were native-born Americans. The parents of the Jewish schizophrenics, were with very few exceptions, all born abroad, most of them in Russia and Poland. Only "old Americans" were included in the Protestant sample. When the record showed that the parents had some affinity towards the old country the case was not included. Classification according to social class was based on the parents' socio-economic status. The lower-class group included those parents who depended on labour—skilled and unskilled—for their livelihood. The middle and upper-classes included white collar workers, professionals and businessmen. Since all case histories had sufficient data on education and vocation it was possible to obtain adequate social class data.

Following several revisions, a special form was devised and adopted to obtain uniform data from the records. Approximately 150 case records of male schizophrenics, who were patients or who had recently been discharged from five mental hospitals in the Boston area, were carefully examined and the required information was transcribed. All consecutive admissions who fulfilled the criteria were selected for our study. All references in the records pertaining to the parents' characteristics and to their interaction with their sick sons were recorded.

The categories of parent-child relationship and family disorganization were based on an evaluation of the problems as presented in the records. Eleven major categories were used in the sorting of the problems: (1) insanity of the parents—if either parent was or had been in a mental institution: (2) extreme irritability, with many inflicting physical punishment on their sons; (3) alcoholism; (4) dullness; (5) rejection or unfavourable treatment: (6) death; (7) dominance; (8) overprotection; (9) passivity; (10) normal relationship; and (11) unknown. Cases lacking information or adequate information for evaluating a predominant trait were included in the unknown category.

FINDINGS

The most striking finding is the difference of pathology existing in parents of schizophrenic patients of Jewish and Protestant lower-class. Almost half of the Protestant fathers were or had been insane, alcoholics, or had manifested extreme irritability, and most of them used excessive physical punishment. The general pattern of a passive and submissive father, reported in the literature, was missing from our sample, which confirms Frazee's[4] findings in her Chicago study. Relationship with the Protestant mothers of the lower-socio-economic class was not ideal since 39 percent of them were found to be overprotective and 16 percent were found to be dominant. However, the overprotectiveness in many instances might have been intensified by the father's neglectful or tyrannical attitude towards their sons. This is in agreement with Lane and Singer's study[13] where they found, using a type of Thematic Apperception Test especially devised for this study, that the lower-class schizophrenic sees his mother as overprotective, and contrary to expectations, instead of expressing hostility he would idealize her.

While pathology seems to be more frequent in the Protestant father than in the Protestant mother of lower-class the trend is reversed with Jewish families of lower-class. Half of the Jewish mothers were categorized as insane, extremely irritable and dull (18%, 15% and 18% respectively). The category of dullness would require some interpretation because of the high frequency found in this group but not in the others. It would be difficult to evaluate the extent to which there was real feeblemindedness among the Jewish mothers, or just an inability to communicate with the psychiatrists who would tend to interpret this deficiency as lack of intelligence. Other dominant traits found in Jewsih mothers were overprotectiveness (20%) and dominance (15%). With the Jewish fathers there was no definite pattern, except that in 25 percent of the cases no pathological trait could be found in the descriptions and we have included these cases under "normal relationship." Little or no data was available on 15 percent of the Jewish fathers belonging to the lower-class. It seems that if the "schizophrenogenic" label were to be used it could more appropriately be applied to the father in Protestant families and to the mother in Jewish families.

In the middle and upper-classes half of the Jewish mothers were categorized as overprotective. The Jewish father, in two-thirds of the cases of middle and upper-classes, was either rejecting (33%) or dominant (27%) which represents a decided contrast to the Jewish father of schizophrenics belonging to the lower-class. The middle and upper-class Protestant mothers tended to be dominant (26%), extremely irritable (20%), and rejecting (16%). The most frequent trait of the Protestant father of middle and upper-class was rejection or unfavourable treatment of the son (22%). In 20 percent of the cases Protestant fathers appeared to have had normal relationships with their sons.

DISCUSSION

We can see from the sample examined above that there are major differences in the familial characteristics of schizophrenic patients belonging to two religious groups and two different social classes. It is not surprising that very little agreement could be found among earlier studies which had undertaken the analysis of the most dominant pattern of parent-child relationship in families with schizophrenic patients. There is no question that the patterns found in these earlier studies were influenced by the norms of the social class and culture to which these patients belonged and that these norms, in turn, may have affected the nature of any pathological relationship that developed.

Generalizations from these reviewed studies should be limited in scope, particularly since there was a wide variation in methodology. Furthermore, a lack of consistency in these findings is to be attributed to a quasi or total neglect of important sociocultural variables. While findings in sociology and anthropology in the past few years have given impetus to the development of social psychiatry as a field of investigation, their effect is still minor, particularly in the regular psychiatric literature. Although the evidence of the importance of family factors in the background of schizophrenics is quite compelling, the patterns of the home environment needs to be more clearly defined and isolated from home patterns which lead to other types of psychoses, neurosis and antisocial behaviour. Furthermore, the nonoccurrence of schizophrenia in the other siblings of the family is another area which needs investigation.

Research in this area can become effective only if a genuine, concerted, interdisciplinary effort is directed toward its solution. The investigator suggests that an international research organization be established to coordinate research in mental illness. Under the auspices of such an international agency it would be possible to set up research programmes in various countries staffed by polyglot scientists in order to provide a basis for more effective communication. An integration of data from research conducted along similar lines and methods with comparable samples in different countries would lead to a greater validity and universality of the findings. The goals are to tackle the problems of mental health and sickness on an international level; on a very large scale and with intensive clinical studies. More scientific answers can be assured if longitudinal studies are conducted on individuals facing different types of stresses and cultural demands over extended periods of time and space.

It is hoped that such studies as contemplated will stimulate professional workers to a greater awareness of the socio-cultural differences which exist in the mental patient population; to enable them to make a better evaluation of the forces which may have contributed to the maladjustment.

SUMMARY

Many studies have shown that mothers of schizophrenics are usually disturbed. The "schizophrenogenic" mother has been described as rejecting, overprotective, abusive, etc., and the father, as weak, passive and ineffectual. Approximately 150 case histories of male schizophrenic patients of Jewish and Protestant, lower, and upper-class were examined to determine the major prevalent characteristics in parent-child relationships.

The Jewish mother of lower-class showed more emotional instability, psychotic breakdowns and dullness than the Protestant mothers. In most of these Jewish families the father was a passive, ineffectual member of the family. In the lower-class Protestant group the pathology was more frequent with the father with a greater incidence of insanity, alcoholism and excessive bad temper. In general it appears from our findings that Protestant fathers and Jewish mothers of schizophrenics belonging to the lower-social classes are more disturbed than their mates. Suggestions for more adequate research in the area of parent-child relationship were given.

REFERENCES

1. Bateson, G., Haley, J., Jackson, D.D. and Weakland, J.: Toward a theory of schizophrenia. *Behav Sci, 1*:251–264, 1956.

2. Bowen, M.: A family concept of schizophrenia. In D.D. Jackson (Ed.): *The Etiology of Schizophrenia.* New York, Basic Books, 1960. pp. 346–372.

3. Delay, J., Deniker, P. and Green, A.: Le milieu familial du schizophrene. *Encephale, 46*:189–323, 1957.

4. Frazee, Helen E.: Children who later became schizophrenic. *Smith Col Stud Soc Work, 23*:125–149, 1953.

5. Fromm-Reichmann, Frieda: Notes on the development of treatment of schizophrenia by psychoanalytic psychotherapy. *Psychiatry, 11*:263–273, 1948.

6. Gerard, D.L., and Siegel, J.: The family background of schizophrenia. *Psychiat Q 24*:47–73, 1950.

7. Hadju-Gimes, L.: Contributions to the etiology of schizophrenia. *Psychoanal Rev, 27*:421–438, 1940.

8. Hitson, H.M., and Funkenstein, D.H.: Family patterns and paranoidal personality structure in Boston and Burma. *Inter J Soc Psychiat, 5*:182–190, 1960.

9. Hollingshead, A.B., and Redlich, F.C.: *Social Class and Mental Illness.* New York, John Wiley and Sons, 1958.

10. Hotchkiss, Georgina D.; Carmen, Lida; Ogilby, Anne, and Wiesenfeld, Shirley: Mothers of young male single schizophrenic patients as visitors in a mental hospital. *J Nerv Ment Disorders, 121*:452–462, 1955.

11. Jackson, D.: Family Interaction, Family Homeostasis, and Some Implications for Conjoint Family Psychotherapy. Paper presented at the Academy of Psychoanalysis, San Francisco, May 1958.

12. Kohn, M., and Clausen, J.A.: Parental authority behaviour and schizophrenia. *Am J Orthopsychiat, 26*:297–313, 1956.

13. Lane, R.C., and Singer, J.L.: Familial attitudes of paranoid schizophrenics and normal individuals from two socio-economic status. *J Abnorm Soc Psychol, 59*:328–339, 1959.

14. Lidz, T.: Cornelison, Alice. and Parker, B.: The role of fathers in the family of schizophrenic patients. *Am J Psychiatry, 113*:126–132, 1956.

15. Lidz, T.; Cornelison, Alice; Fleck, S., and Terry, Dorothy: The intra-familial environment of the schizophrenic patient. part I: The father. *Am J Psychiatry, 20*:329–342, 1957.

16. Lidz, T.; Cornelison, Alice; Fleck, S., and Terry, Dorothy: The

intra-familial environment of schizophrenic patients. part II: marital schism and marital skew. *Am J Psychiatry, 114*:241–248, 1957.

17. Limentani, D.: Symbiotic identification in schizophrenia. *Psychiatry, 19*:231–236, 1956.

18. Myers, J.K., and Roberts, B.H.: *Family and Class Dynamics.* New York, John Wiley and Sons, 1959.

19. Opler, M.K., and Singer, J.L.: Ethnic differences in behaviour and psychopathology Italian and Irish. *Inter J Soc Psychiatry, 2*:11–22, 1956.

20. Reichard, Suzanne, and Tillman, C.: Patterns of parent-child relationships in schizophrenia. *Psychiatry, 13*:247–257, 1950.

21. Sanua, V.D.: Sociocultural factors in families of schizophrenics: A review of the literature. *Psychiatry, 24*:246–265, 1961.

22. Thomas, Rose C.: *Mother-Daughter Relationship and Social Behaviour.* Social Work Series 21, Washington, The Catholic University of American Press, 1955.

23. Tiedze, Trude: A study of mothers of schizophrenics. *Psychiatry, 12*:55–65, 1949.

24. Wahl, C.: Some antecedent factors in the family histories of 392 schizophrenics. *Am J Psychiatry, 110*:668–676, 1954.

25. Weakland, J.: 'Double-bind' hypothesis of schizophrenia and three-party interaction. In D.D. Jackson (Ed.): *The Etiology of Schizophrenia* New York, Basic Books, 1960, pp. 373–388.

26. Wynne, L.C., Rychoff, I.M. *et al.*: Psuedo-mutuality and the family relations of schizophrenics. *Psychiatry, 21*:205, 1958.

27. Yrjo, Alanen: On the personality of the mother and early mother-child relationships of 100 schizophrenic patients. *Acta Psychiat,* (suppl) *106*:227–334, 1956.

Chapter 32

MENTAL HEALTH OF AMERICAN JEWISH URBANITES: A REVIEW OF LITERATURE AND PREDICTIONS

I. D. Rinder

Psychiatry has been broadening its interest from an initial exclusive preoccupation with the disturbed person outward toward the larger social context which produced him. At the same time, the social or behavioral sciences have been focussing down from that larger socio-cultural whole which is their usual level of investigation, to scrutinize the concrete case of the disturbed individual. To the psychiatrist, the type and severity of symptoms presented by the individual seen in the clinic are given psychodynamic depth and breadth when these are related to the family-community-subculture which were the environment of their growth. To the behavioural scientist, the patient population, when classified by categories and computed into rates, becomes an index—symptom, if you like—of social-cultural integration/disintegration.

Research on mental illness can inform us, at least in part, as to how severe are the stresses of life and the resources for meeting these possessed by a given group. A social psychiatric review and analysis of the mental health status of modern American Jews would be one way of learning how the Jewish American fares both in his society and within his body as he leads the unique existence of this social identity at this time and place.

Our analysis will be developed on three distinct levels: (1) *epidemiology*—the incidence or prevalence of mental illness, the

Reprinted with permission from *Int J Soc Psychiatry*, Spring, 1963, pp. 104–109.

distribution of cases among different diagnostic categories, systematic differences or trends taking place in these statistics over time; (2) *socio-cultural* analysis—how and where is this group distributed in society, strengths and vulnerabilities of such distribution, and the functional-dysfunctional potential of particular cultural beliefs, practices, skills, values, aspirations, fears; and (3) *clinical*—results of studies showing individual variations within a group, and differences betwen groups as measured by scores obtained with standardized instruments applied to individual subjects.

Epidemiology: We are fortunate to have at our disposal a piece of work which has systematically assembled most available epidemiological studies.[6] These are brought together under such headings as "Age, Sex and Mental Disorder," "Mental Disorder and Marital Status," "Mental Disorder Among Urban and Rural Populations," "Mental Disorders and Socio-Economic Status," "Mental Disorders Among Negroes," and "Mental Disorders Among Jews." Under this last rubric we find several pages of tables comparing overall rates (hospital populations) of Jews with those of non-Jews; and then comparing rates of Jews and non-Jews on specific disorders, e.g. schizophrenia, paranoia, etc.[*]

The statistics begin as follows: (rates are crude rates per 100,000 population)

Rates: Jews 44.7, non-Jews 69.2 (1920). Jews 42.3, non-Jews 75.1 (1927)— New York civil state hospitals.

Rates: Jews 42.7, non-Jews 81.1—Admissions from New York City to public and private mental hospitals, 1925.

Rates: Jews 31.2, non-Jews 73.6—Massachusetts state mental hospitals, 1926-28.

---

[*] Researchers working with epidemiological rates derived from hospital statistics are alerted to certain possible sources of consistent error or bias. They know that availability of or accessibility to hospital beds may swell some rates, while lack of opportunity diminishes such rates. They also know that religious scruples, cultural biases, ignorance, etc., may dispose some people toward and others away from utilizing psychiatric care facilities. Socioeconomic class becomes a factor to be reckoned with if only public hospital populations are studied, and the more affluent members of society uniformly send their mentally ill to private sanataria and clinics. Better research design has developed from knowledge of these potential distortions.

Rates: Jews 29.6, non-Jews 64.2—Illinois state mental hospitals, 1926-28.

The above and other similar figures consistently show Jews averaging about one-half the mental illness of non-Jews as revealed by the official statistics of hospital admissions. When we turn to the inspection of rates by diagnostic categories, another interesting fact shows. For the psychoses, which are organised under eight headings and reported through 20 sets of rates, Jews have again consistently lower rates with only one reversal of this pattern and this probably non-significant, since it is a matter of only 0.2. However, when we inspect the category Psychoneuroses, we find Jews reported as exceeding non-Jews in two of the three sets of comparisons.

The material compiled in the manner just described was almost all gathered in the years 1926–28, with only one report from 1938 (N.Y., Bellevue Hospital) and another from 1941 (Boston, Selective Service screening). Are the findings of Jewish under-representation in the psychotic population and over-representation in the neurotic population, even if valid for these earlier decades, still applicable or are they now outmoded?

To determine this, we turn to a recent study of considerable theoretical and methodological sophistication—the study of New Haven by the sociologists Hollingshead and Myers, and the psychiatrists Redlich and the late Bertram Roberts.* This industrial city of about a quarter of a million population is approximately 60 percent Roman Catholic, 30 percent Protestant, and 10 percent Jewish. The major finding of this project is that social class is the most important co-relate of rate and kind of treated mental disorder in New Haven. In all three religious groups, it was found that the upper classes comprise a somewhat smaller proportion

* The New Haven study has the deficiency of many epidemiological studies —of taking treated cases rather than true prevalency rates from the community at large. This latter is a desideratum which involves enormous additional difficulties at the present stage of psychiatric diagnostics. However, this research did not restrict itself to hospital figures but sought all treated cases in public or private institutions and clinics, in the care of private practitioners, and those New Havenites who were receiving psychiatric attention in cities and states away from home. In short, their census of treated cases was most thorough and as nearly complete as possible.

of the psychiatric population than they do of the total community, whereas the lowest class in each case contributes about twice its proportionate share.[2]

A somewhat different organization of the New Haven data reveals a number of additional points about both the mental health pattern and social class distribution of Jews.[3] In their social distribution, Jews show greater concentration in the upper and middle classes than is true of other groups. Where they are found toward the lower end of the social spectrum, particularly in classes III (lower middle) and IV, (working class), the Jews show a disproportionate rate of psychoneuroses. In these classes Catholics and Protestants are somewhat under-represented and New Haven's Jews have 2–3 times their proportionate share of psychoneurotics.

That Jews as a group show a lower rate of psychosis in New Haven is attributable to their skewedness in social class distribution. If lower class members are more prone to psychosis (or at least contribute more cases proportionately than other social classes), then Jews, having a smaller proportion of their members in this category will accordingly show less psychosis. However, the findings just reviewed suggest that Jews have not only that greater amount of psychoneurosis we might anticipate because of their higher social class achievement, but an additional amount beyond that.

Having discovered such differences in rates, Myers and Roberts, aware that they are utilizing a psychiatric population of "cases in treatment" rather than a true prevalency sample, review the non-illness related biases which might account for these findings. They recognize that important consequences flow from the fact that groups differ in their awareness of psychiatric symptoms, and in their acceptance of psychiatric treatment. Because of Jewish cultural values encouraging intellectuality, Jews are more knowledgeable about mental illness and psychotherapy; more desirous of the best and most modern in medical treatment; more accustomed to the talking out of troubles with a warmly sympathetic listener; hence more likely to become a voluntary treatment statistic in the area of the psychoneuroses. They then conclude, "In summary, we must state that although these explanations for the high rates of psychoneuroses among Jews in terms of the acceptance of modern psychiatry seem plausible, we cannot be certain that the actual occurrence of the illness is not substantially higher in this group."

Before leaving the epidemiological approach for another, it is both interesting and highly suggestive, with regard to theory, to examine some differences in the distribution of behavioural disorders among the major ethnic groups of New Haven.[4] The Jewish over-representation of psychoneuroses and underrepresentation of psychoses (schizophrenia) is especially pronounced when compared to the Irish, Italian and Negro distributions. Noteworthy is the Jewish and Italian absence from the alcohol and drug addiction populations. The Jewish incidence of senile disorders and other organic disorders also appears significantly lower than the rate of others. This raises the hypothesis that the closing off of other behavioural alternatives through the religious-cultural channelling of learned behaviour may contribute substantially to the high Jewish rate of psychoneuroses. The traditional Jewish emphasis upon sobriety, the control of hostile aggressive impulses, etc., means that these avenues of behavioural expression, hence symptom formations, are less readily available to one socialized in this cultural community. A detailed investigation of precisely this point, i.e. how different sub-cultures apparently contribute to different patterning of symptoms even within the same disease entity has been described by M.K. Opler in his work on Italian and Irish American schizophrenics.[5]

Social-Cultural Analysis: Reference to group differences disposing Jews toward greater awareness and acceptance of psychiatry on the one hand and on the other their location in different illness categories, leads us to the systematic consideration of how different groups create different views of the world for their members. The material we shall summarize here is drawn from an intensive study of the families of Irish, Jewish and Yankee (old family, New England, white, Protestant, Anglo-Saxon) patients in the Boston Psychopathic Hospital.[1] The authors say, "Our goal was to understand the relationship between family social structure and the production of individual stress."

Sons in Irish and Italian families receive less overt affection than those in Jewish and Yankee families. The mother is the dominant figure in the home in all of these except the Italian where the mother's role is buffer between son and patriarchal father. The other maternal roles differ; the Irish mother showing preference toward son but also serving as strict disciplinarian; the Jewish mother being overtly affectionate but over-protective; and the Yankee mother being a moral model. Different types and degrees of stress are felt by sons as a consequence of the varying constellations of relationships just described.

The same is true of role performances expected of these sons. Irish and Italian boys are expected to make financial contributions to the family, while Jewish and Yankee boys are not. For the former, the amount brought in is important; for the latter however, what is important is not how much but the good purposes to which they put their money, e.g. for future advancement. Similarly, Jewish and Yankee boys are expected to be high achievers in school and in their careers. In this they have the support of their families, along with the additional expectations that they will develop the social graces and good social contacts. Irish and Italian families expect their sons to obtain regular jobs with regular incomes, and discourage their jeopardizing this immediate good for the sake of uncertain future betterment through education. The families' social expectations are limited to the desire that their sons "stay out of trouble." For the Jewish and Yankee son, stress may result from inadequately meeting the familially acquired aspiration for social mobility. Conversely, the Irish and Italian sons experience stress precisely when they have somehow incubated ambitions which require their continuing education beyond what the family considers the reasonable amount.

Barrabee and von Mering observe, "Membership in the ethnic group can be a source of stress. This is most frequent with Jewish boys who see their Jewishness as impeding the fulfilment of social or occupational ambitions. Much depends upon the environmental conditions. Indeed, a Jewish boy can select avenues to success that by-pass his Jewishness. However, since this implies a restriction in his freedom of choice, he often cannot shake off a diffuse sense of deprivation about his ethnic membership."

Clinical Evidence: Moving from the social and cultural characteristics of the group to the psychological parameters of the individual brings us to the *clinical* level of analysis. How does the individual Jew compare with the non-Jew on selected variables? We are fortunate here, as we were on the epidemiological level, in having convenient access to a study which has systematized and compared the sprinkling of studies which appeared over the years.[7] Sanua gave both an objective and a projective test of personality to a sample of first, second and third generation American Jewish high school students and to a group of non-Jewish students. His findings cast light on both inter-generational differences and Jewish–non-Jewish differences in certain areas of personality.

On the objective test (the Thurstone Neurotic Inventory) he found progressively better scores moving from first to third generation. Scores from the projective test (The Rorschach Multiple Choice Test), however, arranged themselves as a trend the reverse of the first, i.e. the first or immigrant generation had better scores than the second generation which in turn scored better than the third. To reconcile this apparent contradiction in findings, Sanua, following G. Allpert's distinction, submits the plausible interpretation that the tests get at different levels or aspects of personality: the Thurstone Test probably measures "social adjustment" (through such questions as "Do you get stage fright?") while the Rorschach measures "inner adjustment." Over successive generations, it would appear, continuous acculturation and assimilation results in the learning of patterns of overt behaviour which helps the individual appear adjusted. However, this process is co-related with an increasingly internal malaise, detected by the Rorschach for which there are no conventionally learned "right answers."

By arranging previous studies of Jewish–non-Jewish personality differences in a chronological table, Sanua ingeniously explains previous inconsistencies by showing that from the earliest of such studies in 1929 until 1938, Jewish students obtained scores indicative of poorer adjustment, but that from 1938 until the present Jewish students have consistently scored as better adjusted than their Gentile matches. Since these studies employed objective or self-descriptive instruments, both the initially poorer and subsequently better scores may be largely attributable to the progressive acculturation, hence increasing test sophistication of the Jewish subjects.

When Sanua controlled his subjects for generation, he found that the results just described were not attributable to differences in socioeconomic status or differences in creed (orthodoxy-reform). The generational variable, acculturation, seems to be the most significant factor accounting for the observed differences in personality. When third generation Jewish boys are compared with non-Jews who are long-established Protestants, i.e. their equals in acculturation, the latter obtain better adjustment scores on the Rorschach than do the Jewish subjects. In fact, every Jewish generation group scored lower in adjustment than the matched Gentile group on obtained Rorschach scores.

The inner maladjustment of American Jews, on the basis of this evidence, seems to be greater than that of their Gentile peers; and the greater the Americanization, the greater the maladjustment. This resembles the "heightened self-consciousness" sociologists have described as characterizing the marginal man. Although some fraction of this malaise may become clinical and warrant later treatment, other portions may become chanellized as social, economic, artistic, aesthetic, etc., drive. The crucial question is whether this maladjustment will overwhelm the individual and become pathology, or whether he can harness and utilize it as his private version of a divine discontent.

Summarizing the diverse materials and different levels of analysis adduced, we offer the following by way of integrative interpretation. Jews probably have a higher rate of neurosis and a lower rate of psychosis than non-Jews in the United States at mid-century. The social and cultural liabilities of members of this group include minority status in a predominantly Christian society; the high level of aspiration which is instilled in youth; the concomitantly high expectations entertained by parents concerning their children; the disabilities of minority status which require one to be an over-achiever in order to gain recognition; the ambiguities of identity for the acculturated who never quite leave an older status nor completely realize a new one (the Jew as marginal man); and ironically, success in social mobility, which in itself may be socio-psychologically dysfunctional (numerous studies find the upwardly mobile have higher incidences of neuroses, hostile rejection of parents and family, etc., than the non-mobile).

The social and cultural assets (elements either allaying or supportive against stress) in American Jewish life are also numerous. There is the degree of security children derive from demonstrated parental affection; there is the patient support of dependency during the long years of education; there is the providing of the young with both a "tradition of success" and the skills and values to implement the motivation to succeed. Both of these are very important since in the absence of the latter, failure and frustration are inevitable and the motivation for success becomes a mockery and force for disorganization. Traditional emphasis upon verbal and intellectual skills not only contributes to success and mobility, but is likely related to enhanced skill in self-knowledge, insight, the sustaining of multiple and diversified roles, and the like.

A very modest projection of discernable trends from the past and present into the future would anticipate that if Jewish family patterns persist, if economic stability permits continuing mobility, and if the emphasis upon education and attainment continue to both buttress and challenge the psyche of American Jews, the overall rate of impairment will continue lower than average. As upward mobility, acculturation and secularization proceed, the distribution favouring neurosis and away from psychosis could become even more pronounced. However, should catastrophes such as economic collapse or an ascendance of racial-religious hostility come to the United States the patterns could be reversed, i.e. neurosis would then decrease as psychosis increased.

Regardless of which trend prevails, as the contents of traditional patternings of behaviour become attenuated through acculturation, those disorders which do occur will be more "normalized" (statistically speaking) in their distribution. *Shikker iz a Goy* ("drunken is a Gentile") will no longer point to significant group differences and it and similar expressions will have then become survivals of the folkish social psychiatry of a bygone day.

NOTES AND REFERENCES

1. Barrabee, Paul and Otto von Mering: Ethnic variations in mental stress in families with psychotic children. In A.M. Rose (Ed.): *Mental Health and Mental Disorder*. New York, Norton, 1955. Any effort to generalize from this study must be cautioned by the following considerations: (a) these families did have psychotic children, although their ethnic characteristics may be generally representative of other families of the same ethnic identity; and (b) the Jewish families tended to be lower-class, as opposed to the more typical middle class status of American Jewish families.

2. Hollingshead, August B., and Redlich, F.C.: *Social Class and Mental Illness, A Community Study*. New York, John Wiley and Sons, 1958, p. 204.

3. Myers, Jerome K. and Roberts, B.H.: Some relationships between religion, ethnic origin and mental illness. In Marshall Sklare (Ed.): *The Jews: Social Patterns of an American Group*. Glencoe, Illinois, The Free Press, 1958.

4. *Ibid.*, p. 554.

5. Opler, M.K.: Cultural differences in mental disorders: An Italian and Irish contrast in the schizophrenics—U.S.A. In M.K. Opler (Ed.): *Culture and Mental Health*. New York, Macmillian, 1959.

6. Rose, Arnold M., and Holger, R. Stub: Summary of studies on the incidence of mental disorders. In A.M. Rose (Ed.): *Mental Health and Mental Disorder*. New York, Norton, 1955.

7. Sanua, Victor D.: Differences in personality adjustment among different generations of American Jews and non-Jews. In M.K. Opler (Ed.): *Culture and Mental Health*. New York, Macmillian, 1959.

Chapter 33

ON COMPARATIVE MENTAL HEALTH
RESEARCH OF THE JEWISH PEOPLE

A.A. WEINBERG

MENTAL HEALTH AND BELONGING

Studies on the spiritual, social and cultural life of contemporary Jewry are incomplete as long as we do not sufficiently investigate the impact of socio-cultural and political factors on its mental health. We must at the same time study the influence of mental health on the creation and the moulding of the conditions under which Jewry has to live. Mental health research as a matter of fact is not concerned only with the prevalence, incidence, etiology and symptomatology of mental diseases. It deals in particular with problems of the interrelations between mental health and conditions of life in family, community and society. A study which was recently published deals in particular with problems of relations between mental health and personal adjustment of *olim* (immigrants to Israel).[36] The findings of this study are of interest not only for the knowledge of the social psychology and the social psychopathology of Jewish immigrants and of immigrants in general, but also for the understanding of man's reaction to other kinds of social and cultural change. This study, which was carried out under the auspices of the Israel Foundation for the Study of Adjustment Problems in collaboration with the Israel Institute for Applied Social Research, constitutes an attempt to develop reliable methods for comparative sociopsychological and sociopsychopathological research. In other words, we have proposed research, the data of which can be

Reprinted in edited version with permission from *Israel Ann Psychiatry, 2:* 27–40, 1964.

compiled casuistically as well as statistically, as was the case in a former inquiry among immigrants from Holland to Palestine (Israel).[33]

The methodology is aimed at comparing shades—degrees—of mental health and personal adjustment on the basis of replies to open and closed, scaled, questions on mood, temperament, interpersonal and intrapersonal relations. In this way the unreliable method of comparing standard diagnoses of mental disturbances, which, moreover, in itself does not allow an insight into the dynamics of differing personality development, was avoided.[36,43-45] The methodology proposed opens the way to comparative epidemiological research on mental health and personal adjustment under the impact of social and cultural change.

The data of our study has led us to the operational conception of "positive mental health"[16] as the dynamic steady state of mind, concomitant with free, undisturbed, interpersonal and intrapersonal relations within a primary group of peers, that is, a group consisting of individuals with similar sociocultural background, and, accordingly, with inner security with attendant basic confidence, ensuring gratification of the needs of belonging and self-realization. It is characterized by adequate personal adjustment. Mental ill health is the dynamic, more or less unsteady state of mind, concomitant with unfree, disturbed, interpersonal and intrapersonal relations within a primary group of peers, or concomitant with a lack of interpersonal realtions in the absence of a primary group of peers, with resulting deterioration of intrapersonal relations and, accordingly, inner insecurity with attendant basic anxiety, impeding gratification of the needs of belonging and self-realization, thereby furthering loneliness or isolation. It is characterized by inadequate personal adjustment.[36]

MENTAL HEALTH AND HOMEOSTASIS

This conception implies that a continuum exists from positive mental health to shades of mental ill health. This is in accordance with other authors, e.g. Karl Menninger.[20] Personal adjustment functions as a psychodynamic homeostatic regulator. Severe untoward conditions, as unbearable emotions or conflicts, too many emotionalizing impressions at one time, isolation, persecution, expulsion and resulting flight—in sum, outer or inner conditions threatening the integration of the person or his survival—may necessitate emergency adjustment psychodynamisms. So he tries to exclude from awareness every unbearable emotion.

When repression is deficient or failing, symptom formation occurs. That is, mental ill health is imminent, latent, if not already overt. Lately, an ever more frequent psychodynamism has been described—the alienation from inner self. This has been described by many authors as the result of lack of understanding love in earliest childhood on the part of the parents, especially of the mother (e.g. Ref. 14 and 32). This phenomenon is, in fact, a form of dissociation of parts of the personality by which the ego is built on a smaller or larger part of the self-system while the dissociated part remains infantile. Suffice the remark that in our opinion it is in particular the need for belonging that urges the child to internalize his parents' wishes, to conform to their demands, to identify himself with them.

THE SURVIVAL OF THE JEWISH PEOPLE AND ITS MENTAL HEALTH

This sociopsychiatric conception of mental and psychosomatic health and ill health enables us to come to a better understanding of many basic problems of the Jewish people in Israel as well as in the Diaspora. There is an urgent need for penetrating and systematic research into the mental health problems of the Jewish people. Such research seems to be essential if we want to promote the smooth development of the State of Israel from an ingathering of exiles into a well integrated, as homogeneous as possible, flourishing society. It is also of vital importance for the furthering of the well-being of Jewish communities in the Diaspora.

From the mental health point of view the history of the Jewish people poses to us a number of intriguing questions. How was it possible for the Jewish people to survive in spite of innumerable severe upheavals, discriminations, persecutions and expulsions, with consequent displacement, flight and migration? Could not this tenacity, this indomitable urge for survival, be a sign of a high degree of mental health? But how can we reconcile this tentative diagnosis with the very many statements, made before the Second World War, that among the Jews an inordinately high rate of mental ill health existed, when compared with that of the people in whose midst they lived?[10] Perhaps there are conflicting factors at work, some furthering mental health and others hampering or even damaging it. To my knowledge, very little reliable research, if any, has been done in order to find a satisfactory reply to these crucial questions. Let us try to find a way out on the basis of some facts and findings at our disposal.

The Jewish culture is expressed most strongly in the Jewish religion as is written in the Holy Script. It teaches not to forget, not to repress. Every day, especially the many days of remembrance of disasters, as well as the feasts marking highlights of the year, as a culmination the Day of Atonement, reminds never to forget, neither the good nor the bad days, neither the heroes nor the martyrs, and above all to accept one's sins, as one is sure of the forgiveness of God the Almighty, the good father. It is not our task to tackle the controversial question of how far and in which respects the many centuries of exile, persecution and wandering amongst other peoples had led to exaggeration, to rigid interpretations of the Law, to what is called "chumroth" (restrictions). However, the question seems justified of how far such "chumroth" can be considered as compulsive thoughts and acts which may have unfavorably influenced Jewish mental health.

There is another central factor in Jewish life which has been thought to be of paramount benefit for the mental health of the Jewish people—the synagogue as the central place of community life, praying, learning and jurisdiction. The Beth-Hamidrash and the Yeshiva are manifestations and symbols of the belonging together of the community.[37,38] Not only that. The belief in God, the God of Israel, the reminiscence of common history since the patriarchs, or even Noah, through Moses and the giving of the law on Mount Sinai, the conquest and the building up of the Holy Land, through two exiles, the last for many, many centuries of unparalled suffering, up to the messianic vision of the return to the Land of Israel is all expressed in the feeling of belonging, of all Israel being brethren. It is the conviction of very many psychologists and psychiatrists, and also my opinion, that this feeling of belonging to the Jewish people and to God has saved our people from extinction. Perhaps it could not protect our people against some degree of mental harm, but we are allowed to assume that it has protected it against major mental deterioration (see also the interesting symposium "Judaism and Psychiatry"[23]). However, the warning seems permitted, that we should not confine ourselves to religious, philosophic or psychological contemplations. The problems under discussion have to be thoroughly investigated.

As we have noted above, before the Second World War numerous books and papers stated that the state of mental health was worse among Jews in the Diaspora than among the Gentile majority. However, in most cases a statistical comparison of intake of mental patients in mental health hospitals or asylums has been used to ascertain the incidence of mental ill health. But this does not give a reliable picture of the real state of mental health among a certain population. A few were based on selective service examinations. Recently many sociologists and social psychiatrists have been trying to find better methods of assessing mental morbidity among various economic classes, cultures and other categories of a given population. One method is that of assessing the frequency of psychiatric treatment, not only of patients admitted to mental hospitals, but also of those under treatment of private psychiatrists.[13,15,17,22,26,27] But this method, too, is not reliable enough. Therefore, psychiatric investigations of groups in a population have been carried out lately.[17] We have suggested developing, as we have mentioned in our introduction, a comparative methodology of search, based on the principle used in our recent investigation.[36]

Meyers and Roberts did not find a greater percentage of manic-depressive psychosis among the Jews than among the Gentiles in the United States.[22] The noted statistician Benjamin Malzberg lately has applied an improved statistical method, and his results partly contradict previous findings on the mental morbidity of Jews in the State of New York.[19]

Summing up, we are allowed to assume that is is true that

more investigations with comparative research methods have to be carried out in order to obtain a reliable picture of the state of mental health of the Jewish people in the Diaspora. But one cannot dispel the general impression that the Jews suffer more from functional mental disorders than their Gentile neighbors, although the comparably high morbidity in respect of neurosis may be partly due to a more positive attitude towards the desirability of its treatment. That this assumption may be confirmed by further research seems probable when we take into consideration the conditions under which the Jewish people have lived in the Diaspora.

MIGRATION, INTERGROUP TENSIONS AND MENTAL HEALTH

The Jewish people, ever since its dispersion, has been on the move, except for periods when it lived within the enclosure of the wall-surrounded ghettoes. This migration has increased considerably since the time of the emancipation. Letschinsky[18] estimates that since 1840 some five million Jews have migrated. Recent research has confirmed that displacement and flight influence mental health unfavorably.[21] This is our finding too. There are opinions that migration as such has an untoward influence on the immigrant's feeling of security. I cannot confirm this on the basis of my own research and assume that there exists a confusion of semantics. I have, therefore, proposed to call the immigrant's conscious feeling of doubtfulness in an alien country, whose language, habits and customs he does not know sufficiently, a feeling of uncertainty in contradistinction to a deep-lying feeling of inner insecurity, which is at the root of mental ill health.[36] However, a host of new impressions overwhelming the new immigrant may not only make him feel uncertain, but also instill in him a feeling of inner insecurity.[8] We found, in accordance with other authors, especially Maria Pfister-Ammende,[25] that those who before migration were suffering from overt or latent impaired mental health, are more prone to become mentally ill than others.

The result of the migrations of the Jews was that every time after migration they again formed a minority group among Gentiles—i.e. among a majority with a culture different from theirs. Migrants tend to group in clusters in order not to be alone in a strange and often hostile world. The Jews have always done this, also in cases where they were more or less free to settle where they liked. This fact should not surprise us in view of their strong feeling of belonging together and their urge to cling to their culture, especially to their religion. The resulting tensions between them and the majority groups have led to discrimination, oppression and persecution, and to the development of modern antisemitism. We shall, in the course of this paper, briefly dwell on the impact of these intergroup tensions on the mental health of the Jews. Here it may suffice to point out one of the inevitable consequences of these unheavals—repeated migration. In our time this need for migration has found another, but in fact ever longed for, gratification in the immigration, the "aliyah," to the Land of Israel and the establishment of the State of Israel. Are we not here in Israel confronted with a striking exception? Does not the Jew in Israel for the first time in nineteen centuries belong to a majority in his own county? The reply is only partly in the positive. Manifold are the differences in cultural background in Israel, and in Israel there is a great degree of physical and psychical variation in its population, frequent even cases of psychic and physical anthropological visibility which impedes smooth amalgamation.[2,28] One should not condemn too much the tendency of groups to defend themselves against the intrusion of members of groups with a different culture, as long as it does not impede accommodation, symbiosis and eventual amalgamation of the groups.[34] Prejudice and discrimination are in essence a means of self-defense of the group against disintegration. If it is true that man cannot live in isolation[36] then it is only natural that by the interdependence of the members of a group, necessary for its survival, there is a striving in the group to remain homogeneous. We propose to conceive this striving for homogeneity as a means for preserving the equilibrium in a group and, thus, by the analogy to the similar phenomenon in the mental and physical life of the individual, as symptomatic for the urge of preservation of group-homeostasis. It is one of the main reasons for xenophobia, the fear of the stranger. The symptom of xenophobia which concerns us, in this context, in particular, is antisemitism. Very much has been written on this phenomenon from the historical, sociological, psychological, and psychoanalytical viewpoints in attempts to explain the disastrous and criminal excesses to which it has led and to help forestall future catastrophes, if possible. But too few systematic comparative research projects have been carried out. Since it is not feasible within the scope of this paper to attempt to survey the literature on antisemitism, the reader is referred to References 1,3,6,12.

Let us return to the intergroup problems in Israel. It seems to us that, although tensions undeniably exist, they are not too severe. This appears from the fact that the percentages of "mixed" marriages, that is marriages of Israelis of Oriental communities (originating from Asia and Africa) with those of Ashkenasi communities (originating from Europe and America), are rising from year to year. Discrimination will be at its lowest and least noxious if the intermingling of groups develops as smoothly as possible. Coeducation of children of culturally different groups, with special facilities for children of less educated parents in comparison with the average level in Israel, sound housing policy, language courses for immigrants ("ulpanim" in Israel), information of both immigrants and residents about each other, and equal possibilities for learning and higher occupational training, education for the gifted of all groups of the population, will help solve such problems of intergroup tensions with the nation's mental health, that is its well-being, at stake. For discrimination has, according to our investigation[36] and to those by other authors, especially among Negroes, a bad influence on mental health.[24]

Severe persecution in concentration camps, etc., has raised another question. In how far and in which respect has severe persecution had an untoward impact on mental health and personal adjustment? We found in our material of 99 students at the Ulpan Etzion, Jerusalem, in two courses in 1954, that 28 who underwent severe persecution in concentration camps, etc., tended to better socio-cultural adjustment, or "general adjustment," than those who had not gone through such camps. This is in accordance with what a number of other investigators have found, among them Dvorjetski who, himself, went through many camps. According to

Dvorjetski, there are no definite signs of increased mental illnesses among refugees from Europe in Israel. They try by all means to become integrated into the normal life of the country. Many among them are conspicuous for a certain hyperactivity. How can one explain this striking finding? One of the reasons lies in the fact that those who underwent these terrible sufferings, but remained physically in a more or less satisfactory state of health, had abreacted the not repressed but only temporarily suppressed emotions in the first period after their liberation. This is a well-known, frequent occurrence. Maybe for some reason, for instance guilt feelings over the death of their families, many have succeeded in repressing the memory of their awful experiences rather well, though many suffer still from nightmares reminding them of the horrors of the persecution. Among them are those who were pathologically shocked by the Eichmann trial, because of the failing of this repression. It is remarkable that we, too, in our material, did not find a relation between having been severely persecuted and present mental health. It is quite possible that here the defense mechanisms against appalling emotions helped the sufferers in the camps to hold out.[11] I cannot enter here into a discussion of these mechanisms. It is my personal impression from experiences in private practice that people who, as adults, went through the concentration camps did not suffer from it as much as those who, in their adolescence, when their personalities had not yet been consolidated and matured, were hidden with gentiles or persecuted in camps. Research on this topic is very desirable in order to define how far the undisturbed survival of these people is due to their mental health—survival of the fittest—to good luck, that is by mere chance, or by other causes. In such research the incidence of psychosomatic disorders in relation to successful sociocultural adjustment or to maladjustment has to be thoroughly examined.

Eitinger writes that "case histories of concentration camp survivors give no support to the assumption that those survivors have a higher moral strength than other people as mentioned by Dr. Dvorjetski."[9] In my opinion neither do Eitinger's case histories point to the contrary, since he studied only selected groups of mental patients who had gone through such camps. There is urgent need for comparative research in Israel with large random samples not only of former concentration camp prisoners, but also of other Israeli citizens with similar cultural backgrounds who did not go through such camps.

THE MARGINAL PERSONALITY

There is another prima facie more favorable aspect of group interaction. The most desirable form of living together, where amalgamation, for one or another reason, is not possible, is that of symbiosis, of friendly cooperation of culturally different groups within one nation. However, this interaction has, also in this case, side effects which can be detrimental for mental health. I refer to the development of personalities trying to assimilate themselves to the culture of the majority. This process of acculturation is not without danger for mental health. Victor D. Sanua[29] reports on a research project carried out among three generations of Jewish students in the United States. He found with a battery of tests, an attenuation of the Thurston Personality Schedule, that the students of the third generation were better adjusted to the American culture but were of worse mental health, as measured with the Rorschach Multiple Choice Test. It would be of paramount interest to arrange a comparative study of acculturation of "olim" from various cultural backgrounds in subsequent generations in Israel. Such a study could provide a reply to the question, if, and in what respect, social and cultural distance between immigrants, or, in general, between a minority group and the majority group, influences mental health unfavorably in the process of acculturation.

A frequently occurring effect of faulty acculturation is the development of the marginal character, as described by Stonequist.[31] According to him, "the marginal man is the individual who lives in, or has ties of kinship with, two or more interacting societies between which there exists sufficient incompatibility to render his own adjustment to them difficult or impossible. He does not quite 'belong' or feel at home in either group." He points to the rather frequent occurrence of the marginal character among Jews. It seems worthwhile to examine from the mental health point of view the marginal personality of Jews in the diaspora, its incidence and symptomatology, compared with that of some groups of immigrants in Israel. Research on this topic may throw more light upon some traits, sometimes attributed to the Jewish personality in the diaspora, such as for instance Jewish self-hatred and self-pride, as compared with the Jewish personality in Israel. In this context it seems not to be superfluous to warn against attempts to hasten the immigrants' acculturation because of the danger of marginality or even uprootedness with all the resulting dangers for mental health and thereby for social behavior (see also Ref. 28).

In this acculturation process the roles of the Jewish religion and of other sociocultural factors on mental health and personal adjustment once more become of vital interest. A study of mental health of various communities in the Diaspora and in Israel may reveal a need for religiosity and for Jewish ethical values, far stronger than many people think. It may throw more light on the function of the Jewish religion, especially in the United States, as a factor for strengthening the feeling of belonging within the community and, at the same time, as a form of accommodation to the culture of the majority group, as well as a medium of connection with Israel.

CONCLUSIONS

In conclusion, we believe justified, on the basis of the above mentioned facts, findings and theories, the following working hypothesis:

Individual and group mental health and inter-individual, individual-group and intergroup-interactions are interrelated. It is the task of psychodynamically and psychobiologically oriented, multidisciplinary comparative mental health research to investigate and to scrutinize the validity of this hypothesis. The diversity of the conditions of life of Jewish groups and individuals in the Diaspora, as well as in the State of Israel, seems to be an appropriate object for this kind of research. The outcome of such research may reveal vital aspects of intergroup, interpersonal and intrapersonal psychodynamics of benefit not only for the well-being of this old—and at the same time young—nation, but also for better intergroup and international understanding and collaboration, which means—for improved world mental health.

REFERENCES

1. T.W. Adorno, Else Frenkel Brunswick, D.J. Levinson, B.N. Sanford with Betty Aron, Maria H. Levinson and W. Morrow: *The Authoritarian Personality.* New York, Harper and Bros., 1950.

2. Gordon W. Alport: *The Nature of Prejudice.* Reading, Mass., Addison-Wesley Publishing Co., 1954.

3. Bruno Bettelheim and Morris Janovitz: *Dynamics and Prejudice, A Psychological and Sociological Study of Veterans.* New York, Harper and Bros., 1950.

4. W.B. Cannon: *Bodily Changes in Pain, Hunger, Fear and Rage. An Account of Recent Researches into the Function of Emotional Excitement.* New York and London, D. Appleton and Co., 1920.

5. W.B. Cannon: *The Wisdom of the Body.* New York, W.W. Norton and Co., 1939.

6. Richard Christie and Marie Jahoda, (Ed.): *Studies in the Scope and Method of The Authoritarian Personality. Continuities in Social Research.* Glencoe, Illinois, The Free Press, 1945.

7. M. Dvorjetzki: *Problèmes Bio-Sociologiques de Rescapés de la Vie Concentrationnaire-Immigrées en Israel. Conférence faite au Congrès International sur les effects tardives de l'internment et de la déportation.* Oslo, 1960.

8. L. Eitinger: *Psychiatriske Undersoekelser Blant Fliktinger i Norge,* (Psychatric Investigations among Refugees in Norway) with an English Summary, Green and Co. Oslo, 1958.

9. L. Eitinger: Preliminary notes on a study of concentration camp survivors in Norway. *Israel Ann Psychiatry,* 1:59, 1963.

10. See, e.g., Maurice Fischberg: *Die Rassenmerkmale der Juden.* Munich, Ernst Reinhardt, 1913.

11. Viktor E. Frankl: *Ein Psycholog erlebt das Konzentrationslager.* Oesterreichische Dokumente zur Zeitgeschichte, Ed. Tesarek, Anton Verlag für Jugend und Volk, G.M.B.H., Wien.

12. Saeger Graeber and Steward Henderson Britt: *Jews in a Gentile World. The Problem of Antisemitism.* New York, The MacMillan Co., 1942.

13. August B. Hollingshead and Fredrick C. Redlich: *Social Class and Mental Illness, A Community Study.* London, Chapman and Hall, Ltd., 1958. New York, John Wiley and Sons, Inc.,

14. Karen Horney: *Neurosis and Human Growth. The Struggle toward Self-Realization.* New York, W.W. Norton and Co. Inc., 1950.

15. Charles C. Hughes, Marco-Adelard Trembley, Robert N. Rapaport and Alexander H. Leighton: People of Cove and Woodlot. Communities from the Viewpoint of Social Psychiatry. *The Stirling County Study of*

Psychiatric Disorder and Sociocultural Environment, Vol. II. New York, Basic Books Inc., 1960.

16. Marie Jahoda: *Current Concepts of Positive Mental Health.* Joint Commission on Mental Illness and Health, Monograph Series No. 1. New York, Basic Books Inc., 1959.

17. Alexander H. Leighton: My name is Legion. Foundation for a theory of man in relation to culture. *The Stirling County Study of Psychiatric Disorders and Socio-cultural Environment,* Vol. I. New York, Basic Books Inc., 1959.

18. Jakob Letschinsky: New conditions of life among Jews in the Diaspora. *Jewish Soc, 2:*1939, 1960.

19. Benjamin Malzberg: The distribution of mental diseases according to religious affiliation in New York, 1949–1951. *Ment Hyg, 46:*510, 1962.

20. Karl Menninger: Regulatory devices of the ego under major stress, *Int J Psychoanalysis, 35:*412, 1954 and in *A Psychiatrists' World. The Selected Papers of Karl Menninger, M.D.* New York, The Viking Press, 1959.

21. H.B.M. Murphy, *et al.,* Foreword by J.R. Rees, *Flight and Resettlement.* UNESCO, 1955

22. Jerome K. Myers and Bertram H. Roberts: *Some Relationship between Religion, Ethnic Origin and Mental Disease,* with 15 references, in Marshal Sklare, (Ed). *The Jews, Social Patterns of an American Group,* Glencoe, Illinois, The Free Press, 1959.

23. Simon Noveck, (Ed): *The Approaches to the Personal Problems and Needs of Modern Man.* New York, Basic Books Inc., 1956.

24. Marvin K. Opler, (Ed.): *Culture and Mental Health, Cross-Cultural Studies.* New York, The Macmillan Co. 1959.

25. Maria Pfister-Ammende: *The Symptomatology, Treatment and Prognosis in Mentally Ill Refugees and Repatriates in Switzerland, in: Flight and Resettlement.* (Note 17), page 147.

26. T.A.C. Rennie: The Yorkville Community Mental Health Study. In *Interrelation between the Social Environment and Psychiatric Disorders.* New York, Millbank Memorial Fund, 1953.

27. T.A.C. Rennie, L. Scrole, M.K. Opler and T.S. Lengner: *Urban Life and Mental Health. Socio-economic status and mental disorder in the metropolis. Am J Psychiatry, 113:*759, 1954.

28. Gerhard Saenger: *The Social Psychology of Prejudice, Achieving Intercultural Understanding Cooperation in a Democracy.* New York, Harper and Bro., 1953.

29. Victor D. Sanua: Differences in personality adjustment among different generations of American Jews and non-Jews: *In: Culture and Mental Health,* see[28].

30. Statistical Abstract of Israel, *Demography* (Population, Vital Statistics, Health, Results of Population and Housing Census—1961), Central Bureau of Statistics, No. 13, 1962.

31. E.V. Stonequist: *The Marginal Man. A Study in Personality and*

Culture Conflict. New York, Charles Scribner's Sons, 1937. Everett V. Stonequist: The marginal character of the Jews. In *Jews in a Gentile World,* see[12].

32. Harry Stack Sullivan: *The Interpersonal Theory of Psychiatry.* New York, W.W. Norton and Co., Inc., 1953.

33. Abraham A. Weinberg: *Psychosociology of the Immigrant. An Investigation into the Problems of Adjustment of Immigrants into Palestine Based on Replies to an Inquiry Conducted among Jewish Immigrants from Holland.* Hebrew with an extensive Summary in English. Preface by Prof. Roberto Bachi, Heiliger and Co., Jerusalem, 1959.

34. Abraham A. Weinberg: Mental health aspects of voluntary migration. *Ment Hyg, 39:*450, 1955.

35. A.A. Weinberg: Observations on Psychodynamics of Schizoid Personality. Congress Report of the 2nd International Congress for Psychiatry, Vol. II, Zurich, 1957.

36. Abraham A. Weinberg: *Migration and Belonging. A Study on Mental Health and Personal Adjustments in Israel.* Preface by Prof. Louis Guttman. The Hague, Martinus Nijhoff, 1961.

37. See, e.g., Louis Wirth. *The Ghetto.* Chicago, Phoenix Books, The University of Chicago Press, 1928, 1936.

38. Mark Zborowski and Elizabeth Herzog: *Life is with People. The Jewish Little-Town of Eastern Europe.* Foreword by Margaret Mead. New York, International Universities Press, Inc., 1952, 1955.

Author Index

SUBJECT INDEX

comparison of metastatic adenocarcinomas in Jewish and non-
Jewish females, 169

comparison of mortality for native-
born Jews and Russian-born
population, 156

computation of death rates from,
153

correlation for Jews and non-Jews
in Pittsburgh, 162–163

correlation with cigarette smoking
in Jewish males, 170

correlation with smoking habits
among Jewish females, 168, 170

correlation with smoking for Jewish and non-Jewish females, 167

correlation with smoking practices
of religions, 156–157

duration of smoking influencing,
167

environment influencing frequency
differences between Jews and
non-Jews, 160

epidermoid, 157

epidermoid carcinomas occurrence
with smoking, 165

frequency of metastatic adenocarcinomas among Jewish males,
169–170

glandular types of lung neoplasm
related to smoking, 165

heredity influencing, 169

histological types correlated with
smoking, 165

hospital admissions compared for
Jewish males, Catholics and
Protestants, 151

Jewish male rate compared to
Catholic and Protestant, 160

metastatic adenocarcinomas among
Jewish females, 169

methods used in determining rate
differences between religious
groups, 160

mortality due to, 155–156

mortality by age groups, 154

mortality compared to total deaths,
152

mortality comparison for U.S.-born
Jews and non-Jews, 155–156

mortality for females in Pittsburgh
and Montreal, 168

mortality for Russian-born males,
157

mortality for Russian-born population, 156

mortality rates and cigarette smoking behavior correlated, 159–173

need for better diagnosis, 168

non-Jewish foreign-born groups
compared to foreign-born
Jewish groups, 157

occupational exposures influencing,
152

plastic carcinomas, 157

rate increase for Jews compared
to Protestants and Catholics,
155–156

ratio of male to female death rates
among Jews, 165

ratio of non-Jewish males to females, 165

religious differential in frequency
of, 169

religious differential influence in
metastic adenocarcinomas of the
lung, 171

religious habits affecting smoking
influencing, 162

reversal in comparison of Jews to
non-Jews, 155–156

secondary, 169

sex ratios for Canada, 161

smoking habits affecting, 151

smoking influencing, amount of,
167

smoking influencing, type of, 167

sources for data, 163

studies needed, 157, 169, 170

studies needed to determine difference in frequency between Jewish and non-Jewish females, 171

lung, anaplastic
cigarette smoking influencing, 151
ocupational exposures influencing,
152

Cardiovascular disorders (*see* Coronary disease.)
Castration
women
breast disease in, 135
Catholics (*see* specific topic.)
C-D-E chromosomes
characteristics of shared by Jews, 59
ccddee phenotype
Oriental Jews, 50
cde chromosome
Basque or Berber component indicated by, 50
homozygous combination, 55
Oriental Jews, 54–55
Sephardic Jews, 50
cDe chromosome
African populations, 50
Ashkenazi, 54, 55
comparison with haptoglobins as indicator of ancient African admixture, 60
Jews compared to gentiles, 59
Moroccan Jews, 55
Moslems of the Near East, 59
Sephardic Jews, 50, 55
sources of, 55
Spain, 50–51
Tripolitanian Jews, 55
Tunisian Jews, 55
cDE chromosome (*see* "North European" chromosome.)
CDe chromosome (*see also* "Mediterranean" chromosome.)
Jews in Mediterranean zone, 54
Moroccan Jews, 54
source of ethnic information, as a, 61
Tunisian Jews, 54
Celibacy
homosexuality affected by
Irish, 300
Cemeteries
use in obtaining mortality data, 163
Census
categories used in classification, 6

Census data
difficulties in obtaining from country to country, 7
obsolescence of, 8–9
Census information
retrieval system
Duke University plan, 9
Census returns
United States 1960, decennial, 6
Central Endocrinological Laboratory of the Labour Sick Fund Zamehhof Clinic, 132
Cerebroside kerasine
abnormality in Gaucher's disease, 100
Cervical cancer (*see* Cancer, cervical.)
Charcot joints
familial dysautonomia affecting, 80
neuropathic
familial dysautonomia affecting, 78
Charlemagne
tolerance of
dispersion of Jews due to, 106
Chassidism
relief drinking of Jews before, 266
Chest roentgenogram, 242
Children (*see also* specific topic or group.)
comparison of leukemia between Jewish and non-Jewish, 113
lack of understanding of love
mental health affected by, 322
leukemia among, 175
number of
breast cancer affected by, 128, 129
comparison for New York City Jews, Israeli Ashkenazi Jews and Israeli Sephardi-Oriental Jews, 149
Cholesterol
alpha, 194
comparison for European manual workers and men with myocardial infarction, 194
constancy of, 198
beta, 194
comparison between European manual workers and men with myocardial infarction, 194

Engagements
  protracted
    schizophrenia among Irish affected
    by, 300
England (*see also* specific topic.)
  migration of Jews into, 106
"Enhanced penetrance"
  Gaucher's disease, 100
Enteritis
  regional
    Jews, 182
    U.S. veterans, 184–185
Enterocolitis
  comparison for Jews and non-Jews,
  185
Environment
  alcoholism influenced by, 266
  atherosclerosis influenced by, 189–
  190
  behavioral science studies, use in, 310
  breast cancer affected by, 112, 128,
  134
  cancer in Jews influenced by, 112
  cervical cancer affected by, 118–148
  changes in
    atherosclerosis morbidity and mor-
    tality influenced by, 190
  coronary disease affected by, 203
  coronary disease
    responsibility for ethnic differences
    in, 204
  correlation with corpus, breast and
    ovarian cancer, 149–150
  correlation with mental cases ad-
    mitted to hospitals and religious
    affiliation, 286
  correlation with tuberculosis, 243
  diabetes influenced by, 183, 235
  differences between Jews and Gen-
    tiles
    chemical bases of hereditary dis-
    eases affected by, 67
    differential rates of natural selec-
    tion caused by, 94
  difference in occurrence of genetic
    disease between Jews and Gentiles
    due to, 69
  drinking behavior influenced by, 266,
  267

drug addiction among Jews influenced by, 250
drug addiction influenced by, 266
home
  Class V schizophrenics, 301
  comparison for Jewish and Protes-
    tants for high and low socio-
    economic status, 296
  methods of determining for schizo-
    phrenics, 297
  psychological adjustment affected
    by, 296
  schizophrenia affected by, 302–303
hypertension affected by, 203
  ethnic differences in, 204
inherent in marriage, 120, 125
  affecting gynecologic and endo-
    crine disease, 120, 125
intercourse, in
  gynecologic and endocrine disease
    affected by, 120
interrelationship with genetic factors
  in cancer morbidity, 112
Jews influenced by, 229
lung cancer rate differences between
  Jews and non-Jews explained by,
  160
marriage and pregnancy-related
  cervical cancer rates of Jewish
    groups affected by, 149
menstruation
  gynecologic and endocrine disease
    affected by, 120, 125
mortality affected by, 38
nonaddiction to alcohol of Jews influenced by, 250
occupation and social ambitions affected by
  Jewish boys, 315
penile cancer affected by, 113
pregnancy
  endocrine and gynecologic disease
    affected by, 120, 125
  gynecologic and endocrine disease
    affected by, 120, 125
regional enteritis affected by, 187
selective agents exposed by, 56
susceptibility to cancer affected by,
  113